GEOFFREY MOORHOUSE

The author is a Fellow of the Royal Society of Literature and of the Royal Geographical Society. His books cover topics as wide-ranging as Indian history, travel and cricket, and have been translated into many languages. His most recent book, TO THE FRONTIER, won the 1984 Thomas Cook Award for travel writing.

Geoffrey Moorhouse

AGAINST ALL REASON

First published in Great Britain in 1969 by Weidenfeld and Nicolson

Sceptre edition 1986

Sceptre is an imprint of Hodder and Stoughton Paperbacks, a division of Hodder and Stoughton Ltd

British Library C.I.P.

Moorhouse, Geoffrey
  Against all reason.
  1. Monastic and religious life
  2. Christian life
  I. Title
  248.8'94   BX2435

  ISBN 0-340-38453-0

Printed and bound in Great Britain for Hodder and Stoughton Paperbacks, a division of Hodder and Stoughton Ltd., Mill Road, Dunton Green, Sevenoaks, Kent (Editorial Office: 47 Bedford Square, London, WC1 3DP) by Richard Clay (The Chaucer Press) Ltd., Bungay, Suffolk. Photoset by Rowland Phototypesetting Ltd., Bury St Edmunds, Suffolk.

To
the Little Brothers and Sisters of Jesus
the Taizé Communauté
the Sisters of the Love of God
who, between them, have enabled me to
see the point of the religious life

CONTENTS

ACKNOWLEDGMENTS

I owe a very big debt to a great number of people in religion. I do not expect any of them to share all the attitudes I have expressed in the book; I only hope that none of them is too shocked by some of my comments and conclusions. The largest debt of all is to those men and women – about a hundred of them – who answered a questionnaire primarily designed to find out why they became religious; some of them wrote small biographies in reply and some exposed themselves as very few human beings in my experience are prepared to, at some cost and at some risk of being hurt; they moved me more than I can say and Chapter 7 could not have been written without them, or without the permission of several superiors who generously let me circulate my questionnaire round their communities.

Apart from those helpers who must remain anonymous, people who talked to me as well as people who answered questions in writing, there are others I have to thank. More than anyone, perhaps, Dom Cyprian Martin OSB for his tireless and stimulating correspondence (not always answered promptly, I'm afraid) across three years. I'm also grateful to Fr Vincent Strudwick SSM, who allowed me to see the results of his own questionnaire on Anglican religious deployment; to Mother Mary Clare SLG, for more insights into the religious life than I can count, as well as for permission to reprint the Rule of her community as an appendix; to Dom Ambrose Southey OCSO for negotiating on my behalf permission to reprint the Trappist Usages, as well as for much advice and encouragement; to the Master-General of the Dominican Order, Fr Aniceto Fernandez OP, for permission to reprint the Dominican questionnaire; to Fr Peter Ball CGA, for allowing me to reprint an extract from his community's constitutions; and for various help and counsel to Sister Marcia CSC, Fr Arthur Longworth CR, Fr Hugh Bishop CR, Fr Donald Patey CR, Dom Edward Crouzet OSB, Dom Alberic Stacpoole OSB, Professor David Knowles OSB, Fr Herbert McCabe OP, Fr Peter Hebblethwaite SJ, Fr Brocard Sewell O Carm., Brother Thomas of Taizé, Brother Guy Jarrosson of the Petits Frères and Fr Jonathan Young SSJE. I should also like to salute the late Jonathan Graham CR, who didn't believe I ought to attempt this book, but who told me to forget that and go ahead. Lastly, my thanks to three people outside the religious life. To Mrs Mary Buck, of the Catholic Central Library in London, and to Mr R. K. Browne, Librarian of the Jesuit Provincial headquarters at Farm Street, London, both of whom helped me to find the right books and papers when I was looking for them. And to Ann Shearer who, in the middle of her own writing, made time to translate from the French two books which have not been published in English; the chapter on Taizé is for her.

FOREWORD

This book is not about Christianity in general: it is about 'the religious life' in its technical sense. Much of it is about monks and nuns, but they form only part of the religious world, which is also inhabited by friars, 'sisters', 'brothers' and several other varieties of profession. In crude and worldly terms the book is about those Christian bachelors and spinsters who live together in monasteries, convents or other communities, and who mostly wear medieval clothes. With very few exceptions, which I hope are clear from the context, the word 'religious' in this book applies to them and their life alone; in this technical sense 'a religious' is someone who is 'in religion' as a result of having taken vows or made promises to live in poverty, obedience and chastity with others of a like mind.

This book isn't about all the Christian religious in the world. Except for passing references it excludes the religious of eastern Christianity, of whom the Greek Orthodox monks living on Mount Athos are the best known. It is an attempt to survey the religious life today of western Christendom, of the world under the influence of Catholic and Protestant Christianity. It is an attempt to examine a way of life and a philosophy, the reasons why individuals have taken up that life and the effect it has on them. It is about one and a quarter million human beings. The book has been written at a dramatic point in the history of the religious life, which is changing quite radically for the first time in perhaps fifteen hundred years – since St Augustine of Hippo constructed the doctrine of perfection on which the religious life has been based. No one can yet be sure which way it is going from now on. But it is going. This book, in part, is therefore a last look at a deeply traditional way of life that may not be with us much longer. It is also, in the last chapter, an attempt to see where the religious life might go.

PART ONE

ONE

TAIZÉ

'We must strive for a Christian engagement in the human society around us. We must discover in our own field, in our place of work, the means of radiating – perhaps without a word – the presence of Christ. For you must accept a man where you find him, how you find him, in order to enter into his humanity and understand him from within.'

ROGER SCHUTZ, Prior of Taizé, *Living Today for God*, p. 66*

This is one of the most memorable places in Christendom. Seen from the hillside opposite it is just another attractive French village, slipping off the end of a ridge in a scatter of warm brown walls and pink pantiled roofs, with a Romanesque church tower poking higher than anything else. All around is the rich, cultivated and undulating landscape of Burgundy; patched with woods, with vineyards, with cornfields and with pasture. In a meadow below the church cream-coloured cows idle in the grass. Over a wall a peasant plods up and down his allotment, hand-sowing seed upon the crumbled red earth. It is a very peaceful place and the only loud noise it hears is made by the occasional train passing the maire's cottage at the bottom of the hill, on its way from Dijon to Macon. Seen from a distance the village looks as if it might be vegetating as thoughtlessly as the fields and slopes that surround it. But it is the vibrant centre of an influence which for a quarter of

* Full details of books referred to are given in the bibliography.

a century has been gradually spreading across the world and which is helping to transform one of the most ancient segments of Christian civilisation. Peasants in Chile have been touched by its presence and so have petit-bourgeois in Japan. And when, in solemn conclave beneath the dome of St Peter's, old men at the last Vatican Council attempted to shift the Church of Rome from some of its antique rigidities, they did so at times and in part from an awareness of this place and its significance.

The village's name is Taizé. It is so memorable, so influential and so significant because it contains what the world would call a monastery, but what, by the strictest legalistic canons of Christendom, is more precisely a religious community. It cannot technically be a monastery because to the purists monasteries do not exist outside the Catholic and Orthodox Churches. The Taizé Communauté is Protestant. It is, nevertheless, the home of about seventy men who have renounced the possibility of marriage, abandoned all private possessions and vowed themselves to be obedient to a rule of conduct for the rest of their lives. They have put themselves almost as far as it is possible to go from the social norms of the mid-twentieth century. To most of the world outside their lives must seem a waste or a farce or a mixture of both. To Axel, Léonard, Rudolphe, André, Clément and the other men of Taizé it is something between a duty and a fulfilment; they call it a vocation to a particular form of Christian life. In its essentials it merely follows a pattern established ages ago by men who decided that poverty, chastity and obedience provided a framework within which they would worship their God. Taizé is memorable because of its interpretation of this life, because it is Protestant, because it is dedicated to the destruction of all Christian sects and the revival of a united Church, and because it is effective.

It is the creation of one person, as almost every other religious community has been before it. He is a short, slim man, with shiny and rather damp eyes and a flat nose that may have seen better days. Those who know him best say that he is a timid man, with an annoying habit of changing arrangements at the last moment. He avoids interviews like the plague and refers people who want more than a few words of spiritual comfort from him to his numerous books and other writings. His name is Roger Schutz and one day it may be listed alongside those of Benedict and Ignatius and the other great reformers of the Christian religious life. As a boy, the Franco-Swiss son of a manse, he had been confronted with the Christian divisions which have made humbug of the faith preached on all sides; while coming from a stoutly Protestant home he had been boarded out during his school terms with a Catholic family in the next village. He sees this now as the start of his vocation. It developed further when he became a theological student in Lausanne, where his licentiate dissertation was on 'The Monastic ideal until St Benedict and its Conformity with the Gospel'. At the age of twenty-four he began to organise his friends into study groups, brought them together for spiritual retreats, and called this fellowship the Great Community. It was this only in a loose sense, for its members lived separately in their own homes. Schutz was bent upon something more permanent and more coherent.

When a student leads a band of friends calling themselves the Great Community and then goes on to found a monastery it seems at least possible that a romantic attachment to the past has been partly responsible; the pattern is not unknown in the history of the religious life. Today he is quite clear on rational grounds alone why the step was taken. 'Living the common life at Taizé,' he has written, 'what do we desire but to unite men pledged to follow the footsteps of Christ? To be an existential sign of the unity of the Church? A community is a microcosm of the Church. It sums up in itself the whole reality of the Church.'

Schutz had made his own retreats with the Carthusian monks of La Grande Chartreuse and with the Trappists. In 1940 he crossed the border to look for a house. In coming to Burgundy he was entering a country richer than most in the monastic tradition. On the road to Macon were the ruins of Cluny, which William the Pious, Duke of Aquitaine, founded in 910, which produced a pope (Gregory VII) and which in the eleventh and twelfth centuries was enormously influential as the headquarters of a reformed Benedictine life. A few miles outside Dijon was Citeaux, which after nine hundred years is still the base-camp of an extremely rigorous form of monasticism; a very solid Cistercian barracks which no woman may enter and which, unless they are making a retreat or doing business, men may visit only between 2.30 and 4.30 in the afternoon. Schutz found what he wanted between the two, only just out of sight of Cluny itself. In 1940, though it was in unoccupied France, Taizé was almost an abandoned village; the windows of its seventeenth-century manor house, which had once belonged to the Counts of Brie, were shuttered. But a notary in Cluny had suggested that the manor might be for sale and it was. Schutz moved in and for the next two years lived there alone except for the refugees he sheltered. By 1942 the Germans had taken over unoccupied France and Schutz returned to Switzerland. In Geneva he met three other students – Max Thurian and Daniel de Montmollin, who were theologians, and Pierre Souvairain, who had graduated in agriculture – and until the European war was over the four men shared an apartment. Although none had yet vowed himself to anything, although no rule of life for them was to appear for another decade, this was the beginning of the Taizé Communauté.

The four moved into Schutz's Burgundian manor in the summer of 1944. The first thing they did was to take in twenty orphans. Then they began to organise a retreat house for adults who wanted to spend a quiet day or two in prayer and meditation. They were also busy making friends with the Catholic priests and laymen of the district, which was not an automatic thing for Protestant clergymen to be doing in France twenty-five years ago. It paid off astonishingly. By Easter 1948, with five brothers in Taizé, Prior Schutz and his community had been given permission to celebrate their first office in that Catholic village church with the Romanesque tower. This was henceforth to serve both Protestants and Catholics in the area on the authority of no lesser dignitaries than the Bishop of Autun and the papal nuncio in Paris – who in those days was Monsignor Roncalli, but who afterwards became Pope John XXIII. Given Schutz's vision of a reconciliation between divided Christian Churches, which had led him on ever since his student days in Lausanne, it was perhaps the most important breakthrough of his life. It meant that his chosen purpose had some chance of success and that there could now be total commitment to it. On Easter morning of the next year there were seven brothers in Taizé and together they vowed themselves to chastity, to poverty, to obedience and to community for life.

The place has changed a bit since then. The almost abandoned village is now bulging at the seams with people whose lives have become geared to the community's and with people who are just visiting it. There may be only sixty villagers under M. le maire's authority and seventy-odd brethren under M. le prieur's obedience but except in winter the average floating population of Taizé cannot be much less than two thousand a day. Nuns come plodding up the hill in dozens, clerics go rambling along the ridge road towards the water-tower in foursomes, and coach parties lurch to a standstill on the gravel outside M. Barbier's shop, which does a roaring trade most months of the year in light or heavy refreshments. Neither the manor, the Romanesque church nor the pantiled buildings of Taizé were ever intended to accommodate these numbers, so there have been several structural alterations too. The church is now used by the community only in winter, when few people are about. Most of the time since 1962 worship at Taizé has taken place further along the ridge in the huge Church of the Reconciliation, which from the outside looks like an aircraft hangar or possibly an electricity generating station; with the water-tower it is almost the only ugly thing for miles around. Beyond that is an encampment of white-walled, rather military-looking huts, which is where the community puts up retreatants and other guests it cannot manage elsewhere. And almost everywhere you look in Taizé construction work is going on all the time. In the village proper cottages are being knocked into more habitable shapes. In the field between the manor and the ugly concrete church five great bells hang from a metal frame and men are creating a moat around them so that the visitors can inspect the bells closely from the roadside and yet be kept out of harm's way when they begin to swing. The men wear dungarees and they handle their shovels, their trowels and their cigarettes as though they have been labourers all their lives. Some of them have been. Most of them belong to the community and are therefore a kind of monk as well.

These have come to Taizé, together with their brethren, from a dozen different countries and an even greater variety of religious backgrounds. There are more French, Swiss, Germans and Dutch in the community than anything else; but there are also Scandinavians, an Australian, an American, a Scot and a Spaniard. Between them they cover about twenty different Protestant denominations but they have sunk these differences in the unity of the life at Taizé. About one in six of them is an ordained minister of religion, the rest are laymen, but apart from the fact that the pastors alone can perform certain sacramental functions like administering communion there is no distinction at all in the way they live and are regarded within the community. They are all Brothers of Taizé together. Apart from that first nucleus they have all come to the community, been accepted by it and settled into it along a common pattern.

When a man believes he has a vocation to Taizé he is told to come and make a retreat there for a start. He is given a room in that white-walled encampment beyond the ugly church. He finds himself in the company of a motley gang of itinerants: young men from half the Christian student organisations of Europe; Catholic priests and Protestant pastors; Presbyterian ordinands passing time in their last long vacation at Cambridge. All of them have come partly, as they would say, for the peace and quiet and right atmosphere in which to recharge their spiritual batteries; partly just to satisfy their curiosity about Taizé itself. With the rest of them the man who thinks he has a vocation will do chores about the place, attend the offices in the church, potter around the district, read a bit and spend a fair amount of his time relaxing on his bed. He will then go home but eventually he will return to live with the community in the manor as a postulant. There is no fixed period for this; for some it lasts a few weeks, for others several months. The criterion is in the postulant himself. Everything depends on how long it takes the rest of the community to decide whether he has the potential to become one of them. One day they vote on him among themselves and if the ballot goes in his favour he becomes a novice. For the next three years he will to some extent be a student – of the Bible, of Church history and of sociology – under the direction of a senior brother. 'In order to be trained in the school of Christ,' says the community's Rule, 'the new Brother has need of sound biblical and humane nurture.' He will also be applying on behalf of the community whatever skills he brought with him from the life outside; he will, to the visiting observer, be indistinguishable from any other member of Taizé Communauté. But his most important function during his novitiate will be to learn how to live in common with his new brethren; how to share everything with them; how to avoid getting on their nerves and how to put up with those who get on his; how to discipline himself to unaccustomed periods of silence; how, most of all, to grow into the particular philosophy of Taizé. Towards the end of his novitiate he will be discussed by the prior with the brothers who have been closest to him for the past three years. And on their advice and on his own assessment Roger Schutz decides whether or not to allow the new man to become a fully professed member of the community.

The profession is the most serious step the man has taken in his life and it is invested with all the weight and significance of a marriage ceremony. One morning, preferably on the first Easter morning after he has passed muster, the new brother is taken to the Church of the Reconciliation. He is dressed, like the rest of the community, in the long white cassock with a hood down the back and a cord around the waist which is worn at Taizé only in church. He is required there to renew his baptismal vows and then, while he lies prostrate on the floor, the community sing Psalm 126. Then the prior exhorts him to remember that Christ will strengthen his faith, to walk in the footsteps of Christ for the rest of his life, to surrender himself, to maintain himself in simplicity and joy, to be a sign of brotherly love within the Church. The exhortation also reminds the new brother what he is giving up: home, brothers, sisters, mother, father, wife, children and land. 'This is a way opposed to all human reason, but like Abraham you can advance on this path by faith, not by sight, always assured that he who loses his life for Christ's sake shall find it.' And with this thought in his head the brother takes the vows he is expected to keep until the day he dies.

'Will you,' he is asked, 'through love of Christ, consecrate yourself with your whole being to Him?'

'Will you, henceforth, fulfil the service of God in our Community, in communion with your Brothers?'

'Will you, in renouncing all ownership to property, live with your Brothers not only in the community of material goods but also in the community of spiritual goods, while striving for openness of heart?'

'Will you, in order to be more available to serve with your brothers and to give yourself completely to the love of Christ, remain celibate?'

'Will you, in order that we may be but one heart and one soul and that our unity of service may be fully realised, assume the decisions made in Community and as expressed by the Prior?'

'Will you, while always discerning Christ in your Brothers, be watchful with them on bad days as well as good, in poverty as well as abundance, in suffering as in joy?'

A silver ring goes on his wedding finger after that as a reminder of his solemn commitment. And though several men leave Taizé and return to their old lives when they are in the novitiate, finding the existence progressively less to their taste and temperament, in all the years since it was founded only one fully professed brother has renounced his vows and opted out of the community. He left to get married.

This is the way that all the brothers have come to Taizé. And whatever life any one of them may have left behind it does not look as if he has exchanged it for something that is harsh or bleak or degrading, though these are some of the world's assumptions about the monastic existence. There is a Rule governing the community's life but it does not read like a series of regimental orders; it is a discursive mixture of humane common sense and high Christian sentiment and it has been described as 'a spiritual document redolent of the Gospel'.

In the manor each brother has a room which is simply furnished but which is also comfortable; the bed is well sprung and so is the armchair, there are shelves for books and an ikon to decorate the wall. He takes his meals not in an institutional eating shed but in a more cosy domestic atmosphere with just a few of his brothers, and although no one talks until the soup, the pasta, the salad and fromage are done and the fruit is being passed round, the silence is relieved by a Brandenburg Concerto, an Orthodox chant or something else decently classical coming off the record player in the corner. This small gathering is where the brother hears what is going on in the world outside, for someone is deputed to monitor the papers and the wireless and to bring the news in to the rest. They call these groups 'foyers' at Taizé; the community is divided into six of them, and they are there so that brothers can know each other as brothers and not just as matey members of the same religious commando; but they are reshuffled from time to time so that the community will not become a parcel of cliques either.

The foyer is one small focal point of the brother's life. Another is his work. There is an accumulation of secular skills in the community and they have not been wasted. Taizé cannot afford to waste them when it is a deeply embedded principle of the monastic life that a community shall be as far as possible self-supporting. Gifts of money do come in from well-wishers but the Rule says that 'the boldness to use in the best possible way all present-day goods and, without fear of possible poverty, to lay up no capital, gives an incalculable strength' and so these are put to other uses; as, in the mid-sixties, they were being devoted to a land reform scheme in the Catholic diocese of Talca in Chile. So Taizé keeps going by its own efforts and talents. After the rising bell at 7 am, after the first office of the day in church and after breakfast, it begins to earn its bread and butter.

Some of the brothers will be out on the building work and others will be coping with the perpetual stream of visitors. But for the theologians, like Roger Schutz himself and Max, it means a day of writing if they are at home. For Dominique it means a day in the printery, turning out the books and tracts the theologians have written, which sell like hot cakes in several languages; turning out, too, much distinctly untheological contract work, like the manual on chicken farming which Taizé published for the Cameroons Government some time back. For Daniel and his assistants it means a day in the pottery, making platters and jugs and urns. For Eric and Mark it means designing stained glass to order for churches throughout Europe. They also do abstract wood engravings, ikons, and thick brushy drawings of any subject that has taken their fancy. All these pieces, along with those coming out of the pottery, and the records made of the Taizé Communauté singing in choir, keep the tills ringing in the *centre d'exposition* across the road from the workshops, where the tourists rummage for their souvenirs. A lot of monasteries and even more cathedrals have souvenir attachments and usually the only striking thing about them is how a religion which has produced such a beauty of glass at Chartres and masonry at St Peter's could countenance such shoddy junk on its doorsteps today. But the stuff coming out of the Taizé workshops is modern art and has been good enough for exhibition in Tokyo and elsewhere.

There are times, wandering around Taizé, when the visitor might be forgiven for supposing that he had dropped into the centre of a flourishing arts and crafts movement rather than a religious community. The *centre d'exposition* is packed with gorgeous things. On walls down in the village are neo-Romanesque figures in bas-relief, done by Bernard, who was and still is occasionally a sculptor. Every room in the retreat house contains one of Mark's ikons. Daniel's workshop is not just a place bent on making ends meet; it is an artist's den, with pieces of crystal, stones cut across to show their whorling and tinted insides, and many other utterly uncommercial bits of bric-a-brac. There are white doves fluttering around the courtyard of the manor and a cartwheel balanced beautifully but uselessly against the wall of a workshop. There are even tropical fish tanked up inside the printery. It is as though the whole place were dedicated not to the worship of God but to the pursuit of a very tranquil beauty.

There is, in fact, nothing more beautiful in Taizé than its chief act of worship and its main expression of the common life of the monks. The community is split into half a dozen small factories from breakfast time until 6 in the evening and it eats its meals in separate foyers. But three times a day, and more frequently on Sundays, it gathers en masse in church to sing its offices – at 7.30 am, at noon and at 7 in the evening.

The church may look like an aircraft hangar from the outside but inside Denys, who used to be an architect and who designed it, has made it into a setting for superb theatre. It is cavernous, flat-ceilinged, its walls are white and rough. A little light comes through small windows along one side and through larger ones around the door, whose stained glass has been done by Eric and Mark. There is a promenade around two sides of this theatre and then steps down into the well, where there are rows of chairs for a congregation. In front of them is a low-walled enclosure, where the community will sit in an arc, and its open side faces a great slabby and free-standing altar raised to the level of everybody's head. Yellow spotlights sunk into the floor play on the back wall and throw everything into sharply sculptured relief.

The office is announced half an hour before it begins by those moated bells out in the field, which are controlled electrically by a switch in Dominique's printery. People begin to slip in through the doors, to fill the congregational seats and to squat upon the steps. While they are coming a brother appears from the wings behind the altar, bearing a lighted taper on the end of a long pole. Very slowly he raises this torch to each of the candles on a wide iron circle hanging above the altar; then to a single candle standing alone and high in front of it; then to five others in a row before an ikon to the left of it. As he raises his torch the wide sleeves of his white cassock fall away down his arms and his shadow trembles huge against the yellowed backdrop. For a few moments he has this stage all to himself, until other brethren come in. They arrive alone or in twos, but however they come they move with the pace of men who are sure of every step and know they have all the time in the world to make it. They have what any theatrical producer would instantly recognise as presence and the swish and sway of their cassocks only points it up. There is not an old or a fat one among them and so their entrance is like a meeting of athletes. They go each to his place inside the enclosure, remove a mat from their seats and then kneel on the floor with their heads held high. Last of all, in the almost total silence which has been there since the candles were being lit, Jean-Luc crosses the altar from the wings and climbs up to his silver-piped organ in a loft on the other wall. He looks round, plays six fluting chords, his brethren rise with a rustle of robes, and begin to sing the introit. 'Rendez grâce au Seigneur car il est bon, car éternel est son amour, alleluia. . . .' And if anyone has an ear for sound, for the balance between silence and music, for the tension of the one broken by the other, for the soaring lilt of that opening verse with thin, rather boyish tenor above grounding bass, a shiver goes down his spine at that point.

The office lasts for perhaps half an hour. There are choral psalms in which the congregation joins and there are passages of liturgy sung solo by one of the brothers. There are prayers: for the Church, for the state of the world, for the members of the community who are away from home; for Gérard and Bernard, who are in Africa, for Robert who is in Spain . . . There is a lesson, and the words of the Gospel drift heavy as incense over the church in great rolling French periods and accents. There are also many more silences. The longest silence of all comes near the end when very quietly, almost in a whisper, Roger Schutz says 'Prions-nous'. He says it while everyone is sitting and it would take willpower for a man not to go on his knees with the rest. It is a silence which seems to last a measure of days, in which a man may examine his soul and wonder where on earth he is going, while the candles flicker and the arc of white figures is utterly still and in all that great gathering only the organist sits fidgeting a little at his keyboard. It is a silence which lingers for perhaps five minutes, so that unless a man can pray in it he is towards the end craving a release. It ends to make the heart jump, with a crashing brilliance of chords as Jean-Luc starts his voluntary. The white figures get to their feet and then, in a slow clockwise procession, close behind each other, with cassocks and sleeves undulating in unison, they move away gaunt and long-shadowed against the yellow wall. They have just worshipped their God together, not piously, but with drama and with a rare beauty of sound and stillness and image.

Beautiful as its liturgy is and attractive as so much of the apparatus at Taizé may be, these things are only by-products of its philosphy. They are means being used to achieve a larger end. In worshipping their God the seventy brothers of Taizé have particularly dedicated themselves to unity and reconciliation. The fact that between them they represent two score denominations whose doctrines do not always correspond is itself an expression of this. But within the Christian context the dedication has been carried several stages further at Taizé. In the weird complex of Christian theological differences and Christian political rivalries the unification of several Protestant sects is a comparatively simple matter. The establishment of a bridgehead between Catholic and Protestant until a few years ago had not only been a tougher prospect; for four centuries it had been unthinkable. And a link between these two western camps of Christianity and the eastern Orthodox one was still not a matter for discussion until two or three years back. Even now it is only a matter for very gingerly conversation between the two sides. Yet at Taizé all these bridgeheads have been established. When Denys designed his church he made most of it a great Protestant theatre. He also built into its crypt a chapel for Catholics and another one for Orthodox. They are being used.

Every Sunday there is an Orthodox mass at 8 am and a Catholic mass at 9, and throughout the week the Catholic chapel is packed with people saying the rosary or just kneeling in prayer. There are also five Franciscan friars of the Catholic Church and five bearded priests of the Orthodox faith permanently attached to the community. At every office the community celebrates in its own part of the church these ten men, whose own doctrines and rituals are so alien to those of Protestantism, make their entrance behind the white-robed brethren and take their places in a swither of brown and black cloaking to the right of the altar. Catholic masses have already been said at that Protestant altar. And on Easter Day 1967, which was not their own for they go by a different calendar from that of western Christians, the Orthodox priests celebrated their Easter liturgy there too. Ecumenism, the Christian trade name for this settling of differences, cannot go much further than that.

It is one sign of Taizé's achievement so far. That and the Catholic Dominican sisters who help to man the *centre d'acceuil* which copes with the visitors who have come to stay, and the nuns from a Belgian order who help to sell the souvenirs in the *centre d'exposition*. That and the casual throwaway line of a Protestant brother of Taizé: 'We've just lost our bishop', he said, and he was talking of a Catholic. That and the name given to two of the bells out in the field; one called John XXIII and the other Pacem in Terris, which was the same pope's greatest encyclical. That and the coachloads of nuns and priests who come grinding up the hill from the level crossing by M. le maire's cottage. Nearly two hundred thousand visitors a year come to Taizé now and they aren't all Protestants. Some of them aren't even Christians. 'Haven't we been discovered and recognised by so many agnostics through our liturgical prayer?' asks Schutz. And they have.

This is one part of Taizé's influence. Another is in its interpretation of the religious life. Periodically this has changed and been modified throughout the centuries since it began. Benedict changed it enormously and Francis a little more; Ignatius shifted its direction and so did other men before and after him, with a subtle emphasis on this point and then on that. But of its nature it has tended to become hidebound, with long periods of rigidity between one change and the next. It has been meticulously codified with rules of strict obedience and in varying degrees it has been lived in isolation, which has been death to flexibility. The way of Taizé has gone against this grain. In very small details it has been flexible from the start; so that, although the rising bell goes at 7 in the morning and the community closes down for silence from 10 in the evening, there is at least one brother who gets up at 5 am and goes off to bed early to compensate at the other end of the day; and he is encouraged to do this because he is thus finding the rhythm of days that suits him best. It is not a habit that would be favoured today at Cîteaux. But it is the kind of thing that is being pondered by more and more monks and nuns and other religious all over the world. That and the liturgy, with its great reflective silences which are so alien to the crammed rituals of traditional monasticism. And most of all the religious world is pondering Taizé's attachment to the temporary nature of its life. 'The things that specially distinguish us at Taizé may have to disappear one day . . . when visible unity has been achieved.'

This is not a doctrine in the grand tradition of monasticism, whose insistence has been rather on the eternal and the unchanging and the sureness of continuity. It is a doctrine which depends upon the assertion that a religious community must not be reclusive; that instead it must see itself as part of a world which is always changing; that it must always be taking stock of itself and prepared to adapt itself to contemporary needs. The emphasis is clearly seen in everything that Schutz has written. It is reflected in some of his titles: *Living Today for God*, *A Dynamic of the Provisional*, and so on. Over the past decade this doctrine has more and more been considered and debated and absorbed by the rest of the religious world. The Rule of Taizé has now been translated into German, English, Dutch and Spanish. There is scarcely a conference of religious throughout Europe and in the United States without one of the brothers being present, to whom the Catholics and the Anglicans turn from time to time in their discussions of where the religious life is and ought to be going, to ask what is the interpretation of this or that and the practice of the other at Taizé. This is one reason why there is very rarely anything like the full community of seventy living in Taizé at any one time. Brothers are continually dashing off to conferences and dialogues all over the place.

Another reason is closer to the heart of the Taizé philosophy. For the modernisation of the monastic order of things is not very high on the list of its priorities; Schutz, in fact, resists the suggestion that he has founded a school of theology or liturgy or religious behaviour. He stands pat, instead, upon something with wider implications. 'The Christians of today . . . know it is not possible to separate spiritual and social progress. There is only one thing to do; to work, in the midst of many opposing influences, for the spiritual and human development of the poorest, in fact of all.' Taizé, in short, is not only to be a sign of Christian faith and a meeting point of Christian factions. It is also to be a centre of missionary work, not so much preaching a Christian faith as acting out what it takes to be Christian principles. 'At this point in human history it is important to give freely and never to look for remuneration as representatives of the Church, to be one who is present rather than one who is working for a particular end.' This is the principle that had Robert running a medical practice in the district, when there was no secular doctor for miles around, though now that there is Robert spends most of his time away from home on ecumenical work in Spain. It set Alain to work with the local farmers' co-operative, of which he has been elected a director, not because he is a member of the community – which gets no income from the co-op – but because of his agricultural skills. It has put three brothers into a house in Lyons, where one works as a lorry driver, another as a probation officer and the third in a factory. There are six other brothers in Chicago, two in Réçif, and six more in three different fraternities in Africa. Not all of them are doing workaday jobs like the men in Lyons. But all of them are, one way and another, spreading the doctrines of Taizé. They are present in the world and not in their monastery. And that is what distinguishes them sharply from the tradition they have followed.

Schutz says that they and their brothers at home are not to work for any particular end. If this is a rejection of the proselytiser, the man who would convert the heathen and the agnostic and the merely lukewarm to a fervent belief in a God-man who walked the earth two thousand years go, then this too is a departure from the Christian tradition. Yet there is an end-product to Taizé, and Eric with his ikons, Dominique with his slugs of type, Clément with his trowel, Daniel with his potter's wheel and all the rest believe they are working towards it. It is an end-product that a Buddhist might hope for, or a Moslem or a Jew, or a man with no faith in anything that is not of the here and now and of this earth. It is proclaimed, at Taizé, with all the brash technique of the roadside gasoline advertiser. Outside the Church of the Reconciliation there is a gigantic and gaudy hoarding. On it in three languages is written: 'All You Who Enter Here Be Reconciled. The Father With His Son. The Husband With His Wife. The Believer With The Unbeliever. The Christian With His Separated Brother.' This may not be an original injunction. But by any worldly standards it betrays an enormous, almost a monstrous ambition. To hope to change mankind, to shift perhaps the flux of human nature itself, so much and at so many points: this is what the brothers of Taizé have really set their hands to. Men living lives, as their leader himself admits, whose shape and texture and very essence is against all human reason.

TWO

THE TRADITION

'So the religious life is a help towards saintliness, because it is a life
of burial.'
R. M. BENSON, Founder of the Society of St John the Evangelist, *The
Religious Vocation*, p. 229

The religious life, in its purely technical sense, began with the
hermit and was not a Christian invention. Five centuries before
Christ, Buddha left home at the age of twenty-nine and spent six
years in almost complete solitude sitting under the sacred bo tree
at Gaya while seeking salvation. Long before Buddha holy men of
Hinduism had done likewise. In immediately pre-Christian times
devout Jews were in the habit of taking themselves off from their
fellow men in order to contemplate their God without distraction. Two sects in particular, the Essenes in Palestine and the
Therapeutae near Alexandria, were dedicated to an ascetic and
eremitical existence, practising poverty, chastity, obedience,
contemplation and penance, and setting much store by manual
labour.

It has been reckoned on the somewhat shaky evidence offered
by St Jerome (who has been described as a stylist rather than an
historian) that the first Christian hermit was St Paul of Thebes,
who fled from the Decian persecution in AD 250 and hid in a desert
mountain cave, where he lived till he was 113. After him came St
Antony the Hermit, who was born about the time of Paul's flight.

He was the son of wealthy parents who died when he was young, whereupon he put his younger sister into a home for Christian virgins, sold his possessions and lived alone, first in his own village, then in an empty tomb some distance away, later still in the ruins of an old fort on the east bank of the Nile. He stayed there for twenty years and his days were spent in weaving mats and praying. He was an illiterate but he had learned most of the Scriptures off by heart and so he attracted disciples. A settlement of huts or cells grew around his fort at Pispir, in which these solitaries emulated Antony and sometimes gathered together to listen to his sermons on the principles that should govern their lives. These would be what have since been known as the evangelical counsels of perfection, which have always been the foundation of Christian religious life. They are the ultimate authority invoked in support of a life vowed to poverty, chastity and obedience. They are drawn from a number of biblical texts and the two most frequently quoted both come from St Matthew's Gospel. Upholding the life of poverty there is this: 'Jesus said unto him, "If thou wilt be perfect go and sell that thou hast and give to the poor and thou shalt have treasure in heaven: and come and follow me."' In support of chastity there is this: 'For there are some eunuchs, which were so born from their mother's womb and there are some eunuchs which were made eunuchs of men; and there be eunuchs, which have made themselves eunuchs for the kingdom of heaven's sake. He that is able to receive it, let him receive it.' The authority for a vow of obedience has always been more debatable. Thomas Aquinas suggested that it lay in Christ's words to the young man quoted above: 'Come and follow me'. Others, particularly in recent years, have argued that the only authority is Christ's declared obedience to the will of God on innumerable occasions, a precept which all Christians must follow and not just those with a vocation to the religious life.

At this time the Emperor Diocletian was trying to put down Christianity, ordering the destruction of churches, the burning of books, and threatening torture and death to adherents. Antony and his hermits set off for Alexandria, looking for martyrdom. For some reason they didn't find it, but they did encounter people clamouring to imitate their way of life. Many other eremitical settlements arose in Egypt and in Palestine as a result, and in each of them one hermit was chosen as a spiritual director, after the fashion of Antony at Pispir. The most famous of these offshoots was Nitria, sixty miles south of Alexandria. There five thousand men lived, according to the historian Palladius, each in accordance with his own powers and wishes, so that he is allowed to live alone or with another or with a number of others. Nitria became so popular with visitors that the very basis of the eremitical life, solitude, was undermined and many of the hermits shifted further into the desert and built their huts at a greater distance from each other. Apart from solitude the lives of these early desert fathers were characterised by two things. One was a sparse diet. It is said that Antony confined himself to one meal a day, usually of bread, salt and water; and his imitators don't seem to have fared much better. The other was deliberate and penitential discomfort. Macarius the Alexandrian is reckoned to have sat naked for six months in a marsh, while mosquitoes bit him all over; an Ethiopian named Moses was so determined to exist without sleep that for six years he spent the nights standing up in his cell.

In the first years of the fourth century the centre of all this eremitical activity was still Egypt, with a similar movement taking shape in Palestine. And it was in Egypt in AD 318 that the first detectable move towards a really communal religious life, towards the monastery rather than the hermitage, occurred. Three hundred miles south of Pispir, at Tabennisi on the Nile, St Pachomius founded a new kind of community. It was to be followed, before he died twenty-eight years later, by eight others for men and two for women. They had high walls enclosing a number of buildings and some of them accommodated a thousand people. They were, in effect, small religious towns. With them came two other innovations. Pachomius was an ex-soldier and so he produced a Rule which was to be obeyed. He also put in charge of each community a man whose function more nearly resembled that of the subsequent traditional monastic abbot than that of the eremitical leader. The latter had been no more than a spiritual guide and the hermits had to fend for themselves and could come and go as they pleased. Pachomius's leaders looked after the material needs of their communities as well as their spiritual requirements; Abbot Hor planted trees around his establishment to provide timber, not landscape. In the different houses of each community, which contained perhaps thirty monks, there was an oratory for common prayer and a refectory for common meals, while the entire community would gather twice a week in the principal church for worship. The life was still highly individualistic by later standards; Pachomius allowed his monks to choose what penances they would perform, what meals they would attend, what crafts they would take up. But it was an important development towards the totally communal life. It was a pattern rapidly followed elsewhere. Constantine promised religious tolerance with the Edict of Milan in AD 313 and so created a climate for expansion; Pachomius provided a model. As a result 'Never in the history of the Christian Church has there been such a stampede towards the monastic life as took place in Egypt between the years 350 and 400.' Monasteries also sprang up in Palestine and Asia Minor, along the North African coast, in Greece, Sicily, Italy, Spain and Gaul.

Hermits did not vanish as communities began to appear. The most celebrated of them all, St Simeon Stylites, did not arrive until early in the fifth century, when he mounted his pillar, gradually increased its height from nine to sixty feet, and stayed put on a three-foot platform for thirty-six years. There were many others like him and the eremitical species has never been extinguished. But a norm of religious life was being fashioned and they did not correspond to it. By the last quarter of the fourth century St Basil had tasted the hermit life himself, turned his back on it, and composed a Rule for monks which pointed the way ahead even more explicitly than Pachomius had done. Basil said that the solitary life was against the law of love because the solitary was bound to be self-centred; that it was bad for the individual to be in a position where his faults could not be corrected; that the solitary was in peril much more than the cenobite – the man living in community – of supposing that at some stage he had attained spiritual perfection. Basil's Rule was

stricter than the one Pachomius had laid down. It set the hours of
liturgical prayer and it specified manual labours for its followers.
It discouraged the extreme austerities practised by the desert
fathers but it was at heart a rigorous code. It became the
blueprint of eastern monasticism. The west had to wait nearly
two centuries more before it received and adopted a similar
statute, and in that time the monastic colony on Egyptian lines
had spread across Europe as far north as Ireland. The statute
came eventually from the hand of St Benedict some time between
530 and his death in 543. And for the next six hundred years the
monastic life based on St Benedict's Rule became the norm in
every country of Europe to the north and west of Italy; even in
the middle of the twentieth century purists argued that a substantial departure from the Rule is a departure from the monastic life
itself. In those six centuries the monasteries were a major force
in western civilisation, so much so that J. H. Newman was
tempted to label them 'the Benedictine centuries'; Benedict is to
be seen as much more than the originator of a sub-classification of
the Christian life.

There are few men of such influence of whom we know so
little. We have no idea what he looked like, for a contemporary
portrait does not exist. The Mazzaroppi painting in his old abbey
of Montecassino shows him entirely bald, with a squat and square
head, a patriarchal beard, a generous mouth. A panel in Peri-
gueux Cathedral has him tonsured, clean-shaven, with two scars
on his left cheek, thin lips, small mouth and a huge cranium. We
are scarcely better informed about his life. The only record is in
the second book of *Dialogues* which St Gregory the Great wrote
half a century after his death, and that is sketchy in the extreme.
It begins 'From his boyhood he had the wisdom of age, for with a
virtue far beyond his years he surrendered his heart to no worldly
pleasure. . . .' Benedict's birthday is generally assumed to be
480. He came of a good family in the province of Nursia, was
educated in Rome, but abandoned his school and set off for the
wilderness accompanied by his old nurse. In the village of Enfide
she broke someone's sieve, so Benedict prayed and it was
mended. Whereupon he fled to a cave at Subiaco, forty miles
from Rome, and lived there for three years. One day 'the devil

brought before his mind's eye the image of a woman he had once seen and by this imagination inflamed the servant of God with such a heat of passion that he could scarce control it.' Control it he did by stripping and jumping into a nettlebed, saying later in his life that never again was he vexed by lust. 'Soon after this many men began to leave the world and to put themselves eagerly under his guidance.' In particular the monks of Vicoravo asked him to take the place of their dead abbot and when he did, and tried to reform them, they attempted to poison him. But Benedict blessed the glass of wine before drinking it and the vessel shattered. He took the hint, nevertheless, and became a solitary again for a time. He grew, writes St Gregory, in virtue and miraculous power; once he persuaded a monk to walk upon the surface of a lake and on another occasion made an iron billhook float to the surface. He cured a man with a mottled skin and brought a dead child back to life. He also returned to the monastic existence. He built twelve monasteries before he died, placing an abbot in charge of twelve monks in each of them. About 525 he moved to the abbey of Montecassino, and it was there that he composed his Rule and where, six days before his death, he ordered his grave to be opened. We know nothing else about the patriarch of western monasticism except what is implied in his Rule.

It is a relatively short document of seventy-five chapters, some of them no more than a paragraph in length. It was written to bring order to a religious situation that had become chaotic and in some cases scandalous, as Benedict makes clear in his first chapter by distinguishing four kinds of monks. The first are the cenobites, who live in monasteries under a rule and an abbot. The second are hermits who, after long probation in a monastery, 'having learnt in association with many brethren how to fight against the devil, go out well-armed from the ranks of the community to the solitary combat of the desert.' Third are the detestable Sarabaites, living in twos or threes or alone, whose only law is their own pleasure; 'whatever they think or choose to do, that they call holy; what they like not, that they regard as unlawful.' Last are the Gyrovagues, who wander from place to place 'ever roaming and never stable, given up to their own wills and the allurements of gluttony, and worse in all respects than the Sarabaites.'

Benedict was equally clear about what he was proposing for his followers. They were to establish a school of the Lord's service. The abbot was to be the representative of Christ in the monastery and he was to be obeyed as if he were God. Discipline was to be strict but not invariably harsh; gentle characters were to be admonished verbally and only 'bold, hard, proud and disobedient' men given corporal punishment. No monk should have anything he could call his own 'for monks should not even have their bodies and wills at their own disposal.' A Benedictine monastery was to be completely self-contained and self-sufficient. It was to be supported economically by what it grew in its fields and gardens. Its whole life was to be directed towards the worship of God and the sanctification of its individual souls. Nothing that happened inside its walls was for any other purpose than this; nothing, indeed, had any reference to what might be happening outside its walls. The life was to be utterly regular and quite unvarying in its routine. The average day would see the monk spending about four hours in communal prayer, a similar period in private prayer or devotional reading, and about six hours in domestic chores, manual work or some craft. And at all points it was meticulously planned. The Rule considers how many psalms are to be said at the night offices; at what seasons alleluia is to be said; how the monks are to sleep; how boys – who were offered to the monastery for life by pious parents – are to be corrected; what kind of man the cellarer of the monastery should be; how guests are to be received; whether a monk should receive letters or anything else. It stipulates the amount of food and drink the monks are to take: two cooked dishes at the daily meal with fruit or young vegetables if available, a pound of bread and half a pint of wine a day, no flesh – except for the sick – from quadrupeds. It orders how the monks shall be clothed: a cowl, a belt, shoes and stockings, all to be made from whatever material is locally available and can be bought cheaply. It leaves nothing at all to chance or to the initiative of anyone but the abbot whose responsibility, Benedict warns, is a heavy one. 'And whatever number of brethren he knows he has under his care, let him regard it as certain that he will have to give the Lord an account of all these souls on the Day of Judgement, and certainly of his own soul also.'

This was the charter that brought order to the monastic life in the west. It was carried to England by St Augustine of Canterbury in 597, though there the Benedictine life did not gain a foothold beyond the south-east until in the middle of the seventh century men like Wilfrid of Lindisfarne and Benedict Biscop returned from Rome and began to build communities at Jarrow, Wearmouth and elsewhere in the north; until then monasticism across the Channel had been an adaptation of the Pachomian way, brought in turn by Patrick from the Continent to Ireland and by Columba from Ireland to Iona and the mainland. And by that time in Italy the Benedictine life was already undergoing subtle changes from the pattern envisaged by its founder. By 643 the abbey of Bobbio, which contained about a hundred and fifty monks, owned twenty-eight farms and in one year produced for resale 2,100 bushels of corn, 1,600 cartloads of hay, 2,700 litres of oil, 5,000 pigs and cattle, and 800 amphoras of wine. This may not have infringed the letter of the Rule but it was not in the original spirit of self-containment and absolute separation from the world.

There were other departures from Benedict's precepts and most of them took place gradually over long periods of time. The monastery he planned was entirely for lay brothers (Benedict himself was never ordained) but by the tenth century it was becoming normal for monks to take holy orders. Benedict assumed that his abbots would live the common life with their brethren but by the beginning of the twelfth century in England they had a separate house, chapel and servants. At about the same time the practice of child oblation, under which small boys were taken into the community for the rest of their lives, had ceased. Under the growing patronage of kings, bishops and lesser lords, monasteries like St Martin of Tours, St Philibert of Jumièges and St Denis had enough power and credit to produce their own coinage. During the early Middle Ages the Benedictine monasteries contained the only medical learning to survive in western Europe from the ancient world; Baldwin, who was originally a monk of St Denis, came to Edward the Confessor's court as king's physician and even after being made abbot of Bury St Edmunds was regarded as the leading consultant in the realm. The monasteries produced scholars like Bede and Matthew Paris, a monk of St Albans, whose 'copious chronicles provide a mass of information about contemporary Europe and the Near East which is not to be found elsewhere.' They were the chief repositories of culture and of art; all the greatest examples of book illustration in England before 1220 came out of the cloister. They were so much caught up in the world Benedict had counselled them to avoid that many English abbeys were eventually in the hands of moneylenders, which meant Jews. At Bury in 1180 'matters had reached such a pitch that the tribe had quartered themselves on the abbey, using its strong-room as a bank, lodging their women and children in the offices and wandering about the minster while Mass was being sung.'

The changes that came in defiance of Benedict's teaching were frequently the result of laxity, but as often as not they followed from outside pressure or patronage, either ecclesiastical or secular. The Council of Chalcedon in 451 had ordered that all monks should come under the jurisdiction of the local bishop; in 628 the abbey of Bobbio was exempted from episcopal control and placed directly under the authority of the Holy See. From that date onwards the tide of exemptions ebbed and flowed through history; some popes preferred to regulate the monastic life themselves while others dispensed abbeys freely into the hands of their bishops, which very often meant into the hands of the kings and princelings who had the gift of bishoprics; a movement which did not help the stability of the monastic life. The Rule, moreover, was subject to amendment by subsequent legislation. Benedict of Aniane, a nobleman who fought with Charlemagne and later became a kind of arch-abbot, led a general meeting of abbots at Aachen in 817 which promulgated the *Codex Regularum* and the *Concordia Regularum*. Among other things these considerably increased the liturgical prayer of the community and saw agricultural labour as an extraordinary activity of monks – which laid the way open for the employment of others to work monastic lands. It was the foundation of a social division within the monastery which has persisted into the twentieth century; the literate or well educated priest-monk responsible for the corporate worship of the monastery in choir, and the illiterate or undereducated lay brother whose particular function has been that of labourer and servant.

A further change of direction came from Cluny in the eleventh and twelfth centuries. Under Abbot Odilo and his successor Hugh the autonomy of the monastery, implicit in Benedict's Rule, was reduced by binding dependent houses to the abbey of Cluny. Cluny appointed their superiors, where Benedict had ruled that the abbot of every community should be elected by his brethren. It required the monks of dependent houses to make their profession of obedience to Cluny through their own superior, rather than to him alone. It exacted an annual tribute. By the middle of the twelfth century Cluny stood at the head of 314 dependent monasteries. Its leading figures came from noble families and they were the confidants of kings and popes. Its life was still based on Benedict's Rule but an emphasis had been shifted. The liturgy of Montecassino had been simple and without ceremony, and it had been balanced in the monastic day by equal periods of contemplation and work. At Cluny everything was relegated behind an almost ceaseless worship in the choir, which took up so much time that study was nearly impossible. It was liturgical worship made more solemn and splendid than anything Benedict imagined, by use of chant, ritual and ornament.

Even before the Cluniac reforms there had been pressure in some quarters for a return to the simplicities of early monasticism, and it came in two places: Citeaux and La Grande Chartreuse. The first originated with a group of hermits living in a Burgundian wood. Under the influence of an Englishman, Stephen Harding, who was returning from a pilgrimage to Rome, they set up a house where they intended to observe St Benedict's Rule literally, in the strictest poverty and seclusion. They were to wear a habit of white to distinguish them from the black Benedictine monks. The experiment began in 1098, but within a dozen years numbers at Citeaux had fallen so low that it looked as if it would have to be abandoned. Then St Bernard arrived with thirty companions and from that moment the future of the Cistercian life was assured. Bernard was himself a Burgundian, a nobleman who before his arrival at Citeaux had done time among solitaries in Britanny and had been abbot of St Cyprian. He was a frail man who suffered from chronic stomach trouble which was not helped by the extreme austerities and mortifications he practised. Within two years of joining Harding he was told to found a new abbey at Clairvaux and it was from there that he was to exert his influence not only on the order but on the Church at large. He denounced the persecution of Jews and he preached the Second Crusade. He was the chief backer of Pope Innocent II in his struggles with the antipope Anacletus. He wrote one of the outstanding books of medieval mysticism. But nothing he did was to have such a lasting effect as his rescue and consolidation of the Cistercian life.

There had been no thought of founding a new order when the hermits started their house at Citeaux; essentially they were after a communal life more severe and more remote from society than the one Benedictinism had grown into. Bernard built an order but it stuck closely to those first principles. Powerful benefactors, who had left their mark on the Benedictines, were kept away from Cistercian houses. The monks rejected every evidence of luxury and wealth; cloaks, shirts, warm hoods, bedspreads and combs went and crucifixes were made of wood, not precious metal. They abandoned all feudal possessions, like manorial bakeries and mills, and they disdained any income from church possessions such as tithes, altar and burial dues and advowsons. Their lands were to be cultivated only for their own use and by their own labour, and this meant introducing lay brothers to do the bulk of the work so that the priests could get on with the chief function of the monastery, which was prayer in the choir and in the cloister. Literary work was forbidden by statute, and as a result the early Cistercians had the reputation of being illiterates. In church the services and the liturgy were severely trimmed. The offices of the saints, the litanies, the processions, the visits to the altars all disappeared and the elaborations of chant and ritual which were at that moment reaching greater heights in Cluny and its offshoots disappeared with them. The

Cistercian monks were bent on one thing above all others and that was individual sanctification. So they lived sparely and they conducted themselves in silence except when conversation was absolutely necessary.

It was a life of high ideal and it attracted disciples as rapidly as Benedictinism had in its early years. Under Bernard the abbey of Clairvaux housed seven hundred monks and in England there were six hundred at Rievaulx under Abbot Aelred. But, like the Benedictines, the Cistercians were to shed some of their early fervour and strictness as their numbers began to swell. They were never to depart from the Rule as much as the Benedictines, but by 1200 many abbeys took incomes from sources forbidden by statute. About the same time Cistercian abbots began to build libraries and Cistercian monks started to write chronicles. The white monks in England became the biggest wool producers in the country, having started sheep farming to make their own clothes. In 1325 the abbot of Beaulieu was disciplined by the mother house at Citeaux for drinking with knights, eating off silver plate and having watchdogs tethered to his bed with silver chains.

The simultaneous reform, at La Grande Chartreuse, was to be severer and more lasting. It was the work of St Bruno, who was a canon of Cologne and a teacher at Rheims before joining the same forest hermits who started Citeaux. He spent a couple of years with them before he left with two companions to make his own community at a place in the Dauphine Alps north of Grenoble. The Carthusians were backtracking to an age before Benedict's. In place of the dormitory, which had been the standard sleeping arrangement since Montecassino, the Carthusian monk inhabited a separate cell. He left it only for lauds, matins and vespers in the church each day and for occasional meals and conversation with his brethren. Otherwise he prayed and read alone, ate alone, and worked alone. A hairshirt was as obligatory as the habit that covered it. Silence was total except for the daily excursions into choir and the weekly periods of relaxation. It was a life for contemplative ascetics and it was to be preserved almost entirely in its original state by the most inflexible observation of its Rule. It is the one form of communal religious life that has, even today, scarcely budged an inch from its origins. Because of its inflexibility and its rigours the Carthusian order was never to attract great numbers. It was never to pull any weight in Church politics. Its communities were never to affect the lives of society around them. It is significant chiefly because it was founded at a particular point in time, as a protest against change and decay. It was an emphatic re-assertion of the need to withdraw from a world which could corrupt and come between a man and his desire to contemplate his God without distraction, which had been the foundation of the religious life so far.

For six hundred years after Benedict this, together with the idea of communal life, had been the standard, and an infectious one. It had led the canons of the Church – the priests who long before Benedict had been grouped around a bishop to sing the offices in the basilican churches of Rome and other cities – to reorganise themselves on a comparable footing, with comparable disciplines. The secular priests alone had been untouched by the spiritual fervour and the intellectual growth which, at different stages, characterised the religious foundations. Planted in isolation in the world most of them were in as wretched a condition, morally, spiritually and materially, as the people they were supposed to be ministering to. There was a need for new forms of religious life whose followers, far from withdrawing from the world as the monks had proposed, would go preaching in secular situations while drawing on the strength of the communal life for stability. The first attempt to do this came with the foundation of the Order of Fontrevault at the end of the eleventh century by Robert of Arbrissel, who was an assistant to the Bishop of Rennes. He set up two houses, one for women and another for men, and when he died in 1117 his successor at the head of them was a married woman, Petronilla of Chemaille; not a novelty, for at Whitby four hundred years earlier St Hilda had become the first abbess of a mixed community. Robert's really original idea was to have two groups of religious, one staying within the enclosure while the other went out preaching, the jobs being interchange-able from time to time. Fontrevault was followed within a few years by another double monastery at Premontre, set up by Norbert, a kinsman of the Emperor Henry IV, to begin the

Premonstratensian order which was also vowed to get out into the world and stimulate parochial life.

The twelfth century saw several other attempts to combine monastic life and secular activity. And because it was a time when the Church was deep in its crusades it also threw up the orders dedicated to fighting the Moslems and to protecting the Christian pilgrims on their way to and from Jerusalem. The Order of the Temple was organised in 1120, so impoverished at first that two knights had to share one horse and one mess tin, but eventually, as a result of Pope Alexander III allowing them to keep whatever treasures they looted from the enemies of the Church, it grew into a corporation of colossal and ostentatious wealth. The Order of St John of Jerusalem began by running its hospital for sick pilgrims but then began to fight for them and eventually ended up as a military threat to Moslem shipping in the Mediterranean from its stronghold on Malta, where it remained until Napoleon dispossessed it. There were other military orders, like the Teutonic Knights and the Knights of the Sword, and there were bargaining foundations like the Trinitarians, who existed to ransom Christian prisoners from the Saracens, normally by money but if that failed by exchanging places with them. Between them they took the religious life an unrecognisable distance from what St Benedict had envisaged. If they could be called monks at all it was only because they were based on community and because they began by taking the vows of poverty, chastity and obedience, though poverty didn't last long in the case of the Templars.

They were, though, a response to the times they were living in. If the twelfth century marked a change in the religious life it was even more a turning-point in the European world as a whole. It was a time when merchants and craftsmen began to form themselves into guilds, when wealth from the east began to flow through the market-place in the wake of the crusaders, when people began to travel more freely than ever before, when the troubadours were on the hoof from Provence, when universities began to appear and when traditional beliefs were being questioned by pedagogues like Peter Abelard in Paris. This was a situation the Church felt a need to control and it led in the thirteenth century to the development of the mendicant orders of friars. It produced the Carmelites and the Augustinians, the Bonshommes, the Friars of the Sack and the Crutched Friars. It also produced the Franciscans and the Dominicans. Of the two the Franciscans were the more radical departure from the norm of religious life, and this was in keeping with the character of their founder. St Francis, son of a rich cloth merchant in Assisi, was a frivolous charmer in his youth, bound for a soldier's life, but with a deep streak of tenderness in him. It was to come out revealingly later in his life in his instructions to the ministers in charge of the Franciscan friaries who were, he said, to be as mothers – not fathers – to their brethren. Francis had been captured in a military skirmish in Perugia and experienced conversion while he was in prison. On his release he abandoned his family, became a hermit and one day in church heard the lesson from Matthew's Gospel: 'As ye go, preach, saying, The kingdom of heaven is at hand. Heal the sick, cleanse the lepers, raise the dead, cast out devils: freely ye have received, freely give. Provide neither gold nor silver, nor brass in your purses, nor scrip for your journey, neither two coats, neither shoes, nor yet staves.' And with that, Francis went barefoot into the world and began to follow the instruction to the letter. Like the first Cistercians he had no intention of founding an order, but from a small group of followers a movement began to spread across Italy. It was distinguished from anything that had gone before because the Friars Minor, as they became known, were to attempt life on Christ's own pattern; living and moving among the people without a livelihood, begging their alms, coming unlettered and unpriested on the same terms as those they were trying to convert. It was an effort to convert by providing an example of simplicity and absolute poverty.

This was not the intention of Dominic, a Spaniard who was a priest and a theologian who discovered his vocation when he encountered the Albigensian heretics – who accused the Church of taking New Testament allegories literally – in the South of France. The Dominican Order of Preachers he founded was to attack ignorance and intellectual error by the application of the trained mind. The Dominicans were to propagate the Catholic truths with every means at their disposal and everything was to be subordinated to this end. In a Dominican house fasts could be broken, offices in church were to be said briskly and without elaboration, manual work was abandoned altogether, all to leave the maximum time for study. They were, in effect, to be schools for intellectual shock troops and for this reason each one contained a doctor of theology, while the friars themselves were frequently dispatched to the new university cities of Bologna, Paris and Oxford to preach and to teach. It was the Dominican Thomas Aquinas who brought Aristotle to the defence of the faith, and it was the anti-heretical bent of the Dominican mind that led to the order being used by the papacy as a chief instrument of the Inquisition.

Both Franciscans and Dominicans were founded at the same time and each was to borrow something of the other's ethos before long. The Dominicans became mendicants as the Franciscans had begun, while the Franciscans developed from a completely itinerant and unruly body into one with a central organisation and a growing taste for study which in time was to produce its own sholars like Roger Bacon and Duns Scotus. And because of their mobility, which monks had never officially enjoyed, they were both to be used by the Church as its first considerable missionary force. 'There was no country in Europe into which the Friar did not penetrate, bringing with him the stir of religious revival. For work in heathen countries no missionary was more available. He was to be found in Morocco and Tunis. He preached to motley crowds in Syrian seaports. He voyaged to India and Persia and to the distant parts of China.' A whole collection of other mendicant orders began to develop to such an extent that in 1274 the Council of Lyons banned all but the Franciscans, the Dominicans, the Carmelites and the Augustinians. These, having the field to themselves, attracted great numbers from then on. By 1303 there were 557 Dominican houses, ranging from Britanny to Russia and Africa, containing 15,000 religious. By 1316 the Franciscans numbered about 35,000 in 1,400 friaries. It has been estimated that at this time there could not have been fewer than 80,000 mendicants roaming Christendom.

Inevitably there was friction both with the secular priests and the older monastic orders. Popes issued several bulls which gave backing to the friars, like the one of Martin IV in 1281 which put them under his jurisdiction and exempted them from both parochial and diocesan authority. They were attacked by the seculars for attracting penitents from the parish priest and the monks resented them because their idealisation of poverty reflected badly on the life of the wealthy monasteries. Not that this lasted very long. The friars were no better than the monks had been at sticking to the concepts of their founders. To the irritation of the monks at the engagement of friars to preach in monastic cathedrals and to lecture the monks on theology were added quarrels about the appropriation of revenues like burial dues which had previously gone into other pockets. They watched, moreover, these interlopers progressively acquiring more influence among the hierarchies of the Church. Between 1350 and 1535 no fewer than forty-four Dominicans were made bishops in England. There the friars were subjected to increasing attack. Fitzralph, Archbishop of Armagh, in a series of sermons between 1356 and 1357 criticised the friars for their motives as confessors, for their avarice, their luxurious lives and their sumptuous building. Wycliff not only accused them of immorality but of ruining the nation by begging and sending out of the country a sum he calculated at £40,000 a year.

The truth is that by the end of the fourteenth century the religious life was on the slide everywhere. The mendicants had fallen to the same temptations of acquiring property, benefactors and wealth that had seduced the monastic orders before them. The monasteries themselves were mostly becoming houses of decadence. There were exceptions. There were men like Abbot Thomas de La Mare of St Albans, who would rise before midnight while his brethren still slept, to recite private prayers. He usually ate and drank only once a day and carried out personal fasts and abstinences in excess of those ordained by Church and Rule. He wore a hairshirt and had himself flogged once a week. And though before becoming a monk he had excelled in field sports, at St Albans he refused even to watch hunting or hawking, or to let any of his monks do so. But de la Mare's conduct was no longer the norm. The norm was nearer the practice of William Clowns, Abbot of Leicester, who was said to be the most skilful runner of greyhounds in the country; Edward III, the Black Prince and their attendant lords made an annual trek to the Quorn country specifically to enjoy the abbot's pursuit of the hare. The most common fault, in England at any rate, was that the monks no longer observed the monastic enclosure which was intended to prevent them from coming close to the world and the world encroaching on them. They went out to consort with the towns-folk and they encouraged the townsfolk to come in to visit them. Things became so lax at Daventry by 1433 that the accounts were neglected, the monks were to be found in local taverns and all kept hounds of their own. Women came into the cloisters to do their washing and the prior was charged with adultery. At Dorchester the monks hunted and hawked and in the evening after compline invited women in to help the consumption of ale. The abbot was accused of keeping five mistresses at the expense of the community. A century before, an adulterous abbot would have been deposed and any other monk suspected of immorality would have been punished by close confinement, a restricted diet and various humiliations in choir and chapter. If it did not happen now it was because controls over the monasteries from outside had been relaxed; the diocesan bishop's responsibility for visitation and insistence on at least a tolerable observation of the Rule had generally passed to a royal servant who was very rarely there to do his job, usually being too much involved in public affairs or attendance on the monarch. And for once, the fifteenth century failed to produce from within the Church itself anyone with reforming zeal to restore the religious life to the straight and narrow.

The corruption of the religious life was only a small contributory cause of the Reformation movement, though it undoubtedly helped to give it popular support. Four years after Luther, the Augustinian friar, had nailed his theses to Wittenberg church door he attacked the life, in *De Votis Monasticis Judicium*, not on the grounds of decadence but because the religious implied, by taking vows based on the evangelical counsels, that his was a superior form of life to that lived by other Christians. The

Reformers, in fact, explicitly allowed for the possibility of religious communities in their order of things. In the Wittenberg Articles of 1536 there is this passage:

If certain men of outstanding character, capable of living a life under a rule, feel a desire to pass their lives in the cloister, we do not wish to forbid them, so long at least as their doctrines and worship remain pure, and, notably, so long as they consider the practices of monastic life as things indifferent. We are persuaded that numerous authentic Christians of irreproachable spirituality have passed their lives in convents. It is even certainly to be wished that such convents will exist, occupied by wise and fervent religious, in which the study of Christian doctrine can be pursued for the greater good of the Church. These might be then a place where, by the practice of pious exercises of religious life, young people would receive not only an intellectual training, but a spiritual one as well.

Although monasticism was quenched in most areas of Reform a number of communities, especially in Germany and Scandinavia, where legislation restricted rather than repressed, survived by adopting Lutheran doctrines in place of Catholic ones. At Mollenbeck, on the Weser, which had been an Augustinian house since 1441, the whole community transferred its allegiance in 1558. Its routine remained the same, but its theology was modified and all references suggesting a cult of saints were erased from the liturgy, and everything smelling of sacrifice from the mass. As a Lutheran community it flourished for over a century, until it foundered in the Thirty Years' War, and one of its monks, Conrad Hoyer, published a kind of apologia for monastic life among evangelicals. The Cistercians of Loccum, near Hanover, were another community who made the doctrinal change, practising full monasticism and even saying the offices in Latin till 1658.

The suppression of monasteries was nowhere as thorough as it was in Britain. There the first sign of it came in 1519 when Cardinal Wolsey sent the Austin friars, so far exempt from episcopal control, a set of constitutions he wished them to observe. Two years later he summoned abbots and priors to discuss reform and between 1525 and Wolsey's fall in 1529 a whole stream of royal edicts abolished twenty-nine houses of religious, male and female. This was only a taste of things to come. The Oath of Succession in 1534, which was to secure allegiance to the offspring of Henry VIII and Anne Boleyn as heirs to the crown but which also meant the renunciation of papal authority, let Thomas Cromwell loose on the religious houses, not as Wolsey's henchman but as suppressor in chief. The first tour of Cromwell's commissioners, armed with their question-naires and injunctions, was made with the intention of disciplining the religious houses rather than bringing them down. It pro-duced, among other things, the *Comperta*, a list of sexual deviations which ran the whole gamut from sodomy to nuns having children. The visitations which followed the 1536 Act of Suppression were made to raise revenue for putting down the Irish and Scots and for fighting abroad the enemies of the king's divorce. Even after they had started the king, oddly enough, was granting exemptions to a number of places like the nunnery at Stixwold, so that the religious in them could offer prayers for himself and his queen. But generally Cromwell's brief was clear and carried out scrupulously well. A few monasteries were converted into colleges or cathedrals. In the rest the plate and jewels were sent to the royal treasury and furniture was auc-tioned on the spot. At the house of the Austin friars in Stafford a Mr Stamford picked up an alabaster retable, a door and a high altar for 7s. The buildings were stripped of everything movable, while surveyors decided which part of the structure was to be left standing to create a house or a farm for a new tenant. The religious themselves, by the standards of the time, were not treated badly. They were generally given a pension of £5 10s a year for men and £3 for women; and these were paid regularly by successive governments. One of the curiosities of Elizabeth's reign was that while fines were being collected from Catholic recusants life pensions were being doled out to ex-Benedictines.

Under Mary there was a brief revival of the religious life in England. The monastery at Westminster was restored in 1556 and by the next year four men's and two women's communities had been refounded. These, however, were small pious gestures of a queen horrified by her father's sacrilege and they were cut short with her own death. Protestant England was to make its own gestures. In the seventeenth century John Evelyn was to toy with the idea of starting a Charterhouse, but it came to nothing. In 1626 Nicholas Ferrer and his followers at Little Gidding began to practise a form of religious life which was to last for thirty years, under the patronage of Charles I. Ferrer, a Fellow of Clare Hall, Cambridge, and later an MP, abandoned a promising career when he moved into the manor at Little Gidding with his mother, brother, married sister and about thirty relatives. They devoted themselves to charitable works, ran an almshouse and a school, did needlework and book-binding, and three times a day walked in procession to the village church to celebrate matins, the litany and evensong. A short service was also held every hour in the house and the family took it in turns to keep watch and recite psalms in church every night from 9 pm to 1 am. Little Gidding was no more than a curiosity, though, an isolated exception to the general rule of things. From the time Elizabeth came to the throne the religious life virtually disappeared from England for two and a half centuries.

In the European lands which resisted the tide of the Reformation a succession of popes attempted to bring some discipline to the situation in the sixteenth century. The year before Luther rebelled at Wittenberg, Leo x ended all exemptions and put all religious under the authority of the bishops. Paul IV had the vagrant monks of Rome sent off to the galleys. Pius v suppressed a number of orders, compelled 1,500 abbeys to return to the observance of Benedict's Rule, and forbade the Dominicans to receive any new members. Things were tightened up at the Council of Trent, which ruled that entry to a religious community was henceforth to be a matter of free choice only, that no one under the age of forty or with fewer than eight years in profession was to be made superior, and that no one could be professed under the age of sixteen. The Council also circumscribed more rigidly than before the movement of monks and nuns in and out of their monasteries.

Reforms were made in all the established orders and they were most marked among the Carmelites under the influence of two Spaniards. One was Teresa de Ahumada, who had been a nun for twenty-five years before she founded a more primitive Carmelite community in 1562. The other was John de Yepes, a Carmelite whose urge for a more eremitical life would have turned him towards the Carthusians if Teresa had not dissuaded him and invited him to become confessor to her foundling. Together they created the order of Discalced Carmelites, so called because its members went barefoot or wore sandals instead of shoes. Both were to be canonised, one as St Teresa of Avila, the other as St John of the Cross. Both were mystics, whose insights into prayer and commentaries on its techniques were to become part of the spiritual equipment of the Church.

In the processes of the Counter Reformation the sixteenth century produced other new orders. As the Discalced emerged from the regular Carmelites so the Capuchins (who later on were to establish and man Paris's first fire brigade) sprang from the Franciscans. There were original foundations, too. The Theatines were intended to work for the sanctification of the clergy, the Barnabites were to teach the young, the Camillians were to work among the sick. Philip Neri created the Oratorians who were to convert the world and defend the faith not only by conventional preaching and good works but by music and singing as well. If they had anything in common, these new foundations of the sixteenth century, it was that they all dispensed with the old monastic routine of offices in choir for the sake of mobility. Like the Franciscans and the Dominicans before them they were to get out into the world, at home and abroad, as missionaries in one form or another.

The greatest of them was born in 1534, the year that Henry VIII broke with Rome, when seven students took oaths in the Church of St Mary, Montmartre, and became the first members of the Society of Jesus. Their leader was a crippled Basque called Inigo Lopez de Recalde, whom history was to remember as Ignatius Loyola. Like many religious innovators before him and since he came from a noble family and he was a soldier before ever he became a Christian zealot. The fusion of the two disciplines, military and religious, was to characterise Loyola's Jesuits in a unique fashion.

Loyola trained his men on the *Spiritual Exercises*, which has been described as 'a little pamphlet of icy dryness and purely

administrative appearance', but which is also a means of system-
atically bending the will to a dedicated life. He drilled them to go
anywhere at the drop of a hat and from 1540 onwards, when Paul
III recognised the Jesuit constitutions, it was above all to be at the
drop of the pope's hat; to the normal three vows of religion was
added a fourth, and that was to be always at the pope's personal
disposal. The Jesuits thus became a cardinal instrument of the
Counter Reformation. They were set to rooting out the Protestant heresies by preaching, by education, by confession. They
founded schools throughout Europe to train more young minds in
their disciplines. At the Council of Trent they totally opposed any
doctrinal modifications and so made sure that there would be no
prospect of reconciliation between Catholicism and Reform.
They became confessors to the Hapsburgs and so contrived a
hardening of the Catholic arteries throughout the Austrian
Empire. More than any other group of men, they stemmed the
tide of Protestantism on the Continent. They were just as
vigorous abroad. They went to India and the Far East, they
proselytised in Brazil and Peru, and when the French began to
explore North America the Jesuits went with them. They were to
become so powerful that Catholics were to fear and hate them as
much as any Protestant. Before Ignatius died in 1556 his society
was already being fought in the Spanish dominions of the New
World by the Dominicans, who saw their well established missionary title there threatened by the newcomers. Eventually,
however, the Jesuits were virtually in control of almost a quarter
of South America. And it was partly because of their autocracy
there, because they held the Indians in paternal subjection and
prevented white settlers from exploiting them, that the Jesuits
were to be persecuted by the Church they had served and by its
secular backers. The colonials complained to the kings of Spain
and Portugal. The kings took over Jesuit colleges and churches,
shipped Jesuit missionaries off to the papal states, imprisoned
and executed others at home. In France the Jesuits were
attacked for their opposition to the Jansenists and because it was
believed they taught that the end always justified the means.
Under pressure from the Bourbons, Pope Clement XIV suppressed the society in 1773 and although it was allowed to carry

on its work in Germany and Austria, in Prussia and Russia, it was to remain on the windy side of the papacy until 1814.

In their prime, at the start of the seventeenth century, the Jesuits were the Catholic Church's main hope of regaining its hold over Europe. The Thirty Years' War put an end to that. And the Age of Reason, which the Jesuit-educated Descartes introduced, put an end to any hopes the Church might have had of holding all its people in unquestioning obedience even in the areas where it remained entrenched. The religious orders in the new climate of lay influence began to appear as remnants of an antique universalism. As the Church became increasingly secularised so the religious were more and more under fire from the parish clergy who had always resented their power and their privileges. The friction was greatest in France, where the Assembly of the Clergy in 1625 tried to bring the orders entirely under episcopal control. If they did not succeed completely it was because Richelieu, who imposed a compromise, had acquired a taste for the government of religious orders; within a year or two he had become, among many other things, Abbot of Cluny and Abbot of Citeaux and intended to gather all French Benedictine communities under his skirts as Superior-General in chief. The answer of the religious to these secular pressures was once again to attempt reform from within, as the Benedictines of the Maurist Congregation, two hundred communities in all, did by returning to the strict observance of the Rule. The Maurists were outdone by Richelieu's godson, Jean de Rancé, who entered the Cistercian monastery of La Trappe in 1663, after a fairly randy life, notwithstanding the fact that from the age of eleven he had been titular head of several abbeys. Once in La Trappe, however, he reversed gear and proceeded as operative abbot to make the Trappists a sub-order whose asceticism and devotion to silence was second in severity only to that of the Carthusians.

The seventeenth century also saw the arrival of new societies of priests whose object was to stiffen a secular clergy ill equipped to combat bourgeois rationalism and to train a new and better breed of parish priest. By placing themselves at the disposal of the bishops they avoided, from the outset, the exemption controversies that were plaguing the old orders. They lived in community, but they owned personal property and were otherwise generally indistinguishable from secular priests except that they were not encumbered with a parish. France was their biggest breeding ground. It produced Vincent de Paul's Vincentians, who 'went wherever the bishop sent for them, to preach, to hear confessions, teach the catechism to children, minister to the sick, relieve the destitute. They went from deanery to deanery in the diocese, visiting each parish in turn, and when their words and example had touched men's minds and hearts the bishop came to preside over a general Communion.' An Oratorian missionary named Jean Eudes established seminaries for the improved training of clergy and staffed them with his Eudists. A parish priest of Saint-Sulpice named Olier created the Sulpicians with a similar purpose. A canon of Rheims, Jean-Baptiste de La Salle, started the Institute of the Brothers of the Christian Schools, which introduced a new concept of primary education to France, with instruction in the vernacular instead of in Latin, and with pupils tutored individually instead of en masse. By the beginning of the eighteenth century all these societies were flourishing in France. Similar ones, like the Passionists and the Redemptorists, were starting to appear in Italy.

They were not enough to turn the tide of scepticism that was now on the flood throughout continental Europe. What had happened to the Jesuits by 1773 was no more than an extreme example of the treatment that many more religious societies and orders were to experience in the next thirty years. Throughout the Austrian Empire the contemplative orders were suppressed completely and many others turned out of their houses by the Emperor Joseph II. In France, under the Archbishop of Toulouse, a commission of regulars which consisted mainly of laymen suppressed in 1766 nine congregations of religious, over a third of the monks and nuns. Those that were left survived the Revolution in only token numbers. Many nuns went to the guillotine while most of the male religious simply abandoned their community life and allowed themselves to be totally secularised. The only ones Napoleon countenanced were a few charitable or teaching orders of women. Otherwise, and this applied to every land the Napoleonic armies crossed, disbandment or banishment was the rule. The anti-religious process was to continue well into the nineteenth century in what had been Catholic Europe; not even in Spain and Portugal did the religious orders escape general persecution.

Yet while the religious life was declining fast almost everywhere except in Italy itself, it was beginning to revive in England where it had been virtually absent for well over two hundred years. After the dissolution and after the abortive attempt at revival under Mary most of the English monks, nuns and other religious took the easy way out of their troubles by opting for a pension and a secular life. But a number fled to the Continent, finding refuge in the Italian monasteries of Montecassino and Padua, in the Spanish abbeys of Montserrat, Compostella and Valladolid, in Flanders and in France. A group of English monks led by Blessed John Roberts established St Gregory's priory at Douai, Flanders, in 1605. The monks of Westminster in 1608 founded the priory of St Laurence at Dieulouard in Lorraine. By 1624 English nuns led by a descendant of Sir Thomas More had set themselves up at Cambrai. And during the period of Catholic suppression in England these Benedictines and other exiles formed a kind of underground movement on the Continent, running seminaries for the children of people who were keeping their faith secretly at home, sending missionaries across the Channel to remind them that they were not abandoned. The Benedictines were in 1619 united in an English congregation by papal brief, to strengthen their sense of community against the day when they might return. They were the first of many Benedictine congregations of abbeys, groups generally formed within national frontiers.

Two things brought them back to England. One was the wave of anti-religious feeling that swept the Continent at the end of the eighteenth century, particularly since the French Revolution. The other was the relaxation of Catholic penal laws in England in 1778 and 1791. So back they gradually came. The monks of St Gregory's and those of St Laurence's returned in 1791. They were both at first given house room on the estate of Sir Edward Smythe at Acton Burnell, spent several years after that in a number of places, and then found permanent homes. In 1802 the monks of St Laurence became the monks of Ampleforth. In 1814 the monks of St Gregory became the monks of Downside. In 1838 the women of Cambrai became the nuns of Stanbrook Abbey. By that time the English were well accustomed to refugee religious from the Continent. At the turn of the century there were Benedictine nuns in Hampshire, London, Dorset and Lancashire, canonesses of St Augustine in Suffolk, canonesses of the Holy Sepulchre in Yorkshire, Carmelites in Cornwall, Durham and London, Dominican nuns in Gloucester, Poor Clares in Northumberland. There were even French Trappist monks at Lulworth Cove, set up there on land owned by a wealthy Catholic gentleman, Mr Thomas Weld, in 1796, and they were visited by George III and his family. The spectacle of the monk and nun around the country was therefore no novelty to the English when their own national Church took up the religious life for the first time in the nineteenth century.

Took it up seriously, that is. For the one form of religious life that seems not to have been totally extinguished by the Tudors was the hermit's. In the mid-eighteenth century it was fashionable (purely for decorative purposes, it seems) for landed gentry to recruit hermits to their premises, like the Hon. Charles Hamilton of Cobham, who built a cell in his garden and installed a solitary there. The terms of his service were that he would 'continue in the hermitage seven years, where he should be provided with a Bible, optical glasses, a mat for his feet, a hassock for his pillow, an hourglass for his timepiece, water for his beverage, and food from the house. He must wear a camlet robe, and never, under any circumstances, must he cut his hair, beard or nails, stray beyond the limits of Mr Hamilton's grounds for seven years, or exchange one word with the servant.' For this he was to be paid £700. He lasted three weeks and so didn't get a penny. In 1810 the following advertisement appeared in the *Courier*: 'A young man who wishes to retire from the world and live as a hermit, in some convenient spot in England, is willing to arrange with any nobleman or gentleman who may be desirous of having one. Any letter directed to S. Laurence (post paid), to be left at Mr Otton's, No 6, Coleman Lane, Plymouth, mentioning what gratuity will be given, and all other particulars, will be duly attended.'

These were not even straws in the wind. But the poet Southey's suggestion in 1829 that the Church of England should found sisters of charity on the Catholic model to work among the poor was. This came to nothing. Then on 14 July 1833 John Keble preached his assize sermon in Oxford. It attacked the plan to suppress ten Irish bishoprics, it denounced the spread of liberalism in Anglican theology and it launched the Oxford Movement to restore to the Church of England its High Catholic traditions. It was the crucial step towards the revival of the religious life in the English Church. This was very largely the work of Keble's colleague at the head of the Oxford Movement, Edward Bouverie Pusey, a Fellow of Oriel and Canon of Christ Church. The third leader, J. H. Newman, did in fact dabble with an embryonic monastery at Littlemore in 1842, but he was already on his way out of the Anglican Church which he left for Catholicism three years later. It was Pusey who fostered the Park Village Sisterhood before, during and after its foundation in 1845. In 1839 he had written to the Vicar of Leeds, Dr Hook, of what he had in mind:

I want very much to have one or more societies of Sœurs de la Charité formed; I think them desirable (1) in themselves as belonging to and fostering a high tone in the Church; (2) as giving holy employment to many who yearn for something; (3) as directing zeal, which will otherwise go off in some irregular way, or go over to Rome. . . . It seems best that at first they should not be discursive, as those of the Romish Church in Ireland, but be employed in hospitals, lunatic asylums, prisons, among the females. Do you know any who would engage in it on a small scale, quietly, or one who would be a Mother Superior; i.e. one fitted to guide it?

Two years later, on Trinity Sunday 1841, the daughter of a Gloucestershire clergyman, Miss Marian Rebecca Hughes, took a vow of celibacy in Oxford and became the first professed Anglican religious. She then went to France to find out about the religious life from the Ursulines in Bayeux and the Convent of the Visitation in Caen. Pusey took himself off to Romish Ireland to see how they conducted their affairs. Miss Hughes was, in the event, not to join the first Anglican sisterhood because she had parents to look after at home; she was to become the Superior of another community a few years later when she was free of domestic duties. But on 26 March 1845 two aspirants to the religious life took up residence as Sisters of Mercy at No 17, Park Village West, Upper Albany Street, Regent's Park. One was Miss Jane Ellacombe, who, at twenty-six, had broken off an engagement to free herself for the religious life. The other was Miss Mary Bruce, aged thirty-two, 'a lady of Scottish ancestry and Irish birth, who had been known to Dr Pusey for some time.' At their initiation service, conducted by Pusey and the Rev. W. Dodsworth, they both burst into floods of tears. Their superior in religion did not arrive until May. She was Miss Emma Langston, a 41-year-old governess, 'a lady of great refinement and good-ness, whose very countenance indicated benevolence'; a lady who had never got round to being confirmed until just before she was translated from Miss Langston to Mother Emma. By September there were seven sisters in Park Village. They wore a habit cut in the shape of a sack, of black wool supplied by a merchant who was a good churchgoer in Leeds. They lived under a rule which was basically that of St Augustine, with several other later Catholic regulations grafted on, which stipulated that they were to give six hours a day to works of mercy except on Sundays and holy days, when only the most urgent outside tasks were to be attended to. They were never to retire from a meal without having mortified themselves in some slight way. The superior was to receive all incoming mail and no sister was to speak to any visitor without the superior's permission. They had to be up at 5 am, and said four offices, with breakfast in the middle, before they went off to teach in poor schools of the district, and there were more offices in the evening before they got to bed about 10 pm.

These were genteel Victorian ladies and they were scarcely bred to stand the strain of a pell-mell life of austerity. Miss Bruce was one who had to leave early on. They were also women whose zeal often outran their common sense and their physical ca-pacities, and Pusey from the start saw that if he didn't want to end up as sponsor of a houseful of invalids some of the sisters would have to be restrained from overfasting. This killed off Sister Katherine who one Lent took no food at all except a dish of oatmeal each day after compline. The most zealous postulant of all stayed with the community less than twenty-four hours. She had wanted to imitate St Catherine of Siena by abstaining at all times from all food but the bread and wine of Holy Communion; when the rest of the community sat down to dinner she left in disgust at their self-indulgence.

That was the beginning of the religious life in the Anglican Church. Within a dozen years of their foundation the Park Villagers had amalgamated with another women's order based in Devonport to form, eventually, the Society of the Most Holy Trinity. By the end of the nineteenth century the Anglo-Catholic revival in the Church of England had become strong enough to have produced about thirty orders of women. There was nothing like the same growth rate among men, whose starting point was the eccentric venture of Joseph Leycester Lyne, later known as Father Ignatius. Lyne had been a licensed lay reader and then a deacon of the Anglican Church when he came under the influence of Mother Lydia Sellon, superior of the Society of the Most Holy Trinity. He decided that God wanted him to introduce the Benedictine life to the Church of England and on Shrove Tuesday 1863, at the age of twenty-four, with two companions (neither of whom were priests or had ever been inside a monastery in their lives) he moved into part of the rectory at Claydon in Suffolk. Mr Drury, the rector, celebrated Holy Eucharist for them each morning; otherwise they conducted their own services from a seventeenth-century Catholic breviary which Ignatius, the only one who knew Latin, had to translate as they went along. He also functioned as organist, adapting the Kyrie from Mendelssohn's *Elijah*, the Sanctus and Benedictus from Mozart's second and twelfth masses, and taking the Agnus Dei and O Salutaris from 'various composers'. The locals were scandalised and Ignatius was once badly knocked about and threatened with burning on a bonfire. He was reprimanded by the Bishop of Norwich and his request for ordination as a priest was turned down by the Archbishop of Canterbury. He persevered, bought some land in

Wales, and started to build a monastery near the ruins of a pre-Reformation prior at Llanthony in the Black Mountains.

The life there was penitential enough to have staggered a Carthusian. Every day one or other of the brethren was led into choir with a rope round his neck, was spat upon and walked over by the rest of the community as he lay prostrate in the sanctuary, and had to beg for his food until it was someone else's turn the next day. The reading of anything but the Bible was strongly discouraged. 'We never allow ourselves to think,' wrote Ignatius, 'it is all decided for us.' The community lived there for thirty-eight years, what time Ignatius went through a form of ordination by a roving prelate called Vilatte who had been in turn a Catholic, a Methodist, a Congregationalist and a Presbyterian. Ignatius also subscribed to the flat earth theory, became a Welsh Nationalist, and advertised himself on missionary trips to America as 'the Druid of the Welsh Church'. He died in 1908, and the remnant of his community transferred themselves to the newly founded Benedictines on Caldey Island who were, within a year or two, to convert to Rome.

The first Anglican men's order that lasted was the Society of St John the Evangelist, whose members were to become popularly known as the Cowley Fathers. It was founded by R. M. Benson in 1865 and from the start Benson made it clear that he was not attracted by the picturesque side of the religious life that had so dazzled Joseph Lyne. The men of Cowley were to live simply and unobtrusively. They were to devote themselves to prayer, study and mission work. Benson proposed sending them to the help of any London rector who asked for them; he wanted to start a house in London to be used for proselytising young people; there was to be a house in Oxford where young Christian men might stay while getting their university education; he thought that eventually Cowley Fathers might take up foreign missionary work. Possibly Benson trod carefully in the early years of the society because he didn't want to rouse the same public antagonism that had followed Lyne's experiments. It was not until 1894 that incense was used in the Cowley church, and not until years later that the sacrament was reserved in the Catholic manner. By then the society had a number of bishops backing it strongly enough to have subscribed a high altar for a new church; a great number of Anglicans still contemplated monkery with the gravest suspicions, but the Church's leaders were at least acquiescent even if they weren't all enthusiastic. By then, too, a couple of other men's orders had been started. Under the influence of Christian Socialism, Charles Gore and five other clergymen had taken vows in the chapel of Pusey House, Oxford, in 1892 and founded the Community of the Resurrection, which before the century ended had established itself in a mill-owner's old mansion on a hillside overlooking Mirfield in Yorkshire. Almost simultaneously, a young curate called Herbert Kelly, with an urge to become a missionary, had been persuaded instead by the bishop in Korea to start training youths who were badly needed out there for secular jobs; and that was the beginning of the Society of the Sacred Mission. The century had started with scarcely any religious life at all in England, and what little existed was fugitive; but by the time it ended the Catholic revival was well established, there was a great proliferation of Anglican women's communities, and a tentative start had been made with Anglican men's communities.

Elsewhere the old orders had been having their ups and downs. The Jesuits returned to papal favour in 1814 but were expelled again from Russia in 1820, from Switzerland in 1848, from Germany in 1872 and from France in 1880, though they were never absent from any area for very long. The Benedictines were similarly bounced in and out of favour all over the place. In Germany a community of Benedictines centred themselves on the abbey of Beuron in 1868, were ejected after seven years, took refuge first in the Austrian Tyrol, later in Prague, and returned to Beuron in 1887. The community at Solesmes was thrown out by the French Government four times between 1880 and 1903, found sanctuary in the Isle of Wight, and did not get home again until 1922. And because the fourteen Benedictine congregations were tending to make their own individual interpretation of the Rule – sometimes single abbeys within a congregation doing likewise – Leo XIII in 1893 forced all Benedictines to confederate under an Abbot Primate in Rome. He did the same thing with the Cistercians, uniting the nine congregations of the

Common Observance with those of the Strict Observance (the Trappists) under an Abbot General.

Yet the second half of the nineteenth century was generally a period of growth. As soon as Napoleon was gone from Europe the teaching orders began to appear again, new ones as well as the old. In a spate, Brothers of Christian Instruction were followed by Brothers of the Sacred Heart, of St Francis Xavier, of the Immaculate Conception, of Our Lady Mother of Mercy, of the Holy Family. They came in France, in Holland, in Belgium, in Italy. With them came new missionary orders, to trail behind the white man who was opening up Africa and the East. There was also a New World to be succoured, as America developed and grew. A monk from Montserrat had been with Columbus. English monks had crossed the Atlantic and returned again to their exile on the Continent. When the Jesuits were suppressed by Pope Clement some of them set out for Maryland, where they founded the University of Georgetown. In 1804, after they had been dismissed from nearly all Europe but Spain, the Dominicans followed the Jesuits and founded three provinces in North America. By the middle of the century reports reached Rome that the Catholic immigrants to the United States were in need of some stiffening against various anti-Catholic pressures there. That is what took the Benedictine monk permanently into the Americas. In September 1846, knowing next to nothing of the language, Dom Boniface Wimmer, from the abbey of Metten, Bavaria, and twenty of his brethren, stepped off the boat in New York. They set up a mission church at Beatty, Pennsylvania, and within six years they were joined there by a group of German Benedictine nuns. These were the earliest of many Benedictine immigrants to the United States. They were a transplantation which was to flourish, grow its own firm roots and become the most abundant of all the offshoots issuing from Montecassino and the patriarch of western monasticism. A hundred years after Dom Boniface made his landfall in the Hudson river there were to be more Benedictine monks between New York and San Francisco, between the Gulf of Mexico and the Forty-ninth Parallel, than in any other one country of the world. And by then they and all the other orders, societies, congregations and institutes, which from the moment of their various foundations had experienced by turns expansion and contraction, regression and reform, were to be on the threshold of yet another critical moment in the history of the religious life.

THREE

TOWARDS A NEW DISSOLUTION

'Monasticism in the Church is nothing else than martyrdom reappearing under a new form required by altered circumstances.'
LOUIS BOUYER, Cong. Orat. *The Meaning of the Monastic Life*, p. 54

In 1967 there were 1,405,931 men and women in the religious communities of the Roman Catholic Church. By far the majority – 1,072,934 – were women. Most numerous among the men were the Jesuits, with 36,038. After them came the Franciscans (Friars Minor) with 26,940, the Salesians (a teaching society founded in Turin by Don Bosco in 1859) with 22,626 and the Christian Brothers (another nineteenth-century teaching order) with 17,787. There were 12,070 Benedictines, 10,003 Dominicans, 3,770 Trappists, 4,018 Discalced Carmelites and 1,665 Cistercians of the Common Observance. There were about 500 Carthusians. It is impossible to say how the multitude of women's communities were distributed because the statistical sources which tabulate the men – like the *Annuario Pontificio* – do not keep the same account of women. They are merely tabulated en masse on a regional basis. In 1967 most of them (576,814) were located in Europe, but there were 256,350 in North America. In the same year the Anglican Church had 1,883 women in its religious communities and 328 men.

In spite of its comparatively minute tally the Anglican Church's figures represent a good half-century of steady growth. By 1900 the religious communities of women were firmly established and three years before, the principle of a religious life in the Church of England had been tacitly approved by the bishops attending the Lambeth Conference. Men's communities, though, were scarcely off the ground and it was not until 1935 that the religious became such a significant element of Anglicanism as to justify setting up a central administrative machine in the Advisory Council on Religious Communities. In those three and a half decades the development of communities, particularly of men's communities, took place along two distinct paths. One of them, by far the narrower, meant reproducing as exactly as Anglican theology would allow the ethos and behaviour of one or other of the ancient Catholic orders. The other meant adapting in a specifically Anglican way the basic and traditional principles of the religious life. To an extent the entire early development of the religious life in the Church of England involved a lot of backward glancing at the Middle Ages and the monastic heyday. It was the product of a movement to reassert within the national Church a number of Catholic theological principles which had been eroded by the Reformation; it was also conducted in a period of romantic nostalgia for the fifteenth century and earlier which accounted for the popularity of Sir Walter Scott's chivalrous novels, for the prolific design of neo-Gothic churches and for the curious infection of manufactured Gothic ruins on the estates of gentry from one end of the country to the other.

The Community of the Resurrection is a classic example of the specifically Anglican strain, which can also be detected in the origins of the Cowley Fathers and of the Society of the Sacred Mission at Kelham. On its arrival at Mirfield in 1898 it was easy for the extreme Protestant agitators of the West Riding to mistake the community for a Catholic fifth column planted in their midst. Pamphlets were distributed around the district saying 'Christians! Churchmen! Englishmen! Beware of the Mirfield Monks! The Community seeks to entrap our wives into the hateful confessional! There are papers on confession being handed to young girls which no one with any sense of decency would dare to read in public!' Easy enough to take that kind of line when the Community of the Resurrection did indeed wish to revive the habit of confession and several other things which had been rejected as papist devices three hundred years before.

Yet its origins were unmistakably English, not Roman. Charles Gore was that late Victorian oddity, an aristocrat by birth and a socialist by conviction. It is said that he became the latter on hearing a sermon by Bishop Westcott, who was president of the Christian Social Union, when he was a schoolboy at Harrow. Both he and the five other co-founders of the community were members of the Union before the move to Yorkshire, taking part in demonstrations against slum housing, low wages and factory conditions. Once it reached the north, the community used the quarry which stands in its grounds for frequent Labour meetings. Keir Hardie was once a visitor and so was Mrs Pankhurst, who talked for hours and could not be stopped. What Gore was trying to establish was a community of men 'to reproduce the life of the first Christians, of whom it is recorded in the Acts of the Apostles that "they continued steadfast in the Apostles' teaching and the fellowship, in the breaking of bread and the prayers . . . and not one of them said that aught of the things which he possessed was his own; but they had all things in common."' The only slavish copy from traditional monasticism was the saying of the sevenfold office each day – matins and prime, terce and sext, none, evensong and compline. These were, though, said in English, not Latin. At the beginning the brethren's vows were not made for life. They were asked to make an intention to stay in the community for the rest of their days, but actual promises were to be renewed each year. Similarly they were asked to make a life intention but not a promise of celibacy. They were to hand over all possessions and income to the community but they were to keep private capital untouched as long as they remained there. They were to be generally under obedience to the superior but they could appeal against any of his decisions to the General Chapter; in other words, to the whole community. They were required to do nothing that might offend their individual consciences and they were to be free to leave at the end of each year. Their dress was to be the cassock of the ordinary Anglican clergyman, without a cowl.

Gore had detached himself from the community before it

moved to Mirfield, on being made a canon of Westminster; he was later to become Bishop of Worcester. But under his successor Walter Frere (who also became a bishop – of Truro) and under subsequent superiors the Rule of the Community of the Resurrection was altered and modified in certain respects – life vows were eventually introduced for one thing – without ever losing its distinctive tolerance of individual conscience. Nor was it to lose the streak of social rebellion and engagement in social and political problems that had marked it from the beginning. It was to open outposts in the West Indies and in Africa. In one of these, at Sophiatown in the coloured shanty area of Johannesburg, Fr Trevor Huddleston conducted between 1944 and 1956 his great battles against the South African Government and its apartheid policy. It is doubtful whether his freelance political activities there would have been tolerated to the same extent by any order embracing in their entirety traditional religious concepts which have included, under the vow of obedience, the need to ask and receive permission from a superior for each separate external action. A Jesuit or a Dominican might have got away with it; scarcely anyone else.

A desire to imitate precisely the Catholic religious traditions was to be seen in the Anglican revival from the start. The astonishing progress of Joseph Lyne was the first clear demonstration of this. Two years after he began his version of the Benedictine life a wealthy curate of St Paul's, Knightsbridge, George Nugee, was starting the Anglican Order of St Augustine and it lasted until 1900. It early proved as offensive to local susceptibilities as Lyne's venture had at Claydon Rectory. Not long after Nugee and a dozen others had moved into a house in Hampshire, an aggrieved Admiral of the Fleet, a neighbour of theirs, was writing to the Bishop of Winchester that 'in connection with our parish church there has long been something very like conventual life, and now a Priory is added called "St Augustine's", and from these places are continually issuing forth phantoms, until lately only read of or seen in Roman Catholic countries. Thus our rural population is made accustomed, by the daily procession and perpetual appearance of these "sisters" and "brothers", to Romish institutions in connection with our English

Protestant religion; and our light and beautiful highways are darkened, and to our English sense rendered loathsome and terrible by these associations of the Inquisition.' The Augustinians survived a number of similar representations to Anglican authority over thirty years, and just before their priory was closed and they dissolved upon the death of their founder they helped a much more serious contender for the traditionalist title role. In 1893 Benjamin Fearnley Carlyle was clothed in their chapel as a Benedictine oblate. He was at this time a nineteen-year-old medical student and he had already drawn up detailed plans for an Anglican Benedictine Order with three distinct levels: of oblates observing the Rule but living in the world, of monks on mission work, and of other monks living a strictly enclosed and contemplative régime. All this was based on wide reading about monasticism since the age of thirteen and experience as superior of a 'brotherhood' at Blundell's School which horrified the school chaplain when he discovered the boys at Romish devotions before a home-made altar in a rented room.

The clothing ceremony in the Augustinian chapel was a false start for Carlyle. In 1896, taking the name of Brother Aelred, he went through a similar procedure at West Malling Abbey where Anglican nuns had been living according to the Benedictine Rule for several years. This time the ceremony had the approval of the Archbishop of Canterbury. With half a dozen other young men Aelred for the next year or two was constantly on the move from one dwelling to another, as landlords shifted them on or as local Protestants demonstrated against them. But in 1906 they found a permanent refuge on Caldey Island, off the Pembrokeshire coast. They had also, by this time, found a patron in Lord Halifax and it was doubtless due to his intercession that Aelred was first of all confirmed as abbot by Archbishop Temple and then ordained by an American Episcopalian bishop in Wisconsin on the authority of the Archbishop of York.

Next to the ruins of Caldey's medieval priory the Anglican Benedictines began to build an abbey, with an altar of pink alabaster, with Abbot Aelred's private chapel paved with black and white marble, with a sanctuary lamp hanging from a silver galleon, and with a peacock and two peahens strutting around the cloister garth. The place became the object of Anglo-Catholic pilgrimages from all over Britain. Here one could listen to offices sung in Latin from the *Breviarum Monasticum* as well as a dash of plainchant according to the most highly esteemed Catholic Benedictine usage of Solesmes. Here one could actually see monks with pates bared by a deep-shaven tonsure. And all inside the comfortable embrace of the Church of England. It was not to stay that way for much longer. From the start there had always been some doubt among canon lawyers about the exact legal position of the Caldey Benedictines – being offshore islanders – in relation to the see of Canterbury. And from his adolescence Carlyle had periodically cherished the idea that eventually he and his followers would be in communion with Rome.

In 1911 he invited the Archbishop of Canterbury, Randall Davidson, to regularise the canonical status of the community. Davidson's reply was that the monks should receive Bishop Gore – the Gore who had founded the Community of the Resurrection, who had been Bishop of Worcester and was now Bishop of Oxford – as their official visitor so that he could report to the primate on the spirit and observances of Caldey. Gore was shocked by what he found on the island. He told Aelred that before discussions went any further four things must immediately be changed. There must be a legal assurance that the community's property belonged to the Church of England. The communion rite mut be taken completely from the Book of Common Prayer and the monks who were also priests must say morning and evening prayer according to the same manual, whatever other offices they sang in choir. The doctrines of the Immaculate Conception and the corporal Assumption of Our Lady and the public observance of these feasts must be removed from the breviary and the missal. Exposition and benediction of the Blessed Sacrament must cease. Gore's own community had been vilified for Romish practices but it had never gone anything like the way towards traditional monasticism taken by the Caldey Benedictines. His visitation demonstrated exactly the distance separating the two paths taken by those who wanted to restore the religious life to the English Church. It also made it impossible for Caldey to remain even nominally inside the Anglican Communion. On 5 March 1913, Abbot Aelred and twenty-two brethren were received into the Roman Catholic Church and continued as a Benedictine community on the island until 1928, when they moved to Prinknash in Gloucestershire, which is where Aelred Carlyle died in 1955. Caldey was to be taken over by a community of Trappists, who migrated from the Abbey of Chimay in Belgium, who are still there today and who among other things produce perfumes for sale in that stylish boutique opposite Brompton Oratory in London.

Yet from the wreckage of Caldey enough survived to preserve the Benedictine strain of monks in the Church of England. Three of Aelred's brethren who refused conversion to Rome were taken up by Lord Halifax, who was still hoping that a permanent place might be found for the senior monastic order inside Anglicanism. Within a year premises were found at Pershore, next to the remains of an old Benedictine abbey, and after the Bishop of Worcester had been carefully sounded out the three men of Caldey and a handful of postulants moved in with the blessing of both their Lordships. By 1926 the new foundation was doing so well that a larger house was necessary. A suitable one was discovered in Nashdom, a mansion which Lutyens had built for the Prince and Princess Dolgorouki in Buckinghamshire, almost within chanting distance of the Cliveden estate of the Astors. And at Nashdom Abbey Benedictine monks have remained ever since, with their chapel in what used to be the ballroom, with the princess's shapely head in bas-relief on a wall now discreetly hidden behind a devotional painting. They have become so secure that since 1939 they have fostered a smaller priory at Three Rivers, Michigan, half-way between Chicago and Detroit. Their security demonstrates more than anything else the extreme elasticity of the Church of England now compared with half a century ago, when even the use of the word mass for communion was regarded by many Anglicans as appallingly tendentious. For the life at Nashdom is virtually indistinguishable from that of any Catholic Benedictine community, except in the minor details that mark one house from another within the Order of St Benedict. The present abbot is reported to have said that if Nashdom went

over to Rome tomorrow it would change only one word in its
services; the name of the bishop.

Like every other Benedictine the Anglican monks of Nashdom
prefix their names with 'Dom' – for dominus or master. Their
offices are chanted in Latin from the *Breviarum Monasticum*, and
their masses are celebrated from the *Missale Monasticum*, both
of which are also used at Montecassino. Their rituals conform to
the decrees of the Vatican's Sacred Congregation of Rites. When
a Nashdom monk gets a note or a word wrong during the chanting
of the office he at once makes a profound obeisance by way of
acknowledging his mistake; a mortification that certainly isn't
practised in every Catholic Benedictine community. When a
visitor arrives at the abbey he is met at the door by a strong whiff
of incense, which pickles the whole building; that doesn't happen
in any other Anglican community, either, or in many Catholic
ones if it comes to that. The incense is manufactured on the spot
and occasionally a parcel is sent with Nashdom's greetings to the
pope. Yet this is a piece of the Church of England, under some
inexplicably vague obedience ultimately to the Archbishop of
Canterbury. 'It is', a Catholic writer has remarked, 'such a
normal kind of Benedictine community.'

The Church of England has also, since 1921, had its Franciscans. They sprouted from the now defunct Society of the Divine
Compassion, which originated at the end of the nineteenth
century in the same Christian Socialism that moulded Mirfield.
This society began because a group of Anglican priests decided
that the working classes might be better served by the example
of men living a poverty-stricken life themselves than by any
schemes for social reform that had by then been concocted by
either the co-operative movement, the trade unions or socialism.
They took themselves off to the East End of London and there
they lived among the poor. They were to get their pictures on the
front page of the *Daily Mirror* for marching with unemployed
dockers, they were to tend smallpox victims during the
epidemics of 1901 and 1902 both on the hospital ships moored in
the Thames and in the isolation hospital put up specially on
Dagenham Marshes which at one time housed four hundred sick
people. One of their number, Fr Andrew, was to write to his

mother to say how sad he felt at his catechism class when the
children asked God to give them this day their daily bread, and he
knew that at home there was nothing for them to eat. They
served a small purpose during a bleak half-century of English
artisan life and they quietly expired in the 1950s as the original
members died off and no new ones came to take their place.

But something like the purpose for which they were founded
was by then being served by the Society of St Francis. A novice of
SDC, Brother Giles, had decided before the First World War that
his vocation was to live among tramps and outcasts. On his return
from the army, with two other laymen, he settled in a Dorset
farmhouse leased by Lord Sandwich. They did not take the
Franciscan Rule in its entirety and live it to the letter, but they
aimed to follow its spirit. Others joined them at the Cerne Abbas
friary; men like Douglas Downes, who was chaplain of University
College, Oxford, and Algy Robertson, who had founded in Poona
a hostel in which Christian, Hindu and Moslem students lived in
common. The friars, in those early days, often tramped the roads
themselves, sleeping under hedges or in casual wards, looking
for genuine tramps (whom they preferred to call wayfarers) they
could bring back to the farm for shelter and food. They were,
themselves, allowed 2s a day for expenses while on the road.
Gradually they achieved a reputation for genuine help among
those who in the years of slump needed it badly. They took in a
cat burglar, put him on his feet, and for years after his return to
London he would send down to Dorset lads who were beginning
to get on the wrong side of the law. They led the agitation for an
improvement of the vagrancy laws and the Vagrancy Reform
Society, which was founded in the friary, eventually got the
Ministry of Health to set up a commission which recommended
the need for new homes for young tramps. When the Second
World War started they took over a remand home and looked
after its occupants, and in the past twenty years there has been a
permanently floating population at the friary of men and boys who
have been in need of some sort of help; men drying out after a
stretch of alcoholism, boys being eased back into normal life after
a spell in Borstals. It is all consistent with the Franciscan spirit,
though the Anglican friars have never attempted a meticulous

reproduction of the traditional Franciscan way, as the monks of
Nashdom have aimed for with their Benedictinism. The men of
Cerne Abbas dress like any other Franciscan, in a brown habit
with a thick white rope around the waist, an end of it knotted
thrice and dangling to knee level. But their rule since 1937 has
been an adaptation of the one written first for the Christa Prema
Seva Sangha brotherhood which Fr Algy was once associated
with in India. The offices they say in the chapel, which is a
whitewashed and converted cowshed, come from the Anglican
book *Prime and Hours*, in English, and their communion services
are taken from the Book of Common Prayer. They have managed
a very Anglican kind of compromise, taking what they will from
any tradition that seems to suit their purpose.

If, a century ago, it seemed improbable that by now there
would be nearly fifty women's and seven men's religious communities in the Church of England, the chances were infinitely
slimmer of developments in the same direction among the more
severely Protestant Churches. Fragments of the religious life
had survived the Reformation in the lands which had rejected
papal authority. Apart from the handful of Catholic monastic
communities which transferred their allegiances after Wittenberg there was the odd experiment in community living like that
of the Moravian Church at Herrnhut, in Saxony. This was in no
sense a monastery; it was fraternal village of both sexes which
was created early in the eighteenth century by the pietistic Count
Nikolaus von Zinzendorf. It was governed at first by twelve
elders, eventually by a guardian and his deputy; it was divided
into 'choirs' – for married men, for young unmarried men, for
small boys, for widows, for married women and for girls – which
held separate meetings for prayer and biblical meditation; these
were subdivided into 'bands' of three or four members who
confessed their sins to each other. There was uninterrupted
prayer throughout the twenty-four hours at Herrnhut, taken in
rota by everyone in the community. There was communal
cultivation of the Zinzendorf estate, but everyone retained his
own possessions on joining. A hundred years after the foundation
of Herrnhut, Protestantism on the Continent saw a revival of the
ancient function of deaconess. In the early Church the deaconess

had usually been a middle-aged or elderly woman who cared for the sick and the poor and who also acted as a kind of chaperone when women received adult baptism or when they were interviewed by priests. In 1836, in the Rhineland town of Kaiserswerth, Pastor Theodore Fliedner started a community of deaconesses, who were to be either unmarried or widowed, who were to abandon personal property, and who were to look after the sick and the poor or teach or do miscellaneous parish work. They were, in fact, to be the Protestant equivalent of the many existing Catholic sisterhoods of charity. So were a group of women organised at Echallens, Switzerland, in 1841 by Pastor Louis Germond. So were the deaconesses of Reuilly, in France, who were established in the next year. But all such innovations were rather freakish movements against the general mind of Protestantism, which ran to parochialism and to a strictly domestic conception of community. In 1847 Kierkegaard wrote, 'There is no doubt that the present time, and Protestantism always, needs the monastery again, or that it should exist. "The Monastery" is an essential dialectical fact in Christianity, and we need to have it there like a lighthouse, in order to gauge where we are – even though I myself should not exactly go into one. But if there is to be true Christianity in every generation there must be individuals with that need.' In 1847 Kierkegaard's was a voice crying in the wilderness, that wasn't to be echoed in the Reformed Churches for the best part of a hundred years.

The twentieth century has been a comparatively luminous one among the Protestants. Taizé is quite the most conspicuous lighthouse but a number of smaller beacons have been lit. In point of time the first of them was the Retreat of Pomeyrol which, though it did not take that name until 1940, began in 1929 when Mlle Antoinette Butte settled in a retreat house at St Germain-en-Laye, just outside Paris. It is primarily a praying community and as such was a Protestant novelty when it began. The sisters meet four times a day for common prayer, they take the three-fold vows, and they have recently adopted the Rule of Taizé. Pomeyrol is distinctive in the way that it has shopped for bits and pieces of liturgy from a wide and sometimes curious assortment in the composition of its own.

To the Third Order of Watchers it owes certain meditations and the recitation of the Beatitudes at noon; to the Moravian Brethren the practice of two short scriptural texts and special prayers for each day of the week; to the Federation of Students certain prayers and their manner of intercessions; to the Quakers and to Moral Rearmament silent recollections followed by sharing . . . and finally there are borrowed invocations and antiphonal prayers . . . also the hymns of the Church of the first centuries from the Roman breviary.

Two years after Mlle Butte opened her doors a few women met for a three-day retreat at Grandchamp, near Neuchâtel; it was the first time anyone in the Swiss Reformed Church had ever held a retreat. In 1936, one of the women, who was to become Sister Margaret, opened a permanent retreat home in Grandchamp and by the beginning of the war she and two others were permanently settled there. In 1952 the Communauté de Grandchamp was formally constituted and within a year it had aligned itself closely with the Taizé Communauté. It adopted the Taizé Rule and at the same time Grandchamp's superior, Mère Geneviève, and Roger Schutz drafted a joint document in which both communities declared 'their common vocation to the service of Jesus Christ and the unity of their witness within the Churches of the Reform.' There are now about fifty sisters in the community. Those at the mother house are mostly busy receiving guests and organising retreats which are conducted by local pastors or else by Taizé brothers. Some since 1954 have been running a daughter house at Gelterkinden, in the German-speaking part of Switzerland. A handful have been away on missions in Algeria and the Lebanon. A few have set up an outpost in an industrial suburb of Paris. The pattern of Grandchamp is following very faithfully that of Taizé.

The pattern of the Oekumenische Marienschwestern of Darmstadt – the ecumenical sisterhood of Mary – has been quite unlike anything that has gone before in either Protestant or Catholic Churches. Its preliminaries were commonplace enough: young women attending regular Bible classes given by a Dr Klara Schlink in pre-war Germany, though the political situation meant that classes had to function semi-secretly. By the time the war started Dr Schlink and her friend Frl. Erika Madauss were tutoring about a hundred and fifty girls. What transformed this completely orthodox Lutheran activity into a religious community was the flattening of Darmstadt by Allied bombers on the night of 11–12 September 1944. Dr Schlink and her pupils took this to be a sign of divine judgement. They decided that repentance, reparation and unceasing prayer were called for in response and that it was their duty to offer it. As American troops advanced on the blitzed city a few months later fifteen members of the class went into retreat for three days. The result was that Dr Schlink became Mutter Basilea, Frl. Madauss became Mutter Martyria and that in 1947, under the guidance of a Methodist pastor, they and seven other women began to live together in the attic of Basilea's family home. Within seven years there were over sixty Darmstadt Sisters. They had been given a piece of ground on the road to Heidelberg by the father of one of them and there they had themselves built a chapel and a community house out of the rubble of war.

They are, above all, a praying community. Several times a day they meet in the chapel; in the morning for informal prayer in the manner of Quakers, at noon to pray for Christian unity and for the well-being of Israel, in the afternoon for meditation on the sufferings and death of Christ, and at night for vespers and compline in the manner of traditional monasticism. Every sister also spends at least an hour a day praying alone in what is known as a 'conversation of love' on behalf of one of the Christian Churches, and it is her lifelong responsibility to discharge it; in the guest house every room is named after one of the Christian sects and its decorations and the books on its shelves are relevant to that sect alone. Throughout each day and night at least two sisters are at prayer, relieving each other in couples every hour. Beyond the prayer life there is the missionary work. They have an old bus which they drive to poor quarters of the city and hold catechism classes for children aboard it. They preach at railway stations, in women's prisons and in reformatories. They mount a form of medieval mystery play in their home-made 'Jesu Ruf Kapelle' alongside the mother house. They publish tracts on their own printing press and they make crucifixes and devotional figures in their workshop. They run a house for ailing Jews in

Israel and this is important to them because they partly exist to make reparation for the evils of Nazism and particularly the injury that Nazi Germany did to the Jews. The Darmstadt Sisters are dedicated for life to this existence and each of them wears, on the day of her profession, a bridal wreath and a white gown which is the way a novice in a Roman Catholic convent might make her vows. Someone from the Free Church of Scotland might find it hard to believe, but at that moment, too, the Darmstadt sister is as Protestant as himself.

Like Taizé and like Grandchamp the Darmstadt Sisterhood is superficially, in the basic structure of its daily life, indistinguishable from scores of Catholic communities. It lies, in the total and permanent commitment of its members, at one end of a spectrum which pales off into something as flexible and in a sense sporadic as the Iona Community. Based off the western coast of Scotland, on the route through which the monastic tradition was channelled centuries ago from the Continent of Europe by way of Ireland to the mainland of Great Britain, this is strictly speaking a part-time community. It originated in 1938 when the Rev. George Mac-Leod of the Presbyterian Church of Scotland and seven other people from the Glasgow district decided to spend their summer on the island rebuilding the ruins of its Benedictine abbey. It was a symbolic gesture to start with. This was a time of industrial depression in the Glasgow area; the eight men who crossed to the island decided that the Church was making too many distinctions between the sacred and the secular, that a spirit of community had to be reawakened to relieve social distress and that Iona, with its ancient tradition of a common life, was as good a place as any to exemplify this. The community of about a hundred and fifty, mostly Presbyterian ministers like MacLeod, lives together at Iona only for the three summer months. For the rest of the year it is divided, living and working individually across Scotland, meeting once a month, observing a rule which regulates individual prayer, use of time and use of money. It is, one of its members has written, 'a body of men, ministers and crafts-men, who are committed through their life together, and in their own work, to seek the way of obedience to Jesus Christ, whereby the Church may fulfil her mission in the world today.

The members of the Iona Community are bound together by the common experience of a life shared in work and worship on Iona, by a common intention in their work on the mainland, and by a common discipline.' Devoid of strict obedience to a superior, quite lacking in sanctions for use against the defaulter, utterly open to the world and for most of the time completely fragmented in the world, Iona has scarcely anything in common with the religious life practised at a Carthusian or even a Benedictine level. It is a form of religious life because it is based on a degree of community and fortified by a code of self-discipline above and beyond the norms accepted by any Christian. Its significance is that, in its own local historical context, it is there at all, part of a very recent Protestant trend towards something on which the Reformed Churches had for long turned their backs.

For Protestantism the twentieth century has seen fifty-odd years of unexpected growth. For Catholicism it began with some of the familiar old frictions between Church and State, in which the religious communities bore the brunt of whatever punitive measures were being taken by secular governments. The French passed the Laws of Association in 1901, by which no religious congregations could be formed without the authority of the state. The following year the religious were forbidden to carry on any educational work at all. The result was that most of the men's communities went into exile – the Benedictines of Solesmes, for example, migrated to Quarr Abbey in the Isle of Wight and did not return home until 1922 – while the majority of women's communities transformed themselves into nursing sisterhoods. The Church in France was finally disestablished in 1905 which meant, among other things, that clerics were as liable to military service as anyone else: the Abbey of Citeaux had forty monks conscripted in the Second World War; the Abbey of Bellefontaine lost nineteen of its forty-nine monks in action, collected two Croix de Guerres, and had its abbot, Dom Gabriel Sortais, wounded at Lille, where he was fighting with the 25th French Infantry Motorised Division; even a French Benedictine lay brother of Buckfast Abbey in England was mobilised by his government in 1939.

In Portugal, too, the Church was disestablished in 1911, the religious orders were expelled with their property confiscated, and they were not rehabilitated until the early 30s. And while the Catholic Church survived the Nazi régime in Germany and the Fascist era in Italy rather better than might have been expected, it has borne the brunt of anti-clericalism behind the Iron Curtain since the end of the war; though in 1965 there were said to be 28,000 women religious in Poland, where Catholicism still flourishes under Communist government, 5,870 in Yugoslavia and 59 in Hungary.

The most important single event in the Catholic religious world during the first decades of the century was the foundation of yet another variant of the life: the Petits Frères and the Petites Sœurs, the Little Brothers and Sisters of Jesus, who did not appear until several years after the death of the man who inspired them. He was Charles de Foucauld, the son of a French aristocratic family, who was born in 1858 at Strasbourg in a house which is now the Banque de France and which was where Rouget de Lisle first sang the *Marseillaise*. He was trained for an army career, as a cavalry officer, in the military academy at St Cyr and he became the dashing rake of a crack regiment serving in Algeria until his colonel cashiered him for keeping a mistress. De Foucauld retired with her to the shores of Lake Geneva. He was reinstated with his regiment when a rebellion broke out in Africa and when it was put down he asked for leave to explore the southern part of Algeria. It was refused and he dropped his commission again. He was twenty-three and for the next two years he studied Arabic and Hebrew until he was fluent in both. Then, disguised as a rabbi and with his Hebrew tutor as companion, he vanished into the interior of Morocco – at that time virtually a forbidden land to Europeans – for nearly a year. When he emerged he had mapped a thousand miles of previously unrecorded ground; he wrote a journal of his expedition and it won him the gold medal of the Paris Geographical Society.

But Morocco had given him something of more consequence. It had impressed him with the quality of its religious life. This didn't turn him into a Moslem but it did restore the faith of his fathers. He encountered the Abbé Huvelin in Paris, a priest with a high reputation as a confessor and preacher, and in 1886 he received his first absolution since boyhood in the confessional at St Augustine's church. Temperamentally a whole-hogger, de Foucauld decided that he must live the Christian Gospel to the letter. For the next seven years he was a Trappist monk but found that even Trappist austerities were not enough to satisfy his craving for self-abnegation. He went to Palestine and became handyman to a convent of Poor Clares for three years. That was no good either. So he went back to his Trappist monastery, got himself ordained, and at the age of forty-two set off for the Sahara to live among the Moslems. He did not intend to preach to them or in any recognised sense to convert them to Christianity. He aimed only to live an exemplary Christian life among them in the hope, no doubt, that something would register.

Wearing a white habit with a rough red heart sewn on its left breast de Foucauld called himself Fr Charles of Jesus and settled among the Tuaregs, first at the oasis of Beni-Abbes, later at Tamanrasset, in the middle of the Sahara. The tribesmen accepted him as a benevolent oddity. He lived frugally in a hermitage alongside their camps and didn't meddle in their affairs. But he taught them to cultivate vegetables, he showed the women how to knit and how to make chocolate, and he had medical supplies sent from Europe to treat them with when they were ill. For fifteen years he went on like this until, on a December night in 1916, a band of Senoussite tribesmen raided Tamanrasset. De Foucauld was hauled out of his hut and shot. He appeared to have achieved nothing except to recover his own lost Catholic faith and to have made friends with a crowd of nomadic Arabs. He had built a mud chapel which he called The Fraternity, he had written a rule for proposed Little Brothers of Jesus, and he had prayed that others might follow him from Europe. But when he died he didn't have a single disciple. He had left a number of writings behind him, though, and so he was not to be forgotten.

It was seventeen years before his influence began to bite. A handful of imitators had gone off to live a hermit's existence among the tribes of North Africa before then. But in 1933 a Fr René Voillaume and five other priests recently out of the Saint-Sulpice seminary were clothed in the same habit that de Foucauld had worn and settled in an abandoned Arab building at El Abiodh, on the edge of the Sahara. These were the first Petits Frères. They lived a near-Trappist life there, spending long periods at prayer and in silence, working their garden and running a dispensary for the local sick. It was admirable but it was not what de Foucauld had been working towards during his one and a half decades in the desert. For him a first essential had been to embrace totally the poverty of the most poverty-stricken around him because this was what Christ had advocated to his followers. For anyone likely to join him in his mission de Foucauld had written:

Remembering that our Lord Jesus has said, 'When thou makest a dinner or a supper, call not thy friends, nor thy brethren nor thy kinsmen, nor thy neighbours, who are rich, lest they also invite thee again, and a recompense be made to thee. But when thou makest a feast call the poor, the maimed, the lame, and the blind. And thou shalt be blessed, because they have not wherewith to make thee recompense; for recompense shall be made thee at the resurrection of the just,' we shall then direct our efforts towards the conversion of those who are spiritually the poorest, the most crippled, the most blind, the infidel people of missionary countries; those who know not the Good News; who have no tabernacle, nor sacrifice, nor priest; the most abandoned souls, those who are most sick, the sheep that are indeed lost.

The Petits Frères at El Abiodh were not quite following this injunction; the very fact that they were practising something close to traditional monasticism separated them from the people they were living among. By the time war started ifn 1939, fifteen of them were in the community, which promptly broke up because all its members were conscripted into the army.

The war had a salutary effect on the Petits Frères. It thrust most of them into an atheistic environment for the first time in their lives; none of them had to the same extent before been forced to live as a devout Catholic in isolation from others for a protracted period. They saw something of the world as it really was, uninsulated from them by the protective wrappings of the pious society that had reared them. When they reassembled on demobilisation they came to the conclusion that they must not literally follow de Foucauld into the desert, but that they must follow his example in any situation where poverty and need was to be found. This meant preserving a tension which was clearly present in de Foucauld's life among the Tuareg; a tension between the hermit's solitude and lengthy periods at prayer, and his personal availability to anyone who sought his help. It meant, in their view, that they must turn their backs on the monastic tradition, that they must whittle themselves down into small fraternities living in the middle of poverty-stricken masses wherever these might be found. This has remained their distinction ever since. There are now about two hundred and fifty Petits Frères and they are scattered throughout twenty-eight different countries. There are about a thousand Little Sisters of Jesus living a similar vocation.

The brothers scarcely ever live in groups of more than five. They possess no property at all. In industrialised areas of the western world they rent working-class accommodation wherever they set up a fraternity; in Africa and other underdeveloped parts of the world they move into whatever is the poorest form of local dwelling. They have one fraternity in Great Britain and its address is 24, Autumn Grove, Leeds 6 – which marks it at once for what it is; just another anonymous-looking house in a long, gas-lit and terraced street, which was put up in the nineteenth century by the cloth barons of the West Riding to quarter their factory fodder in. There are rows and rows of Autumn Groves in that part of the city; a high proportion of their inhabitants are West Indians, Ukrainians and other refugees, for this is a slum area, due for demolition as soon as the city can find the funds to rehouse the people, and so its population is permanently at the bottom of the social pile, however that is composed.

Four Petits Frères live at No. 24, which has two cramped rooms upstairs and two more below. They have contrived a chapel in the space between the sloping slate roof and the ceiling of the upper storey; there is room in it for five people to kneel or for three to stand. And when the brothers have their hour of meditation up there, which they do every night after vespers and compline, the silence is broken by the gurgling of the water tank behind the altar, by the sound of next door's television coming up through the thin walls, and sometimes by tipsy laughter from the street outside. The four men in grey cassocks seem oblivious of it all. The noises off are all part of the world they live in. One of them spends his day labouring in a foundry; another has been bricklaying at a local brewery. There they are indistinguishable from their workmates, in blue one-piece boiler suits and heavy boots, and with dirt slowly growing into the pores of their hands. They talk no religion to their workmates unless someone else raises the topic and they do not honestly think that they have induced anyone to go to church who wasn't already going before they moved into the district. But they hope that their presence among the people will one day have some effect. At the moment the working classes of Leeds who come into contact with the Little Brothers of Jesus probably regard them as benevolent oddities, as the Tuareg did Charles de Foucauld; and in local terms they certainly are odd when the four of them exist on one and a half wage-packets and dispose of the rest either to the seminary for Petits Frères in Toulouse or to various charities. The Leeds fraternity is not exceptional in its condition and way of life. There is the Petit Frère who drives a truck in Hamburg, the one who mans a fishing smack out of Concarneau, the one who blacksmiths in the middle of the soukhs of Marrakesh. There are Little Sisters in a third-floor apartment in the coloured quarter of Chicago, others in an Eskimo village outside Nome, Alaska, more living in caravans at Alice Springs in the middle of Australia.

René Voillaume, Prior of the Little Brothers, who now spends most of his time on the move from one fraternity to another when he isn't exhorting them from headquarters in Toulouse, has put their purpose into a paragraph.

Our Lord has asked us to love men exactly as he loved them, and the Petits Frères' way of life might be summed up by saying that they must do their utmost to ensure that what they feel, what they do, and how they live, forms as perfect an expression as possible of our Lord's own feelings towards mankind. This mission is so absolute that everything must be subordinated to it. . . . When a friendship is profound and exclusive, it demands the presence of the person loved and a mutual sharing – as fully as this may be attained – of the particular circumstances of life and especially of any suffering. It must also involve a total and disinterested gift of oneself to the person thus loved for his own sake with a humble respect, in the way God loves each one of us. These demands of friendship define the essential elements in the constitution of a Brotherhood.

This is not unlike the tone of voice used by Roger Schutz of Taizé. There are considerable differences between the Taizé Communauté and the Petits Frères, quite apart from the fact that one is Protestant and the other Catholic. Oddly, the Protestants here are more in the monastic tradition than the Catholics, simply by being based on a central community. But in common both raise the question of the Christian Church's identification with the masses who are poor materially as well as spiritually; and both urge the necessity of the Christian to give himself and to love without expectation or even hope of a return by way of conversion or any other quid pro quo. Because the Petits Frères have gone out of their way to share poverty wherever they can find it, at its lowest level, they have become a thorn in the conscience of the Catholic Church and particularly of its religious communities, whose notions of poverty once they become well established very rarely coincide with its reality as discovered in the Autumn Groves and worse of this world.

There are diehard Benedictines and Trappists who would scarcely admit to even a tenuous affiliation between their own ethos and life and that of the Little Brothers. At the very least they would argue that whereas they are firmly in the mainstream of the religious life the Petits Frères, by their great preoccupation with the world and existence in it, are in some small pond of their own. History has made a nonsense of such an argument. If the mainstream analogy is to be accepted then Benedictinism will be found issuing from somewhere near the source and the Petits Frères from some tributary nearer an estuary which is teeming with scores of different forms of religious life. From other tributaries come the third orders, the sodalities and the confraternities which have since the twelfth century attached themselves in one way or another to the religious communities proper. They are composed of lay people who for some reason are disinclined or unable – who, in the jargon, have no vocation – to become full-time religious, but who wish to identify themselves with a particular order or religious society. At its strongest this attachment can mean that a Franciscan tertiary (a member of the Secular Third Order of Franciscans) will follow a modified Franciscan Rule in his daily life, will make promises for life which include a profession of celibacy, will support the Franciscan order financially and in every other way possible to him, will wear the scapular (a short cloth yoke covering the shoulders and chest) under his ordinary clothes regularly, and the full Franciscan habit on special occasions when Franciscan tertiaries gather with regular members of the order. At its weakest it will mean following something like the associates' Rule of the Confraternity of the Resurrection, which is a kind of supporters' club of the Anglican Mirfield Fathers. The associates of the fraternity (motto: *Consurrexistis Cum Christo*) can be either men or women who undertake to pray regularly for the Community and the fraternity, to subscribe 10s a year to the community's work and to interest others in its special aims – the revival of the religious life in the Church of England, mission work at home and abroad, the supply and training of clergy, and the reunion of Christendom.

At about this level 1947 was a momentous year in the history of the religious life. On 2 February Pope Pius XII issued his apostolic constitution *Provida Mater Ecclesia* which gave official approval at last to the secular institutes. There are well over sixty of these in the Catholic Church today, and they are one of its most significant growth points. A few of them were founded in the nineteenth century, but most have appeared since the First World War. An inclusive definition of them is difficult because while the majority of their members are lay people a few consist only of priests and slightly more include both priests and laity; some are for women only, some for men, others mix the sexes. It is no easier to define their structure and their activity. As one authority has it, 'There are some institutes whose members are wholly, or almost wholly dispersed, living isolated from the others in their own homes or lodgings; there are others whose ideal is to live in small working teams of two or three; there are still others who, through the accidentals of their history and development live entirely in community and are outwardly difficulty to distinguish from some religious communities. There can be no question, however, that the present trend is away from the last pattern.' The members of a secular institute make vows which, while they do not carry the same canonical weight and sanctions as those taken by regular religious, are made with virtually the same life intention. The vow of chastity precludes the membership of married people though in some cases these become attached to an institute through an associated fraternity; the vow of poverty means in this case living inexpensively in the world without actually descending to shabbiness; obedience is made to the rules of the institute which may have a hierarchical structure of government similar to that of a regular religious community, or which may merely be under the ultimate authority of the local bishop. The Catholic Church, whose statistical services are not its strongest point, probably doesn't know itself how many of the faithful are involved in the institutes today; but it is conceivably something over 50,000; one of the institutes, the Secular Ursulines, was reckoned in 1962 to have 16,000 adherents.

Provida Mater in its first paragraph defined the institutes as 'Societies, whether clerical or lay, whose members profess the evangelical counsels in the world, in order to attain Christian perfection and to exercise a full apostolate.' In other words, their purpose is at once to aim for personal sanctification – which is what the monastic tradition started with – and to live a good and influential Christian life out in the world, which is what monasticism has traditionally been averse to. The significance of 1947 is that it gave the Church's fullest legal approval to the institutes, thus raising them above the level of the many fraternities and other pious organisations of the faithful. In doing this it drew into the mainstream of the religious life a movement whose whole character was in its essentials – ordinary unordained Catholics spending most of their time at secular jobs in a secular milieu – alien to the tradition so far. *Provida Mater* and 1947 were yet another great turning-point in the religious life. What began with the solitary whose back was turned completely on the world, and became, first, the community which also hid itself away, later the community which made periodic excursions into the world, later still the community which spent much of its time in the world but always had a bolt-hole for refuge from it, now includes the non-community almost totally committed to the world. And because each successive stage of evolution has had some effect on the forms of religious life which pre-date it, the full importance of 1947 is still to be realised.

It is more than likely that the steady growth of the institutes has had something to do with a decline in the fortunes of the already established religious communities of the Catholic Church. There is no consistent pattern to this but it is there and it has become a major preoccupation of the Holy See. In the past twenty or thirty years there have been a number of growth points, none more marked than the United States. There the ground was fertile enough for Carthusians to plant themselves for the first time in 1951, when they established a community at Whittingham, Vermont. An even more remarkable phenomenon was the increase in the number of Cistercian and particularly Trappist houses in the decade immediately after the last war. In 1940 there had been three Cistercian communities in the USA, two of which dated from 1848; between 1944 and 1956 nine others appeared. The Benedictines flourished, particularly the American Benedictine nuns, who reckon three hundred to constitute a pretty small convent and a thousand a rather large one. About a quarter of the world total of Jesuits is to be found in North America now.

It is also possible for the Church to take an optimistic view of developments in some of its mission fields, provided the dates are carefully chosen. In Colombia, for example, where in 1921 there were only 38 religious houses for men, by 1962 there were 502; where there were only 31 women's houses in 1912, half a century later there were 1,469. Elsewhere the situation has been unhealthy. By 1964 the Belgian Cardinal Suenens was writing, 'Everywhere one hears complaints that recruitment does not keep pace with needs, nor indeed with the growth of population; that religious houses are closing down one after another; that the average age of communities is increasing. . . . Vocations are decreasing everywhere. It is significant that the least affected are the missionary and purely contemplative communities.' Another Belgian, Dom Benedict Heron OSB, Prior of the Monastery of

Christ the King at Gelrode, has estimated that the shortage of vocations runs throughout Europe with the exception of Spain.

A major difficulty in plotting the strength of Catholic religious communities is that the figures issued by the Vatican tend to be unreliable: a fact which is tartly acknowledged in the most respectable Catholic quarters. 'It is instructive,' writes a contributor to the *New Catholic Encyclopaedia*, 'to compare the ecclesiastical statistics of the Roman Curia in the early 1960s with the system that Baumgarten criticised fifty years earlier. Almost all his criticisms appear to be as valid in 1965 as in 1912.' The Vatican's chief directory, *Annuario Pontificio*, appears to paint a more optimistic picture than the current cries of alarm would justify. According to this source, between 1960 and 1966 the number of men in religious communities rose from 311,368 to 332,993; women in religion grew from 999,230 to 1,060,680 in the same period. The authors of the work seem at least to be wrong in their count of Benedictine monks; they suggest a rise from 11,500 to 12,500 in the first six years of the decade. The *Benedictine Catalogue*, which presumably knows its own business rather better, marks a fall of monks over the same period from 12,131 to 12,070 and of monasteries from 236 to 225 – though Benedictine nuns increased from 22,603 in 377 convents to 23,397 in 409 convents.

The position seems to be most serious in those countries – Holland, Belgium, France and Germany – where the Catholic Church generally has been in a state of upheaval, where it has locally been most daring, in the past few years. In the Low Countries, for example, the Church has been conducting experiments in liturgy and in relations with other Christians, and it has been reviewing Catholic social morality virtually in defiance of Vatican ordinances. In France, with half a century of anticlericalism to combat, it attempted to bridge the gap by launching the worker-priesthood shortly after the war, only to be trodden on by the Vatican when it became apparent that the priests were getting too politically involved on behalf of the workers for Rome's taste.

In Holland, where there were 33,350 women in religion in 1958, there were 32,443 in 1964. In the best recruiting year the

Church has had there this century, 1935, about 1,200 girls entered the active communities; by 1958 the figure had fallen to 465 and by 1964 to 231. The real growth period was in the second half of the nineteenth century; there was stability in the first decade of the twentieth but by the 1930s the women's communities were back to the level of the 1900s and today they are back to the level of the years 1860–70.

In Belgium, where one diocese has had to close 78 out of 522 women's houses in the past thirty years, the worst is yet to come. The average age of the women is 54 and only 7.4 per cent of them are under 30. In the diocese of Tournai nearly 30 per cent of the nuns are over 65.

In Germany between the two world wars the number of sisters increased from 61,236 to 97,516 and novices rose from 5,511 in 1919 to 7,488 in 1935, with a fall under Nazi government to 1,865 in 1941. After the war the number of sisters rose to 93,260 in 1957 but had fallen to 86,279 in 1965; novices fell from 3,996 in 1950 to 2,101 in 1965.

In France, where a single diocese saw the numbers of women in teaching and nursing orders fall by 30 per cent in ten post-war years, the age pyramid of female religious generally indicates that, as in the case of Belgium, the bleakest years lie ahead. In 1963 only 8.1 per cent of them were under 30; 24.7 per cent were aged between 31 and 45; 32.5 per cent were between 46 and 60; and 25 per cent were between 61 and 75.

Even in Catholic Ireland the first small signs of a drop-out among women have appeared. It is true that between 1958 and 1964 the number of sisters professed rose from 10,142 to 10,803; but the number of novices declined slightly from 574 to 541. Paradoxically the manpower situation in Ireland – at least among unordained lay brothers – appears to be as healthy as ever. In communities composed entirely of lay brothers the figures rose from 2,538 in 1958 to 2,874 in 1964; in clerical communities, where the lay brother has a distinctly inferior role, there was a rise of lay brethren over the same period from 780 to 836. In England and Wales during those years the number of lay brothers in completely lay communities rose by 15 per cent. In Germany, on the other hand, the number of lay brothers in clerical communities fell from 3,512 in 1960 to 3,372 in 1964, while novices dropped from 268 to 133; in entirely lay communities professed brethren fell from 1,057 in 1960 to 1,028 in 1964 (the novice count here actually rising from 73 to 97). But in Belgium the total admission of laymen to religious communities of any kind fell from 126 in 1958 to 58 in 1964.

Head-counting of Catholic religious at present is an excessively uneven and unsatisfactory business. The *Annuario* cannot be relied upon for accuracy and in any case makes no attempt to plot age pyramids or any other factors that might indicate future movements. Sources which appear to be reliable have so far charted only a fragment of the ground that has to be covered; apart from the figures quoted above there are virtually no others available; there is nothing, for instance, to tell us what the situation has been over a ten-year period among the monasteries of France; or to give us as useful a picture as the Dutch one of women religious in Great Britain. But judging by the general reaction of the Catholic Church's leaders who are most concerned with the religious life the overall pattern in Europe at least appears to be one of decline. Bishop Huyghe of Arras, for example, has said that 'Unless a complete reversal takes place in the present situation, half the convents of religion which now exist will have disappeared by 1980.' And judging by personal observation and reliable travellers' tales the condition of even the most solidly based communities is now a cause for concern. There are enormous Benedictine monasteries, like the majestic baroquery of Melk on the Danube, or Montecassino itself, which was extravagantly rebuilt from the ruins of the last war, which see more tourists than monks; 'both palaces are capable of holding three hundred monks, and both communities are down to forty, rattling like peas in a drum.' At Downside Abbey the Benedictines closed their novitiate in November 1966 for lack of postulants. The decline among women, moreover, is also visible among the comparative handful of Anglican communities. Between 1960 and 1966 the number of men in religion rose by 16 per cent, from 283 to 328; over the same period the women fell by 5 per cent from 1,941 to 1,883. A survey of 37 women's active communities in 1965 showed that they were 10 per cent below their 1939 strength and that of a total of 1,405 sisters only 120 were under 35 years old. Again, as with the Catholic communities, it seems to be the active ones that are suffering rather more than the contemplatives. The Anglican contemplative Sisters of the Love of God, for example, have had a permanent queue of women waiting for admission to their novitiate over the past few years.

However widespread the Catholic decline in vocations may or may not be the first signs of concern came in 1944, when the Sacred Congregation for Religious – the central administrative machine for this sector of the Church – established a ten-man commission representing various orders to study reform projects. A further straw in the wind came in 1950, when the first international congress of religious sat in Rome. By the following year Pius XII was clear enough about the way things were shaping to observe, astonishingly for a man who was temperamentally disinclined to change the status quo, that 'The nun's task in the world today cannot be accomplished without certain modifications in the customs of the classical type of religious life.'

In the years since then a number of modifications have been made. Some of the women's orders have had their clothing restyled, trimming hemlines here and shortening head-dress there. A decree of 31 May 1957 enabled superiors to interpret more flexibly the rules governing the visits of nuns and sisters to the world outside the convent walls. But these have only been modifications when what the religious life in its classical form has required has been an overhaul of its basic structure. The dearth of vocations in so many of the women's teaching and nursing orders has been attributed to the overwork that has usually been the price of membership; but shrewd observers have noted that this alone cannot be held responsible for their evident lack of appeal to young women in the mid-twentieth century, when equally industrious bodies like the secular institutes – mostly the product of the times we live in – have been flourishing. The really fundamental problem has been that religious orders have never been geared to the need for rapid change; slowly they have developed, slowly they have established their traditions and only very slowly if left to themselves have they ever made adjustments to a way of life that has been sanctified by time. A French bishop has written:

There are 118,000 active nuns in France, including 160 small congregations with less than 200 members founded before 1900. . . . Our colleagues in the episcopate consider they have made very little or no progress in the way of adapting themselves or making things more humane. The bishops are right. But they do not always realise how heavy the machinery is and how hard it is to set in motion. During the frequent congresses, which the nuns are always glad to attend, they hear lectures and exhortations which they receive with enthusiastic applause, but in practice scarcely any progress can be observed. The reason is that they are so often fanatically attached to their traditions and customs, which are kept in a sort of secret dungeon. Even the ecclesiastical superiors themselves are often denied access to it, especially in the small congregations. Thus, if there are praiseworthy attempts at adaptation, there are also well-defended strongholds. . . . All the nuns mean well and many see what needs to be done, but none of them dare make a beginning.

The emphasis placed by critics of the traditional and atrophied life upon the women's orders and congregations may say as much about the Catholic Church's hallowed attitude to women as it does about the area where recruitment has most obviously been failing in the post-war years. When Bishop Huyghe wrote his book *Tensions and Change* he pointed out at the beginning that although it was based upon research into the religious life of women 'if any reader likes to translate it into the masculine he will not be far from the truth.' No distinction between the sexes has been made in the discussions of the standing committee of Superior-Generals of religious orders, which was appointed in 1957. And in those discussions proposals put up at the first congress have come up time and again in the years since; they are about the necessity of adapting religious and ascetical discipline to the physical and psychological capacities of modern religious, more modern methods of relaxation, the provision of modern technical facilities insofar as these can be squared with the vow of poverty, raising the age of entry and extending the novitiate so as to be sure that those committing themselves to the

life for life do so in greater maturity than many of their predecessors. At that first congress Fr Lombardi SJ was speaking of
the religious life generally when he said:

When we consider the magnitude of the tasks which these critical
times have imposed upon the orders we have to confess that a great
number of the orders do not come up to expectations. Officially no doubt
they are all very worthy, historically they may have a very glorious past,
but in point of fact many of them are very ill-equipped to meet the grave
responsibilities of today. On the whole, they are perhaps in no way
inferior to the average religious of the past. But when we think of the
tremendous call of the present hour we cannot help feeling that many of
them show little of the ardent readiness of troops on the eve of a death
or glory advance. . . . There are too many of these institutes that
proceed at the same old sedate trot, with no idea of how urgently the
rapidly changing conditions of our time call for new efforts and new
methods in apostolic work and spiritual life. They work to rule and to
follow their routine order of time, which means in fact that they are
sleeping through the time for action.

That was in 1957. Nearly ten years later it was possible for
Bishop Huyghe to observe that

Some have completely accepted this new world along with its
dangers and its hopes. Resolutely detached from the sociological milieu
in which former generations lived, they are alert to the needs of the
people who now expect a new type of evangelisation. Others still cling
desperately to the earlier forms of religious and apostolic life which,
they declare, have stood the test of the years; and, in the shelter of their
institutions which have become for them a sort of artificial Christianity,
they do not see that the world is being formed without them and,
unfortunately, without the message of Christ which they should be
bringing to it.

As an example of the desperately static attitude the bishop
cited the congregation of nuns which in ten years lost thirty per
cent of its womanpower; it didn't close a single house, but left
them all gradually to dwindle and become a faint shadow of what
they had been. There have been more realistic responses to
change and decay than this. A number of federations have been

set up, like the one that soon after the war united forty-six communities of the nursing Canonesses Regular of St Augustine under one Superior-General. As a psychological device federation has its uses. It reduces a feeling of isolation and hopelessness in those houses which are suffering more than most from old age and scanty vocations, and replaces it to some extent with a confidence in being part of a powerful and cohesive organisation. Practically it means that a common policy can be worked out for the running of novitiates, that one novitiate for the whole federation can be established and new blood be deployed where it is most needed. Yet while all this is a help it is, in fact, doing no more than tinker with a structure that really needs changes – many of them major ones – from top to bottom.

Not until the Vatican Council finished at the end of 1965 did the Church officially show any signs of recognising this. But then, in the decree *De Accommodata Renovatione Vitae Religiosae*, it put its finger precisely on the place where the log-jam of tradition must first be made to move. The decree ordained that the organisation of life, prayer and work of religious must be in keeping with their physical and psychological condition; everywhere it must be adapted to the needs of the apostolate, to cultural requirements, to social and economic circumstances. 'Therefore,' it said, 'constitutions, directories, custom-books, books of prayers and ceremonies and other similar volumes must be revised accordingly and brought into line with the documents of this sacred Council, by the suppression of anything obsolete,' In short, the Church saw at last that there was a need for the religious life to change course and that this couldn't be done until the steering orders had been altered.

Which is more than a five-minute job in the most sluggish section of Christian civilisation. Slowly and very cumbersomely the religious orders have begun to crank up the machinery that will overhaul the documents governing their lives. By the end of 1967 some of them were still estimating that it would take a year or two longer before this first stage of adaptation was finished. It wasn't until the end of 1966 that the Dominicans took the preliminary step of sending a questionnaire to every member of the order to find out what the troops thought should be done.

This came from the Master-General in Rome, it required replies in Latin if possible, and it warned that direct answers should not occupy more than five lines of typescript, with supporting proof or explanation worth another ten lines at the outside. This in response to such questions as: 'What is the special character of the spirit and life of St Dominic, and what was his intention in founding the order?' (on which several hefty volumes have been written); 'Should the traditional type of novitiate be altered? At what stage should it begin and how long should it last? And what of the duration and nature of temporary vows?' At about the same time as the Dominican questionnaire was put into orbit another was circling the earth from Cistercian headquarters and the Jesuits of Great Britain were making their own survey of members' thoughts on renewal. By now most orders and societies will probably have a fair idea of the changes their people would and would not like to see; how long it will take them to codify these and then to enact them is anybody's guess.

But time is scarcely on their side. For the mid-sixties introduced a fresh hazard to the stability of the religious life. To the shortage of vocations and the advancing average age of communities was added an increasing number of men (rather more than women, probably, though for obvious reasons no statistics are available) who were abandoning their vows and simply walking out of their communities; sometimes to a marriage but as often as not just to a secular existence. This in the face of an excommunication which is the Church's penalty for those breaking solemn life vows. There have always been some who have accepted the penalty as the price of freedom; but there have never been as many, in the twentieth century at least, as there have been this past two to three years. The movement, it seems fairly clear, is becoming something more than an ominous trickle. In the United States it has been unofficially estimated that two thousand nuns abandoned their vows in 1967. Another source reckons that the membership of American Trappist monasteries, which grew at an astonishing rate just after the war, was by the beginning of 1968 half of what it had been in the peak years of the previous decade; by then the abbey at Piffard, in New York, had dwindled from seventy-six to thirty-six monks. An American

Benedictine has recently written that 'One of the most disturbing phenomena of the last decade in monastic life has been the greater instability of young religious. They come into the novitiate, they take their vows and surprisingly, in a year or two or even earlier, they present themselves to the superior and say that it was all a mistake; they no longer have any inclination to be religious at all. They have no compunction about breaking their vows which apparently have no deep significance for them. This is almost incomprehensible to the older religious, brought up in a different atmosphere.' In Great Britain, according to the local official Catholic directory, there were ten per cent fewer religious at the start of 1968 than there had been five years before; the Franciscans had diminished by twelve and a half per cent to 402, the 883 monks were eight per cent down on 1963's tally; the biggest drop of all – forty per cent – was among the Dominicans, leaving only 143.

Whatever imperturbable face the Catholic Church may present to the world officially when the future of the religious life is questioned, it is well aware now that a crisis exists; the cold truth is that the religious life is now practised by only one Catholic in 1,666, a lower proportion than ever before in the Church's history. Almost the last words of *De Accommodata* demonstrate the Church's anxiety for the future. 'Priests and those responsible for Christian education,' said the decree, 'must make a serious effort to see that there are religious vocations, chosen with due care, to provide for new growth in response to the needs of the Church. Even ordinary sermons should deal more often with the evangelical counsels and religious vocations. Parents must nurture and protect religious vocations in their children, by giving them a Christian upbringing.' The decree, moreover, has conceded that prayer and sermons alone will not suffice to repair the breach that has been opened up; not only are constitutions and rules to be revised wholesale, but communities which offer no hope of any further useful life are not to accept any more novices and where possible they are to be amalgamated with more flourishing bodies which have similar aims.

If there is a note of desperation in some parts of the decree it is no more than is warranted by the condition of the religious life in

general in the 1960s. An attempt to serve and relate themselves
to the world as it really is today has been made by religious in
several quarters, both Catholic and Protestant. These people
have for some time been asking themselves questions which are
fundamental to the life: what exactly constitutes prayer and what
balance should be struck between it and activity; what kind of
activity should religious be engaged in at the middle of the
twentieth century? They have invoked psychiatry to help them
decide whether they are individually fitted for the religious life.
They have even started to wonder whether they have become
religious in order to serve God and his world or just to help
themselves. But these are still a minority. For the most part the
religious life is still clothed and conducted in habits basically
formed in the Middle Ages. It is still regulated by notions and
appliances of authority and obedience which the rest of western
society would have regarded as high-handed at the end of the
nineteenth century. It is still bogged down in a world of its own
that in its essentials has not varied much since it was constructed
fourteen hundred years ago by a man called Benedict, who once
jumped into a nettlebed because he was ashamed of his capacity
for erotic love. It is the most remarkable of all the anomalies in
our society today.

PART TWO

FOUR

THE STRUCTURE

'It is almost as difficult to say what monks do as to say what the
human race in general does . . .'
DOM DENYS RUTLEDGE OSB, *The Complete Monk*, p. 103

'. . . only by living for a while in a monastery can one quite grasp its
staggering difference from the ordinary life that we lead.'
PATRICK LEIGH FERMOR, *A Time to Keep Silence*, p. 27

High in the mountains east of Florence the Sacro Eremo is
perched at the top of a valley bristling with pines. There are about
thirty small cottages here, a church, a guest house, a refectory, a
kitchen and some other outbuildings. A high wall surrounds the
cottages and if it were not for this the whole place would
resemble a village. It is a collective hermitage, the home of the
long-winded Congregation of the Hermit-Monks of Camaldoli of
the Order of St Benedict. It is not substantially different from the
earliest Christian religious communities founded by St Pachomius, an antique survival and a mark of continuity which has
already stretched along sixteen hundred years. Since the
eleventh century, when St Romuald founded the Congregation,
the life at Sacro Eremo has virtually been unchanged and untouched by reforms from within and pressures from without
alike. The hermit-monk of Sacro Eremo is as self-contained as a
man can be in this world. He has his cottage with its four rooms:
one is nothing more than a lobby leading to a porch, where there

is a log on which the hermit can sit and contemplate God and the scenery; another is a bed-sitter, where he eats meals which come to him through a hatch and which have been prepared by more gregarious hands than his in the kitchen; he has a study, with a table and bookshelves; he also has his oratory, with its altar and its prayer desk. He does not often leave his own four walls and his cottage is separated from his next-door neighbour's by a statutory twenty to thirty feet.

There are lay brothers at Sacro Eremo who live a life as communal as that of any other monk; they are the ones who prepare food in the kitchen and push it through the hatches to the hermits: they exist to make it possible for these men to live in solitude, of which there are different degrees among the Camaldolese. Some are so reclusive that they leave their cottage cells only in Holy Week, on the feast of St Martin and on Quinquagesima Sunday, which precede the two long fasts of Advent and Lent, to take part in communal worship in the church, and to dine and speak with their brethren as an act of charity. Otherwise they are quite alone, speaking only to their confessor, spending an hour each day in manual labour, with the rest of their time in utterly private prayer or study. For even the least reclusive hermits the silence and the solitude of each day is relieved only by the offices they attend in the church, at intervals between 1.30 am and sunset, and for the walks they are allowed to take together after vespers on the few occasions when the rule of silence is lifted. Unless he has the special permission of his prior the hermit can communicate with no one else, even by writing. There are perhaps a hundred and sixty men living under the Camaldolese régime in a handful of communities strung out across the northern hemisphere. They range from the Sacro Eremo itself, which is headquarters, to the Hermitage of the Immaculate Heart of Mary, whose unlikely-sounding address is the New Camaldoli, Lucia Ranch, Big Sur PO, California – deep and even more unlikely in the Henry Miller country. There are almost as many living within the similar Congregation of the Hermits of Monte Corona. There are those six hundred Carthusians, whose life is virtually in the same pattern. And none of it is representative of the religious life in the twentieth century any more than the existence of the Little Brothers of Autumn Grove, Leeds 6. It is just the most extreme form of the contemplative life entirely given to prayer. The religious life as a whole has only four common denominators, and they are poverty, obedience, chastity and prayer. The rest is infinite variety.

There are religious communities like the Little Brothers (though they aren't unique in this respect) whose premises are stuck in the sleaziest districts of the most industrialised cities. If they are not actually quartered in a slum themselves they will be surrounded by slums and their own building will be wretched-looking on the outside and gloomy within, full of butter-coloured electric light and an odour of sanctity compounded of central heating, floor polish and elbow grease. Others, like the English Jesuits of Farm Street in London, have revamped the insides of their scarcely less attractive uptown houses with pastel-coloured paint, quietly humming lifts, the most contemporary lettering in the signwriter's manual, and executive-style desks complete with dictaphones. Then there are the monasteries which conform, more or less, to the world's image of them. Some are so remote that, like the abbey of Gethsemani which the Trappists built in an empty corner of Kentucky, they have their own postmark. Some have been carefully sited as though their incumbents wanted to feel themselves half-way to heaven before they had actually started, like Montecassino, which sits arrogantly on the peak of its mountain so that you get a pain in the neck looking up at it from the town almost vertically beneath: a great white rambling shrine containing St Benedict's bones (though it doesn't do to say so to the monks of St Benôit sur Loire, who think they guard his remains) which was bombed to rubble during the war and carefully restored with a rapid grant from the Italian Government the moment the shooting stopped. Some, like Melk on the Danube, are baroque palaces with state bedrooms and grand staircases surviving from the days when the Emperor of Austria and his retinue, or another potentate, would call in for a drop of Benedictine hospitality. A few can number themselves still among the world's great treasures of art and books. At Kremsmünster, the biggest Benedictine community in Austria, the library holds 100,000 volumes, 400 manuscripts, 792 incunabula and the eighth-century Codex Millenarius; there is also an art gallery with work from the fifteenth to the nineteenth centuries, an armoury full of weapons dating from the Turkish invasion of 1683, a museum of astronomy in an eighteenth-century observatory, and collections of geology, stuffed animals and birds. But, then, there are monasteries like the Trappist abbey at Ogden, Utah, which was constructed in 1947 from United States Army surplus Quonset huts; and the Trappist community at Nunraw, Scotland, whose monks are living the same way, in Nissen huts, while they build themselves a permanent abbey from stone. There are also monasteries whose premises have at one time or another had curiously unmonastic histories. The Benedictines of Worth Abbey, in Sussex, inhabit a house which once belonged to the man who invented the torpedo and which was taken over by the military to become the headquarters of the Canadian Corps before the invasion of Normandy.

If the religious life can be divided into parts which each have some kind of unity then the line must be drawn between the contemplatives and the actives; the contemplatives who, in greater or lesser degree, keep themselves apart from the world so as to concentrate on prayer and the actives who have, more or less, embraced the world so as to spread their Christian fervour. The distinction between the two is becoming blurred today, as religious themselves begin to question their ancient definitions and attitudes. But it still makes more sense than one between monks and nuns proper (who alone, in purist language, inhabit monasteries and convents and are subject to varying degrees of enclosure) on the one hand and the remainder of the religious world on the other – the Franciscan and Dominican friars, the Jesuits, the Sisters of Mercy or Charity and all the rest. It is more sensible if only because it cleaves in two the senior monastic order, the Benedictines. There are two hundred and twenty-five Benedictine monasteries and forty-three of them are contemplative. In these the monks are subject to strict enclosure, which means that they rarely leave the premises. The life is not so strict as that of a Carthusian or even a Trappist, but it follows closely the Rule which Benedict composed. In effect the contemplative

Benedictines have more in common with the Cistercians than they have with active monks of their own order.

These would prefer to say that they are living a mixed régime of contemplation and activity if only because their day traditionally has been punctuated seven times by attendance together in choir for the offices in addition to their times of private prayer; moreover the monastic life at any level is a way apart from that of many religious because it is lived largely in common: even when the average Jesuit occupies a house with several others he does very little in common with them apart from eating meals.

Contemplative actives or active contemplatives as a label for most Benedictine monasteries? It is a very private Benedictine debating point. Whatever you call those 182 remaining communities the fact is that they are scarcely cut off effectively from the world any more. The world has a habit of coming to the monastery, if it is famous enough, irrespective of how it sees its function. There are abbeys like Montecassino and Subiaco in Italy, like Beuron in Germany, like Maria Laach in Austria and like Montserrat in Spain (which, besides owning a painting of Mary reckoned to be by St Luke, and being the place where St Ignatius hung up his sword after conversion, is also a centre of Catalan and therefore anti-Franco patriotism) which count their annual pilgrims in scores of thousands and spend a fair amount of time accommodating them and catering for them. There are others, the eighteen monasteries of the Solesmes congregation, which get many visitors because they have specialised in liturgical prayer and become the great masters of Gregorian chant. Among the actives the greatest activity is in running schools and parishes. St Benedict visualised the education of small boys specifically to populate his monasteries and at Weingarten, Germany, the abbey still runs a school for this purpose. The saint might have taken less kindly to the spectacle of a hundred Benedictine abbeys – like Downside and Ampleforth in England, like St Scholastica's in Kansas, St Leo's in Florida and St Benedict's in Minnesota – educating children merely to be good Catholics and citizens. While a proportion of boys attending Benedictine schools do end up as monks, this is scarcely seen by an abbot and his teaching staff to be the main point of the exercise. St Benedict's objection would have been based on other grounds, though. The monk who is a teacher cannot function as a monk in the grand tradition. He cannot attend some of the offices in choir, as by St Benedict's Rule he ought, because at those times he is in the classroom instead; and so he has to read his offices alone, compressed into a bunch at the beginning or the end of the day, so as to fulfil his quota of prayer. At a place like Downside – where twenty-five of the forty-seven resident monks are teachers (together with forty-five laymen) in the abbey's public school – this means that only half the community are keeping to its conventional routine during term time. The rest are throwing themselves wholeheartedly into their teaching jobs, extra-curricular activities and all. On Fridays at Ample-forth, which is the day the combined cadet force is on parade, half a dozen variously pipped and crowned figures in battledress turn out not to be officers and gentlemen at all but merely monks of the order of St Benedict who have temporarily swapped one uniform for another.

Ampleforth, by far the largest of the English Benedictine abbeys (153 monks compared with Douai's 73, Downside's 65 and smaller numbers descending to Worth's 24) is a good illustration of the parochial taxation of a community's strength that can occur nowadays. Of its total number only seventy-seven monks live in the monastery. They rest are serving singly, in twos, threes and foursomes, twenty-three different parishes from one end of the country to another, from the diocese of Cardiff to the diocese of Middlesbrough. There they live as any other Catholic parish priest does, following their Rule as far as their work allows, catching up with their offices just like the monk-teachers at home. They are not unique; 115 of the 225 Benedictine monasteries in the world are now involved in parish work. This may not coincide with Everyman's assumptions about the monastic life but, then, you find that riddled with anomalies whichever side of the contemplative-active line you look. Even the most strictly enclosed Trappists – whose Cistercian ances-tors were so dedicated to isolation that they forbade members of the order to confess, bury or administer communion to anyone unless he happened to be a guest of the monastery, would not educate boys even to become monks, and walledup doors leading to the tombs of canonised Cistercians so that pilgrims should not come – even the Trappists, who have stuck quietly and closely to the letter of their founder's law, have been known to run a public school in the United States. At Mount Melleray, in Ireland, they have a reputation for curing dipsomaniacs, which they do by gradually decreasing a man's consumption of the real stuff until the poor lost soul is drinking unadulterated water.

The activity of Benedictines, however, is nothing compared with the works and functions of most religious communities. When, in 1965, the Catholic Church mounted a vocations exhibition in London 57 communities for men and 142 for women advertised their presence in the British Isles. This is a list, avoiding duplication as far as possible, of the ways in which they saw their vocations:

MEN'S COMMUNITIES
The evangelisation of Africa.
To seek God, living a common life under a rule and under obedience to an abbot.
Preaching and hearing confessions, the publication of eucharistic periodicals and giving Fifty Hours, eucharistic weeks and triduums in parishes.
The society seeks to work closely with the laity in reviving the faith in already Catholic countries and spreading it to missionary countries.
Wherever priests are scarce Pallotines strive to establish missions and parishes, schools and retreat centres.
To seek God in a balanced life of prayer, manual labour, reading and study.
Contemplatives intent on prayer and sacred study.
Spreading the knowledge of God as preachers, lecturers, missionaries and writers.
Run parishes, give missions, retreats, teach in schools, organise broadcasting, act as hospital and prison chaplains.
To send members to lowly and difficult fields of the apostolate for which the Holy See has difficulty in finding missionaries.
Especially for the evangelisation of pagans and, above all, of the black race.
To make known Mary's apparition and to combat the evils that Mary

complained of – violation of the Sunday, blasphemy, religious in-difference etc.

Keeping alive the faith of Italians abroad by means of spiritual and social assistance – builds churches, halls and clubs, opens mass centres, distributes Italian magazines and helps in the long and difficult process of integration with the local community.

To promote the greater glory of God and the personal sanctification of its members through the care of the sick.

Embraces every work of charity for boys; it has schools of all kinds – primary, grammar, agricultural and technical and labours earnestly for vocations and the 'Good Press'.

Tries to provide a homelike atmosphere where priests with problems, physical, mental or spiritual, may rebuild insofar as is necessary health of mind, body and soul.

To serve Mary and spread devotion to her Seven Sorrows.

Essentially missionary; special emphasis is placed upon Africanisation and in particular on the creation of African clergy.

Varied works of charity, the education and instruction of children of all classes, especially the poor, the destitute, deaf, dumb and blind – and the care of the sick and mentally afflicted.

Sharing the social conditions and manual work of the poor.

Conducting approved schools for delinquent boys in England.

The practice of holy slavery to Jesus through Mary.

WOMEN'S COMMUNITIES

To form a family entirely consecrated to the heart of Jesus, adored especially in the Eucharist.

The sanctification of all its members for the glory of God by prayer and works of mercy which include clinics, helping the aged, social and parish work, including dispensary work.

A contemplative order but undertaking also farming, religious instruc-tion, art work, the teaching of languages and the running of a guest house for ladies as well as printing.

The Christian education of girls in all types of schools and apostolic work connected with it.

To promote the glory of God and the sanctification of its members through the care of the sick in hospitals and homes for convalescents, the chronically ill, children, the aged and maternity. The sisters specialise in all phases of hospital work and may be doctors, nurses, technicians, radiographers, secretaries, dieticians, pharmacists and physical therapists.

To educate young girls, while giving them a good modern education and striving to instil something of old-time courtesy and consideration for others.

To give glory to God by a life of contemplation and penance, seeking God alone for His own sake; all the ordering of the life is but a means to this end.

Saviour-mindedness is the distinctive spirit as each sister aims to become all things to all people.

Work on the missions, teaching, nursing, undertaking catechetical work, the care of the aged, church needlework, child care work in Salford and Lancaster, including social works of adoption, fostering, family welfare and preventive case work.

The re-education of girls in training homes, approved schools under the Home Office, special schools under the education department, homes and hostels for unmarried mothers and the rehabilitation of children from broken homes.

The practice of Christian charity towards the sick . . . to all classes of sufferers with any kind of infirmity no matter how contagious or repulsive and to all denominations, Catholic and otherwise.

To provide the religious life for girls wishing to care for and educate children from birth to seven years of age, helping unmarried mothers and teaching young girls who wish to become children's nurses.

Provides residential centres for university students, business and working girls, economical restaurants, free evening classes, dispensaries in mission areas, relief centres in slum areas, homes for immigrants, recreational clubs and social service centres.

Nurse the sick in their own homes without fee, preference being given to the poor.

To act as a living link between the Church and the Jewish people.

To help our separated brethren back to the true fold.

Spreading the word of God by means of social communication – the press, cinema, radio, television and by any other means that human progress supplies and the necessities and conditions of the times demand.

Benedictine monks and nuns (To seek God, living a common life under a rule and under obedience to an abbot) were represented in that exhibition, of course. So were Franciscans, Dominicans, Trappist nuns, Little Brothers and Sisters of Jesus. So were the Congregation of the Sisters of Jesus Crucified, who are contemplatives founded in Paris in 1930 to make the religious life possible for sick and invalid women, who 'wish to give greater glory to God by accepting their sufferings joyfully and helping other souls to draw benefit from the Cross.' For the list is not a peculiarly English one; almost every community in it originated outside the British Isles; every vocation represented there will be found in any other country where the religious life is practised. It means that there is practically no social situation in which active religious are not involved. Some of them are tasks which few people but religious, with their dedication and their vow of obedience, care to take on. The Anglican sisters of the Community of St Mary the Virgin, for example, run the only hostel in Great Britain which cares for women who are slowly being rehabilitated after drug addiction; the Ministry of Health doesn't provide one yet. The Community of the Sacred Passion, another Anglican sisterhood, staffs one of the two leprosariums in England, the other being a Ministry establishment.

There are very few skills which are not to be found in one cloister or another, often badly neglected by superiors who do not know how to employ them, but often encouraged to flourish as best they can in the context of a religious life. With a tradition of study so deeply embedded in monasticism it is scarcely surprising that theological journals everywhere are peppered with contributions from religious; some of the best of them are edited and published from religious communities. At the Vatican Council almost all the heavyweight *periti*, the theological experts whom individual and less scholarly bishops took to Rome to keep them briefed and up to scratch, were religious; Edward Schillebeeckx, Yves Congar, Jerome Hamer and M. D. Chenu were all Dominicans, Karl Rahner and John Courtney Murray were Jesuits, Gregory Baum was an Augustinian and Bernard Haring a Redemptorist. All of those eight pressed hard for a more liberal Church and between them originated some of the ideas which have been put into effect and changed Catholicism since 1965. Other forms of scholarship, sometimes distinctly untheological, occur here and there. The Jesuit Father Wilson Brown, in London, is a botanist who identified a whole crop of new plants which now bear his name in Guyana, where his society sent him as a missionary a few years back. Dom David Knowles was detached from his abbey (Downside) many years ago to become an academic in Cambridge, where he was at first Professor of Medieval History and then Regius Professor of Modern History. The Abbot Primate of all the Benedictines, the American Dom Rembert Weakland, is a distinguished musicologist. Sister Mary Corita Kent, of the Sisters of the Immaculate Heart of Mary in California, has had paintings hung in the New York Metropolitan Museum of Modern Art. Father Martin Jarret-Kerr, of the Community of the Resurrection, has written a study of D. H. Lawrence ('a serious piece of criticism of Lawrence,' wrote T. S. Eliot when it appeared in 1951, 'of a kind for which the time is now due.') and Father Peter Levi SJ, like Father Manley Hopkins before him, has produced poetry which gets published in the most discriminating anthologies; so does the American Daniel Berrigan SJ. But the Jesuits, after all, have a reputation for exploiting a man's talents to the full, even if they don't always feel comfortable with the results and deem it necessary to sit on them for a year or two before the world outside gets wind of them and more or less insists on publication. Teilhard de Chardin spent a large portion of his Jesuit vocation as a biologist and palaeontologist, pottering around China (where he was partly responsible for the discovery of Peking Man in 1929) not so much as a religious as a scientist; and because his scientific writings questioned so many fundamental and orthodox Christian beliefs he was an embarrassment to his Society, which forbade him to publish. There is no end to the odd and worldly things in which a man might be engaged when he has settled for the withdrawn and obedient life of a monk. There is a monk of Belmont, Dom Laurence Beers, whose address in his community's directory is given as c/o Ministry of Defence and who at the moment is residing in the officers' mess of an RAF station, where he acts as chaplain. At Buckfast Abbey there is Dom John Stephan, who has been president of the Devon Association, and Dom Paul Patterson, who has been chairman of Exeter's branch of the Association of Superintendent Electrical Engineers on the strength of his acquaintance with the monastery's generators. Whole communities can be roped in for extra-curricular activities. The Anglican Franciscans have become guardians of a bird sanctuary off the Northumbrian coast because one of their friaries happens to be best placed to do the job. The monks of Nashdom have been asked by doctors experimenting with an antidote to german measles to allow themselves to be inoculated and then to remain as enclosed as the deepest contemplatives for a fortnight to help find how to stop women having deformed babies.

The huge majority of monks, nuns and other religious, of course, do not enjoy the ups and downs of having a book suppressed, then published, or even the mild excitement of presiding over the local historical association. They live, most of them, a life of interminable similarity; of offices in church each day, of domestic chores, of private prayer, of whatever is the particular vocation of their community; if they are priests their days are more varied with the obligation to hear Confessions, to conduct retreats, to administer sacraments outside the community, perhaps to act as spiritual director of nuns. They may enjoy occasional robust relief, like the Franciscan who defends the faith on a soapbox in Hyde Park every Sunday afternoon, sandwiched between Lord Soper, who is preaching an omnibus Christianity, and the gentleman who damns it all with his preference for Black Power. But the relief is only occasional. Unless they are enclosed they can and do travel, though.

In the Anglican Community of the Resurrection a monk is required to be officially in residence at Mirfield for about eight weeks of the year, in company with three others. During that time the four of them must stay at home, to wait on their brethren at meals, to lay tables, to prepare afternoon tea, to answer the telephone and the door. They each have to write a newsy letter to one of the community's overseas houses. Every member of the community in Britain gathers at Mirfield for the General Chapter, at which the community's affairs are discussed and regulated, and this lasts for three and a half weeks in July, nine days after Christmas and a week after Easter. That is a general pattern into which everybody fits. Most men have a special job assigned to them in addition to their general community functions; one will be the custos in charge of the garden, another director of the Fraternity of the Resurrection administering much paper work to keep in touch with the lay friends and supporters of the community, two or three will be teaching theology to

ordinands in the College of the Resurrection. This is the
year's engagements of the novice-master at Mirfield for 1967;
on dates left blank he is at home.

January 31– February 1		To Chester to hear confession of nuns and to give an address.
February	2	To the women's community at Horbury, of which he is warden.
	3–6	Theological conference in London.
	23–24	Warden's visit to Horbury.
	25–26	A weekend preaching engagement in Nottingham.
March	8–29	To New York to conduct retreats for communities of nuns.
April	17–19	Warden's visit to Horbury.
May	1–3	Chester to hear nuns' confessions and give an address.
	8–12	Conducted a priests' retreat at the community's retreat house in Huntingdonshire.
	13–15	Gave talks and led discussion at a 'holy party' for inquirers at a country house in Surrey.
June	2–19	On holiday (members of the community normally take a month a year, usually with relatives).
	20–21	Meeting of the Religious Communities' Advisory Council at Oxford.
	22–24	With other members of the community took part in discussions with Methodist theologians at Mirfield.
July	3–6	Attended conference of religious communities at Oxford.
	26–27	Warden's visit to Horbury.
July 29–August 7		With other members of the community ran a summer school at Wantage, giving lectures and sermons.
September	2–3	Warden's visit to Horbury.
	4–6	Oxford for meeting of Advisory Council.
	12–13	Theological conference in Oxford.
	14–28	On holiday.
October	3–7	Conducted retreat for nuns near London.
	13–16	Another 'holy party' in the Surrey country house.

November   2   Talk to local branch of the Mothers' Union.
              10–13   Conducted retreat for men and women in
                         Huntingdonshire.

That is the year of a fairly senior member of an Anglican
community. It probably represents greater mobility, though not
all that much, than more junior Mirfield men enjoy; it certainly
leaves the average Benedictine standing, or the religious of
either sex whose community is almost totally committed to
teaching, nursing or local relief work of one kind or another. But a
Jesuit or a Dominican or a handful of other religious in Catholic
communities might find it comparable to their own routine.

It is from communities such as Mirfield, both Anglican and
Catholic, which have never been fully geared to engagement with
the secular world on its own terms (as the Sisters of Charity, the
Sisters of Mercy and many others have), that in recent years
there has been growing talk of greater activity outside the
community in ways the world would recognise as useful.
Basically it has involved rethinking the meaning of Christian
commitment, a process which has been speeded by the example
of the Petits Frères and of the French worker-priests. The
worker-priesthood was started in 1944 as a means of bridging the
gap between the Church and a suspicious and almost completely
anti-clerical working class. It was backed by Cardinal Suhard of
Paris and it meant that priests were to live as manual workers,
not in an effort to proselytise those around them, but simply to
demonstrate that the Church too was prepared to dirty its hands
and be on the dole as well as to starch its linen and cash its
cheques; what mattered most of all was not conversions but
simply *la présence* – just being there. At the height of the
movement perhaps a hundred men were involved, some of them
secular priests, others religious. The trouble was that they
eventually identified themselves so closely with the workers
politically that the Church took fright and in 1959 finally banned
the worker-priests altogether. Some of them obediently returned to their religious duties; others either abandoned their
orders formally in defiance or else just carried on as if nothing had
happened. One of them was Henri Perrin, a Jesuit, who left the

Society when it became an issue. At the time matters came to a head for him he was working as a navvy on the construction of the Isère-Arc dam. There was a strike over poor pay and bad working conditions, which the men won, and a letter Perrin wrote just after it was settled (March, 1952) indicates clearly the position that he, a Jesuit, had adopted by then:

Dear Everyone, Here's another collective letter, which is a way of avoiding repeating the same things over and over again to individuals. We are now fully out of the strike, and the results regarding my pay are gratifying. I earned 6,000 francs in the last three days; that is to say, for thirty hours' work. But above all what we have gained is that the management has really got going, that the worksite is running better than ever before, that there are constant adjustments in the organis-ation of the work, and that the 'township' is growing under our eyes. Better still, the bosses, far from trying to make reprisals, treat the strike leaders with obvious respect. They consult us and listen to us. In a word, the situation is good. A new fatal accident that occurred four days after our return to work (one of us was crushed by a tractor in the tunnel) served to reinforce the attitude of the workers and the situation I have just described. As far as I am concerned, all is well, and Christ seems to be taking a guiding hand in events. . . . The funeral of our workmate also marked a new stage for me. Inevitably, I had to officiate at it myself. All the workers were present, when I appeared all dressed up and ornamented, before a great number of workmates who were not yet aware that I was a priest. Half of them came into church; the other half stayed outside. When we emerged, some of them came up to me and said that in the view of all, or nearly all, the ceremony had increased the trust they felt in me. . . .

At the Vatican Council the Catholic Church discovered a lot of truths about itself; one was that it had been ill advised to end the worker-priesthood. Quietly the experiment was restarted. By the middle of 1967 there were fifty-one priests working full-time in French factories. Half of them were men from religious orders, including five Jesuits and a couple of Dominicans. Essentially their aim is the same as that of the Petits Frères: identification with the poorest sections of society. Their ultimate effect on the religious life as a whole is so far incalculable, but in the long run it is likely to be enormous. Already some communities have begun to conduct their own tentative experiments. One Anglican sister-hood has closed the workshop in which for several generations it has sewn church vestments, retrained its womanpower, and started a chiropody practice for old people with sore feet. The Sisters of the Church (another Anglican community which has spent most of its time teaching so far) in 1967 sent a clutch of women to Australia to live in a house in downtown Sydney and get whatever jobs they could find locally; within a week or two one of them was a kitchen hand in a hospital and another was packing cosmetics on a Max Factor production line.

This reappraisal of function is accompanied in some cases by a searching look at the meaning and practice of religious poverty. St Benedict was quite clear what he meant by it in the sixth century. 'The life of the monk,' he wrote, 'should at all times be Lenten in its character.' Not only were the first Benedictines forbidden to receive presents and ordered to share all worldly goods from a communal chest, but the abbot was instructed to make regular searches of mattresses to be sure that no one was concealing private property. And though the saint was, in fact, noncommittal about the extent of communal ownership it is implicit in the Rule that while a monastery would do well to be solvent it had no business to accumulate anything beyond necessity. Like a lot of other things in the religious life, the conceptions of poverty were to be modified by the centuries.

There are communities which still appear to be living the Benedictine Rule to the letter, even though they have no affili-ations with the order, and to wear their poverty like a talisman. The Poor Clares, for example, determined to look the part, pad around in bare feet unless they are out of doors or standing on stone floors, when they are allowed to wear sandals. Some of their houses, it is said, never know where next week's budget is coming from; and the Anglican Franciscans make sure that they have no more money in the bank than will see them through the next six months. Cistercians sleep fully dressed, and though poverty is not the motive for that – it has more to do with always being prepared to meet their Maker – it amounts to an economy of sorts. There are monks who lengthen the life of fraying habits by sewing leather on the elbows and the cuffs. But for every

Cistercian sleeping rough there is probably another religious somewhere who will not be above slumbering in a pair of silk pyjamas donated by a reverent relative at Christmas. And for every abbot with leather-bound elbows there will certainly be two who permit themselves the odd cigar when they are away from home and on their travels. It all depends which community a man or woman belongs to, how the rules are written and how they are interpreted. There are some communities which give every member a few shillings a week pocket-money, with a bob or two extra for the smokers, and some which give them nothing at all. There are some so flush with money that if a man takes a fancy to a book in a shop window he can walk in and buy it, reimburse himself from the community's general fund, and put the volume in the library when he has read it. There are some which will provide a typewriter or a dictaphone at the first time of asking and others in which a religious reckons he is lucky to have a fountain pen he can call his own. 'We are taught,' says a Benedictine of my acquaintance, 'in the novitiate – but don't always remember after – to live simply and not to ask for expensive and unnecessary gadgets. There is a danger in letting people have what they ask for. The trouble is that it's all covered by obedience if they've gone through the proper channels.' There are many places where they have to live more austerely than that implies; where every single item has to be wheedled out of the superior, where every member of the community carries a notebook in which he enters to the nearest halfpenny everything he has spent, and where a man is encouraged and even expected to hitch-hike his journeys rather than travel by public transport. There are places apart from Trappist monasteries – where they never eat flesh meat on principle as a penitential gesture and go totally vegetarian during Advent and Lent – whose meals are adequate and only just. The Mother Superior of a contemplative community recalls that the first thing she did on taking over from her unduly ascetic predecessor was to install central heating and make sure that everyone got at least one square meal a day 'because this life is hard enough without fainting from cold and hunger'. She was a sensible woman. More sensible than the abbot of the Benedictine house in which I watched the most

staggering display of excessive food I have seen anywhere
outside a metropolitan expense-account restaurant. It was Saturday lunch but, I was told, nothing out of the ordinary. There was
soup, a meat course, a heavy pudding, cheese and biscuits, fresh
fruit, beer and coffee. Everybody, so far as I could see, waded
through the lot. Rather more than half the monks accepted two
helpings of one or other of the first three courses. They were all
offered a third.

An American Benedictine has remarked that it is possible for a
monk to be as poor as a church mouse while his community is as
sleek as a city cat. And so it is. Kremsmünster Abbey's assets
must amount to millions in either dollars or sterling, however its
monks may be individually placed, and Montecassino will be
worth a penny or two. 'Monasteries and convents,' writes Dom
Columba Cary-Elwes, 'have almost a natural propensity to become wealthy. They pay no taxes; friends lavish upon them gifts
of land, buildings, art works. By their very profession their
inmates are industrious and abstemious; as with the early Puri-
tans riches come unsought but inevitably. Even if these institutions pass through hard times, they have by their corporate
nature a better chance of survival to better times than private
individuals, farmers or small businessmen, for example. History
bears this out; monasteries and convents, particularly the former, accumulate wealth as dams water.' He is writing from a
priory seat in Missouri, and American religious institutions
doubtless fare as amply, compared with those elsewhere, as
anything else in the United States; in England it is only the active
communities which go untaxed; the contemplatives, which are
not regarded as charities, have to pay up like the rest of us. But
Dom Columba's comment will not be a wild generalisation whatever the context.

Anyone who in Italy, Spain or Malta has watched religious
quartering a town street by street with their mendicant bowls in
hand knows cynically well one way the funds are raised, though
barefaced begging is probably beginning to wane everywhere.
Within the past decade a French inquiry into a hundred and fifty
Carmelite convents showed that the nuns had to earn between
sixty and seventy per cent of their income themselves, instead of

the twenty-five per cent which had at one time been the custom. Good Churchpeople, however, are in the habit of giving alms whether solicited or not and no group of them is more regular in its donations than the Churchpeople who attach themselves to the fraternities and other support bodies belonging to religious communities. Gifts roll in not only by cheque, banknote and coin but often in kind as well and sometimes the generosity can be tiresomely misplaced, so that a conscience-stricken superior has to issue reminders of vocation and planned giving and other Christian principles. 'We do not,' write the English Benedictine nuns of Burnham Abbey in their monthly journal, 'want to appear ungrateful but we often receive large and beautiful boxes of chocolates which we have to give away. I am sure this is not what the donor intended. We are grateful for a limited number of plain sweets or plain chocolate as we may eat sweets on Feast days. Otherwise we would be glad of small book tokens . . . or garden tokens . . . Or it would give us great pleasure to know that any money which would have been spent on us was sent to the fund for refugees.' And then a tactful reminder of real needs: 'For the Mother House – a few Ancient and Modern hymn books, with or without music. A garden rake. Teacloths for Guest House. *Old* plastic mackintoshes, plastic or polythene bags.' Not that every women's community turns up its nose at boxes of chocolates; among the British lately it has become quite an ecumenical gesture for neighbouring Anglican and Catholic convents to exchange bumper boxes of 'Black Magic' or some other brand on each other's patronal festivals.

Although the Sisters of St Joseph of Cluny, for example, are careful in their recruiting publicity to point out that no dowry is required of their postulants, many communities still set high hopes on what a newcomer can be expected to bring to the cloister with him or her. In some places they may still canvass a fixed sum, but in these tight-fisted days a more common practice is to accept gratefully whatever a newcomer can offer. There are communities which insist on acquiring only the income from a member's capital, which must remain intact in case there are family claims to be met on his or her death. There are modern-minded communities which would prefer to have nothing at all to do with the money anyone might have owned before coming inside. The Community of the Glorious Ascension, an Anglican teaching order for men which is not yet ten years old, orders this side of its affairs like this:

1 If a postulant or novice has money of his own, or owns property, he should deposit the money in the bank before entering the community, and make arrangements so that his property may be administered with the least possible concern to himself. The income from these sources should also be put into deposit in the bank and may be allowed to accumulate. No one may be received into any grade of the community who is in debt.

2 Before profession (in temporary vows) a novice must make a will. He shall also deal with any money or property he has in the following way:

(a) He shall make arrangements for the disposal of any income from these sources. He is at liberty to do what he likes with this income, though he may not have it for his own personal use, neither may he allow it to accumulate in his own account.

(b) He must inform his superior as to what he has arranged and the superior may make suggestions. Also the superior may order him to appoint an executor if he consider that the administration of the income or property is going to need considerable amount of work.

(c) He may not rid himself of his money and property.

(d) He may make over the income from the money and property to the community. If, however, he do this, he has no say in the way in which the money is spent, but it shall be put into the community fund in the normal way.

(e) If he has made over the income to the community and later he be released or removed, then he is at liberty to re-adjust the disposal of his income as he wishes. He may not, however, reclaim any money which was paid to the community from these sources while he was a member.

(f) In his will the brother must make quite clear what is to happen to the money and property and the income from these, in the event of his death.

3 Before profession in solemn vows a brother must dispose of all

money and property which he owns. If it be in trust he shall make arrangements for the disposal of the income from this trust. In the disposal of this the rules set out in (a), (b), (d) and (f) above apply here also. (e) above also applies here with the addition that if at solemn profession the brother gave all his money and property to the community he may not reclaim it should he be released or removed. The community, however, if it wishes may return some or all of it to the released or removed person.

A major source of income for any order which teaches, nurses or performs any other recognised social service is the wages its members collect from the state, the local civil authority or the Church itself. Monks can abide by the Burnham scale as much as any grammar schoolteacher with a wife and two children to support. For the non-teaching, non-nursing community, for the *real* monks and nuns who don't collect wages from anyone, other shifts must be made as best they can. Happy the community which has a prolific and best-selling author in its house – and there are one or two here and there – whose royalties come in like a benison every six months. Lucky the prioresses who have those singing or guitar-strumming nuns under their care, talent-spotted by the record companies and at the top of the hit parade before you can chant 'Ave Maria'.

The Cistercians are still farmers, taking St Benedict's injunctions about manual labour more seriously than most these days. They always have been more consistent agriculturalists than any other order. They not only fed and clothed themselves off their own lands through the ages, but in their heyday, by developing a system of outlying grange farms manned by peasants, whose sons as often as not ended up in the monastery, they were of considerable economic influence in their localities. The American Trappist Thomas Merton* has remarked that their sheep-rearing, wool-growing activities in the twelfth century were on such a scale that in the north of England the role of the Cistercians was comparable to the role of General Motors in the States

* Died December 1968

today. Their role is much diminished nowadays, though Wilhering and other Austrian abbeys still run the monastic granges which generally disappeared with the Reformation, and they still look to the large farming families who work them for a lot of their vocations. But every Cistercian monastery runs a farm of some kind, both to fulfil its vocation and to pacify the bank manager – and sometimes to clean up the prizes in agricultural shows against the local farmers. Among the big news emerging from the American monastery of New Melleray in 1966 was this: 'The farm department won the 1965 Dubuque County corngrowing contest (125 bushels per acre); the alfalfa dehydration plant is functioning smoothly; the dairy (Holsteins) and the beef cattle (Angus) departments have improved their stock; the garage department invented a revolutionary alfalfa chopper; and 10,000 lbs of honey and 5,000 lbs of liturgical incense were produced . . .'

A Cistercian farm may run to a thousand acres and more, like Nunraw's in Scotland, or it can be two hundred acres and less, like Mount St Bernard's in Leicestershire. It may be so big that it keeps every man in the community busy when he isn't in choir or saying his prayers; it can be small enough to be left mostly to the lay brothers while the choir monks get on with their studies except when harvest time comes and they are required to reinforce the farm workers.

From their two hundred acres, their market garden and their orchard, the seventy-five monks of Mount St Bernard produce almost but not quite all their food. There are vegetables from the garden and fruit from the orchard; there are eggs from the six hundred birds in a deep-litter laying unit; there is milk from the herd of pedigree Ayrshires – 2 bulls, 45 cows, 27 heifers, 14 young stock. Most of the land, 120 acres, is under grass for the cattle; but there are 25 acres of root crops, 55 acres of corn; the Mount St Bernard harvest is mostly kale, potatoes, oats, barley and wheat. There is also a twelve-sow pig unit producing about 215 porkers a year. All this is run very professionally for the monks have become farmers down to the tip of their cowls. They have installed a six-point herringbone milking parlour and their cows are part of the brucellosis eradication scheme. You can't be more professional than that. And although the only newspaper entering the monastery is a single copy of the *Daily Telegraph* (extracts of which are read out to the community during the evening meal), the *Farmer and Stockbreeder* and other journals of the trade press are almost required reading for anyone working on the farm. The monastery's solitary wireless set – in the possession of Father Abbot, who listens to it to find out what prayers of intercession the world has need of that day – was originally acquired not to get the news but to have the BBC weather forecast for the benefit of those two hundred acres. If it were not for those white figures, cassocked and overalled above their muddy gumboots, gesticulating like the deaf and dumb to each other (for these are Cistercians of the Strict Observance, Trappists, who are among the least conversational of men) if it were not for them, and the great crucifix high on the whitewashed wall at one end of the cowshed, you would never dream down on the farm that you were well outside the jurisdiction of the National Farmers' Union and the National Union of Agricultural Workers. But everything around the dungy yard – the tractors, the trailer combine, the baler, the disc harrows, the fertiliser spinner, the corn drill, the spraying machine and the forage harvester – everything here is here for the greater glory of God and no other purpose. Except for those 215 porkers, which are flesh meat, and therefore fated for a less discriminating market in the world outside to bring in revenue to the monastery along with the surplus milk and eggs.

The Cistercians have their farms. They sometimes have more exotic forms of income. The Trappists of Caldey are in the perfume business, retailing anything from Caldey Number One ('a sophisticated perfume in the modern idiom') at 63s a bottle to Island Rose hand lotion ('incomparable "body" and soothing qualities') at 4s 3d a time. They run a mail-order business, as well as one scent shop in London and another in Los Angeles, to keep trade on the move, aided by publicity material that looks as if it has come straight off Madison Avenue. ('When the monks began to make perfume they trained in the best schools of perfumery, consulted the leading authorities, and Number One was their first outstanding achievement. . . . When the Caldey gorse is in full bloom the evening air is heavy with its fragrance. The monks, repeatedly asked by visitors to capture this scent, offer Island Gorse as a fine fully balanced perfume. . . . The matching After Shave and men's Cologne differ from those found on today's market, reflecting the simplicity and ruggedness of island monastic life. . . .') There are other communities which keep themselves afloat on the liquor business, from the thin red wine produced by the Salesian Convent in Bethlehem off those bony and sand-blasted Judaean terraces, to the tonic stuff that comes from gentler slopes in Devon by way of the Benedictine Abbey at Buckfast ('People write: "It is indeed a wonderful tonic and in my estimation incomparable. . . . I am so delighted with BUCK-FAST that I am recommending it to my many friends. . . ."') The Benedictines of Nashdom make incense (Tintern at 6s 6d a lb, Sherborne at 9s, Rievaulx at 13s, Evesham at 16s, Glastonbury at 19s) and the Benedictines of Prinknash make pottery with trading outlets in dependent houses, in London stores (Harrods, Barkers), and even in the souvenir shop at Upper Canada Village, Ontario, where Prinknash ware lies among the Crockett caps, the Redskin moccasins and the picture postcards of the St Lawrence river. There is a shop in the Boulevard de Tirlemont in Louvain which sells nothing but the varied produce of Benedictine and Cistercian houses in Belgium, whose shelves are loaded with cheese, liqueurs, mustard and mayonnaise as well as missals. And so somehow the monasteries get by. Just occasionally, when the harvest has failed maybe, or when the faithful are laggardly with their alms, an abbot will have to examine his treasures and sadly dispose of some antique rarity, the better to keep his monks in holy poverty. It was so not very long ago at the Abbey of St Rupert in Salzburg, which stripped itself of two twelfth-century prizes, a chalice and a vestment. They were gobbled up expensively by American museums.

The fact is, of course, that a monastery is like any other institution with mouths to feed, bodies to clothe, work to be done and fabric to be kept in repair. Even if it found the notion utterly abhorrent, money would have to pass through its hands and a balance sheet would have to be kept. The Petits Frères themselves cannot escape the menace of housekeeping. And the way they live involves the simplest housekeeping of all. For the Father Bursar of a full-scale community, keeping the accounts puts him in more or less the same position as a company secretary. This is what it amounts to in hard cash at one British monastery:

There are over forty monks at the mother house, another twenty in dependent British houses, maybe another thirty in four small communities overseas. The overseas houses keep their own balance sheets, they get annual allotments from the mother house, but as the monks in them have teaching posts they have some local income of their own from the governments employing them. The only earned income of the monks in Britain comes from the royalties on their writings and work done on parish missions or in conducting retreats, which often brings in a cheque. Individually the monks get 4s 8d a week pocket money (a few shillings a week more if they are smokers) and a £25 allowance for their annual holidays. In 1967 the monastery in Britain spent £46,724. Provisions cost £7,393, salaries for the five full-time and odd part-time employees (for whom it runs a non-contributory pension scheme) £7,527, lighting and heating £4,108, allotments to overseas dependencies £6,300, travel overseas by the superior and other brethren £3,881. The tobacco allowance amounted to £207. The monastery had a working deficit that year of £7,152. Its main source of income for 1967 was the £12,605 it collected in subscriptions and donations from people who support its work. It did almost as well – £11,565 – in dividends drawn from the capital brought to the community by brethren when they joined it. Guests and retreatants left a voluntary £3,934 in return for monastic hospitality. Royalties came to £2,038. That was how the monastery's general fund, from which it attends to its running costs, shaped up.

It also has what it calls a joint fund, from which it takes the money for capital expenditure. Out of that in 1967 it spent £9,383 on repairs and renewal of equipment in Britain and £50,100 on various subsidiary works of the community, mostly overseas. Into it came £12,934 in legacies to the monastery, £13,299 income from its investments, £7,623 on the sale of some investments and £10,918 in recoverable income tax. Its investments

are put into about 140 different firms and they have a book value
of £484,252. The monastery does not play the market itself (even
the bursar wouldn't know how to do that) but it has some good
friends in the City of London, Churchmen all, who buy and sell on
its behalf. At the moment it has shares in almost every sector of
industry. They run from Associated TV Ltd to John Brown and
Co., the shipbuilders; from Woolworths to Allied Breweries;
from Thorn Electric to ICI, Imperial Tobacco, the International
Publishing Corporation (owner of the *Daily Mirror* and the
People) and de Beers. What with one thing and another the
monastery has half a million pounds in the bank. It sometimes
worries about the placing of its investments, about the morality of
some concerns whose stock look good. It searched its heart a
long time when its City advisers suggested backing the South
African diamond miners de Beers; in the end it wrote to Bishop
Huddleston of Masasi, who belongs to the Anglican Community
of the Resurrection, who made his reputation as an opponent of
apartheid in South Africa and who would be expected to provide
an impeccably Christian judgement of the problem; he said that
de Beers were among the best employers in the Republic, and
that if they went out of business the people to suffer most would
be their native workers; so the monastery thanked him and
invested in de Beers. It has other problems of high finance. It has
to juggle with its joint fund, spending no more than a tenth of its
capital a year on capital works because the flow of legacies is
uneven; in 1967 £12,934 came in, when in 1966 there had been
£32,000. That at least is likely to balance itself out over the years.
The income that is certainly running out is the dividends on the
money brought to the monastery by newcomers. They are
obliged to leave their capital outside the community in case there
are family claims on it after death, so the monastery can't bank on
more than the interest. This has been pretty handsome in the
past but as more families claim the capital of dead monks it is
dwindling steadily. In 1967 the interest amounted to £11,565;
in 1966 it was £18,020. It will never be a growth point
because wealthy young bachelors with a vocation to be monks
seem to be a thing of the past. 'It's quite a blessing these
days,' says the bursar thoughtfully, 'if a man comes to us

with £100 he can call his own.' So the monastery watches its half-million carefully, wonders how long it will last, spends its four-and-eightpences with abandon, and remembers to say its prayers.

The economies of the Poor Clares and the Petits Frères are nearly light years distant from that one, for the spectrum of the religious life is almost as broad as that of life in the world outside the convent or the community house walls, and its breadth can be measured in every particular of the religious vocation, in every moment of the religious day and night. Even inside the two divisions of contemplation and activity there can be strange distances of habit and usage. A Trappist sleeps in a dormitory which is divided into cubicles with only a curtain to be drawn across the open end, because St Benedict ordained community in everything and the Trappist of the twentieth century adheres more strictly to St Benedict's Rule than any Benedictine does. Yet a Carthusian, who is also contemplative, has a cell which is his very private retreat from the moment he enters his Charterhouse until the day he dies. A monk or a nun may inhabit the same room from the beginning to the end of their vocation or they may be constantly flitting from one cell to another, every six weeks or every six months, as an act of obedience which has been invoked to prevent their becoming too attached to any one set of four walls, to make sure that there is absolutely nothing in this world that they can begin to regard as their own. There are monastic and conventual cells which are bereft of anything but a bed, a table, a hard chair, a hook behind the door, a crucifix on the wall, a missal and whatever spiritual reading is at the moment on loan from the community's library. There are others where the chair may be easy and well sprung, where if the incumbent's tastes run to Hokusai prints one will be framed and hanging opposite the crucifix, where there will be photographs of a nephew or a niece or a wedding group on a mantelpiece, where shelves and table will be an untidy sprawl of books, periodicals and papers which have been begged, borrowed or bought from a variety of sources both inside and outside the community. The English Trappist nuns of Stapehill in Dorset sleep on mattresses stuffed with straw. The Anglican nuns of Fairacres in Oxford, whose purpose in life is identically contemplative, lie on boards covered with thin foam-rubber Dunlopillo.

A community sometimes proclaims its flavour the moment the visitor walks through the front door. At this convent the waiting-rooms, where the nuns are allowed to converse with callers, will be named 'Watchful' and 'Faithful' and the rooms where guests are bedded down will be a series of 'St Uriels', 'St Gabriels' and other archangels. In the waiting-rooms there will be volumes of Trollope and Scott behind glass and you can be sure that nothing intellectually more invigorating or disturbing is to be found in the hinterland. The sisters and the atmosphere they make will be gently smiling, a little brisk, a shade pious. But at that monastery across the town, where the rooms are numbered or left entirely anonymous, where there is no waiting-room but a kind of hanging-around space instead, the first thing the visitor encounters is a revolving rack of recent paperbacks. The reading matter will proceed from the Bishop of Woolwich's latest at the threshold to Alex Comfort on *Sex in Society*, and the opaque psychiatric pronouncements – sprinkled, here and there, with four-letter worded case histories – of Dr R. D. Laing further along in the interior. And the fathers will be suitably sophisticated, very knowing about life outside, sometimes just a bit too hearty in their laughter.

A community can usually be depended upon to give itself away in the literature it publishes. This may run to nothing more than a cyclostyled newsletter aimed at a handful of friends and well-wishers; it may go to thickish volumes (in addition to hardback stuff written by individuals and handled by secular publishers) which are intended to be a source of research and argument in the highest intellectual echelons of the Church as a whole. As an example of the former here is an extract from the small magazine circulating from the Community of St Laurence, an English sisterhood which chiefly looks after incurable invalids and old people:

Dear Friend, Again it is time for us to be writing our letter, that is if you are to receive it in time for Easter. How quickly the days and months fly by. What an endless time it seemed, when we were small, from one

Christmas to another. But now the seasons seem to follow one on top of another in the twinkling of an eye. By the time you receive this it will be that Queen of all Festivals, Easter Day, and a very happy one indeed to all of you. We hope you have managed to steer clear of the flu. Perhaps it is too much to expect you all to have done this. If you were so unfortunate as to become such a sufferer we hope it is now only an unpleasant memory. We here have been very fortunate. We did not entirely escape, but we only had one or two isolated cases and for this we are very thankful.

In our last letter we were very sorry to forget to tell you about the loss of one of our treasures, old Mrs Gratton, better known as Gran, not that she was the eldest of our little family but she had so many grandchildren that it seemed quite the thing for all of us to refer to her as 'Gran'. . . . One day we were most interested to find Belper had suddenly come possessed of a Washetaire, and what a wonderful and useful place it is too with its lovely pastel shaded washing machines and tumbler dryers. How reasonable the cost. We worked out that we could do the whole of our wash there for the price we now pay for sending our sheets to a laundry in Derby. It's 2s 6d for the use of the washing machine and sixpence for the tumbler dryer, more sixpenses if you want things bone dry. Several of the community have spent several happy hours there. There is always an audience too, the other side of the window!!! We sometimes wonder whether these people are plucking up courage to come in themselves!! . . . As I write this we have 26 boys and girls staying with us from Whinshill. They are preconfirmation candidates and what a happy little crowd they are. Some of the girls had a wonderful time in the night, six of them were discovered in one room and four in one bed!! Smothered laughter and suppressed giggles betrayed them. They leave us after dinner today and we hope they take with them memories of their visit which will be of lasting value to them. . . .

A religious community can still be one of the last repositories of adult innocence, but it can also be as sophisticated as ever they come in the world outside. In an issue of the Benedictine *Ampleforth Journal* you can light on a ballad by Bob Dylan, alongside some pretty solid theological correspondence and book reviewing. In one copy of the English Dominican monthly *New Blackfriars* you can find articles on Black Power, Rhodesia, French political thought, God and suffering, redemption and revolution. In its issue of October 1967 the Canadian Dominican review *Maintenant* spent itself entirely on the French-Canadian question, and demanded a socialist republic of Quebec with its own president and a special relationship with the rest of Canada. In the September 1967 number of the *American Benedictine Review* the main articles were entitled: 'If St Benedict were alive today . . .'; 'Psychological hazards of young religious and semi-narians'; 'Freedom in the age of renewal'; 'Julien Green and his search for truth'; 'The meaning of the term "Father" as applied to Catholic priests'; 'Liturgical symbol and reality in the poetry of George Herbert'; 'The psychology of American foreign policy'; 'Renewal – the key to the vocation crisis'; 'Meeting today's vocation crisis'; 'Pattern of medieval monastic reforms'; 'Aphorisms for a teacher'; 'The gyrovags, or wandering monks'; 'God is friendship – the key to Aelred of Rievaulx's Christian humanism'; 'Unity day at Coventry – Benedictines participate in "Vision of Unity Week"'.

The quality of the paper, however, is not always a guide to the standard of the contents; the English Sisters of the Love of God publish a good deal of tough-minded spirituality with the aid of a stencilling machine and a stapler. Nor do the contents always represent the mood of the order backing them. The English Carmelites sponsor a literary quarterly which mostly reflects the individual preferences of the friar, Fr Brocard Sewell, who edits it; it is strong on Henry Williamson, Colin Wilson and the adventurous sort of poet whose writings are set down like this:

> 1 auricle/the wheel sounds
> turn to (turn ovah TURN
> fly a tern corner up out
> TURN to drumz

Even though the tradition of monasticism, and especially of the contemplative life, is one of withdrawal from the world the insularity of a religious community can still astonish when the community is physically not so very remote from the rest of society. It is less of a shock to find a Camaldolese hermitage blissfully unaware of current affairs when it is stuck in isolation high upon an Italian alp than to discover only slightly smaller ignorance in a Trappistine convent situated a few hundred yards from an English main trunk road. But when, in the 1960s, you ask the Abbess of Stapehill just how aware she and her nuns are of what goes on outside their walls, and she replies, 'Oh, we knew when we had a new pope; and we heard about the Coronation', you realise just how much the world is passing them by. At Stapehill they took, said the abbess, just one periodical and that was the Catholic weekly *The Tablet*. No newspapers, no wireless, certainly no television. One or two of the recently professed nuns had been acquainted with TV in their former existences but for the majority of the abbey the device might never have been invented. Yet the device is among the equipment of some contemplative houses which are physically just as enclosed as Stapehill. And the guest-master of a Trappist monastery in the English midlands is so anxious to demonstrate his awareness of what is going on outside that within a few minutes of a visitor's arrival he is artfully steering conversation towards the most recent movement on the pop record charts. There are communities which pride themselves on their conversational ability in the currency of the times they are living in, just as there are communities which cherish their ability to communicate in Latin. A Benedictine monk borrows a book from one of his superiors and pencils on the flyleaf 'olim Fr Prior nunc ad usum Br A—'. Not that all Benedictines can communicate as deftly as all that. One of the delegates to the 1967 congress of Benedictine abbots in Rome lamented when he got home: 'All the abbots would nevertheless agree that the sessions were sometimes boring. The speeches were mostly in Latin and had to be translated into English (for the benefit of the Americans, so my fellow-Englishmen insisted). Occasionally a speech in French would have to be translated into both Latin and English. I confess I sometimes wrote letters: other abbots admitted to having used the time in the same occupation.'

The insularity of a community does not necessarily correspond to the degree of its enclosure; it depends much more upon the alertness, the open-mindedness and the readiness of the order, the congregation or the superior to assimilate by all means available within its rule the facts of life and the flow of affairs

outside its walls. A community can have its mind broadened while
it is eating its meals. In monasteries it is customary to have
someone reading from a lectern throughout dinner and supper; it
happens in a lot of other communities, too. But while in one
Benedictine house there will be at dinner an excerpt from the
Rule, a piece of Old Testament and then an extract from some
saintly biography, in another the biography will be supplanted by
the latest non-fictional best-seller. The educative process is
sometimes continued in the recreation period; and sometimes
the period set aside for this purpose is neither educative nor
obviously recreational. Recreation can amount to a solid half-
hour's gossip over the coffee after lunch in a Jesuit house, with
the talk skipping as nimbly from one topic to another as in any
University common-room. It can be three-quaters of an hour in
the mid-afternoon with everyone sitting in a prim half-circle
around the superior like a lot of third-formers up for special
treatment from the head, in a less stimulating climate. The
head/superior reads a postcard he has just received from Fr X,
who, everyone will recall, visited the community some time back
and is now on holiday in Greece; he then describes a visit he
himself made to a community of nuns the day before; and then he
gives a potted account of what he has read in that morning's
newspaper; and no one is much encouraged to get a word in
edgeways. The dead hand that lies over many a religious recreational period is nowhere better exemplified than in the Rule
drawn up by the founder of the Anglican Society of St John the
Evangelist, the Cowley Fathers. In recreation, wrote R. M.
Benson, 'controversy and party spirit must be avoided, for party
spirit is the bane of conversation.' Yet in the formal daily
recreation periods of an enclosed convent not a mile from
Cowley, where the nuns are only allowed a free-for-all chatter for
three hours on a Sunday, Mother is liable to promote a general
and vigorous consideration of anything from the news coming out
of Vietnam to Mr Muggeridge's latest televisual perambulations
around Christianity. Which is only one more example of the
breadth of the religious spectrum. And though that is so broad
that it can have a Dominican clambering into bed after a long
evening's wrangle with university students, at about the same

time that a convent of nuns is rising to chant the night office; that it can contain both Benedictines living in the priceless treasury of Kremsmünster and Petits Frères subsisting in the gas-lit slums of Leeds; that it can embrace Spanish Carthusians to whom the infallibility of the pope is still almost an article of faith and French Protestants of Taizé who have never believed this and to whom it is not even a matter worth debating with Catholics any more – although the religious life is as broad as all those things suggest, there is one element above all others, above the poverty, the chastity and the obedience which all profess, which spans it from side to side and from end to end, which holds it together and gives it a unity. It is as vital to the Capuchin friars who are bearded in imitation of St Francis and Christ himself as it is to the Trappist monks who are tonsured in a symbolic reference to the crown of thorns. It is as central to the life of a Brigittine nun, whose habit is grey, whose shoulders and face are framed in a white linen wimple, whose head is veiled in black with a white linen crown in the form of a cross with five red drops on it, as it is to a Daughter of the Heart of Mary, who does not look like a nun at all because she dresses in ordinary clothes. One thing alone supports those who falter in the relgious life and kindles fervour in those who live it confidently to the end of their days. That is prayer.

FIVE

PRAYER

'Prayer means thinking of our Lord with loving attention.'
RENÉ VOILLAUME, Prior of the Petits Frères
Brothers of Men, p. 81

'That is the meaning of the contemplative life . . . to remind us of
what we are and Who God is – that we may get sick of the sight of
ourselves and turn to Him.'
FR LOUIS (THOMAS) MERTON OCSO *The Seven Storey Mountain*, p. 446

Let nothing, said St Benedict, be put before the Work of God.
The Work of God, the Opus Dei, was the saying of the Divine
Office in the monastic choir once during the night and at seven
different times during the day; at lauds and prime, at terce and
sext, at none, vespers and compline. These were the punctu-
ation marks of a monk's existence. This was when the common life
was lived at its most exalted level, when all gathered together in
the monastic church and devoted themselves to the most solemn
and carefully regulated liturgy, which was at first merely a
recitation of prayers but which later was to be ritualised into a
pattern of movement and refined into a haunting sound in the
intricacies of the Gregorian chant. The moment the monk heard
the signal for Divine Office he was to abandon whatever he had
been doing and assemble with the greatest speed, yet soberly, so
that no occasion might be given for levity. If he was late he was to
stand in a place set aside by the abbot for careless persons so that

all should know him for what he was, and he might not presume to join the choir until he had done penance. For nothing else was of the least importance when set beside the Work of God. And though Benedict defined this strictly as prayer and worship in the choir it was, by extension, something from which the monk was never entirely free. The monastery was to be a school of the Lord's service and the Lord was to be served best by prayer at all times, in all places and in subtly different forms: in the choir, in the cloister, in the cell and even when a monk was doing some work of God's out in the fields. Fourteen hundred years after Benedict one of his followers was to write:

> Underlying all Benedictine structures of life is prayer . . . the ground of a monk's life: it is that foundation, those piles which are driven deep into the earth to support the mass of activity above. It is the profoundest act of created man and no prerogative of the monk, except in his perseverance, extension and intensity. Without prayer the rest is straw. Prayer belongs not to monasticism, but to that Christian life which is more generic, the life of the soul seeking the face of God, sharing the Cross and the sufferings of Christ.

Prayer may not be the monk's prerogative, but it is his profession, more than that of any other man whether he be priest or not. And for any religious it has a theoretical primacy which in magnitude at any rate is scarcely to be expected of any other Christian outside the priesthood. It is the channel of communication between a man and his God; and however much modern apologists for the religious life may insist that theirs is only one of several Christian vocations (the married couple with three children and a very worldly job to attend to being another) the religious is distinguished from any other Christian by the totality of his commitment to God; by what, according to the norms of society, he has dispensed with to make it. Prayer suffuses a monastery for nearly twenty-four hours a day; and at the other end of the religious scale it is seen as the indispensable qualification for the life of the Petit Frère, whose day begins with mass if there is a church remotely at hand, and ends with vespers, compline and an hour of silent prayer before the altar he has contrived in his lodgings. The prior of the Petits Frères, René Voillaume, has asserted that prayer is such an essential to that vocation 'that unless we were convinced that it alone provides a sufficient reason for embracing such a life we should not have the courage to carry on. Is it not the tale of an idiot to embark in this way, in the flower of one's youth, upon a life in which one will do nothing useful by human standards, and very often by the standards of one's own intelligence?' For the Petits Frères one of the justifications of their prayer life, sandwiching, like two pieces of bread, a filling of completely unspiritual industry, is to demonstate that contemplative prayer is possible even in the most arid and brutalising conditions of the twentieth century. But its main justification is that it allows them to carry on the work they have taken up; and so every brotherhood is counselled to build itself a hermitage in some lonely place within reach of its house, an equivalent to the desert sought by the early fathers of the Church, to which in turn they can go for a weekend of solitude and undisturbed contemplation.

There are many different definitions of prayer, of what it consists, of its purpose, of how it is executed; possibly the only common ground is an agreement that it is communication with God. A French Oratorian has implied that for the monk it is an antidote to lurking evils that would poison his system.

Obviously the monk's life is a hard one. And perhaps what is hardest about it is the constant presence of these fundamental renunciations . . . the renouncement of earthly possessions, of earthly affections, of his own will. If the monk does not want to be tempted to seek shameful and unlawful compensations for these renouncements, one way alone is open to him, and it is precisely to force himself to engage in it with all his being that he has finally blocked up all other ways. This way, which leads him forward to the heights, all horizontal issues being closed to him, is prayer. In prayer he will breathe the supernatural atmosphere which will purify him, which will relieve him of all his weariness. . . . His life is no longer anything but prayer – prayer is his life.

The Benedictines of Buckfast Abbey see the monk's devotion to his prayers as an essential social service.

Every man is bound to worship God, both as an individual and in common with his fellow members of society. Worship implies a social act. This obligation of worship arises from the realisation that man did not make himself; that he is a creature made and belonging to a superior being which we call God. From the relationship of creature with creator there springs the necessity of praising and giving thanks to God by mankind as a whole. It is clear that a great many people because of their work have got little opportunity and perhaps as many again have little inclination to spend time in the worship that is due to God from his creatures. The monastery, as the Rule says, is a school of divine service and exists for the purpose of carrying out that duty officially as a social act on behalf of society.

Seen as a social service one of the most easily appreciated forms of prayer, apart from that implying a statutory quota which must somehow and by somebody (monks if everyone else is too lazy or uninterested) be offered to the Almighty by society at large, is the prayer of intercession with its special intention for a person or an event. In every monastery and most houses of religion there is an intercession board hanging on the wall of the sacristy, where the vestments are kept. It is usually a-flutter with pieces of paper bearing the intercessions which people would have the community make for them in its prayers. 'For Agnes S—, lying grievously ill with cancer and afraid of death.' 'For John and Mary P—, whose marriage is going through a difficult time.' 'For Peter J—, who after years of loneliness and despair, has just rediscovered his faith.' And the community remembers these people and their predicaments in its excursions into choir and commends them, one by one, to God's mercy. A contemplative nun, a Sister of the Love of God, explains just what that means to her:

If I am deeply involved, for example, in the pain of a friend who is suffering, in the anxiety of a mother whose son is fighting in Vietnam, then how am I to pray for these needs? Worship and intercession are both founded in perfect trust and this is the meaning of faith. We can trust perfectly in the goodness of God. He wills that all men are to be healed, that is made perfect with him, which is salvation. We can therefore trust through all and every circumstance and in that trust we hand over our care for our loved ones, or for the world in its needs, to his loving will – and this willing our will with his is our intercession. This act of trust will not take away the pain but it uses the pain and turns it into a positive act of love, which is a continuing intercession. It stills the anxiety which is the reflection of the bit of our wills which is not really in union with his will. Let's be honest, when we are caring most deeply so often we would still hold on by our emotions to some bit of possessiveness in our prayer – that beloved son and what we think is best for him – we cannot just completely let go of him into God's purpose. It is so understandable and we are doing it all the time, but really to intercede we must give our wills to be transformed to be one energy with God's creative purpose. As creatures we shall only truly be what he means us to be as we let go of our own human standpoints.

That woman listens to the BBC news at ten o'clock every night, just before she goes to bed, to see if any last-minute prayer of intercession for the world ought to be made.

Prayer can also be an act of reparation for all the sins in the world, as well as an output with a target figure per shift. A Benedictine nun says that 'Behind the grille of my enclosure, which protects me exteriorly from many temptations, I am jointly answerable for all the sins of the world, even the most gross and revolting ones. It is this which throws me on my knees to ask pardon of God in the name of the culprit or culprits whenever I hear any crime spoken of.' It can be the vital part of a concentrated personal and implicitly exclusive relationship with God. 'The monk,' said Cardinal Newman, 'proposed to himself no great or systematic work beyond that of saving his own soul. What he did more than that was the accident of the hour.' A century later he is echoed by a monk of Downside: 'Benedictinism stands or falls not as a civilising influence which brings the Christian culture to mankind but as a means of individual sanctification.' And because prayer is directed towards God, who is a spirit among other things, surrounded by the innumerable good spirits which are the angels, it is also something which must axiomatically find its way to God through the incalculable forces of evil. 'It is,' say the Sisters of the Love of God, 'our great joy and privilege to recite the Night Office at 2 am, a time when the powers of darkness are very active and the suffering needs of mankind and the souls departing from this life are specially needing to be held to the Love of God.' They see their contemplative life as an intensely positive and creative one, 'for it seeks to deepen by prayer and offering the will of man to be participant in the will of God in order that the Divine Will may flow back into the world.'

Prayer can be the recitation of psalms by an abbey full of Benedictines in choir. It can be a Jesuit spending his obligatory hour a day of private devotion, lying on his bed in what one of his predecessors, Jerome Nadel, called contemplative inaction. It can be a mental ejaculation, 'All for Jesus', repeated by a Trappist with every forkful of dung he heaves out of his cowshed. It can be the click of a rosary to break the heavy stillnes of a cell. It can be a solitary figure kneeling or lying prostrate, utterly fixed, upon the cold stone of an otherwise empty church; and you very rarely go into a monastic or a conventual church without seeing somebody at prayer. It can even, say some wide-minded souls, be a conversation between one of the fathers or the sisters with an outsider in the guest wing; because the talk goes on with God in mind. There is no end to the possibilities of prayer.

There are techniques of prayer, to be pursued in private. Simone Weil once remarked that there was a certain way of writing a Latin prose or solving a mathematical problem which, by training the mind to be attentive, could constitute a preparation for prayer. Most spiritual directors say that the first step is to pacify perfectly the body and mind; to quieten even the rhythm of the breathing. When that point has been reached the moment is ripe for the recitation of the Jesus prayer. This originated among the mystics of Sinai, was much cultivated by the Orthodox monks of Mount Athos, but has since circulated throughout western Christendom. With his breathing coming slowly and quietly the man at prayer murmurs 'Lord Jesus, Son of the living God . . .' as he inhales; and then '. . . be merciful unto me, a sinner' as he releases his breath again. He breathes his Jesus prayer indefi-nitely until the rhythm of it is something he would find difficult to shake off, so that it promotes a tranquillity in all that he does. He can achieve the same effect by repeating the Hail Mary slowly and fervently. And this, which in its essentials is a technique that either a Buddhist or a Hindu might identify with his own, can be a prelude to meditation proper.

There are written meditations which, the sages argue, are especially suitable for intellectuals accustomed to setting their thoughts down on paper but which, of course, can easily degenerate into mere literature if a man isn't careful. There is the meditation on the rosary, which was first devised to satisfy the groping piety of illiterates who could not join in Divine Office, but which can also be of use to more sophisticated souls. The rosary devotion in full consists of reciting 'Our Father' fifteen times, the 'Gloria' fifteen times and 'Hail Mary' a hundred and fifty times. While these formal prayers are being recited the mind dwells in turn on the Five Joyful Mysteries (the annunciation, the visitation, the nativity, the presentation, the discovery of Jesus in the temple), the Five Sorrowful Mysteries (the agony in the garden, the scourging of Christ, the crowning with thorns, Christ carrying the cross, the crucifixion) and the Five Glorious Mysteries (the resurrection, the ascension, the descent of the Holy Ghost, the assumption of the Blessed Virgin Mary, the coronation of Mary and the glory of All Saints). 'The simple recalling', suggests one commentator, 'even quite implicit, before each decade and throughout its recitation, of one or other of these mysteries and of all, one after the other, continually charges and recharges the names of Mary and Jesus for us with all their meaning, all their reality. Thus, finally, in the single name of Jesus, united by his mother to our humanity, is concretised everything that makes him the unique but total object of our faith; the living word of God who creates and recreates us in his image.'

There are more complex methods of meditation than that, the beginnings of those spiritual gymnastics in which the true contemplative hopes to achieve utmost proficiency. There is none more celebrated or daunting than the Jesuit chapbook, the *Spiritual Exercises* of St Ignatius; a very dangerous piece of literature, as any Jesuit will tell you, which should only be used under the guidance of a spiritual director who knows all the ropes the untutored might easily throttle himself on. It is a slim volume of three hundred and seventy paragraphs and St Ignatius decided that four weeks were necessary to get the best out of either it or the user. It starts by establishing some fundamental principles, like the daily examination of conscience. The moment you get up in the morning, says St Ignatius, you resolve not to commit a particular fault or sin that day; after your midday meal you recollect how many times you have transgressed and you make a mark for each occasion in a notebook; you do the same thing after supper; and every time you catch yourself sinful or faulty you lay your hand on your breast in a token of sorrow. The book ends with a number of tips for the devout – on Three Ways of Praying, Rules for Distinguishing between Different Spiritual Influences, About Scruples, and The Mind of the Church. In between the daily examination of conscience and The Mind of the Church come the Exercises proper. The four weeks are divided into four broad subjects of meditation: first one's own sins, second the life of Christ up to Palm Sunday, third the sufferings of Christ, and last the resurrection and ascension, with the Three Ways of Praying as an appendix.

The first exercise of the first week is a meditation on the first three sins – pride, covetousness and lust. It begins with a prayer asking God to direct one's whole self to his service, and this is the preparation for every exercise in the book. It is followed by an imaginative effort to picture the subject matter; later in the exercises this may be Mary riding towards Bethlehem, nine months pregnant, and the cave where she will have her child, or it may be Christ leaving Nazareth to be baptised in the Jordan; but in the first exercise it is necessary to imagine 'that my soul is a prisoner in this corruptible body and that my whole self, body and soul, is condemned to live amongst animals on this earth, like someone in a foreign land.' Then comes a petition appropriate to the subject matter; if that is the resurrection the prayer will be for a share in Christ's joy; here 'my prayer will be that I may feel wholly ashamed of myself, thinking how often I have deserved eternal damnation for my frequent sins, whilst many have been lost for a single sin.' There follows the application of memory, reason and will to the subject matter, here dwelling on each of the sins in turn, on their origin, on their results and on their presence in oneself. Finally there is a colloquy with Christ, what an Anglican curate of the caricatures might call a straight talk with God, and a final 'Our Father . . .'

That is the first exercise. By the end of the first week the whole gamut of sin has been reviewed, winding up with a meditation on hell which is very clearly the starting point of that most hair-raising passage in all English literature, the Jesuit sermon to which Stephen Dedalus is subjected in Joyce's *Portrait of the Artist as a Young Man*. A handful of additional practices are recommended before the second week starts. It is proposed that on going to bed, just before falling asleep, the thoughts be turned, for the length of a 'Hail Mary', to the next day's exercise; it is suggested that all light should be excluded from the room except when reading or taking meals, that the body should be chastised 'by wearing hairshirts or cords or iron chains, by scourging or beating ourselves and by other kinds of harsh treatment.' This is the broad pattern of all the *Spiritual Exercises*, though they become progressively more sophisticated as they consider, besides images and implications from the New Testament, such by-products of the spiritual life as Three Ways of Subjection, The Making of a Decision, Rules for Achieving Self-Control in the Future with regard to Eating, and suchlike. As a manual of self-discipline there will never, in any philosophy, have been anything to improve upon the *Spiritual Exercises* of St Ignatius Loyola. As an instrument for achieving obedience in a subject there is probably nothing to touch it outside the realm of drug-gery; it is doubtful whether the most cultivated psychological methods of persuasion known to the twentieth century could better this product of the sixteenth. And someone has called it a little pamphlet of icy dryness and purely administrative appearance.

Somewhere there is a frontier to be crossed between medi-tation and contemplation. The capital difficulty for any stranger to this territory is that those who appear to navigate it with confidence scarcely define it in terms he will understand. 'Meditation, laborious by nature, is the activity of beginners in the spiritual life,' says Fr Bouyer, 'or of those who have not progressed very far in it. But normally one ought to attain a phase of spiritual progress in which meditation no longer adds anything, or even becomes psychologically impossible to carry out. Then, it would seem, contemplation will flower of its own accord.' And without pausing to varnish this cryptic signpost the experts are off on a debate of their own about whether contemplation is infused ('the effect of a pure influx of grace, taking hold of the soul independently of any effort – or at least any conscious one – of the soul's') or acquired ('obtained by the soul itself, progressively simplifying and unifying its meditation and thus entering of its own accord, by a calm effort of concentration, into a state of spiritual tranquillity'). Then, having dropped the name of St John of the Cross into the heavy atmosphere of dim perception, they are away and lost to sight in a rarefied spiritual climate of their own.

St John of the Cross was another product of the Spanish sixteenth century. He was a religious reformer, co-founder with St Teresa of Avila of the Discalced Carmelites. He was a considerable theologian and a poet of some note. He was also a great ascetic. But he was canonised and finally named a Mystical Doctor of the Church, because of his contemplative insights; and for this he is remembered best. His reputation rests almost wholly on three major treatises: *The Ascent of Mount Carmel and the Dark Night of the Soul*; *The Spiritual Canticle*; and *The Living Flame of Love*. And of these it is the first, the *Ascent-Night*, which is most widely used as a manual of contemplation.

It begins with a poem of eight stanzas, each with five lines to it. The first of them is

> *One dark night*
> *Fired with love's urgent longings*
> *– Ah, the sheer grace! –*
> *I went out unseen*
> *My house being now all stilled;*

The whole poem is allegorical, a woman singing her good luck on having gone to her love one dark night, and of their rapturous union. It ends:

> *Upon my flowering breast*
> *Which I kept wholly for Him alone,*
> *There he lay sleeping,*
> *And I caressing Him*
> *There in a breeze from the fanning cedars*

When the breeze blew from the turret
Parting His hair,
He wounded my neck
With His gentle hand
Suspending all my senses

I abandoned and forgot myself,
Laying my face on my Beloved;
All things ceased; I went out from myself,
Leaving my cares
Forgotten among the lilies.

Carmel then consists of ninety-two chapters of commentary elucidating the spiritual matters buried in the poem; it is followed by a similar treatment of the poem in *Dark Night*, which runs to a further thirty-nine chapters.

St John's thesis is that the aim of the spiritual life is the state of perfect union with God through love, not obedience; this is the summit of Mount Carmel. And though on one short line of verse he builds a mountain of ambiguous meaning, hanging whole chapters on the significance of a single word, the poetic images alone are insufficient for his purpose. He uses others. He likens God to the sun and the soul to a window; when the sun shines upon a smeared or grimy window its full light cannot penetrate; so God cannot fully benefit the soul smeared with inordinate affection for creatures and worldly things. The soul, argues St John, is divided into sensory and spiritual parts, each with its own faculties and powers; to the first belong sight, hearing, smell, taste, touch, fantasy and imagination; to the second the intellect, the memory and the will. In passing from the initial stages of the spiritual life to perfect union with God the soul must deny its appetites by the purification of its two parts and by advancing in faith alone. To advance towards God a man 'must lean on dark faith, take it for his guide and light and rest on nothing of what he understands, tastes, feels or imagines.'

In *Carmel* St John instructs the beginner in the ways the soul must purify itself at its own instigation, why it must do so, the recognisable stages of progress and the methods of proof. In *The Night* he describes how God purifies the passive soul and brings its faith and love to perfection. He makes it plain that the whole progress of the soul towards God is a hard and at times a terrible one. There are moments of illumination which are followed by periods of black despair. There are dark nights when the soul imagines itself in purgatory or hell. But at the end of it all the soul in blind faith has ascended the steps of a ladder of love. On taking the first step 'As a sick person changes colour and loses his appetite for all foods, so on this step of love the soul changes the colour of its past life and loses its appetite for all things.' On the second and third step the soul is regaining its strength and slowly making progress, but on the fourth it is again seized with a weariness; if it can overcome that then the soul is well on its way to God. At the fifth it experiences an impatient longing for God, at the sixth it runs swiftly to him, at the seventh it becomes bolder in its affection and at the eighth it lays hold of him without letting him go. The ninth step is reached only by the perfect and on leaving it the soul departs from the body. On the tenth and final step it is assimilated completely with God.

St John of the Cross is not the only spiritual guide engaged by religious to lead them into the intricate ways of contemplation; the list is a long one, starting with St Clement of Alexandria who lived within two hundred years of Christ, taking in St Teresa of Avila, St Augustine of Hippo, St Bernard and Charles de Foucauld among others. But no single manual has greater currency, perhaps, than the *Ascent-Night*. And if the non-contemplative, with his alien concepts, his limited vision and his temporal inhibitions can make nothing of the spiritual life at this elevated level, then he must hold on to any simpler signpost he discovers in the hope that this will point to a glimmer of intelligence in it all. He can turn, for example, to the indispensable Fr Bouyer again.

Our personal assimilation of the gift of God, our personal association with the prayer of all in unity, can take many forms. . . . It may be nothing more than the appropriation of a word, of a phrase of the liturgical prayer; it may give free rein to an outpouring all our own, set in motion by this phrase but overflowing it; it may lose itself in the simple gaze of mystical contemplation. This matters little; what matters essentially is that not only our mind – our intellectual attentiveness – be engaged, but also our heart; that core of our whole personality, that centre not only (nor primarily) of our emotions and our feelings, but of our most intimate decisions, those most thoroughly involving our whole being. . . . While such a prayer normally needs silence for its birth or at least its development it should also normally end in silence. As with all conversation between persons in whom mutual affection, knowledge and comprehension have attained a certain depth, so in such an exchange there must soon come a moment when no word can suffice to express what is in our hearts, a moment when all words are by the same token unnecessary, being both inadequate and superfluous. It is this moment in prayer which we usually call 'mystical'. And there is no true prayer which does not tend towards it. . . .

Even for the man or woman who has accepted a contemplative vocation neither St John of the Cross nor any other mystic is a touchstone to the summit of Carmel. The reputation of some convents as places whose nuns are so jolly and joyful, put about by pious retreatants on their return from a weekend in the guest wing, is not always reliable propaganda; what is evident from the guest house and from the side chapel of the conventual church does not always tally with what might be seen in the cloister garth or the refectory, much less in the privacy of the cell. It is perfectly true that a contemplative convent can radiate, even in its inner recesses, a happiness and calm which seems unaccountable to the outsider who is preoccupied with the physical restrictions and monotony imposed upon the nuns. But it is also a fact that there can be islands of despair which have resulted not from the bleak routines of the conventual environment but from that same spiritual journey which St John of the Cross and others promise shall end in the glory of God and perfect union with him.

This is what has become of a Carmelite nun of sixty-six years old:

When Père B became my spiritual director he encouraged me to study the *Treatise on God*. When I reached the chapters on predestination and the smallness of number of the elect they were really a stunning blow from which it took me a long time to recover. It was not that the question of my own personal salvation troubled me, but it seemed to me that up till then I had regarded the loss of souls as solely due to their own perverse will, I was nearly saying as if God could do nothing to prevent them. Aquinas focused the matter for me in a way that was terrible because it was the source of temptation to me no longer to believe in love in the same way. Nevertheless, I have never regretted having been led in this fashion to a more correct idea of the transcendence of God; of his inaccessible mystery. I got over this crisis by adoration, but I feel that the naïve audacities of a child who feels she may ask what she likes of her Father are a thing of the past with me. In fact, I can hardly bring myself to ask God, either for others or myself, even for what he wishes to give us. No doubt this attitude is more authentic, but there is no longer the same spontaneity; and I must admit that, on coming back to those texts of the Gospel such as: 'Ask and you shall receive, that your joy may be full' which used to be the whole ground of my confidence, I feel tempted to say to myself: 'That is no longer true for me.' Now I am old, and everything that could have been a light to me is extinguished; it is in total darkness that I see my contemplative life – or what that should be – alternated by periods of doubt which make it very painful. Having no feeling at all of the presence of God or of the reality of the divine life in us, which demands an act of positive faith of me, I am confronted mostly with this mystery of evil which pervades everything and seems to submerge all the rest. It is the most habitual suffering and nothing comes to counteract it.

That is a woman who has spent most of her life struggling with St John of the Cross up the slopes of Carmel.

Anyone who imagines that to be a religious, especially to be a holy monk or nun – as some reverent outsiders do – is automatically to be possessed beyond doubt of all the blinding truths of the Christian faith, is living in hope of the impossible. Among the inhabitants of the religious world are to be found very nearly all the shades of belief and disbelief – ranging form pure Vaticanism to near-agnosticism – as occur these days among Christians generally, though doubtless not in the same proportions. A religious is not even much likelier to have a standardised impression of God than the man in the street or the Bishop of Woolwich. When, a few years ago, some Dominicans canvassed practically every contemplative convent in France – houses, that is, of the most rigorous spirituality within the religious life – they obtained an impression of God-imagery that might just as well have come from the market place. A 52-year-old Dominican said: 'I have neither an "idea" nor a "mental picture" of God. He is God, someone undefinable, of unimaginable beauty. When I hear God spoken of I feel I must drown myself, get out of my depth, not even try to understand any more. . . . Then I am satisfied because completely overwhelmed, I say to myself that I am too stupid to understand but that it must all be true.' Another nun reported that

between the ages of four and seven the presentiment became impressed on my mind that one day the world would come to an end when God would appear in the clouds and that we would all go to meet him. . . . Since then the vision of God-Man coming in majesty on the clouds of heaven has always been with me, and I have never ceased ardently to desire the end of the world and the coming of our Lord. This impression, this expectation was so strong that I had got into the habit of looking at the sky whence our deliverance was to come, and one familiar corner of the sky has remained engraved on my memory as the ideal place from which our Lord should reappear. Even now, when I think of God, I see this patch of sky.

For a Dominican nun of eight years' standing 'The image of God which comes most readily to my mind is the image of light or of water.' A Carmelite for thirty years replied: 'How does the face of God present itself to me now? The same as it has always done: no face at all – only love, that is all. If, however, I should wish to picture God to myself, I would think of him as fire and flame, life overflowing, an ocean of peace.' And a sixty-year-old Carthusian said, 'I can find no other (image) than that of my father, a man as wise as he was good and as just as he was wise. . . . I have only to extend this portrait to ultimate perfection and add the omnipotent and creative intelligence of a God to have the most beautiful image I can have of God.' Oddly, not one of the people questioned, nearly two thousand of them, saw Michelangelo's God, aquiline and limber, supported by angels as he creates Adam with a casually imperative finger in the middle of the Sistine Chapel ceiling; or the God of any other painter.

The only thing that can be said about the spiritual life of the religious with any assurance is that he or she spends more time and effort in trying to develop it than the Christian living out in the world. That is part of the profession. And nowhere is it professed as thoroughly as among the contemplative orders, the Cistercians and the stricter Trappists, the Carthusians and the Carmelites, the second order of Dominican nuns and the Benedictines who are relatively inactive, plus those dozen or so communities in the Church of England, the Society of the Precious Blood, the Order of St Anne, the Sisters of the Love of God and the rest. These are the monks and nuns proper, papally defined as such as far as the Catholics are concerned, and apart from the active Benedictines there are few outside their number who may lay claim to the same purist title unchallenged. Of the million or so women in religion in the Catholic Church today it has been estimated that about 60,000 are contemplatives; and of the 332,000 men there will not be more than perhaps 16,000 in the contemplative life. These are the people living the life of strict enclosure, though there can be and are degrees of strictness. Among the men there is nothing more confined than the life of the Carthusians, who properly speaking are hermit-monks like the Camaldolese. They, too, live in separate small cottage cells which they leave only three times in the average twenty-four hours, first for the office of vigils at 10.30 pm in the church, later for conventual mass in the early morning and finally for vespers, which are said communally in the middle of the afternoon. There is also, once a week, a communal walk lasting three hours, complete with the only conversation the Carthusian has except with his confessor. It is taken in the country around the Charter-house and everyone is obliged to join in. In a wayward exception to the general rule of such things the Carthusian nuns – all a hundred and fifty of them, in two French and two Italian houses – are less confined than the monks of the order. They eat in common and have a daily recreation together.

Generally, enclosure for a man is far less rigid than for a woman. It means scarcely ever leaving the monastic grounds, except in emergency or as a senior member attending a confer-ence. But places are provided where visitors may be received and talk freely to the monks at certain periods. There is nothing resembling the grille, which is still more than a talisman of most contemplative convents. There is at least one convent in this world where it has been abandoned; where the only thing resembling it is the barred peephole in the front door with the notice underneath, 'Please do not ring unless expecting an answer'; where, if you do pass muster with the custodian of the peephole, you may converse with Mother or one of her sisters in an anteroom, in easy chairs, with chrysanthemums on the table and a lingering flavour of furniture polish. There may conceivably be other convents which have also felt winds of change. But generally the grille is still there; an appliance introduced, it is said, by St Dominic after the family of Diana D'Andolo had tried to abduct her from her thirteenth-century convent, breaking one of her ribs in the scuffle to extract her.

A formidable thing it can be, too, a heavy wooden grating running the width of the only room an outsider is allowed to enter; he sits on one side, the nun sits on the other, and so thick is the wooden latticework, so comparatively small the openings in it, that the pair of them can have a little difficulty in the first few minutes agreeing on a position from which they can look each other in the eye. There is another one in the church, cutting off the community from the sight of any visitors who may be joining them in worship from a side chapel. And this is the reality of a nun's enclosure; a barrier which very often not even the parents of nuns are allowed to pass; so that when parents visit their daughter on her birthday or the anniversary of her profession they must hold conversation through the grille, unable even to touch each other and certainly prevented from exchanging any-thing so improper as a kiss. There are even some communities where it is forbidden that other nuns below the rank of superior shall cross the grilled frontier. And the Catholic penalty for breaching the enclosure, for a nun stepping outside the grille without permission, for an outsider breaking in, is ex-communication.

Grilles are still being installed. One community of nuns in the South of England felt it necessary, in 1964, to explain to the world at large why, when certain structural alterations were being made to their premises, they had decided to ask the architect to provide them with a grille in the new parlour:

A grille is a symbol of our voluntary withdrawal from the world, in response to a particular call from God, in order the more effectively to pray for it. No suggestion is intended of protection from the world represented by our guests nor any idea that the community is imprisoned and physically unable to get out. But a grille means more than this. There is always the danger that we put love of man before love of God and that the ties of personal affection will take priority over our consecration to God. Our dedication to intercessory prayer, our love for people which grows as one prays, our close contact chiefly through letters with those for whom we pray all increase this pull and it is so easy for it to undermine our primary consecration. The grille symbolises the priority over all things of our consecration to God (our having been set apart by him). It prevents physical contact and expressions of affection without involving rudeness or coldness or withdrawal. It helps us to give ourselves wholly in the way God means us to and emphasises the fact that all we have to give to others is God, not our persons, which are wholly given to him to use. . . . It reminds us that we have only what God gives us to give others and keeps our face to face encounter with people in its proper, second, place. Our real meeting with people and our real work for them is in our prayer.

The other cachet of the contemplatives is the almost everlasting silence. Precious thing though it is – and no one from outside a religious community can ever value it properly until he has experienced the blessed relaxation of eating his first monastic breakfast, where the only sounds are those made by a few elderly dentures and milk being poured over the cornflakes – it is here carried to almost punishing lengths to the normal ear. Silence is rated highly in any community, not only as a necessary accompaniment to private devotion. It is generally unbroken in every religious house, except in case of the most urgent communication, from after compline in the evening until after breakfast the following day. Among contemplatives it tends to stretch through most of the twenty-four hours, a practice followed elsewhere only on particularly solemn occasions such as the period between Maundy Thursday and Easter Day. In some of the strictest contemplative communities a monk or a nun is forbidden to speak to anyone at any time, unless it is to the superior, or unless special permission has been granted. The Trappists, who were the first to adopt a rule of total silence, were also the ones to devise a system for getting round it, holding conversation without breaking the rule. They have developed to a dexterous art their own variation on the deaf and dumb language. If the first finger and thumb of each hand are touching with the knuckles of the little fingers joined you mean 'mass'; if only the first fingers and thumbs are making a diamond shape the word is 'God'; 'coffee' is the first two fingers of the right hand placed on the left pulse; 'food' is all right-hand fingers on the mouth; and so on. A Benedictine has circulated the story of the Trappist who, wanting to tell a brother that some mutual acquaintance had found his vocation in a Spanish Charterhouse, did so by turning a pirouette and striking an imaginary tambourine; he might, suggested the Benedictine, have conveyed the message less energetically and with more decorum simply by hissing the word '*Burgos*'. Which was rather naughty of the tell-tale, for Benedictines, too, have been known to employ sign language to get the bread passed in refectory during the silence of their dinner.

It is a Trappist, Thomas Merton, who has outlined in realistic terms the cardinal burden placed upon the monk of his order.

It is after profession that the Cistercian really begins his training as a mature monk. He is simply thrown more or less on his own in the community. . . . He sees his abbot once a week or so, speaks to his confessor once or twice a week, and he might sometimes open his conscience to the Father Prior as well. But on the whole he is left face to face with a huge, inscrutable, and perhaps terrifying force which surrounds him on all sides and which is the community, the common will. This can develop into a terrifying trial to a young monk who does not realise what it is all about. To live in a house full of a hundred or a hundred and fifty completely silent men who are always together yet never speak to one another; to move about in this amorphous yet vital mass which stirs into action at the sound of bells rung at precise intervals of the day and applies itself with a mysterious energy to all its communal activities. . . . If you do not acquire deep faith and supernatural common sense, a couple of years in a Trappist monastery will do strange things to you.

The contemplative life can be hard enough at a less rigorous level than that of the Trappists. A nun says that it is literally hard on the body for a start, with a hard stool to sit on in the refectory, a hard chair and a hard bed in your cell, hard stone or wood for you to kneel on at prayer. And her convent is lenient enough to allow the nuns to cast their votes outside at elections or to visit the oculist in town; to give the young sisters a fortnight's holiday a year, which they spend in bungalows in the convent grounds, where they can gossip with relatives for two hours each day and with friends for one hour; to pack the holidaymaking old ladies and anyone recovering from an illness off to a cottage by the sea at the other end of the country. But except during a holiday, when you are obliged only to attend mass on Sundays and first-class feasts, and vespers every day, says the nun, there is so little time to do what you would choose to. You're either at work or prayer or spiritual reading all day from 5.30 in the morning to nine o'clock at night (as well as being up from 2 am to 3.30 am for the Night Office) except from 3 pm till 4 pm, when you get a cup of tea; but even in that time you've to put in half an hour's gardening. That hour is the day's formal recreation period and just before it ends you may be asked by another nun to walk with her round the garden. 'She may be the last person you want to walk with but you go in charity.' Then back to work, which means either the kitchen, an office, cleaning, sewing or the sacristy, where the vestments and the vessels and all the other paraphernalia of liturgy is kept. But work isn't nearly as trying as the fact that with the silence and the enclosure, modified as both these are by Cistercian standards, 'you have nothing in the convent which allows you to get away from facing yourself and God. You can't coax away a depression with a cup of tea just when you feel like it, or by taking a night out at the pictures. You just have to stumble through it.' The hardest thing of all, though, is the praying. 'One of the bad times is when you say I'll pray for an hour and nothing happens, your mind keeps wandering and you have to pull it back but it won't stay put. A consciousness of evil or suffering or intense pain is when I know that something's happening. It's a very simple and exhausting thing. I get nothing out of praying verbally at all. I might just as well talk to myself.' She doesn't know what her sisters recognise as something happening in their prayer life. The nuns, she says, don't talk to each other about that sort of thing.

A hard life and a very remote one from the patterns which have been established by the world outside the conventual or the monastic walls. This is where the hard fasting takes place. A plain and not overfilling diet is the best that a contemplative can expect; until recently, when the rule was modified very slightly, a Trappist would never taste fish or meat from the day he was accepted as a novice till the day he died unless he was very ill or weak; a Carthusian will still see no eggs or milk foods either in Advent or Lent and will eat only one cooked meal a day from 14 September, which is Holy Cross Day, until the following Easter; and though an active Benedictine may well enjoy a measure of beer or cider with his dinner his contemplative brother will probably have to make the best of water. This is where the silence and the restriction and the small discomfort of it all are fervently embraced in penance for the injury done to God by man and in some mysterious, supernatural and utterly contemplative way to heal the souls of poor sinners aware of neither God nor monk.

There is a compelling attractiveness to it which is partly romantic, partly aesthetic. There never was an occasion when time and place and event were more spellbindingly fused than when a column of Cistercians come pacing two by two along their Gothic cloister, their feet hidden in a swirl of white hems, their hands concealed within the deep envelope of their sleeves, their faces lost in the shade of their pointed hoods. That moment by those men in that setting makes a myth of the passage of centuries. St Bernard may be broken into a multitude of holy relics scattered across the face of a faithless earth, but nothing has really changed. The Opus Dei still goes on according to the precepts of St Benedict. Seven times a day is God to be praised in choir, for that, the saint reminded his monks, was how the psalmist ordered it; and once in the night as well. And every week every one of the hundred and fifty psalms is to be said, beginning with the twentieth at the Night Office every Sunday. And so it mostly still is. And though a conventual mass has its own gorgeous beauty, when the church is vivid with its seasonal colours, on altar cloth and cope – white for the great festivals, red for Whitsunday and the commemoration of martyrs and apostles, purple in Lent and Advent, green at other times; when it is stained aromatically with its eddying incense, it is not *then* that you catch the peculiar essence of the monastic or the conventual life. That comes during the periods of the Divine Office at the seven different hours, when all colour is muted and sound is almost the only perceptible sensation. When the monks sit in their stalls and recite the psalms across the choir to each other, *cantores* answering *decani* verse by alternate verse, in a murmuration that quietly rises above misericord and corbel, triforium and clerestory, to lose itself in the vaulting of the roof. When the Benedictines of Beuron, who are unexcelled in the art of plainchant, move in long, drifting Gregorian phrases, crescendo and diminuendo, from Gloria to Credo to Te Deum; and it is unthinkable that they should chant in any tongue other than Latin, the dead language that is quite palpably bridging the interval between the living and the dead. When the monks of La Pierre Qui Vire sing compline by heart from the blackness of the choir, for the only light floods the altar in the middle of the church and night is everywhere around it. Or when, at any Night Office, the candles seem to flicker more erratically than during the day, the great wooden covers of the office books seem to squeak louder, and noses have to be blown and throats cleared more frequently. At any of these times the religious life is translated from a philosophy or a strategy or a profession into an unfathomable mystery, and faith is almost tangible in its presence. And every day of his life a Cistercian monk will spend between five and six hours at this numinous Work of God.

So will a Cistercian nun, whose day begins when a bell rings in her dormitory at a quarter to three in the morning, summoning her to the Night Office of vigils. In the church the cantor breaks the silence of the night with the salutation 'Ave Maria, gratia plena, Dominus tecum' in the commemoration of Mary which precedes every portion of the Divine Office; and while she does so her sisters kneel and bow with their knuckles on the ground, in a peculiarly Cistercian devotion made especially to the Mother of Christ. The office is sung, there is half an hour of silent prayer, then lauds and the angelus follow one after the other. Twenty minutes later there is a Low Mass and Holy Communion. This is dispensed by a priest through a square hole in the grille, the sisters moving up to it one by one and bowing to the knuckles before lifting their heads to receive the Host. Then, in turn, they bow profoundly and move back to their stalls for more quiet prayer before they go to the refectory for the breakfast which Cistercians call 'Mixt'.

At 6.15 am they are back in choir to sing prime and when that is done they move into the Chapter room, where the Abbess reads from the Rule of St Benedict, gives a commentary on it, and then proceeds to the business of the day. First the Chapter of Faults, where the nuns accuse themselves publicly and sometimes (in charity, of course) each other of infringements of the Rule or customs of the community. They receive penances for this; so many 'Hail Marys' for Sister A, who failed to keep proper custody of the eyes in the garden yesterday, having looked up instead when an aircraft passed overhead; an extra term of waiting at table in the refectory for Sister B, who allowed the door of the library to close behind her with a bang. There is a space for spiritual reading after the Chapter before terce and conventual mass are sung at eight o'clock. Then comes the manual labour: a squad doing the weekly wash if it is Monday; household and garden chores any day of the week for some; handicrafts which range from weaving to book-binding for others, who will thus bring income to the convent. At 11.15 there is sext to be sung, with an examination of conscience at the end of it. Then comes dinner, with a prayer before and after the eating and some spiritual reading by a sister in a pulpit during the meal. Grace, which is said when the last piece of pudding has been consumed and the last napkin tightly rolled up in front of each place, is so long and so fondly intoned that it is broken into two parts; one in the refectory, the other in the church, with the miserere chanted en route from one place to the other. Washing up then, followed by reading or prayer, or just a stroll round the garden or anywhere else within the enclosure; except for the novices and the lay sisters who at this time must receive instruction in the Rule or the usages of the house, or some spiritual exercises from the Mother Mistresses. At 1.20 pm it is back to the choir for ten minutes of none, and then work again until 3.30 in the afternoon.

There is an hour after this for *lectio divina*, the spiritual reading which St Benedict placed high in priority after the Opus Dei. Before vespers are sung, fifteen minutes of silent prayer are spent, and supper is taken at 5.15. In another hour there is a public spiritual reading in the Chapter room before compline, the final office of the day. It ends with the evening angelus, with a last few moments of silent prayer, and a sprinkling of holy water upon each nun as she leaves the church from her abbess standing by the door. Then the nuns return to their dormitory to sleep as they have worked and prayed, fully dressed, on their mattresses of straw.

This is the life they have chosen and it is the life they are obliged to live unvarying except in its seasonal changes of liturgy, its professions of novices and its burials of the dead. A life of communication with no one but God and the two superiors of the convent, the abbess and the prioress. There is no such thing for the Cistercian nun as general conversation for the order does not approve of even stilted recreation; no Cistercian nun knows anything about the background of her sisters, whence they came and why, even after a lifetime of standing and kneeling alongside them in choir, washing dishes with them in the kitchen, pottering round the garden with them in a subsidiary work of God. There is no reason to know such things for all is directed towards God alone and everything is a preparation for death. And when death comes the nun lies on a bier in the choir, clothed in her habit, crowned with flowers as she was at her profession, without benefit of coffin, while two of her sisters kneel beside her, reciting the psalms in turn. Without coffin she is committed to her grave, and as the earth covers her body her sisters in God kneel and put their knuckles to the ground and cry three times on her behalf for mercy: 'Domine miserere super peccatrice!' There are religious in this world who will take the visitor into their community's cemetery, where the crosses with their triangular tops stand like rows of gable ends, and flippantly refer to it as the parking place. No Cistercian ever took such a liberty; nor Carthusian, whose end is chillingly anonymous. Just a piece of earth without even a cross to mark that anyone had ever been. But then the Carthusians are so fiercely concentrated on God to the absolute exclusion of all else that they will make no special intention in their intercessions lest these defile the purity of their prayer.

A Cistercian's represents the most extended pattern of worship among all religious but the hermit's, whose timetable is the one most curiously at odds with that of the world outside. For the monk or nun of a less rigorous order like the Benedictines, the devotions will be similar but the chronology will be more of a piece with the times we live in. Instead of a Night Office, matins will start the day at 5 am and compline may occur any time between 8 pm and 9 pm, for there tend to be small differences of routine from one house to another within the same order. Basically the structure of all monasticism has not changed in any essential since Benedict composed his Rule. For the severest contemplatives even the timing of the offices, the *lectio divina* and the other periods of the day coincides almost exactly with that of the Middle Ages. This, for example, was the monastic timetable according to the *Regularis Concordia Anglicae*, a document promulgated by abbots meeting at Winchester in AD 970 in an attempt to bring stability to an English situation which was threatening schism at the time; it was the schedule for summer, the winter one starting an hour later and finishing one and threequarter hours earlier:

1.30 am: Rise, trina oratio, gradual psalms. **2.0** am: Nocturns, psalms for the royal house, vigils and lauds for the dead. Short interval. **3.30** am or **4.0** am: Matins, miserere, psalms for the royal house, anthems of the Cross, the Blessed Virgin Mary and the patron saint of the church. Matins of All Saints. Change and wash. **5.0** am: Trina oratio, reading. **6.0** am: Prime, psalms and prayer, morrow mass, Chapter, five psalms for the dead. **7.30** am: Work. **8.0** am: Terce, sung mass. **9.30** am: Reading. **11.30** am: Sext, psalms for the royal house. **12.00** noon: Dinner. **1.0** pm: Siesta. **2.30** pm: None, psalms, for the royal house, drink. **3.0** pm: Work. **5.30** pm: Supper. **6.0** pm: Vespers, psalms for the royal house, anthems as in the morning, vespers and matins of All Saints, vespers, vigils and lauds of the dead. **7.30** pm: Change into night shoes, collation (a snack). **8.0** pm: Compline, trina oratio. **8:15** pm: Retire.

The Church has traditionally regarded the contemplatives as an élite compared with the actives, has seen them, in modern terms, as a sort of religious Brigade of Guards or United States Marine Corps. To some extent it is because the contemplatives have clung closest to the origins of the religious life, have maintained after a fashion the purity of the line. But at bottom it derives from St Augustine of Hippo's theology of perfection (of which more must be said later on) which he applied to the Church as a whole. Contemporary exponents of the view point in justification to five verses in St Luke's Gospel:

Now it came to pass as they went that he entered into a certain village: and a certain woman named Martha received him into her house. And she had a sister called Mary, which also sat at Jesus' feet and heard his word. But Martha was cumbered about much serving, and came to him and said: 'Lord, dost thou not care that my sister hath left me to serve alone? Bid her therefore that she help me.' And Jesus answered and said unto her: 'Martha, Martha, thou art careful and troubled about many things. But one thing is needful: and Mary hath chosen that good part which shall not be taken away from her.'

The contemplatives have tended to be equated with Mary, while the actives have become identified with the industrious but plaintive Martha. Pius XI was much given to discriminating between the two forms of religious life. 'It is not hard,' he said in his apostolic constitution of 8 July 1924, 'to understand that a much greater contribution to the growth of the Church and the salvation of mankind is made by those who are constantly occupied with the duty of prayer and mortification, than by the workers who till the fields of the Lord; for if they did not bring down from heaven an abundant rain of divine graces, the evangelical labourers would gather but a meagre harvest from their toil.' Even Pope John XXIII, who has been reckoned to have had broader vision than most of his predecessors by people both inside and outside the Church, even he on one occasion quoted a contemplative puff of Pius's and added, 'There is the guarantee of the value of the contemplative life in the eyes of the Church. Let others like Martha give themselves to the work of the external ministry. But it was Mary who received from the Saviour's lips the assurance that she had chosen the best part. That part is yours.' Perhaps the fact that he was addressing the Abbot General and the Reformed Cistercians on their home ground had something to do with it; possibly the speech had been written for him by some contemplative member of the Curia. It is conceivable, of course, that if you are enduring a Cistercian existence your morale needs such flattering boosts from time to time and that popes are sensitive enough to be aware of it. Nevertheless, the perils of taking the Martha–Mary implications for granted – not least the spiritual peril of pride – seem to be considerable.

The possibility of a developing arrogance has been pointed out most vigorously by one who is himself a Cistercian, Fr Thomas Merton. He has considered the Vatican Council's injunction that the Church should nurture greater 'openness to the world' and particularly what this might mean for religious living the most enclosed régime:

To some contemplatives the idea of 'openness to the world' is incomprehensible. It contradicts what they believe is fundamental to their vocation. The essence of the cloistered life consists in their being 'enclosed'. They argue that the cloistered life cannot be open in any real sense without ceasing to be cloistered. This seems to them a matter of simple logic. When you embrace the contemplative cloistered life you turn your back on the world, you renounce the world, you forget the problems and concerns, you pray for it without needing to know what you are praying for. You turn away from the world to God, because the world is opposed to God. The cloistered ideal then becomes an ideal of 'pure contemplation' in which everything is organised in view of a state of perfect recollection; everything is arranged so that one will be entirely purified not only of attachment to the world but even of all interest in it, all concern for it, all memory of it.

But 'openness to the world' means involvement in the affairs of people outside the cloister, identification with them in their desires, problems, struggles, dangers; it means vital concern about a world of total war, genocide, race riots, social injustice, misery, poverty, violence, lust, every kind of disorder. All this is wicked and ungodly. Far from divine, it is diabolical. How can one think of such things and maintain the inner peace, the purity of recollection, the serenity of spirit in which one will hear the sweet, ineffable call to divine union? 'Rejection of the world', 'contempt for the world', then results in a crudely automatic polarisation; everything that happens inside the cloister and according to the sacrosanct rules of the cloistered life is wise, pleasing to God, full of redemptive power and supremely significant. The God who is nauseated by the actions of worldlings outside the cloister is consoled and delighted by the actions of observant religious within the cloister. This distorted interpretation of the gospel texts about renouncing the world in our own hearts becomes an excuse for pharisaical complacency. Contemplatives despise the world because they imagine themselves to be superior to it in every way. The cloister is the guarantee of that superiority. If they resume contact with the world they lose their superiority and become like everybody else. The beautiful image is tarnished. They no longer feel secure in the thought that God loves them better than anyone else. Obviously this is a caricature. But this distortion has been made positive by a valid traditional concept of the contemplative life – one which has been taken for granted for sixteen hundred years. Yet there are many things which have been taken for granted longer than that which the Church is now questioning.

This obviously *is* a caricature of some contemplatives. It will scarcely fit the image of the Mother Superior who listens to the 10 o'clock news before she goes to bed, whose convent takes a couple of daily papers and a sheaf of serious periodicals, and who illustrates the meaning of intercessory prayer by referring to the Vietnam war. It tallies rather better with the abbess to whom current affairs means first and foremost papal and royal coronations. Or with the Anglican contemplative monk who writes: 'The conditioning to which modern man is subjected, in the subtle brainwashing technique of advertising or political propaganda, or the latest craze for distortion in art and literature, cannot touch the mature contemplative. He is an adopted son of God through his baptism, and now knows by experience that he is free to claim the paternity and fellowship of his heavenly Father, and to be a servant for the redemption of all God's children.'

Elite or not, the contemplative has accepted a vocation which is less common than any other and which can be as much of a puzzle to some active religious as to any agnostic who has been brainwashed by admass. It is possible for a religious who says his offices every day, who is in much demand as a lecturer on various

forms of the new Christianity, and who has a respectable amount
in print both periodically and in paperback, to declare that he just
doesn't see what the contemplatives are getting at. Such a man
has told me so. For many more actives it is a matter of tempera-
mental unsuitability to the enclosure and the pressing silence. A
friar of my acquaintance was sent during his novitiate to his
order's retreat house for a concentrated period of spiritual
instruction and formation. Except for the offices and the confrontations with his spiritual director the course was wrapped in
total silence so unbearable to him that he would go for long walks
in the woods far from the retreat house and there bellow every
ribald song he had learned in the army, merely to relieve the
tension that had built up in him.

Yet it is not at all uncommon for active religious of many years'
standing to experience a strong attraction to the contemplative
life at about the age of thirty-five. It is possible for some that by
then their spiritual development has taken them to the threshold
of true contemplation and that they want to give themselves to
this more completely than their first vocation will allow. For
others it is almost certainly a reaction against overwork which
has pushed them to the point where what they need most of all is
peace and quiet for an extended period if they are not to break
down. The first thing to suffer in any thoroughly active community dedicated to teaching or nursing is the time to pray, whether
that is interpreted as a prostration in front of the altar in church or
merely an hour spent torpidly on a bed. In some congregations of
active sisters the only form of Divine Office each day is the
recitation of the complete rosary; and, as Bishop Huyghe has
pointed out, 'there is no prayer that so easily becomes mechanical when fatigue prevents concentration and control of the
imagination.' It is also possible for the liturgy in choir to become
mechanical, for the monk or nun to tick off their five or six hours
of office a day, their hundred and fifty psalms per week, with the
blank steadiness of a metronome. There is a monastic joke about
an abbot who was reciting Divine Office in choir with his community when a violent thunderstorm broke outside. He shut his
breviary with a snap and said, 'Brethren, let us pray.' Religious
are apt not to laugh too much at that one nowadays because it cuts

a bit too near the bone for many of them. It is even on record that some, when asked why they practise daily prayer, have replied, 'We do not know' or 'It is advantageous to us.' There are superiors who distrust any form of prayer life other than the simplest forms of meditation and the verbal formularies of the office books, presumably out of a nagging anxiety of quietism – a seventeenth-century French heresy which held that for perfection man must become so passively 'given' to God that he was indifferent to heaven, hell or his own salvation, and that once he had reached this state of mystical perfection it was impossible for him to sin any more, whatever he did.

There are others, growing in number, who are restlessly reviewing prayer, its techniques and its possibilities, its bases and its applications. They are reacting most of all against a quota of prayer in choir being crammed into a fixed timetable which leaves little space for reflection on what is being chanted or said. They are introducing silences in which there is time to think between the prayers of intercession, between the epistle and the gospel, between the Sanctus and the Agnus Dei. They are beginning to wonder whether it is vital that a nun should have to make her mental prayer in church with her sisters, where she can too easily be distracted by their presence, rather than in the privacy of her cell. The monks of the Maurist Congregation of Benedictines are now allowed a week of solitude every few months, free from Divine Office in choir, in which they can find their own rhythm of prayer and return to their brethren glowing with spiritual health.

The most radical departure of all from the established systems of prayer in western Christendom has been taken in Africa by Benedictine monks and others. There they are now accepting the local dance as a form of worship.

If some night you were able to get into the convent which the Poor Clares have recently founded in the Cameroons, you would be present at a form of adoration which is completely novel to us Europeans. With the Blessed Sacrament exposed, the sisters sing the Divine Office to the lively rhythms of the local music and accompany their prayers with sacred dances of equal originality. With the exception of the prioress the forty members of the community are all native vocations and have invented this new way of praying precisely in order to be able to praise and adore God with their whole being. In fact, music and dancing are for the African the essential means of expression. How could these young women who wanted to consecrate their whole life to God in an enclosed convent, forget this simple fact? Their decision has led to a sharp increase in vocations. Many young women were hesitant about entering a contemplative convent, for they knew of the life only in its European form and did not feel that this was in harmony with their own spiritual needs. But now that the contemplation has in some way become 'African' they have brushed aside their doubts and the number of applications is growing daily.

Which only adds to the enormous and bewildering complexity of prayer, though this is said by the prayerful to be such a simple thing. One commentator will say that it is possible for a highly consecrated person to meditate faithfully every day of his life without making the slightest spiritual progress. Another will claim that the most spiritually advanced can derive much benefit merely from turning the Lord's Prayer over in his mind. Prayer is the ecstasy of the mystic who has reached the summit of Mount Carmel and it is the dark night of the poor soul who is still slogging up its slopes in despair. To some it is thinking of Christ with loving attention; to others it is being so sick of the sight of ourselves that we turn to God. In a multitude of conceptions, Christ-God is its only common denominator and its threshold, so they say, is when God becomes 'you' and not 'him'. No one but a man of prayer can possibly say how that happens. Sometimes not even he can.

SIX

AUTHORITY AND OBEDIENCE

'The monastery is a school – a school in which we learn from God
how to be happy.'
FR LOUIS (THOMAS) MERTON OCSO *The Seven Storey Mountain*, p. 446

In the *Codex Iuris Canonici*, the Catholic Church's code of canon
law, some lengthy consideration is given to the religious life. At
the outset the three evangelical counsels of perfection are noted
as obligatory for all religious. Significantly, obedience is given
priority over poverty and chastity. It could hardly be otherwise
when God himself is to be obeyed before, and as well as, being
loved and worshipped. His Church has grown upon the assumptions of authority and obedience. In no part of the Church are
these assumptions taken more seriously or savoured more
carefully than among the religious. Prayer may be the element
that binds their spirits to the Lord but it is obedience, with all its
subtle implications, with all its variety of practices, with all its
thoughtful penalties, that orders the pattern of their lives
and sometimes holds their bodies in fee until the moment they
die. It was by invoking obedience that St Benedict brought order
out of chaos. It is only by snubbing it in carefully chosen places
and at artfully picked moments that the religious of today can
begin to change the shape of the society he fostered. And the
pressures against their doing so are greater than any others in
Christendom.

For a start there is the weight of canon law itself, binding on all Catholics at various perils to their souls. There are 2,414 canons all told and nearly 200 of them – canons 487 to 681 – are devoted to the religious life. These begin with some definitions. Canon 488 points out that:

an institute is a society approved by legitimate ecclesiastical authority, the members of which, in accordance with its laws, make public vows, either perpetual or temporary, provided they intend to renew the latter after their expiration and through these means tend to evangelical perfection. An institute whose members profess solemn vows is an order. Vows are solemn when they are recognised as such by the Church with definite juridical effects. A group of independent monasteries united under one superior constitutes a monastic congregation. . . . The union of several of these monasteries into a monastic congregation, although establishing a mutual bond among the various houses, leaves them all independent.

Canon 489 notes that strictly speaking a 'rule' refers to one of the ancient Rules – of St Benedict, St Basil, St Augustine, St Francis and others – while constitutions in the strict sense mean particular statutes added by various orders or congregations to the ancient Rules.

After the definitions, every avenue of the religious life is explored. According to Canon 504 no one can become the superior of an order or a congregation unless he has been professed for ten years, was born in lawful wedlock and is at least forty years old. He can become a local superior at thirty. According to Canon 531 there are only two exceptions to the general rule of common ownership of goods; the property used by the Friars Minor of the Observance and the Capuchins belongs not to them but to the Holy See. Canons 547 and 549 declare that in monasteries of nuns, postulants shall bring in a dowry fixed by the constitutions 'or determined by legitimate custom' but that it is absolutely forbidden for a community to spend more than the interest on a dowry until the nun has died. Canon 551 lets a religious take her dowry outside if she leaves her convent, even if she is dismissed or decamps and 'if the day on which the semi-annual interest is due be June 15 and the religious leaves on June 14 the interest for those six months is hers; if she goes on June 16 it is the institute's.' Canon 559 decrees that a novice-master or mistress shall be at least thirty-five, professed ten years and 'distinguished for prudence, charity, piety and faithful observance of the Rule.' Canon 598 positively forbids any woman, even a relative, to enter the enclosure of monks under any pretext unless she is the wife of a king, regent or president. As for the major enclosure of contemplative nuns Canon 600 is full of safeguards. The only people allowed in without the Holy See's special permit are the local bishop or the regional superior on his visitation, the confessor to administer sacraments to the sick or dying, 'the highest actual ruler of states . . . with their wives and their retinues', cardinals and, 'with due precaution' at the Mother Superior's discretion, physicians, surgeons 'and others whose services are needed'. The bishop making a visitation 'must be accompanied by one and preferably two clerics . . . of mature age. The companion or companions must not leave the visitor during the entire time he is in the monastery.' If the confessor is admitted 'two nuns must accompany him to the cell of the sick nun and after confession directly to the exit of the enclosure.' A footnote to the canon observes that 'should a consecrated Host be dropped within the major enclosure the priest may enter to pick it up; or a nun may pick it up and consume it or, if she has already received, give it to the priest.' Canon 601 says that after profession no nun may leave her major enclosure even for a short time unless she has special permission from the Holy See or unless she is in danger of 'death or other very serious evil'. According to Canon 602 'by general law nuns are not forbidden to see the altar. This may be forbidden them by their own constitutions, however. In any case the nuns must not be seen by the faithful.' Canon 624 states the rules for women religious collecting alms. They must go in twos, not remaining away from their house for more than a month. They must travel by rail and make sure they arrive and depart during daylight. They must try to find lodgings with other women religious, or at least with some charitable benefactress. 'The modesty owing their state undoubtedly requires not only their avoiding taverns, but also their staying away from sporting events, particularly horse races.'

The Church is an obedient society if it is to live in the image of its founder. It is also a hierarchical society and this is nowhere a greater imperative than among the religious. Standing just below the pope, as far as they are concerned, is the Vatican's Sacred Congregation for Religious and Secular Institutes which (under various titles) since 1586 has been the chief agent of religious government, the penultimate arbiter and court of appeal. At the last count it consisted of a Cardinal Prefect and 29 other cardinals, a secretary and an under-secretary, 48 consultors, 13 commissioners, a treasurer, an archivist, three writers, 22 assistants, 93 experts on ecclesiastical affairs and seven counsellors on civil matters. The entire congregation meets on occasions so special that no one is sure of the last, but once a week the Cardinal Prefect, the secretary, the under-secretary and the commissioners get together. The Anglicans have nothing comparable to this organisation any more than they have any rule book as heavy as the *Codex* – they can only muster 151 canons to cover the whole of their Church government; and their Advisory Council on Religious Communities, consisting of a bishop appointed by the primates, six people appointed by the bishops at large and six by the religious communities, is exactly what its title suggests, without any coercive powers. In fact, on all but the very gravest matters of discipline or unless the Church as a whole has an interest in the point at issue the religious, either Catholic or Anglican, are left to run their own affairs without interference from above, though they can never be free from superior influences.

There are some religious institutes with a central command post which directs policy in every one of its houses throughout the world. There are others which offer their houses virtual autonomy and erect a pyramid of central authority more as a token of unity than anything else. There are some orders who elect their superiors for life and others who offer them only limited periods of authority. There is nothing more centralised than the structure of the Jesuits. Sitting in Rome is the Superior-General of the Society, at the moment a Basque, Fr Pedro

Arrupe, who is after the pope himself possibly the single most powerful man in the Catholic Church. He rules without any internal counters to his authority other than those imposed by the Jesuit constitutions and the general congregation of Jesuit superiors, which meets in effect only on the General's death to elect a successor. Otherwise he has an absolute right of decision on all issues within the Society. He appoints personally the superior of nearly every Jesuit house and as these are changed every six years this means about a hundred and fifty appointments a year. He has an advisory 'cabinet' of four men to reduce the amount of work he is faced with: the monthly account of local affairs that each Jesuit provincial has to submit to the General, the similar report that every superior must send from his house twice a year, and the ones that come annually from the four 'consultors' in every house. There is a further buffer of eleven assistants, one to keep an eye on each of the Jesuit regions throughout the world. But though the general congregation appoints the men of cabinet rank, while the General chooses his own regional assistants, all of them are disposed only for his consultation. His word is final on any matter under the Jesuit sun.

They order things differently for Benedictines. The oldest monastic foundation has coagulated into a confederation since Leo XIII in the nineteenth century decided that there was a danger of too many local interpretations made in isolation fragmenting the Order of St Benedict beyond repair. Every twelve years every Benedictine abbot in the world gathers in a confederal congress to elect an Abbot Primate, who is now the American Dom Rembert Weakland, from Latrobe, Pennsylvania. Half way through his term they meet again for a general conference about the order's affairs. It can never be more than that because much more power is invested in the individual congregations and even in individual abbots than ever resides in the congress or the Abbot Primate. This is no more than following the spirit if not the letter of St Benedict, who never visualised anything but individual monasteries looking after their own affairs and nobody else's. Below the confederation come the congregations: the Cassinese and the English, the Bavarian and the Brazilian, the Beuron and the Subiaco and the rest; eighteen of them altogether, with their strings of related monasteries and dependent priories and their subtly different emphases on individual aspects of the Benedictine life.

Subiaco with 35 has more monasteries than any other, the American-Cassinese the most monks with 2,045. The 21 monasteries and 1,078 monks of the (Solesmes) Congregation de France specialise in the liturgy and the Gregorian chant. The twelve monasteries and 599 monks of the English have a reputation for running fine schools for the sons of gentlemen. And although the congregations mostly follow national boundaries this is not invariably the case; a small handful of Benedictine houses in the British Isles do not belong to the English congregation, which is the oldest in the Benedictine Order. It is also one of those which submits its abbots to periodic elections, every eight years here; Subiaco puts a man in for life.

The English run their congregational business by means of a Chapter which meets every four years to elect a new Abbot President if it wishes. To this come all the abbots in the congregation, together with one delegate from every abbey. In a religious world that is once again beginning to change these Chapters will have had more really thoughtful work to get through in the 1960s than for a long time. Normally they haven't exercised themselves much more than was needed to make minute alterations in the local style, or to bestow titular abbacies and priories upon the various monks of long service and good conduct. Dom Herbert Byrne, monk of Ampleforth, is also Titular Abbot of Westminster; Dom Sigebert Trafford, monk of Downside, is Titular Abbot of St Albans; Dom Oswald Dorman, monk of Douai, is Prior of Peterborough; and Dom Vincent Fogarty, monk of Belmont, is Prior of Worcester. And though each title refers to an unimpeachably Anglican see, it is also a reminder, to take a perfectly wholesome Catholic view, that the premises were pinched from the original owners by Thomas Cromwell and Henry VIII.

The infrequency of the congregational Chapters points to where Benedictine power really lies. It is with each abbot sitting on his own throne in his own abbey church with St Benedict's Rule to support him and to remind his brethren that he is the representative of Christ himself in the monastery. He has all the power of a sea captain who may have to answer to his company when he is ashore but who commands as he pleases when his ship is afloat. He has his own brethren in Chapter to refer to and a Chapter meeting can be conducted with the studied formality of the Buckfast Benedictines, who use a ballot box with white beans for 'yes' and black beans for 'no' when they are voting on anything important. It can be as informal as sometimes it is with the Trappists of Caldey, who, it is said, are apt to hold Chapters on the spur of the moment, merely sending the novices out of the room after mass and getting down to their discussion. In some places a Chapter can be so democratic that it goes on for hours so that anyone who might possibly want to speak has had every chance to say his piece. But however democratic the processes of Chapter may seem to be it is in the end the Benedictine abbot, and most other superiors too, who pass judgement and who, if they are careless and determined enough, can ignore that some-times nebulous but otherwise latently powerful force they call the mind of the community. Fortified by tradition and with the constitution or the Rule behind him a superior can hold a religious in obedience as strictly or as leniently as he pleases.

Exemption from this chain of command only comes when a man is made a bishop or a cardinal and is answerable only to the pope. This happens, but not very often. A handful of religious have been plucked from their vowed life and exalted in some Curial capacity. The Jesuit Cardinal Bea* is in the Curia, and the Benedictine Cardinal Gut and the old Master-General of Dominicans, the Irish Cardinal Browne, and one or two others. About sixty bishops from the orders were mustered at the Vatican Council, with about two hundred Superior-Generals who were there in their own right to have a finger in ordering the general affairs of the Church. But the way to preferment for the monk or the friar is a very narrow one indeed. And for the nun or the sister it does not exist at all.

There is a weight of canon law above the religious state and there is a pyramid of power. There are also vows, which hold the

* Died November 1968.

individual to the life. A Catholic parish priest takes a vow of
celibacy and a promise of obedience to his bishop, the one being
virtually irrevocable with the highest penalties, the other being of
some smaller account and with sanctions well short of excommunication. The religious is much more involved than that. He
has to obey, besides canon law, the Rule and constitutions of his
order, which lay down the larger principles of its life; he also has
to keep his eye on the customary (sometimes called the usages or
Consuetudines) of his community, which details the minutiae of
his timetable. If he is a monk proper this will tell him when and
where he is to sit or stand with his cowl up or down in choir; in
what order he shall process to the Divine Office; what response
he is to give the brother who wakens him in the morning – 'Deo
gratias' as often as not in exchange for 'Benedicamus Domino' but
with longer variations on particular days like Good Friday, when
the knocker-up does his rounds murmuring 'Christus factus est
pro nobis obediens usque ad mortem' and expects the sleepy
voice to answer 'Mortem autem crucis'.

Religious obedience is mostly made not by a promise but by the
much more serious vow. There are several different varieties.
The temporary vow is the one taken during the novitiate, which is
binding only for that period. Simple vows and solemn vows are
then taken for life, the difference between them being a very fine
juridical one that only canon lawyers can appreciate properly; it
concerns degrees of poverty and the obligations of the Divine
Office more than anything; it means, in effect, that the strictly
enclosed life of the monks and nuns proper obliges them to take
solemn vows, while less rigidly circumscribed souls are put under
simple vows. But there are also societies holding to a common
life, mostly products of the seventeenth century, like the Oratorians, the Sulpicians, the Sisters of Charity of St Vincent de Paul
and a few others, which take no public vows at all but instead
make promises with a life intention, in much the fashion of the
parish priest making his promise of obedience. To anyone outside
the religious life these may sound artificially fine distinctions. To
anyone inside they may mean the difference between eventual
dispensation into the secular world again with nothing more than
a few hurt feelings all round, and a life sentence which cannot be

reduced by one minute – unless the circumstances are so pressing that the pope issues a special dispensation – except by the soul brave enough to face excommunication and the Church's promise of eternal damnation.

Religious vows and promises are generally to the three principles of poverty, chastity and obedience but there are exceptions. Neither the Benedictine nor the Cistercian makes them in that form. They vow themselves first to stability, which means that they will stay in the same monastery all their lives; although occasional exceptions are made today, a Benedictine monk is generally expected to remain a monk of Downside or Bec, or wherever he was professed, to the end of his days – unlike a Jesuit or a Dominican, who is liable to have dropped anchor in a dozen or more communities of his order by the time he is through. The Benedictine secondly vows himself to *conversatio morum*, or a serious attempt at progress in virtue, which implicitly means both poverty and chastity. His third vow is one of plain obedience to his abbot. And while three vows are the general rule some religious have to take a fourth. The most famous of these is the Jesuit vow of instant obedience to the pope's personal wishes; in recent years this has been invoked to put Jesuit missionaries into Japan close behind General MacArthur's conquering Americans at the end of the Second World War, and to staff most of the positions in the Vatican radio station. The canonesses of St Augustine vow never to let the education of girls be neglected.

The religious is also living under a caste system infinitely more artful and complex than that devised for the general rank and file of the Church. It has many more ramifications than a simple division between the contemplative Marys and the active Marthas, the celestial doves and the plodding mules. Canon 491, to start with, declares that while all religious enjoy an undefined precedence over laymen, within the religious world itself there is further stratification. Canons regular – Premonstratensians, Lateran Canons and the like – take precedence over Benedictines and other monks. Monks take precedence over other regulars – Dominicans, Franciscans, Jesuits, Barnabites and so on. Regulars take precedence over all other religious –

Redemptorists, Passionists, Oratorians, Brothers of the Christian Schools and the rest. Only women in religion are spared the embarrassment of knowing their place and trying to keep it in this class-conscious society; they aren't even considered for membership. They have their own hierarchy within their own orders and congregations, though, just like the men. Canon 564 codifies part of it. The novitiate, it says, shall be separated as far as possible from that part of the house inhabited by the professed brethren so that the novices shall not be brought into contact with them. 'Separate quarters shall also be assigned the novices preparing to be lay brothers, that is separate even from the quarters of the other novices.'

At the very bottom of the religious pile, just below the novice who will eventually be a priest as well as a monk, is the monastic lay brother. Though monasticism started without benefit of priests, within three hundred years of St Benedict monks were taking orders as a rule, concentrating more and more on worship in choir and less upon the necessary chores around the establishment. The way for a servant population was opened by Benedict of Aniane at Aachen in 817 and the practice was generally adopted by the Cistercians two centuries later. Since then a cornerstone of the monastic life has been the recruitment of men (and in convents, of women) sufficiently educated to have a hope of becoming priests (or in convents, to keep up intellectually and vocally with the choir nuns) but perfectly suitable to toil away at the less cerebral monastic exercises, like stewards in an officers' mess. With a few exceptions the lay brothers have traditionally found themselves excused not only from the full Divine Office, in place of which they have had a modified liturgy of their own, but also from meetings of Chapter – which has deprived them of any say in the government of their houses. There are, of course, many religious congregations which were built from their beginnings in the nineteenth century specifically for the unordained who wanted to take up the life; it is, for example, laid down in the constitutions of the Marists and the Brothers of St John of God that the superiors shall not be chosen from among priests.

One of the changes starting to creep into the religious life is the status and function of the monastic lay brother and sister. The current position was perfectly expressed by the Benedictine Abbot of Prinknash at the end of 1965:

In July we held a Chapter of the English Province of our Subiaco Congregation. Among other decisions made then there is one of special interest, namely, that our Brothers be admitted to solemn vows; moreover, we hope that at the General Chapter next year they will be given full Chapter rights and the same monastic habit as the choir monks. The aim of course is to integrate the Brothers completely with the community so that they share fully in its life and have just as much say in the running of the monastery as the clerics. For too long the Brother has been looked upon as a kind of lesser Religious whose main duty is domestic work. This is far from true. Here at Prinknash most of our Brothers hold responsible offices; they head the various industries and in fact often enough the choir-monks work under them. Of course in a monastery domestic chores have to be done as in any other house, but all alike, priests and Brothers, share them. The Brother's vocation is a very special one. He comes to the monastery because he feels drawn to the monastic life but he does not feel called either to the priesthood or to choral duties; and there is surely a place in monastic life for such vocations. There are many young men who would like to dedicate their lives to the service of God in this way; craftsmen and artisans and men who wish to work on the land. And, thank God, we have been greatly blessed in our Brothers. It must be admitted, however, that in recent years there has been a falling off in vocations, due no doubt to the general turmoil of these present days. I should, however, point out that it is an altogether mistaken idea that those unfortunates who are backward, mentally retarded and the like, are suitable candidates for the Brothers; for such is not the case. The Religious life is so completely unsuited for neurotics; when such people are accepted, the usual result is disaster. Monastic life can never be looked upon as an *escape*.

Though the notion of obedience has been implicit ever since the teachings of Christ it was not specifically invoked as a distinctive trade mark of the religious life until Pachomius established his Egyptian communities at the beginning of the fourth century. It was not regarded as an essential until St Benedict compiled his Rule. For his monks there was not only to be obedience to the abbot who represented Christ in the house;

there was also to be a complete resignation to its corollary, humility. In chapter seven of the Rule, Benedict distinguishes carefully the twelve different degrees of humility he wants to see in his followers. The first degree of humility, he writes, is always to keep the fear of God in mind. After that the monk is to renounce his own will; he is to subject himself to his superior for love of God; he is to bear with patience all the difficulties, contradictions and injustices arising from obedience; he is to confess humbly to his abbot any evil thoughts or secret sins; he is to be content with the meanest and humblest in everything; he should not only talk of himself as the lowest of the low, but he should believe it, too; he must do nothing but what is exemplified in the Rule and his superiors; he is to keep his mouth shut until spoken to; he must not be ready or prompt in laughter; when he speaks it must be gently, seriously, sensibly and briefly; and he should not only be humble but take care to show it, by always bowing his head, casting down his eyes, pondering his sins and considering that sooner or later he must be judged by God.

This was to serve as a rule of thumb for religious for the next seven hundred years. It wasn't until the thirteenth century that a more sophisticated, fully developed theology of obedience appeared from the hand of the Dominican Thomas Aquinas. It was Aquinas who first gave priority to obedience over the other evangelical counsels of chastity and poverty because, he argued, 'great is poverty, greater is chastity but the greatest good is obedience if it is observed inviolably. For the first rises superior to material things, the second to the flesh, but the third to one's own mind and will.' To Aquinas obedience induced subjection, striking at the heart of the ego, beating down the pride which survives when all other vices have been vanquished. It also liberated the individual from the anxieties of independence. It sacrificed man's greatest treasure, free will, and thus became the most handsome gift a man could make to his God. And the Thomist doctrine has been accepted, woven into the fabric of the Church and embroidered by the zealous ever since.

It is recognised, of course, that there are limits even to religious obedience. 'It would not,' according to a recent commentator, 'be disobedience to refuse to keep a fast to death imposed by an imprudent superior . . . the sphere of religious obedience . . . does not extend to acts contrary to the rule or unrelated to it. A religious who fulfils his voting obligations has not to go to his superior for guidance on the way he is to vote. A superior may not . . . give orders on technical points to nursing sisters or social workers who depend in this respect on a professional authority.' And then, in one of those delightfully vague Christian loopholes, 'there can be no culpability in a breach of the religious rule whose motive proceeds from the pursuit of a greater good; it would be culpable if it proceeded from some ill disposition, idleness, gluttony, negligence, for example, but it would not of itself imply an offence against obedience in particular. . . . It goes without saying that a religious who gives practically no heed to the rule he is vowed to is on the downward grade towards contempt and is liable to commit actual sins at least against the requirements of the common good and the respect due to superiors.' Basically, though, obedience still means what Aquinas meant it to mean. 'The perfection of obedience consists in entering totally into the will of the superior, that is to say, in conforming oneself in all that is licit in his will, forestalling his commands, seizing with predilection on painful occasions of obedience because in them the will has less likelihood of its self-seeking, and because a maximum contact is thus guaranteed with the superior's will and this, in the last resort, means with God's.'

This is an important piece of every novice's inheritance when he or she first attempts the religious life. Canon 542 says that no one may enter a novitiate until he or she is at least fifteen years old; but before anyone takes the temporary vows of a novice he will have done time as a postulant, to see if even the limited period of the novitiate is something he can cope with. The Carmelite friars will accept boys of twelve for their juniorate, allowing them into the novitiate at seventeen; a child of eleven can begin the long life of a Scalabrini Father under certain conditions. On the other hand, the Benedictines of Downside try to discourage anyone from even tentatively trying out his vocation until after he has been to university; and there are not many Anglican orders who will take in anyone under twenty-odd. Most orders are not prepared to start making a religious out of anyone older than about thirty-five, though some accept what they call late vocations. Curiosities, of course, tend to crop up all over the place; the English Fr Laurence Bright was an atomic physicist before becoming a Dominican. According to Canon 542, the only people positively disbarred from starting the religious life are bishops, people in debt and people whose parents or grand-parents are in dire need; widows and widowers are normally welcome as long as they can fulfil the general conditions of the institute.

The qualifications sought most of all tend not to be educational ones. Look through any directory of the religious life and the same requirements are made over and over again by institute after institute: a sincere desire to serve God as a priest and a religious; good health; a good moral character; a deep personal love of God that manifests itself in great love of our neighbour; a supernatural motive; good common sense and an ability to live happily with others; a sense of vocation and a well balanced character; a spirit of generosity and courage; a zeal for souls and a cheerful disposition. But the Sisters of Notre Dame de Bon Secours de Troyes require postulants to have 'normal appear-ance and legitimate birth' among other things. The Missionary Sisters of Our Lady of Apostles, who sound as if they've had their troubles, are on the lookout for females between fifteen and thirty 'of legitimate birth, belonging to an honourable family; having an unblemished reputation; good health; no remarkable deformities; an upright mind; sound judgement; sufficient knowl-edge, good disposition and qualities suitable to give assurance of service to the congregation; not to have been sent away from another novitiate or any other religious or lay establishment whatsoever.' Inevitably, Carthusian nuns must be virgins.

When the postulant arrives at a community's doorstep he is usually given what in the more unsophisticated circles they call a guardian angel; a novice experienced enough to guide the new-comer round the premises and introduce him to the routine and the rules. The postulancy may last a few weeks or a few months; unless a child has been taken in very young indeed it will scarcely last longer. At the end, if the aspirant is to join the novitiate, there is a clothing ceremony. For a girl joining the Franciscan Missionaries of the Divine Motherhood it means walking to the altar in something much like a wedding dress, complete with veil, and there, having made her temporary vows, having a few symbolic locks of her hair cut off; this is later cropped short enough to be comfortable under a tight-fitting guimp, when she is dressed in her novice's habit; and there is an iced cake to be cut and a party to be enjoyed. For men the structure of the temporary profession is more or less the same, though the party trimmings are less decorative. Novitiate periods vary. They cannot be less than one year and in some institutes the novice is in for life after that. Two years is more common. At Ampleforth the budding monk makes a temporary vow for a year and simple vows for three more before committing himself to solemn vows. And at some time in the period leading up to those final vows he is sent to university partly, as one of the brethren puts it, 'so that he can see what a skirt looks like again.' It costs them something in lost vocations at that point but they take the view that it is better to discover a worldly streak in a man then than later on. They reckon to keep for life about half the people who enter the novitiate.

The Jesuit training period is notoriously longest of all. It is not true that a man cannot become an ordained Jesuit until he is thirty-three, though he rarely manages it before then. The curriculum varies from province to province in some details but in general the pattern begins with two years' novitiate, in which the man's character is probed, while he is subjected to those daunting Ignatian Exercises in all their sidelong complexity, and while he himself weighs up the Society. After that, three years hard labour in philosophy. Then three years at university for a degree in almost anything and as often as not in what the man himself wants to read. During those six years he will have been given his first few crumbs of theology but no more; and before he is allowed to make a meal of it he is dispatched, straight from university, for another three years as a teacher in a Jesuit school. Then he gets his main course of theology, four years of it; and after that he spends what the society comically calls the 'third year of probation', in which he grapples with the Exercises once again and takes part in various 'experiments', which may mean anything from acting as a prison chaplain to giving retreats to schoolgirls. Then, and not before, the Jesuit is considered fit for ordination. A moment, as someone has remarked, which 'could seem like the reward of a well-spent life, rather than the beginning of a priestly career.'

The Benedictine will have long since committed himself to his monastery for life. At Buckfast Abbey the novice will have gone through his initial year on temporary vows and will have assumed the name by which he will be known for the rest of his life if he is to remain a monk. Not everyone is obliged to change his or her Christian name on becoming a religious; it very often depends upon whether the same name is already installed in the community. But the changes that do occur are strongly in favour of the saints, and particularly the monastic saints. Every Catholic monastery on earth has its ration of Benedicts, Cyprians, Mauruses, Aidans, Dunstans and Dominics; most convents will be sprinkled with a Scholastica, a Teresa, a Hildegard, a Mechtilde. After his first twelve months the Buckfast novice is required to take simple vows for three years. And for the next three years he will be studying more closely than before St Benedict's Rule and all its implications; he will be receiving instruction in the fundamentals of spirituality; he will be learning the rituals and chants of the Divine Office. He will also be learning to strip himself of all the things that formerly expressed his personality; he will have long since lost his civilian clothes and his way of wearing them; he will take longer to learn the alien but now approved ways of moving his body, of greeting his companions, of having nothing that he can call his own.

And at the end of the three years, while the aspiring Jesuit is still only a quarter of the way to his ambition, the young Benedictine, having been accepted by the vote of the professed monks, will be led one morning during mass to where his abbot sits enthroned below the altar steps. He will take with him a sheet of parchment on which his vows are written and he will read these aloud. He will show the script to each of the monks in turn and then he will lay it on the altar and sign it. His abbot will bless him then, and each of his brothers will give him the kiss of peace before they continue with the mass. All but he, who will now lie prostrate before the altar with a black funeral pall covering him, with a candle at his head and another at his feet, while high above in the abbey tower a bell tolls to signify his death to the world. 'Let him understand,' says St Benedict, 'that according to the law of the Rule he is no longer free to leave the monastery, or to withdraw his neck from under the yoke of the Rule, which it was open to him, during that prolonged deliberation, either to refuse or to accept.'

Neither he, nor the Carmelite nun who promises 'obedience, chastity and poverty to our Lord God, to the most Holy Virgin Mary of Mount Carmel and to you, reverend Mother Prioress, and to those who shall succeed you, according to the primitive rule of the Order of Barefooted Carmelites and our constitutions', nor the Jesuit still plodding through his studies can ever decently, in the eyes of the Church, have a will to call their own again after they have reached that point. Nor can anyone vowed to the religious life. They have given it away and a terrible weight of law and authority has been accumulated over the ages to see that the Church exacts every jot of their obedience from them. And this great weight is the rock on which the religious life stands.

It is an Anglican superior who has said that 'There is undoubtedly a Jansenist strain in the spirituality of some religious communities which dies hard, and under its influence the vow of poverty can be made to appear grim and joyless and austere, the vow of chastity cold and loveless and inhuman, the vow of obedience tyrannical and unreasonable and opposed to human dignity and responsibility.' It is a Catholic abbot who has written that 'a novice-master or novice-mistress who can and dares to enjoy things, or who can and dares to love someone, is practically unknown.' Fairly swingeing indictments, both of them, and though neither could be sustained as absolute generalisations to be applied to every community in the world both speak of a tradition that once was universal and that today is still widespread, even though erosion has recently set in. The tradition is clear enough in documents such as the *Manual for Novices*, which was published in 1921 for use by the Discalced Carmelites, and which may still be seen in Carmelite library shelves. Chapter 3 is devoted to mortification, and under Section II – Mortification of the Exterior Senses, there are these admonitions:

ARTICLE I – *The Sight*

1 Do not raise your eyes more than is necessary even in your cell.

2 In passing the cells of others or on entering them, also the sacristy, the church, the garden and the various offices, repress all notions of curiosity; do not seek to find out who or what is there, or what is going on.

3 In the streets especially, and in the houses of seculars, be particularly careful to observe modesty of the eyes, and do not examine curiously the buildings or the persons you meet on the way.

4 When you are speaking to any person do not look at him fixedly in the face, at least without a serious cause, especially if he is a superior or a man of dignity.

5 Never allow yourself to be drawn from your solitude in order to see the palaces of the great, public gardens, exhibitions, pictures or other objects remarkable for art, antiquity or novelty, or in general those things that serve for the vain display and amusement of seculars. Our Lord Jesus Christ had nothing but contempt for these worldly vanities. . . .

ARTICLE II – *The hearing*

2 Do not give ear to profane music or to worldly songs, however artistic their style may be.

3 You should pay no attention to news of current events, much less seek for it, not even what is going on in the Convent or Order, unless it contributes to your edification or regards your particular duty.

4 Avoid as poison of the religious spirit news and accounts of wars, treaties etc. between earthly princes. . . .

ARTICLE III – *Smell*

1 Do not smell fragrant herbs, fruit or flowers etc., much less bring them into your cell, or keep them for their pleasant odour. . . .

ARTICLE IV – *Taste*

4 When you eat or drink, think of something unsavoury in order to mortify the taste, especially if you take things agreeable to the palate.

8 Sometimes mingle a little water or bitter flavouring with your food.

9 At intervals put the body to some inconvenience, such as keeping one foot raised etc., in order that the discomfort of the body may impede the gratification of the taste or moderate it, that so each morsel may be dipped in the gall and vinegar of Jesus Crucified. . . .

ARTICLE V – *Touch*
6 In summer do not seek the refreshments of air, water, cold drinks, shade or change of garments etc. Be very careful, however, to shake off the heaviness caused by the heat.
7 When an occasion of suffering occurs, seize it eagerly as a jewel from heaven. . . .

Section III concerns the Cultivation of Chastity on which, among other things, the manual offers this advice:

10 Touch no one, and do not allow yourself to be touched by anyone without necessity or evident reason, however innocent. . . .
11 Repress and fly from as a mortal plague, even though spiritual in their origin, particular friendships and familiar conversations arising from an attractive appearance, pleasing manner, or an agreeable disposition in which you feel a certain sensual gratification; avoid with the greatest care the occasion of being in company with those who are the object of such friendships.

There is, finally, advice on what to do when retiring to rest, in which this direction appears:

10 Sprinkle your bed with holy water on all sides as if it were your tomb and lie down with crucifix in hand and your arms folded in the form of a cross, as if you were never to rise again.

That tradition is not yet dead. Mortification is much older than the organised religious life; it was as much a distinguishing mark of the first hermits as solitude; and it was as much an instrument of self-abnegation as a device to quieten sensuality in order to develop and release the spirit for a flight towards God. Religious are still apt to rationalise it on the same grounds. Over thirty years after the appearance of the *Manual for Novices* it is possible to find someone arguing that mortification should mean a refusal to satisfy nature and what is natural, should mean forcing the body to remain in the world as though it were out of place there because 'the nature of present-day man is a nature which has been vitiated. If we do not wound it, it wounds itself. . . . It should be noted that the three essential mortifications, in food, in comfort, in sleep, are aimed at the same thing under different forms. They attack peaceful and satisfying accommodation, installation and enjoyment in the world.' And this because 'the material privations which lie at the root of the monastic life . . . presuppose that the life we call natural, if it is not bad in itself, in its substance, for this was created by God, is in any case bad in its actual exercise, for which we are responsible.' So the mortifications continue in the 1960s under obedience. And though one English Mother Superior reports that before Lent in 1967 she was getting letters from people asking if her convent supplied disciplines, because they had tried half a dozen monasteries up and down the country without success for the first time, this doesn't mean that the discipline has suddenly vanished from the religious life. The discipline is a small whip with which penitents scourge themselves. 'I was,' Mother recalls, 'brought up on the discipline myself but I hadn't been superior ten minutes before I realised that it didn't mean a thing to the novices we were getting. And, after all, I should have thought it a pretty well established fact by now that there's a distinct correlation between self-inflicted pain and sexual gratification.' That brisk dismissal will not be common yet, even if the discipline is beginning to wane – which is about all one dare say of it at present. The Trappistine nuns of Holy Cross in Dorset still apply it to themselves once a day. And according to a Madrid newspaper two thousand hair-shirts and a thousand disciplines had been supplied to the faithful of the Spanish capital by local religious shops and monasteries within five days of Ash Wednesday 1967. At a more ludicrous level there is still in the English midlands a convent whose constitutions forbid the use of anything other than soda for washing either pots or clothes.

There is one kind of penitential gesture required, so the argument goes, to purify the spirit. There is another demanded by a superior merely to break the will and test the obedience of a religious. The precedents for many of these have an honourable place in Church history. The desert fathers used to weave rush baskets in the morning and undo them again in the evening to provide themselves with a virtuous occupation. St Antony obliged one Paul the Simple to empty a well and pour the water on the ground for the sake of obedience and nothing else. St Teresa of Avila used to recount with pride how once in refectory she was served with a small cucumber which was rotten at the core. 'Unperturbed I called one of the sisters, one who had most discretion and intelligence, and in order to prove her obedience I told her to plant it in the little garden we had there. She asked if she were to place it upright or on its side. I replied she was to place it on its side. . . . I once happened to give a sister six or seven incompatible offices simultaneously. She accepted them all without a word, ready to believe she could fulfil them.' These have their counterparts today when, according to the religious grapevine, instead of rush baskets, it is sewing that is done and undone; instead of water emptied from a well, it is dry leaves to be swept from the priory path in a howling gale; instead of planting rotten cucumbers, the fashion is now for planting walking sticks or cabbages upside down. Much of this sort of thing, where it happens at all, takes place in the novitiate. But the breaking-in process there can be a good deal subtler than that.

This is a novice-mistress giving an account of her stewardship:

To accustom them to submission in the practice of obedience they are not allowed to question an order as soon as they receive it; if they do they are cut short; they must do their best and leave explanations till later. We avoid demanding anything seemingly unreasonable or, when correction is required, discouraging penances. These penalties vary according to the subject and the state of her soul. We send them sometimes to kneel at the communion rail with arms outstretched, or to make the first part of the morning meditation there; it is clearly a public humiliation, but the sister can retain her composure from her proximity to our Lord. Sometimes they have to listen on their knees to the spiritual reading in the refectory, or something of that sort.

And this is a novice who has been on the receiving end of a similar process:

My stumbling block and battleground were my confidence in myself and my own judgement. I found no great difficulty in obeying, in doing this or that, or conforming to observances. But not to give my opinion when I considered things went a little awry or would be better otherwise, was too much for me. . . . Humiliation in every form came as an almost complete daily trial: humiliating penances to be performed in the middle of the refectory, being proclaimed by others. . . . I ought to have been the life and soul of recreation, but I was rarely allowed to finish anything I had begun. On the contrary, our mistress encouraged others whom she found dull or uninterested to take the lead in conversation. Her one objective all the time was to mortify private judgement and self-will, the ego in fact, in every form.

The attitude of the mistress in question would have been moulded not only by her own training and experience but by a conditioning process which has been preserved carefully for centuries in the tablets of the *lectio divina*. 'There is,' a superior protests, 'a class of ascetical literature, not intrinsically contemptible, and in its day effective, which speaks of us as worms, refuse and other such flattering terms. This only upsets the young people of today. Why should we persist in maintaining this obsolete and repulsive vocabulary?' There is also a class of literature that would persuade the religious to imitate the sufferings of Christ by almost all means short of actual crucifixion. And so in the period before Easter Day not only are long and heavy fasts undertaken and greater periods of silence than normal observed, both of them commonplace mortifications and doubtless useful ones, but the zealous individual may go so far as to slash his wrists with a razor blade so that he, too, may bleed freely with his dying Lord. 'Excess,' a Benedictine has remarked, 'is never very far, as it is never very far from intensity in other fields, from religious enthusiasm.'

Strictness may relax a little when someone has left the novitiate, but obedience is still to be observed. It is a rule among Jesuits that a man must be given a humble job after filling an exalted position, in order to control his pride; the superior of a house thus finds himself drafted to an uncomfortable mission station when his term of office is up and the head of a province can be demoted to the third curacy in one of the thousand parishes he has just commanded. The Benedictines, too, have been known to adopt the same procedure; the last abbot of Ampleforth, Dom Herbert Byrne, is now a parish priest on the outskirts of Preston. More antediluvian symptoms of obedience than those, though, are also to be seen outside novitiates. The woman who for two and a half years was not allowed outside her own section of the community without asking the superior's permission and explaining exactly where she wanted to go and why may have been a novice in a French teaching order. But the women who after acquiring a degree or any other qualification from an outside body are quite deliberately sent to work in the kitchen for the next twelve months to prevent them from getting too much above themselves, are the fully professed sisters of an American community. In some monastic orders there is a ceremony called the mandatum, a form of liturgy in choir accompanied by the washing of feet. Among some Benedictines the tradition is that the abbot washes the feet of his brethren, as Christ washed his disciples' at the Last Supper; in some Cistercian houses the monks go through the ritual in pairs in the cloister every Saturday. At Holy Cross Abbey it is used as yet another opportunity to emphasise the lowliness of the individual. There, where the abess is saluted by her nuns with a profound bow every time they encounter her, the sister who has waited on the rest at table finishes her week's service by washing their feet as well. Life at Holy Cross is not by any means the most abject to be found in the religious life. The Bishop of Arras reports that there are continental congregations where the sisters still kneel before the superior as vassals once knelt before their sovereign. These are the places of which St Teresa, perhaps, might have approved most of all; places where obedience consists in the first instance of 'a bias, a voluntary inclination to accept reasons which favour the superior's decision, which is to be seen in its best light. Then if in good faith, despite the most sincere good will, these reasons seem to have but little weight, and are overpowered by arguments of considerable validity, one must have recourse to blind obedience.' That is a voice from the middle of the twentieth century.

Obedience is to be summoned for every conceivable reason

and applied to every imaginable situation at that level. It is invoked to preserve the chastity of the religious, sometimes by means of the most astonishing precautions. There are houses where the nuns have been forbidden to pass each other on the stairs in case they touched, as this would be against chastity. There are houses where a nun is never allowed to be alone with a visitor in the parlour for fear of some indiscretion, verbal or tactile, passing between them. There are houses which insist that if a nun has to go to the doctor for a physical check-up she must be accompanied every inch of the way by one of her sisters. There are houses which still prohibit their nuns from visiting art galleries, lest their eyes fall on some immodest painting. There are houses where, if a sister is attending university or some other establishment of higher education, she must take someone else from the community with her as chaperone, to spend the day knitting alongside the struggling intellectual. It was at the turn of the century that in Teilhard de Chardin's novitiate young Jesuits had to step into their baths in a blue serge robe, which they then removed under cover of a white linen tent; but it was in 1965 that a novice-mistress replied, when a postulant asked her some question about sex, 'I do not speak of such things. I am a virgin.'

While some nuns have acquired such a horror of the opposite sex that they will not even speak to a man on the telephone, let alone in person; while generally the most stringent precautions against besmirching religious chastity are taken in the case of nuns, authority also keeps a careful eye on what the men are up to. It sometimes forbids the monk or other male religious to enter anyone else's room. It invariably, in the novitiate, issues vague but very definite warnings against forming what in the vernacular is always referred to as the 'particular friendship'. It rationalises this as a potential serpent in the breast of the community life; as something that will prevent the individual from sharing his affections equally among his brethren, as in charity he is bound to do. It is, in fact, born of nothing less than a quaking fear that active homosexuality will break out in every corner if two men are given the slightest chance to get on better terms with each other than with any of their fellows.

Homosexual relationships are certainly not unknown in the

religious life; within the past few years one English men's community has lost many of its members because of the chaotic tensions that arose when the superior decided that the traditional restrictions had been ridiculous and that henceforth love was to be the watchword of the house; from one extreme of behaviour the community swung conclusively to the other, a number of people paired off in and out of bed, jealousies formed almost as fast as fond relationships, and the whole thing became a caricature of what the well-meaning superior had intended. On that scale homosexuality is doubtless rare; the rules are generally too restrictive to let it develop to anything like the extent a cynical outsider might imagine.

What the rules are doing to individual insiders is another matter. It has been held by one religious authority that the staggering prudery which envelops most communities is nothing less than an inducement to the thing they fear most of all. 'It is easy to see,' writes the dean of students at the Catholic Notre Dame University in the United States, 'how the superior, subjects and the individuals themselves create an atmosphere which forces them (two individuals) to take consolation in one another because no one else "understands". The fear of homosexuality has ironically created an atmosphere in which any hint of homosexuality will readily grow.' Not that the topic is very often discussed as bluntly as that by religious anywhere outside a university; homosexuality is still such a dirty word that it has to be diluted to 'particular friendship'. And obedience has been recruited so massively to subdue any thoughtful consideration even of the euphemism that when advice is given as often as not it is so inadequate that it would be comical if individual tensions and worse were not at stake. 'Beware, however,' suggests a Dominican, 'of those doting and obsessive enthusiasms, often called forth by external or superficial qualities, called particular friendships. They are bad, and if you entertain them they will separate you from God. If you find anything of the sort rising involuntarily within you, withstand it from the beginning; do not give it any voluntary gratification, and entrust your heart humbly to God. Quiet resistance, relying on grace, will usually drive it away quickly enough. A few words about it with your confessor or superior will help.' If only the good Father had also provided sound advice for the confessor to pass on that might be of some value; but he didn't.

Obedience is also invoked to preserve the security of the order or the community against the world outside, to prevent mere seculars, incapable of understanding, from knowing what goes on in the small world inside. In recent years this side of religious obedience has been flouted perhaps more than any other, both in print and out of it; if it had not been so, this book could never have been written. But censorship is still vigorously applied in places. A Jesuit writes that 'It is common to find among the regulations of religious communities, often as part of their constitutions, a provision which limits the reception and sending of mail at the discretion of superiors. Religious superiors or persons delegated by them are thus entitled to read letters addressed to or by their subjects and to decide on the basis of their reading whether or not to transmit these letters to their addresses.' Another Jesuit talks of telephone conversations being tapped by inquisitive superiors. There is certainly one community, and there are probably others, where no novice is allowed to write to anyone – fellow novice or fully professed brother – who has opted out and returned to the secular life, for fear that he will be unsettled by the contact. Essentially, censorship is carried out in the spirit outlined by R. M. Benson, the founder of the Anglican Cowley Fathers, towards the end of the nineteenth century. 'The brethren,' he wrote, 'must not speak to strangers of any matter relating to the state or condition of the community, nor to one another without serious reason, unless it be to the Superior-General, the Assistant General or the Provincial Superior. . . . People are often anxious to know the numbers of the society and what works are being undertaken. It is of no concern of people at large to know these things.'

Under obedience it is possible, it may even be common, for women in nursing and teaching orders to be grossly overworked. There is the case of the nun who, in an understaffed school, already simultaneously teaching two classes with eighty children in each, was told to take on a third class. There is the exhausted cry of the nursing sister who after twenty-five years' hard labour wrote that 'Our life is not one of service but of bondage. Since we can no longer dominate our work we have become slaves to it. What should have proved a source of daily spiritual strength has become a cause of daily dying.' It is easy enough to exact that price from a religious who under obedience is on call at any time, when there are not enough secular nurses – who in any case have regular negotiated hours – to fill the staff rotas. It is also easy for a superior whose mind is so blanketed by tradition and the habit of obedience herself, not only to suppose that her sisters can do tasks which may be quite beyond some of their capacities, in the belief that anyone acting under obedience can even perform miracles, but to misuse the talents that are actually available to her. Like the provincial replacing a sister who, for six years, had been warden of a girls' hostel with excellent results; the Mother Superior deplored the difficulty of finding a successor who would be half as good. When asked why, then, was she putting the sister in another post, she replied that Sister had finished the two triennial terms permitted by custom of the congregation.

The largest indictment that can be made out against religious obedience as it has so far been generally practised is that it encourages the passivity of a babe in arms in those to whom it is applied unconditionally. This is particularly marked in the case of nuns. There are strong grounds for arguing that the Catholic Church must bear a heavy responsibility for the inferior status of women generally in western civilisation, which in the most under-educated areas of society still continues. The influence of Tertullian is seen by some to be at the bottom of this. This early Father of the Church could neither forget nor forgive the mythology of a paradise lost through Eve. Addressing womanhood in general in the third century he cried: 'Do you not know that you are Eve? You are the devil's doorway. It was you who profaned the Tree of Life, you who dragged down with you him whom the devil dared not attack directly. It was you who thus disfigured the image of God which is man.' But St Paul must bear at least some of the blame and it is in Pauline tones that religious commentators sometimes today address women in general and religious women in particular. 'The place of women in the Church, then,' says one, 'is not at the altar with the priest and the clergy, but among the

faithful. The function of woman is not to govern, at least not primarily. Even if she is a superior, she remains in subjection to the priesthood, to the canonical visitations made by men. She is expected to listen with docility to the conferences she ought regularly to attend. The function of woman in the Church includes no right of speech, but she must listen in silence, as St Paul says.'
It is after centuries of similar injunctions that infantilism among religious women has become widespread enough to constitute a problem so big that even a pope can recognise it: significantly, most of the books which in the last few years have started to look critically at the religious life and most of the papers which have been read at one conference after another, have concentrated on this problem almost to the exclusion of every other one.

Various attitudes encourage it, some of them trifles; for example the names of individuals in a men's community frequently appear in published lists of one kind or another; in almanacs of the order or in intercession leaflets for the commendation of the faithful. I have never yet seen a similar list of women, and whatever purpose is served by this discrimination it cannot help the sister or the nun to maintain a feeling of individual identity. It may be, as some argue, that woman is psychologically disposed to obedience and submission; certainly the majority of women who think they have a vocation are built this way. The methods of the convent would generally induce the characteristic if it were not there already. For when the novice arrives she is in a state of uncertainty about every new thing she encounters; she is also likely to be nervous about her eventual acceptance or rejection by the community; she feels clumsy and helpless for the first few months in this alien environment. She is confronted in the persons of her superior and novice-mistress with people who are older than she, whose titles, positions and experience make them utterly maternal figures. If they are benevolent and attractive they will, within a system that does everything possible to discourage individualism and promote anonymity, become models in the eyes of the novice; their attitudes and physical mannerisms are going to be imitated unless she is an uncommonly mature and strong-minded young woman. The novice-mistress is in a particularly influential position. From the day the novice comes in it is she to whom the girl has to go for advice, for help and for consolation at every turn. It is she who encourages each of her charges to share every thought with her because she herself has been taught that to be a real mother in God to them, which from the highest motives she wishes to be, nothing less than bearing every responsibility for them will serve. She stands in this relationship with every novice for anything up to three or four years. In that time, with the best will in the world, she can cripple their development as human beings by over-mothering alone.

Where that does not promote infantile behaviour the chances are high that authoritarianism will. It was Pius XII who had become sufficiently aware of this problem to say that 'What psychology teaches is doubtless true, that a woman in authority does not manage as easily as a man to strike the exact balance between severity and kindness.' The precise nature of authoritarian deficiencies in women superiors has since been remarked by a number of commentators from Cardinal Suenens downwards. It seems that these are more or less the same as those anyone can spot in the world at large. There are superiors, timid by nature, who let things slide until they blow up disproportionately over some trivial matter and their sisters become either aggressive or huffy. There are others with a natural taste for power, who believe like St Teresa in obedience for its own sake, who reduce some of their nuns to abject fear. There are some who think and even talk in terms of 'annihilating' the will of their subjects. A chaplain reports that 'During a conversation a superior let out the word annihilation. She checked herself and said she had been recommended not to use the word but to replace it with humiliation.' If such a superior has under her some nuns strong enough to withstand this philosophy she will have a house which is divided into a resistance movement and a group of humble servants; she will cultivate the latter to inform upon and to isolate the former, whose days will be marked by increasing bitterness.

Whatever kind of superior a convent may have, there is a built-in tendency to perpetuate either herself or like-minded sisters in positions of authority. The Central Council of a women's congregation has made its own point on this:

It is noted that with few exceptions most female congregations have a Central Council composed of a majority and sometimes a totality of older members. Commonly enough elections for renewal of terms of office have their own particular psychology: a nun very easily feels that she must not be ungrateful to a retiring Superior even if there is an obviously competent candidate to take over her office, and so she votes for the present holder. Another point is that although freedom to vote as one wishes is theoretically guaranteed there is often a fear, founded or unfounded, that in the end the votes do not remain secret, and this obviously inhibits freedom. Finally, most of the time a serious renewal is almost impossible, owing to the fact that the Superior-General, once in office, nominates at her discretion all the general staff of local Superiors who are therefore devoted to her and who are ex officio members of the next General Chapter. Thus it follows that the tendency to maintain the status quo can easily prevail.

Manifestations of infantilism are about as diverse as you would expect to find in the average primary school. At a community level the processes which produce this phenomenon can be responsible for a degree of uniformity in conventual demeanour and decorum that a middle-aged man's great-grandmother might recognise as contemporary. Someone has said that the convent is the last stronghold of the studied middle-class manners of the nineteenth century; women who have lived fifty years together call each other 'Sister' and not by Christian name; a nun I once met said that no she certainly wouldn't dream of kissing a sister who had come home after a long time on a foreign mission 'because we don't want to be effusive'. At an individual level all forms of childish behaviour have been remarked upon here and there. In the nun whose whole day focused on the moment when she would intercept the superior at the top of the stairs, take her apron from her and fold it for her. In the nun who became utterly distressed because Mother forgot to congratulate her on the anniversary of her profession. In the nun of forty-odd who burst into tears the first occasion she was given a job without precise directions for every stage of it; she had performed the task a hundred times before, but before there had always been someone to lead her through it from start to finish. An American priest has noted another kind of infantilism. 'There are people who feel like ducking when they see a sister coming. They love the sisters but they say "They will wring you dry. They will take your car for every and any occasion. They will use your gas and oil with no thought of the inconvenience to you. They are about as responsible in these matters as adolescent youngsters are. As the adolescent brings the car home with the tank nearly empty, so also do the sisters."'

There has been such a concentration – mostly by men – upon infantilism and authoritarianism among women in the last year or two that outside observers of the religious life might well have concluded that such problems were exclusively feminine. They aren't, though they may be more prevalent in the convent than in the monastery. There are men as neurotic about physical contact with others as any nun; it was Father Raymond Raynes, Superior of the Anglican Community of the Resurrection until 1958, who 'had a way of becoming completely impersonal at moments of stress, or when he had to make physical contact. When a woman cried on his shoulder he put his arm round her and held her with the flat of his arm but kept his fist clenched so he should not grasp her. When you helped him out of a chair he would not take you by the hand, you had to hold him by the wrist.' It was a friar who once told me that as you grew old in his community hypochondria set in and nearly everyone worried about his health and was dabbling with special diets by middle age. It is a Jesuit who has said that members of the Society don't mature much psychologically during the first seven years of their training because they are given no serious responsibility in that time. There are male superiors who exact obedience as strictly as any Mother, whose doors are constantly being opened by a succession of brethren asking Father if they might do this, that and the other, for permission to do almost everything short of going to the lavatory. Even in Taizé, that launching pad of the avant-garde, a streak of authoritarianism, doubtless benevolent in its operation, is detectable. Although nearly a quarter of a century has passed since the community settled down, although its observances were codified in the early 50s, Roger Schutz has still not established a procedure for the substitution of anyone else in his own place as prior; and when a brother arrives late for the office he strides past both altar and cross without so much as a glance in their direction and makes straight for Prior Schutz's seat, where he kneels and receives a paternal hand upon the shoulder before he takes his own place in the choir.

Thomas Merton, the Trappist, describes what may await the monastic novice in terms which echo the writings of Suenens and Huyghe on women religious:

Too often they see men who have abdicated their human identity and reality (in good faith) and are leading lives without human authenticity, simply passive, evading responsibility, and humanly impoverished, often to a serious degree. For example, they see men who have been in the monastery for years and whose simplicity is not that of spiritual childhood but frankly that of neurotic infantilism. They see men who seem to be obeying and who, in fact, are simply the products of a life of over-control (the idea that every slightest move of the monk and even his inmost thoughts are not supernatural and monastic except when subject to complete control is disastrous for modern man. False supernaturalism). These people cannot be entrusted with the simplest job without expecting instructions and commands at every step. They lack sound judgement and even common sense. They are often eccentric and their spirituality tends to be both naïve and bizarre. Yet because they maintain a servile attitude they are praised and rewarded. In point of fact the emptiness and futility of their lives are a real scandal to the young monk. How often do we not hear novices and young monks say 'If I remain in the monastery will I become like Father so-and-so?' This is one of the main problems of the young monk today.

It is a problem which for men and women springs fundamentally from conceptions and applications of obedience and authority that are about as old as Christianity itself. In spite of all its colossal weight there have from time to time been a few brave enough or reckless enough to flout the unequalled authority and risk the unique sanctions which the Church imposes upon its religious. When the Council of Trent forbade any more convents of nuns to be opened (which, in fact, at that time meant that no more women's communities could be started because the convent was the only kind open to women) St Vincent de Paul still founded an institute to care for the sick by sidestepping the rules. 'It cannot be said', he remarked, 'that the Sisters of Charity are nuns because if a woman is a nun she must be enclosed. Being a nun means being enclosed and the Sisters of Charity have to go everywhere . . . For monasteries you have the houses of the poor, for cells your rented rooms, for chapels the parish churches, for cloisters the streets of the town, for the enclosure obedience, for grilles the fear of God, for veils holy modesty.' When the Vatican Council of Pope John XXIII began it was under an oath of secrecy not to allow anyone but participants to know what had happened at each day's session. A religious who is now generally acknowledged to be the American Redemptorist Francis Xavier Murphy got round that one by publishing in four volumes a report on the daily proceedings of the Council, whose accuracy has never been challenged, under the pseudonym Xavier Rynne. But these are scarcely norms. And even when a religious order is prepared to tolerate the critical voice within its ranks it can be overruled by the Vatican itself. The most notorious example of this in recent times concerned the English Dominican Herbert McCabe. At the beginning of 1967, as editor of *New Blackfriars*, he wrote a leading article which considered the defection of the theologian Charles Davis; in it he agreed with Davis that the Church was 'manifestly corrupt'. A little later he was removed from the editorship and for a short time he was suspended from his priestly functions, all on orders from the Master-General of the Dominican Order in Rome. Although the case has never been proved there is strong circum-stantial evidence to suppose that neither of these sanctions would have been applied if pressure had not been put upon the Master-General from some quarter inside the Curia, the papal court through which the Catholic Church in general is governed.

The norm, however, is less spectacular than that. It consists of men and women enduring a régime based upon authority and submission to it with varying degrees of difficulty and different measures of sacrifice; for some it is a matter of easy acquiesc-ence and for others it is nothing less than a painful slog from one day to another. It means moments of crisis which attack different people at different times; for some who have entered a novitiate at the earliest possible age there can be a crisis in high adolescence, which has something to do with a physio-psychological rebellion against chastity, but which is also a rejection of control over other than sexual powers which the individual begins to feel might be limitless if only they could be released; for women there is often a crisis in the mid-thirties, by which time they normally should have borne children but here recognise subconsciously at last that they never will; for anyone there can be a crisis between ten and fifteen years after entering a community, when the first enthusiasm has dwindled and the religious life at last assumes its correct perspective as a monotonous routine which is not always going to provide the elevation of spirit necessary to bear the individual serenely through difficult patches which will surely recur, maybe growing longer each time, for the rest of his life. And all these crises in some way or another mean a clash with authority, either submission to it or defiance of it. Once acquired, religious obedience, which is rubbed in so deeply from the beginning of a vocation, is hard to shed. If it is true that there is no such creature as a lapsed Catholic who in his marrow does not have a lurking fear of hell to the day he dies, it may also be true that there is no defected religious who can ever shake off completely a disposition to be obedient.

After twenty-three years in a convent Monica Baldwin obtained her release and returned to the world outside. She wrote a best-selling book about her life inside and outside the nunnery and she called it *I Leap Over the Wall*. Twenty-five years later she concluded, in a spirit of some repentance, that she had defected in 1942 after a long period of self-will in which she had never really understood the true nature of religious obedience. 'I deceived myself,' she said, 'I now realise. Obedience was my stumbling-block.'

Obedience is a stumbling-block to many who have remained inside their convents and their monasteries. Because it has been so often a stumbling-block, and an apparently senseless one at that, the reformers are abroad in the religious life today, who would modify the existing conceptions of authority, making them more humane where they seem to be tyrannical, more intelligent where they appear to be brainless. The reformers must, and they know it, go gently; not only because the Church is conditionally and deeply averse to revolution and change but also from a charitable consideration of the ageing and the old in religion who have spent their springs and their summers and sometimes their autumns, too, in a pattern which has been fixed for generations; these cannot be expected as a matter of course to accept, much less to enjoy, radical changes now. This is not to say that the reformers are entirely youthful and the opponents of change are all approaching pensionable age; the most revolutionary and the most luminously spiritual religious I know will never see sixty again. A superior who has already changed much in her order in the past few years and knows very clearly what changes she would still like to see refuses to do more until half a dozen or so of her old ladies have died. 'They've put up with a lot since I took over,' she says, 'and they've put up with it generously. But this place has been their home longer than it's been mine and I think they have a right to recognise something in it of the home they first came to as long as they're here.'

It is impossible to guess the proportions of religious who are hot for change, who are implacably opposed to it, or who would obediently acquiesce whichever party gained the upper hand. But just as an increasing number of religious have abandoned their vows in recent years and walked out rather than put up any longer with things as they have been, and just as an even greater army might defect if they did not think that a substantial adaptation of the religious life to the twentieth century were imminent, so there is an incalculable number of people who are fighting to preserve the status quo. One of them is Brother Gregory O'Donnell, of the Institute of the Brothers of the Christian Schools, a teaching body founded in 1680 by John Baptiste de la Salle. Since the 39th General Chapter of the Institute ended its long deliberations in Rome in 1967 and decided to make alterations in the Rule, Brother Gregory has been frantically busy trying to stop this happening. Quite apart from the representations he has made within his institute he has showered his objections and supporting arguments in sheaves on no fewer than forty-one newspapers throughout the world, from the *Salford City Reporter* to the *New York Times*, from the *Cork Examiner* to the

Indian Express of Bombay. He has also lobbied the British Broadcasting Corporation, two members of the British Government and his local Member of Parliament. His defence of the old Rule is a very simple one. It was, he says, the code by which the institute's founder wished the Brothers to live. It was, moreover, something which he, Brother Gregory, solemnly promised to keep for the rest of his life when he was fully professed in 1956. Not only did it carry the express wishes of de la Salle, but it was backed by the full authority of Benedict XIII, who was pope in de la Salle's day and who issued a Papal Bull of Approbation to ratify it.

In the Bull we hear the ageless voice of the Church's authority at its most dogmatic and its most florid:

We ordain, moreover, that these present letters shall be and continue, always and ever, in full force, and obtain their full and entire effect; that they be not compromised under the revocations, limitations or suspensions of any similar or dissimilar favours whatever, and any other contrary dispositions whatsoever, but shall always be excepted therefrom; and that as often as such contrary arrangements shall appear, so often shall these presents be and continue to be restored, replaced and fully re-established in their original and most effective state; and that so and not otherwise it is to be decided and pronounced in all the premises by all judges whatever whether ordinary or delegated, even the Auditors of Causes in the Apostolic Palace and Cardinals of the Holy Roman Church, even Legates 'a Latere', Vice-legates and Nuncios of the Holy See. And if anything to the contrary should be attempted in or about these matters by anyone under whatever authority, whether knowingly or through ignorance, We declare the same to be null and void, any Apostolic Constitutions or Ordinances to the contrary notwithstanding.

Which seems a fairly conclusive point in Brother Gregory's favour. Which also illustrates the ass that authority can make of itself when it is as inflexible as religious authority so often is, with its talk of observing points X, Y and Z for ever and a day, without leaving itself a loophole for reappraisal later on. Brother Gregory, of course, will not win because his superiors are bent upon reform and they have authority over him. He doubtless realises this. On 2 February 1968 he wrote to the pope.

Dear Holy Father, I am writing for permission to come to Vatican City to work there, if necessary for the rest of my life, at some useful task even in the garden. For four years I have been objecting to changes in the de la Salle Rule which I have promised to observe for the rest of my life as I had it in 1947. . . . Since in conscience I am unable to change my will I think I would be less of a burden on others doing something useful in Vatican City and trying to observe the Rule alone. I am, Holy Father, Your most humble and obedient inferior and subject, And loyal subject of Her Gracious Majesty, the Queen – *Gregory O'Donnell.*

There are more than one and a quarter million religious in the world today. A lot of them will be as dismayed as Brother Gregory at the winds of change that are now starting to gust through their lives. Many will be in the same daily humiliated condition as the novice who was perpetually sat upon by her Mother Mistress. The religious life at present is on the change and it is not a comfortable time for anybody except the ones with unshakeable calm and self-possession and hope, with certain faith and a capacity to endure all things. These are not the commonest ones. And among the rest the casualties are occurring all over the field of battle. The dichotomy of the religious life today, the tensions and strains which at the moment run from end to end in conflict with each other, were not so long ago illustrated grimly in an English Anglican convent. In 1967 it lost two of its nuns. One was an old lady who had lived most of her life under an unchanging system and who could bear the confusing new reforms no longer. The other was a young woman driven to despair by the humiliations of the novitiate. Within a few months of each other they committed suicide.

SEVEN

VOCATION

QUESTION When did you become a monk?

ANSWER When I was fifty. I was a soldier from 1912 until 1924 and then I worked in the leather trade.

Q Why did you become a monk?

A God lit up the way and I came here.

Q Were you married?

A No.

Q Are women a bad thing?

A Yes.

Q But look, I'm married; what should I do?

A You should tell your wife you're going to God and then you live together, like brother and sister, not in bed. The best thing would be to tell her to go into a convent and come yourself to be a monk.

Q What about children?

A Put them in an orphanage.

Q But nobody loves them there.

A Of course there must be love in an orphanage, like there is in a monastery.

Q What was your life like before you became a monk?

A In the army I smoked fifteen cigarettes a day, women, drink, went to the theatre – but those were bad things.

Q Why is the theatre bad?

A Because you see naked women and that's scandalising.

Q But sometimes the actors wear clothes?

A Yes, but such light ones you can see what's underneath.

Q How do you see the Devil? (meaning what image do you have of the Devil?)

A I've never seen him – only great saints see him. How should I see him?
Q Yes, but what do you think of him?
A He makes us like the bad things, women, smoking . . .
Q Why must a monk not smoke?
A Because it makes him think of other bad things he could do.
Q What do you think of life here?
A If you have good will it is easier than life outside – you have a roof, food, clothing, and you go to church often.

That is a conversation with a Greek Orthodox monk on Mount Athos, the eighty-year-old porter of the monastery of Dyonisiou; it is said to be fairly representative of Athonite attitudes. No doubt more or less the same answers could be elicited from cross-questioning a chosen section of the monastic population in the western Church. At any rate, it reveals a state of mind – unintelligent, illogical, bigoted, prudish, narrow, and extreme – which a cynical world is very ready to accept as a normal mark of the monk or the nun; it suggests a form of escapism from Life with a capital L which much of the secularised world understands to be the sine qua non of the religious life.

The disbelieving, and certainly the cynical, can scarcely be expected to make any other assumption when there is nothing which has been so wrapped in mystery and secrecy as the reasons why human beings become religious and so, by taking vows of poverty, chastity and obedience, put themselves socially and morally at right-angles to the rest of the race. To a large extent this follows from incompatible vocabularies and concepts. The language religious employ more often than not to explain the attractions of the life to them is the language of mysticism and theology; they are forming their explanations within a super-natural context which the outsider generally has either rejected or simply cannot comprehend. There are other reasons. One is a perfectly understandable reticence on the part of a religious to share, unless it is absolutely unavoidable, the most intimate details of his or her life; it is not a habit that any but the neurotic acquire in any section of society in normal circumstances. And reticence here tends to be heightened because the religious is defensively aware that he has defied the norms of a society which harbours a number of derogatory suspicions about his motives.

There is also an element sometimes not so much of self-deception as of inadequate self-awareness; a failure to analyse oneself either deeply or accurately enough. It all adds up to a failure in communication which is no greater and probably no commoner than the failure of anyone to explain why and how he fell in love with someone. The chances are that unless the individual is extremely articulate and analytical he'll utter no more than a string of clichés about love; and unless he is uncommonly honest and aware of himself and his motives he will gloss over some significant detail either from ignorance or from a fear that it might be interpreted as unworthy of him.

The religious life abounds in its own clichés about discovering a vocation and the most common of them tend to be that 'I knew God wanted me', that 'I knew I had come home when I first visited the community', that 'I wanted to give myself completely to God.' Even with the best will in the world the explanations can sometimes sound heavily muffled. A 32-year-old monk writes: 'From the age of fifteen or sixteen I was quite certain that I was meant to be a priest, and also that the priesthood involved for me some form of poverty and celibacy. I knew virtually nothing about monastic life and had very little interest in it until I was persuaded to take part in a parish mission run by my community when I was an undergraduate. On this mission another member of the team (a woman) told me that I should offer myself, she thought, to the monastery. This came as a complete surprise to me, but nevertheless seemed exactly the right thing, and I knew at that moment that this was what I had to do.' A 63-year-old nun writes: 'During the years in which I was seeking the will of God as to vocation, and following where he seemed to be leading, I was not brought face to face with marriage. Had I been so brought I could only have considered it in the light of vocation.'

Largely because the modern world has mostly viewed the monastic or the conventual existence with scepticism, the defensiveness of religious themselves has become as traditional as the habit of obedience. It is unlikely that a quarter of a century ago even a tartly qualified concession to the popular view would have been allowed. Yet in the 60s a French Oratorian is prepared to concede that 'If the romantic vision of the monk who has become such out of disappointed love is an over-simplified caricature, it is quite true that certain people need as it were to have actually experienced the vanity of idols we fashion for ourselves if they are to realise the unique value of God alone. Of others, on the contrary, it might be said that it is the very purity of an affection denied by circumstances or destroyed by death which leads them to go beyond it, perhaps when threatened by despair.' It is certainly difficult to imagine that until very recently one of the most crucial issues to be settled by a vocation to religion would have been confronted as boldly as it has been by Bishop Huyghe. 'It is not sufficient to reject the world,' he has said. '. . . What would have been the candidate's attitude towards marriage if she had not had a religious vocation must be discovered. One who is incapable of genuine human love cannot consecrate herself fully to God. . . . Only one who would have been capable of the fullness of human love in marriage can engage herself in the religious life with the certainty of finding therein the full flowering of her chastity.' And then, in extension of this principle, he adds: 'One can enter religion to care for the sick or the aged, or to teach; one can even enter for less worthy motives. But unless these motives are eventually transformed one cannot persevere long in the religious life.' And it does indeed take all sorts to make a religious world.

There are some religious who can tick off precisely the moment they decided that it was for them, like this 51-year-old who has been in her Anglican convent for more than twenty years. She had been brought up in a nominally Christian family, in childhood had a vague idea of becoming a missionary, in adolescence had a notion that she might take up religious education and go to work among natives in South Africa.

My first job on leaving college was as children and youth worker in a parish and it was when I had been there, very happily for three months, that this appalling idea of religious vocation simply settled itself in my mind with a ghastly sort of conviction after I had read something about it. For about a year nothing happened, no further thought of it came, and

I hoped I had imagined the whole thing, though always with a sense of something hanging over me. Finally, on All Souls' Day 1940, about 7 pm on a wet evening in the middle of an air raid, I just 'knew' absolutely clearly and unmistakably that this was what I had to do, and that I was to get going on it at once. For about half an hour I walked up and down regardless of falling shrapnel, with a certain degree of exaltation, but after that it was sheer going against the grain. It cut across everything I had planned to do – all *my* ways of using my life, quite good ways, too, of serving God as I thought – and going to a convent just seemed the end (well, I mean, just think of the clothes; no suggestion of a reformed habit twenty-five years ago!). But short of deliberately refusing what God asked and so cutting him out of my life, there was no alternative. I had to go forward along this way that was now so painfully clear.

There are others for whom there never was such a clear-cut moment of decision. This 64-year-old nun, for whom the religious life was a recurring prospect over a long period, for example:

My parents were happily married for nine years but were childless. They believed my birth, when both were forty, was a direct 'Yes' to their prayer to God. Accordingly, I having been born on my mother's birthday, I was given a Christian name meaning 'Gift of God' and when I was christened the occasion was for my mother the real dedication of her child to God for His service. I cannot remember a time when I did not know this, and in an infantile manner was aware of God, Jesus, heaven and angels as a real part of my whole life, and of myself as truly belonging primarily to my heavenly Father. So, when between 7½ and 8¾ both parents died, my real life and comfort lay in that verse 'When my father and my mother forsake me, the Lord taketh me up' (Psalm 27).

Within a few years she had decided to become a teacher on some foreign mission; at sixteen she toyed with the idea of becoming a nun but 'life was opening up and I wanted to enjoy it, and I knew enough of one religious community to realise how hard they worked, what few relaxations or pleasures they enjoyed, how tied they were by obedience. But I saw, too, their deep joy, their kindness, patience, compassion, and I was much attracted by the liturgical side of the religious vocation.' She went to university, however, 'fell in and out of love' with boy friends who were mostly ex-Servicemen older than herself, and 'though I looked young and unsophisticated many of these grown-up boys came for advice. They got advice with no foundation of human experience. This was really, I believe, the religious vocation; the committal of one's whole, fully alive, fully natural and super-natural self to the love of God made known in Jesus, through His spirit's direct action. It was something which made communication with others, at a deep level, easier and not difficult and it brought in an element of detachment from any particular person which contributed to the foundation of a wide and varied circle of *real* friends. These friendships (one can count at least twelve, off-hand) have remained with *very* infrequent communication of any kind, especially during the twenty-four years of life in an enclosed community.' In her fourth year at university she fell in love with an ex-Serviceman several years older than herself. 'Again, there came the challenge – "Whom do you most desire, him or me?" It was as definite as that on one particular evening. My real love for Our Lord drove me to leave the decision in His hands, so I antedated my offer for service abroad and was accepted by the missionary society to whose missionary union I belonged.' She was twenty-four and she had not been in the missionary training college a month before 'as I knelt in the chapel one evening, the realisation of the religious vocation was suddenly clear, as it had been eight years earlier. This time I said "Yes".'

The history of the religious life is studded with examples of people who had some mystical or visionary experience while in a secular condition, which changed their whole course of action from that moment. It still happens, even though the individual has difficulty in conveying the exact nature of the vision, just what it was that he or she felt so vitally. A woman in her thirties who for several years had been teaching religion in her diocese, steeping herself in St John of the Cross and other mystics, began to feel that for her an answer to the cosmic struggle between good and evil which she identified with the Second World War might be the religious life of prayer and contemplation. It was not a straightforward choice, though.

In spite of the satisfying nature of my vocation in religious education there still persisted in me an interior sadness due to a desire for marriage. This was finally resolved for me in 1947 by a spiritual experience, the authenticity of which I have never once doubted. Our Lord (in what St Teresa would have called an intellectual vision; i.e. nothing seen with the human eye) asked me to give to Him this thing which lay at the heart of my sadness. In the one moment I gave and He took, at the same time giving Himself to me in a moment that was superlatively satisfying and at the same time radically painful. I have never since been troubled by the sorrow of unfulfilled human love.

A Benedictine monk sheds a little more light on the vision as he experienced it.

The call in part was started off as a live question for me in 1953. My first visit abroad – Portugal. The weather was superb, although it was January, and I was staying with friends on a farm behind the Estoril coast, overlooking the Atlantic. In a peaceful moment drinking in the scenery and my good fortune, the thought crossed my mind that if the world and its beauty could produce this foretaste of happiness, what would heaven be like. Surely the sacrifice of everything this world can offer would cost little? Personal economy, maybe; but it was a profound experience which stimulated a haunting question. Until that moment I had always considered marriage as my way of life, with lots of children, to the exclusion of a priestly or a monastic vocation which I did occasionally think about and reject from time to time. Now the vocation question became an open one. About a year later, during night prayers, I was reflecting on the day's happiness and I looked out of the window at the myriads of stars; aware of them, perhaps for the first time, as each being in the mind and care of God. Again the wonder of God surprised me, and his generosity. The thought then struck me that a return of generosity and service to God, be it a token compared with his, was possible. I immediately shrank from the implications of this thought; but, again, it would haunt me and I knew it raised a question which, if I failed to face and answer it, I might regret all my life. But slowly I accepted that the only way to see if God wanted me to devote my life to his service was to try out my vocation as a monk, which I regarded as a more difficult calling for me than being a secular priest. And this I did.

Whatever else may have propelled them towards the life there is, for some, the realisation that it has offered a form of security that was important to them and might otherwise have been missing. An Anglican monk who was a solicitor and then a priest before taking vows as a religious six years ago, and who says that only a second dissolution of the monasteries would now drive him to any other life, can see several pressures which helped to put him where he is.

My age [he is sixty-five]; the fact of having sipped at so many flowers and found the experiences delicious but unrepeatable – two gorgeous goes at university, the enjoyable experience of a loose war-time discipline with the Royal Marines, clergy house life under a wise vicar, with regular offices etc. weaving into an unpredictable menu of cosmopolitan work and pleasure; contact with a number of religious communities; and the knowledge that I am incapable of directing (efficiently or amicably) a staff of housekeeper, parish worker, secretary, assistant priest (and their husbands and wives); and the inability to know how either to spend or save money.

A monk who has been with his order for thirty years thinks that his vocation

was, in a sense, an escape from a world which seemed to me to present almost overwhelming difficulties in my case. I also think very strongly now, that in spite of periodic wobblings since profession, I feel very much more sure of the vocation than I did at the time of profession, at times almost overwhelmingly sure, but it's because of a kind of strengthened weakness. My life before I began to think about the community was one of revolt against a revolt in my family life from respectable Victorian belief and church-going. My father had broken with religion at an early age and become an agnostic and, furthermore, had separated from my mother. I felt incredibly the lacuna in life left by the absence of family ties and bonds. I do not think this made me *sure* that the life in community was my vocation, but it led me to suspect that I might find an anchorage here, and I think I have.

An unhappy home is a recurring factor in the development of a vocation, even though the individual sometimes seems to be barely aware of this. Here is a nun of sixty-seven, who entered her convent in her fifties.

I would say that the call was present in embryo in childhood, in that God was wholly real, first as a refuge from fear, then as a compelling voice of conscience. After confirmation he flamed into a new dimension – Creator, Source of all life, Lover of men, Light. He streamed into my little life and my whole being went out to him in a love so absorbing that I really ceased to want anyone or anything else. Through years of light it persisted, then through years of loss, darkness or intellectual doubt. It was some years before I recognised it as prayer, but it filled life. . . . I was immature but the desire, the search, the love, remained central, however faulty the attempts to live by it. Bad health, frustrating circumstances, family claims piled up in seemingly endless succession and wild ideas steadied down to two firm alternatives: contemplative life in an enclosed community or prayer in the middle of the mess, i.e. doing an ordinary job completely identified with my fellow workers. . . . I never thought of renouncing the world, but of helping to draw the world back to God through the deepest identification in prayer, in whatever outward setting God chose to put me. . . . God settled the choice through circumstances. For years it was the ordinary job in the middle of the mess. Then the circumstances changed, and with them the inward pressure. Family needs had been met, health had improved, and work which had hitherto been an instrument of service and growth turned into an obstacle to the new response demanded. Total commitment now pointed to obedience and silence in an enclosed community. What made me sure of the truth of this vocation? The persistence through all circumstances of the central purpose, and the recurrent, recognised pressure of God in many earlier decisions of life. My attitude to marriage was one of personal detachment from the age of about eighteen, because I knew that God had claimed me to give myself directly to him. There must have been unconscious influence at first from the fact of my own immaturity and the disharmony of my parents' married life. But even after I discovered myself as a woman I continued to be much more conscious of relationships with people as human beings than as specifically men or women.

A 49-year-old nun, professed in her convent for twelve years:

When I was confirmed I just knew that God wanted me to be a nun, but I did not. So I did nothing, but God did not leave me alone. I soon saw that I should have to try sooner or later and then I began to make excuses. I said I was too self-willed, too undisciplined, too unstable, too proud and that these things would have to be put right before I could possibly try a possible vocation. But of course they did not get right and I began to realise the reason – I just was not doing what God wanted, and therefore of course nothing went right. In the meantime I did nursing and midwifery and moral welfare work and eventually at thirty-two found myself running a home for young girls who had venereal disease; while we treated them medically we tried to help them rehabilitate themselves. Here I found myself up against evil as I had never met it before. The best of the girls were often so in the power of evil that if and when they wanted to go straight they had a terrific struggle and spiritual battle. Then I began to see why God kept on saying 'be a nun'. The Lord provided two people to whom I could speak – a nun and the chaplain of the house – and so at the age of thirty-two I eventually found my way to my community, the Lord smoothing out one mountain after another.

I have had no experience of human love in terms of the man-woman relationship; in fact I grew up terrified of men and frightened of marriage, though I did think it would be rather nice to have a home and family of my own. This attitude was the result of strained relations between my parents; my father, having been a spoilt posthumous child, was inconsiderate and demanding; my mother thought the way to cure him was to deny him and so there were rows. Secondly my mother was a cold sort of person; she made little show of affection and so, being an affectionate person myself at heart, I became ashamed of it. Thirdly I was indecently assaulted by an uncle at thirteen years – hence the fear of men and the setting up of a great tension because (a) I had no one to tell about it and (b) the incident itself was pleasing and I was not able to reconcile this with the knowledge that it was wrong. However, when I started nursing I made some good friends among the nurses but none among the medical students, from whose advances I shied like a frightened cat. In particular I made friends with the family of one nurse and this home became a second home to me and showed me what affectionate family life was like, and community life has just continued that.

A 54-year-old nun, professed in her convent for thirty-two years:

I had no ordinary home. I do not remember my first home. As a small child of about two I went to live with a woman who took in children for a living. There were about ten of us, all ages. She was cruel and unkind to all of us. We were sent to Sunday school to get us out of the way, but there was no religion in the home. At the age of six I was sent to a new home where there was a husband and wife and one son. At this time he was in good work and they had a nice house which was in great contrast to what I had been used to, but this did not last, as in 1919 times were difficult and he lost his job and they had to move to a new place. There was no practice of religion here either; his family were Wesleyans and there were relics of Nonconformist practices – no pleasures on Sundays etc. At the age of nine I went to a Church school but was not allowed to go to the church. But I must have got some glimmerings of teaching in the day school as I asked if I could be baptised and was refused. At twelve I came to live with my 'aunt' who had paid for my keep and was no longer able or willing to do so. I had always disliked her and was very unhappy with her and disapproving of her way of life, although I did not fully understand the implications of it at that time. No religion here, but very anti-religious.

On leaving school at fourteen and having to produce a birth certificate before I could get work I discovered that the 'aunt' was really my mother and that I was illegitimate. This was a very great shock indeed and made me even more disapproving of her way of life. When I was fifteen I got knocked down by a taxi on my way to work and was taken to hospital. The people for whom I worked gave me letters for a convalescent home run by a community of Sisters. On arriving I astonished them by inquiring if I could be baptised. So I was duly instructed and baptised in their chapel. It was at my baptism that I first became conscious of the call to the religious life. I had an overwhelming sense of God and His claim upon me as I stood at the font, this call to serve him alone, but I did not speak to the Sisters about this as I thought that they would regard it as impertinent of anyone as ignorant and lowly as myself even to think of such a thing. The Sisters were anxious for me to remain at the convent but I thought that as a Christian it was my duty to go back and see if I could do anything to improve matters at home; we are terrible optimists when young and think all things will come right if only we make an effort to do something about it. So I went back and got a fresh job, but there was very little I could do. One night when my 'aunt' was lying on the floor hopelessly drunk and I was sitting up with her till she regained consciousness, as she was liable to do violent things like upsetting the oil lamp, this thing happened.

It was 12 pm and she was lying there muttering about rats and mice when I became aware again of that same compelling Presence which had claimed me at the font; and the voice said to me, 'This is the result of sin. This is what sin does to man. For this sin I died and you must give your life to Me in prayer in union with My Offering.' And I could see the crucified Lord reaching out His hands and knew that in some way there is really something that a person can freely give and that it is of value to and accepted by God in and through His Son. This was a most tremendous experience; it seemed to embrace not only what was before my eyes as the spoiling of a human being but all the sin and sorrow of the world which lay upon His heart as He hung upon the cross. . . . It soon became clear to me that I could do no good living in that house and that if I wished to remain a virgin I must not stay. So after a night when the lodger tried to come into my room and the next night when my 'aunt' in a drunken fit smashed my bedroom windows I ran away and went to the people who had brought me up. I very easily got work and began to go to church. Here I was again overwhelmed with this sense of vocation. I began to find out about the religious life in its various forms but was rather frightened of the enclosed kind, being a very energetic and active person. I thought that I would serve God just as well if I became a missionary. In those days I was not old enough to go to a really good hospital for training, this being the only possible way, as I had no money and would have to earn while learning, so I went to a convent of nursing Sisters for a period of preliminary training. Getting into the religious atmosphere of a convent just brought up this inescapable vocation again and I began to read books like *Holy Wisdom* etc. and spend all my free time in chapel.

Eventually she was put in contact with the Mother Superior of an enclosed convent.

The Mother was marvellous and most understanding when I told her the history of my call, and said the convent accepted people on their merits and not on their family history and I could come as a postulant as soon as I was free. So I came on the day after my nineteenth birthday and found in the Rule all those things to which I had been drawn; this life of prayer in union with the Saviour, the offering of one's whole self to Him to be used according to His pleasure. *How* this helps the world is a mystery but I do not think it matters that one cannot give an exact explanation. I have never doubted the reality of this call and the urgent need to answer it in this way and at this time. I have often doubted my ability to fulfil it, but somehow the Lord has held on to me through thick and thin. It is a bit like marriage if you have a vocation, you have to go on with it for better or for worse till death – but in this case death will not be the parting; only the parting from the old self that the new life may begin.

You will see that I had no desire to reject the world but to reach out and embrace it with the Divine Love – to become a channel for all men to receive this Divine Love. I think that modern inventions help us to understand this a bit – you need a wireless set before you can receive a message which is all the time going through the air – so the Divine message for men can be picked up and transmitted through those set apart and called to this work. It is not to be heard for oneself alone but for the world.

When I went to get my medical certificate before going to the convent the doctor said to me, 'But why go into a convent? You have got a perfect body for child-bearing – it really is your duty to marry and have children.' I should have loved to have had a large family of children and have always been glad that I had a perfect body in this respect; why should not God have the offering of a perfect thing? As I came so young I had no ordinary experience of the human love between men and women. I took special care to avoid it as, being red-headed, I know that I am attractive to men and I wanted to give my whole virginity to God, especially in view of my family history and the call to reparation. I have often wondered if this was a mistake, and if I should have become a fuller person with some such personal experience, but it seemed at the time to be most necessary. I have not found this lack of experience to prevent my sympathy and understanding of those who have.

A positive urge to give themselves without at first focusing on an object or a means of their giving is a fairly common denominator among women in religion, rather commoner than among men; though sometimes at an early age they have decided to direct their energies towards God. For one woman 'the call' came while a child 'in the form of a strong desire to follow God in the closest, costliest and most direct way I could. It seemed to me natural to turn to the traditional way of life under the vows of religion.' For another, 'When I grew up I had a great urge to give myself entirely to something – as a governess to a family, or as a teacher to a school, but both were disappointing.' So was something else. 'Human love did not seem to be satisfying. It had a way of breaking down. I wanted something total. The human relationship in religion is of quite a different quality. It tastes of eternity.' Sometimes the giving is evidently required by family circumstances. A seventy-year-old nun 'had a great longing to go to university but had no thought of anything like the religious life. When I left school it was my obvious duty to look after an old arthritic aunt who had been so very good to Mother and all of us.' When the aunt died she was twenty-six and finally got to Oxford, where she was happy but where she also made a retreat and decided to test her vocation. As for the possibility of marriage, 'I do not know what might have happened if I had met anyone I could have cared for enough. I lived a quiet life and did not meet many people. I think most normal women have a sort of background longing for a husband and family. I was eighteen in 1914, so I grew to maturity with those awful casualty lists coming out every day, and said to myself "My aunt needs me and there are too many women to have husbands. It is reasonable I should be one of them".' She is not the only nun of her generation to have been affected by those casualty lists. For a woman of seventy-six 'the few "boy friends" as they are now called, to whom I was more intimately drawn, were killed in the First World War. But my attraction to the married life was really based more on love of children and mothering, the essence of which is love in sacrifice.'

There are many religious who seem to have by-passed any love relationship which might have ended in marriage or who, with varying degrees of consciousness, have avoided it. For one sister: 'Before coming into the religious life my chief experience of human love was in my own family and home, to which I was very devoted. When I left home to earn my own living I found the world a somewhat hard and unloving place. I enjoyed the friendship and intimacy of a few kindred souls. I had no boy friends. I think I was always looking for the ideal man who never existed. When I took up nursing I found much satisfaction in caring for the sick, for whom I discovered I had a special love.'

For a nun, 'Questioning about marriage hardly entered my life. I was one of a family of six and I think I hoped that I would marry. I was very fond of children. My life was full, I liked my work, I played games a great deal, so I came into contact with people quite a lot. I had good friends and friendship meant much to me (mostly with people of my own sex). When I went to the mission field I made no promises not to marry, but at the age of fifty, on coming to this convent, I just thanked God that I was single and so able to enter.' For another nun 'the experience of human love has always been unsatisfactory, though there was a brief period when I thought that as a married woman it would be possible to live a Christian life almost parallel to that of a religious if one's partner were of the same persuasion. I now know that this would never have materialised in the given circumstances, and that God allowed me to have that experience even while he was preparing me for this life.' For a third 'marriage seemed to be a very beautiful way of life, as witnessed to by my own home, but I knew it was not the Will of God for myself. There was an urgency to love God in a more direct special way. I was aware also, of course, of the many sorrows experienced through unhappy marriages etc., having come into contact with such while visiting in parishes in earlier years. These sorrows, I feel, can best be alleviated and supported in intercessory prayer.' For a fourth there were

deep friendships with one or two schoolgirls when I was between seven and seventeen years old, but no friends among the other sex, partly due to the circumstances of my education, which was in all-girls' schools or colleges except for my years at prep schools; partly because I had no brothers and because as a family we did not mix much with other people; and partly because I knew very early on that my life should be a celibate one entirely given to God; this was an entirely satisfying thought to me. I did not, of course, realise at an early age the deep psychology of one's emotional and sexual make-up. This came later through sharing in my sister's experience of these things as we grew up together; for unlike me she went to a mixed school and fell in and out of love several times before she finally married. I realised ultimately, of course, that I was giving something up, but it seemed a small *personal* thing (for which I felt myself unsuited) in face of taking one's place in the Purposes of God which would be what one would be doing in taking one's place in the religious life. Moreover, having seen what hypertensional crises could be raised in a family by two highly emotional people such as my father (Anglo-American) and mother (Irish) getting married, and knowing myself to be the heir of both these temperaments, I did not consider myself a very suitable woman to marry any man, certainly not to pass on a hypertensional temperament to children. I also thought God had arranged my nature like that on purpose so that I should realise and see the way to following the religious life without having any confusing side issues about whether or not to marry.

There are others in religion who have tasted a kind of love and found it wanting. A monk decides in retrospect that

fear of commitment to any relationship was partly responsible for my lack of progress in two matrimonial possibilities, but neither was vested in enough romantic quality to have been seriously considered. I had considerable promiscuous relationships, particularly during the war and after, with people to whom I hope I shall remain always grateful. Promiscuity was brought to an end by a far deeper relationship for two or three years with someone with whom a complete involvement would have been thoroughly unsuitable on either part. Since then, ten years ago (*he has been professed for five years*), there has been no sexual involvement or tension.

Since leaving school and being ordained [says an Anglican monk], I had a series of girl friends with most of whom I engaged in passionate love-making. In each of them I was seeking one to whom I could commit myself body and soul, but in vain. It was much more a case of restless lusting than of genuine love, though on their part there was an obvious desire for marriage. The only time I fell in love was with a nun (already doubtful of her vocation before we met) shortly before my call to the religious life. We still write and meet when we can, now that all passion is spent, and we are so grateful for God's merciful dealing with us and for our continuing friendship. I may add that the understanding and achievement of true celibacy comes hardest of all the demands of the religious life. Since joining my community, knowing my susceptibilities, I take care (I trust!) not to allow any relationship to develop to that point where in other circumstances marriage might seem natural.

A nun, now thirty-four, recognises that

On one level, I was always surrounded by loving care; I loved my home, enjoyed school and university, and made many friends – boys, girls and older people. I also learned compassion for people through various vacation jobs. But there was another level. I was seduced at the age of eight and from then until I came to the convent I was sexually promiscuous. I had these affairs frequently and of course that led to other vices, but I managed to keep that side of my life very strictly hidden. I experienced fear and pain and frustration and loneliness, and sex became for me a sort of greed, unconnected with love or life. I was so amoral about this that at first I did not even mention it to the community. I did not come as an escape – the escape would have been not to come but to have gone on in unreality; nor did I come as a penitent. I simply decided to give myself wholly to God. It is difficult to remember how one felt long ago, but I think I felt that it was the only real thing I could do, to hand my life over to God, who was the only one to know the real me under the outward show. It did not occur to me to 'give myself' by doing good to others; that would have seemed a sort of presumption. It had to be all or nothing and God only; so I chose the strictest religious order I could and asked them to have me at once.

It is possible for someone to experience the shock of love for the opposite sex for the first time after becoming a religious. This is how it happened to a seventy-year-old priest in an Anglican community. He was one of seven children whose parents were devout Christians. 'In 1915, when I was nearly nineteen, I joined the army and soon dropped most of my religion. I was very ignorant of sexual matters but I was full of curiosity and longed for erotic experiences, and the upshot of that was that I learned to masturbate.' Some time after demobilisation he had 'a conversion experience which . . . was like falling in love. And, from then on, I have always known that my life was God's.' He became ordained, worked first in a parish and then overseas as a missionary, before deciding that 'I needed the mutual help and support of a regular community.' He became a monk in 1933 and since then has had no doubts that it was his true vocation. But

the one difficult sacrifice I have had to make as a religious has been not to have a wife and children. This has sometimes been hard, but I feel sure that in my own case the sacrifice has been right because it has been spiritually fruitful, and in accordance with Matthew 19.12. I tried to accept celibacy as a vocation from the time I was at my theological college. I had never been in love with any woman before that date. After profession I was twice very strongly attracted to two women, one at the age of forty-three and the other when I was nearly sixty. I fancy that either of them might have consented to marry me if I had embarked on a courtship, and on each occasion I felt nearly overwhelmed. On the first occasion I told a prayer group of my dilemma and asked for their prayers and on the second occasion I talked it out with one of my brethren and asked for his prayers; and on each occasion the temptation passed away from me.

It is possible for an uneasy love affair not perhaps to continue or to mature but to swing into a quietly satisfying friendship after one partner has taken religious vows. The case of the man who fell in love with a nun before himself becoming a monk was one example of this. Another is that of a nun who was forty-two before she tested her vocation in the convent which was finally to become her home. She had sensed her vocation while she was working as a medical missionary in Africa

and I found this incompatible with marriage to the man I would have wanted to marry. As I knew I could not marry him and thought it would be wrong to let a man propose if you did not mean to accept him (I think now it would have been better and kinder to have let things come to a head) I held him off so that he cannot have known where he was with me at all. Consequently we had an uneasy friendship until I came to the convent. Then I had to explain what I meant by vocation and told him that I had previously had one to be a missionary. This made him realise how things stood and since then we have had a very satisfying relationship. My Superiors know about it and he comes to see me each year and I am allowed to write to him once or twice between visits. Apart from my letter to him about vocation and his answers we have never referred to our personal relationship; we just sit together when he comes and talk about this and that in an atmosphere of relaxation and peace. This sounds rather dull but isn't. Christ said that if anyone gave up wife or child or parents for Him they would have a hundredfold. This is not just an exaggerated way of putting things for emphasis, the relationship *is* stepped up a hundredfold. Christ also said that in heaven there would be no marrying or giving in marriage but we should be as the angels of God. I used to think 'How dull!' But now I know that it would be worth anything to love one another with the burning love of the Cherubim, and although we haven't got there yet I can see it as a possibility in heaven.

It is also possible for the homosexual to find in a religious community the framework within which he or she can be more at ease than would have been likely in the world outside. A lay brother who had been in teaching and in show business before taking vows says:

I should never have got married even if I had not become a religious. I am completely homosexual. Before becoming a religious and before I was a schoolmaster I had been very promiscuous and found no satisfaction in it at all. The only human love that was in any way successful was with a coloured boy of my own age, who was a revue dancer, as I was at that time. We were in different shows. We lived together for several years completely platonically and were very happy – nearly all our interests being shared. Since joining the order I have had two very intimate and close friendships, both with men much younger than myself and both in the community. They run simultaneously and are completely satisfying.

In the case of an Anglican priest who is a monk:

My love for others has been for those of my own sex. There was one instance at university when marriage might have been a possibility, although from my point of view this was much less strong than the girl's. There was a good deal of affection on my part, but nothing like a love so strong that marriage could have been an outcome. This kind of thing happened again in a parish. But before becoming a religious the deepest human love I have experienced in either giving or receiving has been from those of my own sex. Since discovering my vocation and following it the pattern of human love in my life has not changed. It has, however, deepened. I think that I can best express it by saying that in the religious life I can be as God made me, and accept myself as God made me. There is a great sheet-anchor of love in a community which I find satisfying. By nature I am a very affectionate person and can fully give and receive the kind of brotherly affection which is necessary to me.

A woman who entered her community sixteen years ago at the age of forty-seven 'would probably have married had not circumstances seemed deliberately to circumvent it. I had two friendships with women, both circumvented in the same way. Since being here I have been allowed a friendship with another Sister, and have grown increasingly close to my large family and outside friends.'

Inside the community the experiences of warmth, friendship, love in any recognisable sense and form, are about as varied as they have been for the individuals concerned in the world before taking vows. Whether it is out of loyalty or not it is rare for anyone to concede that in these particular terms the life is as bleak as some have found it outside; there is, rather, just an occasional hint of disappointment borne bravely and then sternly overcome. A nun who had known several good friendships before her profession says that 'Perhaps at first I expected to find the same kind of friendship and was a little disappointed. But that was just foolish and didn't last long. Love and kindness was there, expressed perhaps in a different manner, but quite honestly human affection is not needed in the same way. Living and growing together, giving oneself to the whole in God, is wonderfully satisfying.' A Benedictine monk who as a youth never went round with girls except one, a Jewess, with whom he fell in love and was later to meet after his profession when she was married to an American businessman, seems to suggest that a vacuum can be created between the monastery gate and the cloister. When he met his old sweetheart during his annual holiday at home, 'She was well and happy and I was glad. I have no regrets. My experience of human love since then? It's difficult to describe. There are many friendships both within and outside the community. I still feel the thirst to give and receive human love and affections – perhaps more than ever.'

But a nun of sixty-seven, on becoming a religious, 'found a warmth and depth of human love quite beyond anything I had known before, an openness to each other and a true sharing in all our joys and sorrows, and in difficulties something on which you know you can always depend.' For another there has been 'much happiness in human relationships, with my family, friends, those I cared for in the course of service, and most especially my Sisters in religion and pre-eminently Superiors, of both sexes. I think a fearlessness in human loving has grown with the years in religion.' A third speaks of 'the amazing joy of having so many sisters. I rejoice in the loving naturalness of our life together at recreations – both formal when conducted by Mother and informal when we wander together in the garden or sit and talk together in the common-room. We are encouraged to be natural and really human. I find great richness in the pooled experience of so many women of varying ages, backgrounds and interests.'

It is almost commonplace to find in a relgious community people who have been there for half a century and more. And there is maybe nothing more astonishing to a secular world which is permanently and continuously in a state of vivid flux, which is forever packed with incident, where high contrast in every form shapes the pattern of days, than the fact that there are many people who have lived for so long a life of comparative monotony and immobility and who can say at the end of it that never for one moment have they doubted that this was indeed their vocation. But there are. More frequently they will say, like this monk of three decades, but they have not *always* felt absolutely sure of their vocation but that 'on the whole, by and large, I have grown more sure. I have, indeed, been through experiences of very considerable abandonment by God but this, I think, is very usual in the religious life.' A nun who has just celebrated her jubilee says that she has never seriously doubted the rightness of her option for the religious life: 'Occasionally I have wanted or tried to do so in moments, hardly even hours, of stress, but have never succeeded.'

Stress usually derives from some personal friction or else from some collision with the vow of obedience, in which case it can take the oddest forms. A septuagenarian nun recalls that

It was not until 1945, when I had been professed fifteen years, that I had a terrible shake over the question of obedience. We had been told that, although we were enclosed, the Bishop had given us permission to go out to vote for Sir Winston Churchill in the general election. Greatly as I admired Sir Winston as a War Leader I could not vote for that Conservative programme. So I stated my difficulty and was of course allowed not to vote (the Labour candidate was divorced and in favour of easier divorce). No one was unkind to me, but it gave me a queer sort of shock. It was only a priest who said to me, 'Remember – "Ye have not chosen Me, but I have chosen you"' that brought me back to the certainty and wonder of vocation.

A wavering vocation is more likely to be felt by the young, rather than the old in religion. A 31-year-old Benedictine monk

says that 'Of course, one still has moments of doubt and dissatis-
faction with oneself. But reflection and prayer usually seem to
restore the balance. My doubts and misgivings are about my own
inadequacy, not about the certainty of my vocation.' An Anglican
monk of thirty-eight does not think that his vocation has ever
seriously faltered 'though there was a time not long ago when I
did have a depressing stretch. I am sure that this was owing to
the kind of work and the place where I was. As the tensions were
not just something that I felt myself, but were common to the
other brethren in that particular house, I did not take seriously
any temptation to throw in the sponge.' A 45-year-old contemplative nun who has been professed with her order only two years
can say:

that almost from the beginning of my life in the community I have had a
deep, underlying conviction that this was God's call for me. But at all
stages I have had times of rebellion and been tempted to give up and
return to an easier life in the world, because I was unwilling to bear the
cost of the necessary purgation of my inherent selfishness. Thus, as a
postulant or novice and since profession, at times an inner voice has
said, 'Why carry on what seems a stupid waste of my life when I could
have a good job, be successful in the world, comfortably off financially?
Why not return home to my mother and so prove my love for her? Why
not use my medical training and experience in the world and have the
satisfaction of knowing I was helping people?' And at times there has
been the whisper, 'Is there a God at all?' I am sure that those times will
go on, as faith will only grow and mature as it is tested; but knowing
that the testing will never be beyond what God knows each one can
endure.

A 42-year-old sister, professed with her community for ten
years, says briskly: 'Since becoming a religious the conscious
certainty of my vocation has been almost entirely absent. This
is neither unusual nor important. It was a functional thing
which served its purpose in enabling me to know God's will
for my life – it was not intended to be a permanent prop of
reassurance.'

And the purpose of it all? There are some religious who see it
almost entirely in personal terms, like this monk.

There is no particular virtue in living the Christian life in community as opposed to the world of the parish, the factory, the commercial undertaking, the Services or the home. Neither is there any particular virtue in living it in those worlds rather than in the cloister. There is no more virtue in working in freedom from the worry of making ends meet and coping with the income tax than there is in trying unsuccessfully to cope with these things and paralysing the rest of one's work. There is no more virtue in accommodating one's idiosyncrasies, talents, opinions and inabilities to the mind and milieu of the community than to that of the office or family. The commitment for life certainly plunges a brother into the joys, distresses, responsibility and creative activity of a family; into the work of a corporation or co-operative society; into a freedom in which he is relieved of many difficulties which he is by nature incapable of solving; into a brotherhood in which he is supported by corporate prayer and intention. The immediate worship and service of God (which is the first requisite of all Christian work) is not the monopoly of the monastic, but is practised among all the faithful, priests and laity. For me personally, the religious life has made this practice possible again. I might also add that it has given an untidy mind a framework in which to pray, think and live.

Others see their life as a signal to the rest of the world. A monk says:

Although we reckon to have certain aims in the order I would say that we are here to demonstrate the truth of learning obedience by the things we suffer. We appear to give up all sorts of things, but if this is where we should be, then we are happy with the things that are provided for us here, we are the praying heart of the Church, and therefore the worship of God is first in our lives. Everything that people see, and by which they mostly judge our lives and our usefulness, is the outcome of this life of worship and prayer. Our founder said that we were a lot of men trying to be good. I think that this still holds – because it is what we are that is more important than what we do.

A contemplative nun compares the convent to

an experimental laboratory into which some are called to work out in a particular way the problem of how man can give himself to God and to his neighbour, and if this is the basic spiritual need of human life, then it is worth doing. This experiment involves every part of one's being – physical, mental, emotional and spiritual. If any part is left outside the experiment goes wrong, the gift of oneself to God is incomplete, and we have nothing authentic to give to others. People come to us either in person or by letter, expecting to receive the results of our experiences in Christian living and community, that they may work out the principles in their own particular vocations. This is part of the overspill from our prayer which they have a right to expect from us.

Another nun appears, in the more conventional language of piety, to collect all these ideas and wrap them into one general-ised diagnosis of the religious life. The object, she says, is

that all the members of the community should become mature persons, unified in themselves and in ever-deepening relationships with God and so with each other; and so be a family of love, and by doing so to fulfil the purpose for which they were created, and so to give glory to God. By their increasing growth in sanctification and union with God to be channels of this love to the world, participants in this thirst that all men and all creatures should be drawn to unity, to respond to his love for their healing. Thus called to share in God's reconciliation, to stand in the centre of the world's forces of evil in the victory of Love's triumph on the Cross.

So far, we have had religious talking piecemeal about a number of sides to their vocation; the quotations have been deliberately extracted from often lengthy answers to a questionnaire in order to form a coherent pattern of experience and belief in a highly complex subject. By contrast, here are three unedited state-ments of vocation and what it means to two men and a woman.

1 THE JESUIT'S STORY
(He is a Scholastic, aged twenty-five; which means that he is at that stage of Jesuit training in which he is grappling with philos-ophy and theology before eventual ordination as a priest. He took his vows four years ago.)

I joined the Jesuits on leaving school; before that I could have been described as a pious Roman Catholic schoolboy. I came from a large family and with a very religious atmosphere. Weekly mass was taken for granted and occasional weekday mass was encouraged. Everyone took morning and night prayers seriously and the family normally said the rosary together in the evenings. Both parents were active members of our parish. My father was very active in the Legion of Mary and all the children joined the Sodality of Our Lady as they grew up. Out of the six children so far to have left school, two are Jesuits and one is a nun.

I was never very sure that the religious life and no other was my vocation. I realised that there was a shortage of priests and I regarded the priest's work as being extremely important. I also realised that I had the necessary academic ability to be a priest myself. With the encouragement of my elder sister (the nun) I reluctantly admitted to myself that there was no excuse for me. I thought of the Jesuits partly because I was at a Jesuit school and partly because I thought that they, more than any diocese or order I had come across, would be able to use my academic ability. I did not consider very seriously the difference between religious priests and the diocesan clergy. When I tried to discuss the matter with a priest at the college it soon became clear that he had already made up his mind that I had a vocation to the Jesuits. After that I went through the formalities required for entering the noviciate, never quite sure that I was doing the right thing. I might add that the fear of hell was a predominant driving force in my life at least until I joined the noviciate.

Before I joined the Jesuits I considered celibacy to be merely an unwelcome condition of becoming a priest. I was never very steady with one girl, but I enjoyed dancing and mixed social functions, and I had a few close friends who were girls and one in particular of whom I was very fond. On the other hand I was singularly short of friends among my contemporaries at school.

Since becoming a religious I have been able to make close acquaintance with a number of girls. One of them is a particularly close friend, and is also very fond of me; I am not sure of the exact meaning of the term 'in love' and whether it applies or ever did apply to my relations with this girl. I can say that at a time when I was reconsidering my commitment to religious life I discovered that thoughts about her were considerably influencing my judgements, and I found myself unable to accept the fact of my vow of perpetual celibacy: this state of affairs was, however, of short duration and I was able to correct it almost as soon as I realised that it had arisen. I do not regret the relationship, which has been a stimulus both to my work and to my religious observance. So my experience of human love has been limited, what I have experienced I consider to be very valuable in my life, but I do not believe that any person's desire of, and need for, love can be satisfied by any one person. I might also remark that one of the main considerations which have kept me in the order over the past couple of years is the help and stimulus I have found from friends within it, and my commitment to them.

On a number of occasions I have found it necessary to reconsider the value of and my attitude towards religious life as practised by those members of the order with whom I have come into contact. I now regard the concept of 'choice' to be more fundamental than the concept of 'vocation': the idea of some inner call I regard as irrelevant – what matters for me is that I have chosen and can continue to choose to live the religious life, and that the order chooses to have me. Every time I have reconsidered either the value of religious life as I have found it (taking into account the possibility of my own particular adaptations) or my own suitability for it, I have decided that I would do more good within than without – or more harm by leaving than by staying.

One doubt I have about religious life is that it gives me an authority and status in the Church which I have not really earned for myself. This can create a tension between my own convictions and those of the superiors who have given me the status. Each has in some way to take responsibility for the statements of the other and the question arises as to whether this is possible with the fairly radical differences of opinion that exist and whether honesty is being sacrificed. One objection I have to the living of the religious life in the order to which I belong is that the religious life seems to become in the minds of many an end in itself which has to be preserved as such. Certain practices and customs are held by many as binding on all irrespective of their usefulness to particular individuals or communities, and the situation in which they find themselves. Religious life becomes a particular style of life rather than a group of persons living for a common goal, so that 'common life' achieves a status out of proportion to its value. This is not to deny the need for some regularity, and I am reasonably content with the community in which I normally reside – but I am not content with the attitudes of many who are in positions of authority.

This over-emphasis on religious practice does seem to produce in people an odd scale of values. The concept of 'supernatural' is not supposed to be in any way contrary to reason, but in the minds of many it has become so distinct from reason that it does in fact result in attitudes and conclusions which to most people would seem to be unreasonable. Friends of mine have been put onto work simply in order to 'give them experience' or even 'to test their obedience'. Their

suitability to the work, the 'natural' value of the work, or the responsibility towards those outside the society for whom the work is intended –
these considerations were apparently deemed irrelevant. In one case
this involved two years at the prime of his life. Other examples are the
expensive and long training without consideration of the usefulness for
the individuals concerned – the long academic training for priests even
in the case of non-academic persons seems to me absurd, and to have
people doing degrees at university which they do not use seems to me
to be a scandalous waste of time and of benefactors' money. I am also
out of sympathy with teachers of morals who have had little pastoral
experience, with hours of rising and retiring unnecessarily out of
conformity with the society in which we live, with injunctions on
wearing a very distinctive dress and other difficulties imposed on social
contact with non-religious, etc.

This slightly odd 'religious logic' becomes, to my mind, a more
dangerous influence owing to our over-rigid rule about staying with
non-religious, and difficulties imposed on eating outside one's house of
residence (at least during the dozen years of formation). Religious tend
to become isolated even while living in very populated areas, and
over-concerned with the particular problems of religious life which are
rarely examined in relation to other people's problems. In this way, for
example, realistic attitudes towards the value of money can be completely lost, apart from more serious topics such as the possibility
and limits of authoritative government, the nature of social problems,
etc. Many have gone through the prescribed training and come out
extremely human but many, to my mind, have not, and the danger to
one's own personal development – a danger which is not simply
overcome by a critical frame of mind – does create a certain amount of
moral concern.

I understand the primary aim of the founder of the order to have been
to serve the Church in any way the Church requires, and this is
fundamental to my understanding of religious life, though I would give
less importance to the hierarchical Church than he did and would
emphasise that the Church goes beyond explicit Christians. Thus I
demand of myself a utilitarian justification of my life and my work. I
regard the purpose of my religious life as being to make the best
possible use of my talents, taking into account the needs of the society
in which I live: if at any stage I decided that I could make better use of
my talents outside the order I think I would leave. But this should be
understood in a very broad sense, taking into account the effects of my
change in status, and of the various interpretations that might be given

to my action, the betrayal of trust that many, both inside and outside the order, may feel. A realistic assessment of what can be done outside the order is required, and also a realisation that human happiness is more important than material welfare.

As for the function of the public vows I have taken, it seems to me that primarily they are a witness and a challenge to the world and their main purpose is to provoke a rethinking of attitudes and values; this applies as much to the religious himself as those with whom he comes into contact. The vow of poverty is a challenge to the rat race; how effective this can be when one is a member of a large organisation with substantial funds remains questionable, but living slightly below the standards of one's associates can suggest that happiness can be obtained as much by having a little less as by having a little more. A recent interpretation of poverty as being more concerned with working hard than with the standard of living is also relevant. The vow of chastity is, I think, an effective challenge to the place of sex in the modern world. I would like it also to result in a greater availability – which at the moment is true of major tasks, but unnecessarily limited in daily life by rules of residence, and a tendency to require an over-particular exercise of the superior's sanctions – and a witness to a distinction between sex and love, though we cannot simply draw a line between them. The vow of obedience is a challenge to the value placed on independence: I would like it also to suggest that we can go a long way by trusting men who make mistakes like everyone while remaining realistic about the mistakes – a public acceptance of the fact that nothing can be perfect and that we must do our best with what we have. The religious life as a whole is my witness to my beliefs in the importance of religion (in some form) and the value of a commitment to serving rather than personal gain.

I might also point out that although my answer is stated in secular terms I am not entirely in favour of a 'secularised religion'. My own interest in philosophy results in a personal tendency towards a secular language, and I am very sceptical of anything that completely prohibits some sort of translation into secular categories.

2 THE NUN'S STORY
(She is sixty-one and she has been professed for thirty-nine years, first in an active order of Anglicans, later in an Anglican contemplative convent.)

Born in a university city in an intellectual milieu, reaching the age of adolescence in the reactionary years of the First War period, at an early age I developed all the tendencies of revolt against traditions and conventionalities which was so typical of the age. Deeply involved with the moral and psychological distresses of one of my brothers and violently opposed to the idea that there was a God of Love because my eldest and much loved brother had been killed in the war, I made an absolute fetish of chucking over all religious observances, very largely to make a show of my independence and probably also as a form of shocking my parents, which was one of my chief aims of life.

This form of self-determinism carried me well into my own university years. I have no doubt at all that any psychologist would have summed me up as a good example of the will-to-power complex, as my un-doubted gifts of leadership had ample scope on every level to be given expression to. It is all the more remarkable, therefore, that when the Lord caught up with me, it was through the overwhelming cosmic pressure of suffering and frustration by which the years of the middle 1920s were so characterised.

In the vacation I went down to the East End and saw something of what those years of unemployment meant, and the moral decline of the brother mentioned above so overwhelmed me that it became obvious that something more than a philosophy of self-determinism was needed to provide an answer to the problems of the age.

If religion was to be the answer it had to be all or nothing, and therefore when I returned to the sacramental life of the Church and the practice of prayer there could be no half measures and the religious life presented as far as I could see the most complete self-committal to God in the service of others. At first I revolted against the idea and tried to escape from it; to no avail. I tried my vocation in an active teaching order the year after I got my degree and twelve years later was transferred from the active to the enclosed life of my present community.

This transference must again be seen in relation to the world conditions of the time in which I was living. By 1940 I was a Mission Sister and participated to the full in all the suffering and emergencies arising from the German bombing of the area I lived in. This was the culmination of a gradual process which had been there from the beginning – a realisation that the Christian is called not only to try to ameliorate the *effects* of man's selfishness and depravities, but to go far deeper, to be in God's process of reconciliation of that evil which is the source from which sin as we know it is derived. In terms of Christian commitment this means the witness to the power of prayer and the transforming grace of Christ's Passion being brought to bear on the world's deformities. This is the primary essence and function of the contemplative life and it was the challenge of World War Two that made me realise that for me personally the contemplative rather than the active life was the only way to fulfil my vocation.

Probably in the process of translation of Mgr Huyghe's book the unfortunate word '*reject* the world' has given a wrong impression. Religious vocation can never be negative, but for those so called the most positive way of serving the world. If there is an element of escapism then the religious life has no more virtue than any other form of negative way of life. I think it is quite wrong to put the question of human life in opposition to the call to the religious life; the two are not in opposition.

If a candidate for the religious life has had first-hand experience of sexual love in its fullness, it would be far truer to say that the call to the religious life is the completion of the human experience. In my own case I was engaged and can truly say that the experience was one of complete satisfaction at every level of one's being. We both realised there was a call from God not to abandon our love for each other, but to take it into the most complete form of dedication of which we were capable. This meant in effect that before we could think of marriage I had to try my vocation to the religious life.

My biggest query was not the rightness of what we were doing, nor even shrinking from the cost of it, but whether I was asking more in terms of sacrifice from the man who loved me and whom I loved. The whole thing was obviously only made possible by the fact that he as well as myself could sincerely and with a sense of complete fulfilment put the will of God first before any desires and wishes of our own. But the point I want to make is that we found each other by giving up each other, and certainly I can say now that this completely satisfied experience has gone on with me all my life, as I know it has with him, and has been the foundation of my fulfilment of human relationships within the religious life, and with all the manifold needs and problems that are brought to a contemplative community to pray for and to help resolve. In other words, having known human life at its best I was a fulfilled person, and so ready to be more completely sanctified by religious life if I let it. A religious community should be a place where human relationships can be fulfilled in depth, united as we are by a common aim and purpose, and with the consecration of the whole man and woman to God, life is balanced and all the faculties and emotions are redirected and thus gradually reach their full potential.

My years as a religious from 1929 to 1968 must be seen against the background of the changes in the world and in the religious life itself.

There have been peak crisis points – e.g. from 1938 to 1941 and from 1948 to 1954, when I would have given anything under the sun to have got out of the religious life. This was *not* that I doubted my own personal call, but that I doubted profoundly whether the forms of religious life as we know it, either active or enclosed, could meet the challenge of the times or provide the setting where the real Gospel life of service of God and man could be fulfilled.

One was brought up against extreme forms of autocracy in government, outdated and outmoded social traditions which had been brought into being and absorbed by religious custom, the right initiative and freedom of the individual thwarted, and a general lack of Christian love and trust which seemed shattering and incompatible with the aims and ideals which religious life professes. Therefore as a younger nun I have been both frustrated and disillusioned, but somehow never doubted that the call for me was a true one and that the religious life as a whole was a microcosm of the whole macrocosm of the Church, in its stuckness and blindness. That is why for the last ten to fifteen years it has been increasingly thrilling to be aware of the spirit of renewal and reform within the whole Church, and to realise that our community has its part to play in this ecumenical age, in cutting right out from the clogging conventionalities which have bogged down the Church's and the religious life's witness, and to get down to the fundamental principles which are both biblical and patristic in origin.

The purpose of our community is that of all contemplative enclosed life. (1) To bear witness to the primacy of God and to actualise this Godcentredness right through the whole life, so that nothing lies outside the ordinances of his will, as revealed through the Christian premises and the Rule and Constitution of the community. This means in actual fact the sanctification of the whole life so that the prayer and relationship – in fact the whole lot – are seen as one whole, and one human activity is not put in opposition to any other. (2) Prayer is the life and work of the community. (3) The overspill of the prayer is the love and caring and compassion of God's love for mankind, and an expansion farther through ecumenical channels (personal dialogue and encounter). Therefore (4) Love of the brethren, the giving of oneself to serve the community and, through the community, the Church and the world, with all that means of self loss, is the primary purpose of the contemplative life.

Religious life and probably contemplative life in particular has from the second century stood for the challenging and counterbalancing of the conditions in the Church and world in any given age. It is not higher than nor better than any other form of Christian witness, but it should provide for the individual the conditions under which he or she can more completely give him or herself to God and show forth to the world in terms of love and joy and self-committal what it means to be a Christian. This community is taking full part in the aggiornamento which means an ever-expanding form of apostolate as a proof of prayer, but the fundamental principles do not change in any age, and it is to these principles each successive generation must turn and see how far its practice is answering the needs of the time.

I do not think I have stressed here sufficiently that religious life should be seen in terms of *relationship*: man's relationship with God, perfected in and through vocation; man's relationship with man in God, perfected in and through vocation. This is only the Gospel – thou shalt love thy God, body, soul and spirit, and thy neighbour in God. Religious life is *Relationship* – not a code of moral life and behaviour; therefore it is organic and progressive.

3 THE MONK'S STORY

(A Benedictine monk, aged thirty-two. He took simple vows eight years ago and solemn vows five years ago.)

About the age of thirteen I was conscious of a desire to do something large and generous with my life. I had no notion what this could be, and the desire itself was completely formless except that, having had from my Irish mother a 'good Catholic upbringing', I felt the Church to be the biggest thing around, in fact the only true thing. Therefore my life must in some way be involved in it. I didn't equate this with being a priest, but because my then Jesuit form-master at the local Catholic grammar school was the most loving and lovable person I had so far met I wondered whether his life was the thing for me. The 'religious' and priestly ideal meant nothing, or at least was completely remote; but this man somehow broke the conventional Jesuit behaviour pattern by showing an unconditional and disinterested concern for us, for our growth. I remember in particular that he took what I said with complete and unaffected seriousness in a way no one else quite did, which may explain why my one-year contact with him left a deep impression which still remains. Without moralising he communicated a sense that life, our life, was intensely worthwhile, wholesome, and could be terrific fun. I don't think there was much, if any, romanticism or fantasy in my view of him; I wasn't shattered, though naturally puzzled and dismayed, to hear of his very severe mental breakdown soon after leaving us. He remained for me a vital person.

Through later school years and two years' National Service, I had no deep desire to do anything in particular with my life. My non-Christian father, remote in childhood owing to physical separation during the war years, was a solicitor and joining him seemed a sensible thing to do, especially as his business was self-made and the idea of a son inheriting it meant much to him. So it was with this fairly formed intention that I went from National Service to university, yet with a sense that this career, and indeed any career acceptable to most people I knew, was not quite real for me, somehow not adequate to my deepest desire and need. My father had very generously made it clear that any desire to be a priest would have his support, but this was not then appealing.

At university my only intimate friends were Old Boys of the school run by my present monastery. Through them and some of the younger monks also at university I came here first, largely out of curiosity to see the place which had produced my friends. The sophistication of their minds and the depth of their thinking about religion were a revelation after the prosaic and second-hand quality of religious instruction at the grammar school. Coming to the monastery for a few days was a deeply moving experience; a glimpse of a new, strange and curiously attractive world of which I wanted to be a part. I had no intellectual notion of what the monastic life was about – I wanted to be whatever these men were. Very simple so far.

At school I always moved happily in a like-minded group of friends, free of any emotional intensity. This pattern more or less repeated itself on National Service, except that the RC bit gave me a certain sense of apartness in this new irreligious atmosphere. My faith now demanded at least some degree of nonconformity to the group ethos, at least in terms of Sunday Mass and saying night prayers by my billet bed, scrutinised by at least one hostile witness. But I was on easy terms with almost everybody, and very dependent on a group of new but firm friends. It was at university (age twenty-one) that I first consciously and intensely loved anyone in particular. My narrowly formed RC conscience turned this experience into a morbid, guilt-ridden infatuation. This temporarily fixated relationship clogged the vocational issue because the person I loved (A) intended to join this monastery after university. This was at once a draw to the monastery and a repulsion from it; while desperately wanting to be always with A I felt guilty about this desire, which seemed a radical disqualification for the monastic life. Another friend, whom I now realise I loved more deeply (B), joined the monastery a year before

I left university. I missed B very much in my last year and the thought of him in the monastery was a terrific pull, unclouded by the increasingly paralysing guilt associated with my immediate contemporary. My desire to be with my friends won out, although I seriously considered joining another monastery.

It seems clear to me now that it was quite simply human love which brought me here, although the attraction and inspiration of the place as a whole suggested a larger worth-whileness in living the life my friends proposed to lead. In letting my love lead me in this way I wondered very much whether I was really escaping, doing the nearest and most immediately appealing thing instead of something less congenial and more mundane, like my father's job. I couldn't exercise this doubt, and entered the monastery hoping rather desperately that all this would be resolved positively or negatively in the noviciate. It wasn't!

Things were further complicated by the noviciate-induced feeling that the search for and service of God were paramount, with love of other people as a kind of by-product of the God-and-prayer business. This made my emotional involvements a worry, a distracting irrelevance; yet I could never feel in my bones that they were no more than that. The fact that other people were absolutely important for me suggested that I was really in bad faith and should leave, or at least make the kind of psychological break with my friends which others seemed to find workable but which I felt to be beyond me. The recognised guides (books and older monks) had things to say about 'the problem of particular friendships', but they weren't adequate; they treated this as a *problem on its own*, never suggesting how such a relationship could be creative.

Sex was a closed book, so that the fact that my love included sexual attraction and desire made me think, at least with a part of myself, that it was outrageous, sinful, lustful, sacrilegious even. Words like 'sublimation', heard occasionally in the monastery, suggested there was an answer to be found, although the word itself was never enlightened in any practical way by the speaker. But I could never feel in my bones that loving another monk in this way was simply taboo, although often thinking that I ought to leave because of the intensity of the emotional-sexual pressure in the rather hothouse enclosed noviciate atmosphere. A further complication was the sense of not-quite-really about so much of the God-and-prayer business; this, I felt, was something I had to be able to take on and make my own, yet it never really connected with the rest of my life in any satisfactory way.

The first glimpse of anything I could honestly call 'certainty' about my vocation came in my fourth year here, when I began to be deeply influenced by an older monk. This was the year in which I had to try to reach a final decision about solemn vows, due that September. The terms in which superiors posed the problem – 'Do you really want to serve God in the monastic life?' – were artificial, presenting me with what I felt to be an unreal and therefore artificial question, although part of me felt this *ought* to be the real, decisive question. So it was a flash of light when this older monk (C), who had recently taken a more genuinely personal interest in me than any other older monk, suddenly said: 'The real vocational question is "Do you want to share the problem of this community?"' This struck home because it pin-pointed the sort of bond I already felt with the monastery in a way which seemed to unify all my hitherto fragmented concerns. The tension involved in my love for B was by no means resolved, but here at last was a conviction which made sense; a desire to help and serve this community in any way I could. In particular I thought of the commitment as helping the monks to resolve a spiritual crisis which their communal and personal history had clearly left radically unresolved at the time. I don't know what I thought I could do, but I wanted to be in on anything that happened. C communicated a strong sense that out of so much darkness and confusion some tremendous good would surely come. A deeply intuitive person, this conviction possessed him. Then, in the pre-solemn vows retreat, an old monk with the reputation of a highly intelligent eccentric, suddenly said, 'The eyes of the heart should be on all the brethren all the time.' I wondered why I had had to wait four years to hear this from a monastic preacher: I took solemn vows.

Subsequently I became ever more involved in C's struggle to articulate his new-found conviction about the Christian life and the monk's life ('You either marry or go it alone – if you take the second option it turns out to be going it with everybody.') His preaching was the service of the community as the key to what it meant to be a Christian and a monk. Deeply influenced by Teilhard de Chardin, he discerned a unity in the whole of creation and in personal experience, which was for me a liberation. I could never understand how I was such a help to him, since I seemed little more than a sounding-board for his ideas. He was so conscious of the mawkish sterility of even the most positive elements in the received teaching on particular friendship that he seemed to deny the relevance of emotional intensity between people, despite a message of love. So while giving me a firm conviction that we were working towards a re-birth of our own community in an unimaginable oneness of mind and heart, he couldn't fully resolve my personal uncertainty. I thought he would have been dismayed and outraged had I told him of my real feelings towards my contemporaries. There was very great emotional intensity in his talking and teaching, but a very deep inhibition prevented any clear articulation of this.

His inability to find any adequate way of expressing his own intense feeling for others led to a severe mental breakdown, at the height of which he took his own life. I spent the last night of his life with him in hospital, and so witnessed in a very purgative way the disintegrating effects of emotional frustration. Shortly before his death he had seemed suddenly to contradict all his earlier preaching by saying, 'It must be with one person in the end.' This, plus the circumstances of his illness and death throwing light on his life, set me furiously to think. I wanted to find some unity beneath this apparent contradiction. I never for one moment doubted his transparent and fierce integrity, and his death if anything increased my sense of the wholesomeness and significance of his teaching. In his life he had given me an increasing sense that I had a key part to play in our community's future; witnessing his illness and death gave me a vocation to see this thing through, to go all-out to resolve the communal problem of which his anguished life was symptomatic and which his death at once pin-pointed and left unresolved. Some of my contemporaries, but not those I most loved, shared spontaneously my conviction about the significance of all this, and my euphoric certainty that what had occurred was not a tragedy. To the rest of the monks it was that, and it is still a painful subject between us.

Since C's death almost four years ago, those of us who felt this way have sought to develop and implement his insight here. This had its painful aspect for me, since in the name of the loving service of the brethren and the boys in our school I was deeply divided from B. I longed for him to share my conviction and help us to change things; he didn't seem able to, and the whole C-business produced great conflict in him. I tended to attribute this to his pride, selfishness, etc., not realising that his reaction revealed a delicacy of feeling which saw my conviction as somehow impersonal and dogmatic.

Recently we have been given a new insight into the equation of the communal and the personal which simplifies the whole business and leaves me with a new and deeper certainty that the love of one another is the only worthwhile thing, that it is this and only this which creates community, that only growth in this love will equip us for service in the wider world beyond the monastery to which we must increasingly look. This is no longer a largely notional conviction, still less a maudlin sentimentality, but an increasing intuitive awareness of the reality of others and of how we can in fact help to create each other's lives. The obverse of this is an increasing realism about the impossibility of really loving, the recognition that whatever real further change we can initiate in one another will be, like what has happened to us so far, a gift to us all.

This, then, is my present vocation certainty: a clear-headed involvement in the creation of a community to serve the world in a way which will hasten its end. I see this as the unification of my hitherto fragmented experience in the ability at last to begin to love others straightforwardly and wholeheartedly without fear or scruple. One consequence is that the options are now open in a new way: I am no longer worried as to whether or not I am a 'queer', but neither am I worried about what would happen if I were to fall in love with a woman. Ultimately I doubt whether full spiritual freedom can be reached without an intense man-woman relationship, but I don't see the sexual consummation as essential. Indeed, it seems that relationships which by-pass the immediate consummation have a special function in building up the whole human community and precipitating its final fulfilment in God – this is what I mean by the end of the world.

I should add that what has brought me to my present certainty is a sense of *being loved* unequivocally. The sense of being wholesomely and unconditionally loved has begun to release in me the power to love, so that more and more people are now clear to me as growing vessels of the Spirit, in whose growth is my salvation. This may sound a piece of abstract or pietistic wishful thinking, but I am writing out of an experience which has rapidly stripped me of many illusions and self-defences, out of a newly-discovered sense of my own real self and others' real selves which is deeply unromantic and open-ended (but emphatically not *unfelt*). An older confrère not at present resident in the monastery has called this the recovery of sanity; if it reads like the belated discovery by a deeply neurotic person of a basic human truth familiar in childhood to more normal people then my language has failed me.

This is a love which *is* for ever; I am certain of my brethren, whatever they may do, say or think, now or in the future. This certainty works outwards into other relationships, producing for instance a new and exciting freedom in family relationships and leading to an increasingly direct and genuine contact with a wider range of people. It was the refusal to compromise either on this fully personal quality of loving or on the traditional communal obligations which destroyed C, because he could not fully express the problem in terms of his own experience of love, lack of love and inability to love, which I now see clearly to have lain behind his teaching on loving-service. This teaching I accepted and regurgitated in its drastically inadequate form because I loved and trusted him absolutely. What often looked and felt like a divisive ideology was in fact the best expression he could manage of a profound conviction born of personal experience, as he often said ineffectively to outsiders. I feel now that his spirit lives in us, and that I have his support in at least frankly loving B, whom his teaching had seemed to forbid me to love. So a human love which had for years divided me against myself now comes newly alive at the centre of my life as a growing point, carrying with it a wholly new certainty, a wholly new sense of oneness with everything and everybody. A conviction which is *me* at last. This doesn't, of course, mean that monastic life is suddenly and totally unproblematic: I find myself exposed now increasingly at every point; this is simply the obverse of coming out into the open in the way I have.

As hinted above, I think the purpose of our life together is to bring the world to an end by the practice of an all-embracing, open-ended love. Few monks would accept this without cavil – many would find it incomprehensible or shocking. And this conviction would be an absurd, delusive fantasy if it didn't illuminate Christian and monastic tradition. But all the classical monastic doctrines now take on a new fullness of meaning: the search for God, loving obedience, communal prayer (effective sign of our love's present achievement and future fulfilment), so-called private or personal prayer (to facilitate some depth of reflective awareness of reality, of all that is and how it moves), the flight from the world (i.e., the darkness, whatever requires exorcism in Harvey Cox's sense, of *The Secular City*). The world is intensely present in the monastery; this stripped-down way of living together heightens consciousness of what is truly dark and unresolved in all our lives.

The monk least of all can avoid the burden of consciousness of the whole human spectrum and the insistent challenge to new ways of spiritual action which that consciousness provokes. Perhaps we can define the monastery's function as exorcism. True, that is the Church's function – but the monks are explicitly and consciously committed to this task. If a monastic community can be exorcised, what task is beyond it? I have known sufficient exorcism to believe total exorcism possible.

EIGHT

THE TURNING-POINT

'Suddenly, the fact of being a human being seems wildly liberating.'
SISTER MARYELLEN MUCKENHIRN CSC
American Catholic Exodus, p. 119

'Monks are found to view the question of reform in different ways.
The seasoned religious will tend to see it as the rusty turnstile
through which we all at one time or another must want to pass. But
he will be quite happy at having himself turned back in time. To him
it represents an artificial device which does not so much introduce
to the promised land as separate from it. He has so often seen
monks getting stuck in that turnstile for good. He thinks of sound
men wasted on a superficial cause, going round and round, with self
leaning nearer to the centre of it.'
DOM HUBERT VAN ZELLER OSB, *The Benedictine Idea*, p. 81

There have been many great turning-points in the history of the
religious life. Benedict was responsible for the first of them,
when he brought order out of chaos, when he introduced the idea
of a closed community life, when he composed the theme which
has been developed and rearranged but which has never been
substantially challenged as the basis of monasticism from his day
until this. Francis and Dominic led another change of direction
by taking their disciples and their faith out into the world, to convert it by exhortation instead of praying for it and for themselves
within the security of the monastic walls. Ignatius founded a

society to defend the faith against all comers and by all means
when it seemed likely to be demolished by the Reformation; it
was the first time the Church found itself with its back to the wall,
attacked by an enemy from within its own ranks on its own terms;
and that was a turning-point, too. Yet none of these shifts and
changes are of greater significance than the ones taking place
today. History may eventually see the middle of the twentieth
century as the moment when the religious life lurchingly rounded
a bend much more acute than Benedict navigated fourteen
hundred years ago. It is so sharp a turn, and the vehicle
traversing it is so top-heavy with tradition, so uncertain in its
steering mechanism, that some gloomy souls at present wonder
whether it will, in fact, make it safely; they can foresee the awful
possibility of flying off at a tangent half-way round and ending up
catastrophically in some utterly irreligious ditch by the side of the
road. This is, of course, no more than the predicament of the
Church at large, writ small in the microcosmic world of
the cloister and the wimple and the threefold vow.

Like the Church as a whole the religious have seen the need for
changes in the structure of their lives, some of them fundamental. Reappraisal has nowhere been more agonising than in
the matter of religious poverty.

Religious poverty as it is generally interpreted today entails the
inability of the religious, the monk or the friar, the nun or sister, to
possess anything. Whatever they need is provided by the community,
in many instances frugally enough, in others on a more lavish scale. The
individual's poverty consists in not owning anything in the sense that he
(or she) has no dominion over what is provided for his (or her) use.
Communities, as such, may be considerable property owners, powerful
corporations with large resources. Now poverty as it is experienced (as
distinct from practised) outside the monastic enclosure is somewhat
different in scope; it embraces a whole family, not just individual
members of it, and although it consists in a lack of property (in this it is
the same for the private individual as for the monk or nun) it includes
also the consequences of such a lack, among which is to be numbered
insecurity and dependence on others – and also dependence on a weekly
wage packet or, in unemployment, on the allowance made by the state
insurance system, if any. It is probably in this last respect that the

contrast with religious poverty, as it is interpreted by canon law, is particularly obvious. A solemn vow of poverty, provided the religious is not guilty of some heinous offence, nowadays amounts in practice to security for life. All this is not to say that canonical poverty is meaningless or has outgrown its usefulness, but the contrast between it and actual poverty has been shown in this way in order the clearer to show the ideal of poverty practised by the Petits Frères. They *share* the poverty of those among whom they live – lower-paid labourers, peasants in under-developed countries, casual agricultural workers and the like. This 'witness to the poverty of Christ' (in de Foucauld's words) is the clearer because it is easily understood by those whose lives they share.

That, as it happens, is the comment of a layman. But much the same attitude is today being struck by priests and by religious themselves. The Bishop of Aras has pointed out one traditional offence against real poverty which has been perpetrated under the guise of fortifying chastity. He has cited the example of the nun travelling from a community in Paris to another community in Lyons, who has been obliged to take two sisters with her – one as her chaperone, the other as chaperone to the chaperone on the return journey; which has made the cost of her journey five times what it need have been. An English Benedictine monk, recalling the vast baroque palaces like Melk, inhabited at great expense, these days by brethren of his order, has observed that there seems to be something wrong with an economy which requires an income of about £1,000 per head to keep a monk in holy poverty. An American Benedictine has pointed out a local flaw in the system.

Trips away from the monastery or convent are a problem. Custom varies. In some congregations a time away each year is regularised, ten days or more either in a mountain retreat owned by the community or with the family or friends. For those who are allowed to 'go into the world' for a period in the summer a real problem exists. . . . In our sophisticated society eager friends want to give the returned solitary a good time, meaning an entertaining time. Friends are so generous; trips to Florida or Cape Cod or Europe may not cost the monastery a cent. Of course, it would be against poverty to be spending all that money on a first-class fare to the south of Spain, but if the friends pick up the bill . . .

the Superior may be nonplussed or a little hesitant, especially when friends have been good to the house – perhaps built the library and set up a fund for further education of the young religious; it would be ungrateful to refuse. After that a precedent has been set. Next year there are other tempting offers, which can hardly be refused when the first has been accepted. People tell us that these trips are very economical. But economy is not the same thing as poverty.

An English Carmelite prioress has detected another jarring note.

What convents and institutions should be interested in today is the tableware used by the average unpretentious family: deal tables instead of oak benches; stainless steel rather than hand-carved or turned wooden spoons; not pottery platters and earthenware ewers that look charming and medieval, but Woolworth's china, glassware, or even that ultimate abomination of our century, plastic.

And René Voillaume, Prior of the Petits Frères, has suggested a more subtle danger to the life of poverty as it is known in real rather than religious terms. He has written that:

We need a clearer idea of the relationship between the priestly calling of a Petit Frère and the general mission of the priest in the Church. This calling of a Petit Frère to be a priest involves its own difficulties. The reason which made Brother Charles of Jesus hesitate when he was thinking about ordination to the priesthood is today as valid as ever; it is the difficulty of reconciling the status of a cleric, and the signs of a dignified position which the Church attaches to it, with the social status of poverty and toil essential to the calling of a Petit Frère.

Alongside poverty the religious concept of obedience is being re-examined. Nothing has struck more firmly at one tradition than Cardinal Suenens's insistence that the chief consideration 'is not the abdication of one's own will nor the submission to a person, it is loyalty to the common good as an expression of God's will. . . . The superior has the final decision, the last word – but not the second-last word. . . . To think that one obeys in the first instance in order to renounce one's own will, is to start on a path that leads nowhere. . . .' And, taking him at his word, religious have started to make their own caustic observations on the application of obedience. An Anglican deaconess has written that 'For a religious to have to telegraph to England from Africa before accepting an invitation out to a meal even in connection with the work suggests a caricature not only of obedience but of religious poverty.' The criticisms have begun to produce results. Some of the greater deferences to superiors have now been abandoned. In the Belgian Congregation of Benedictines the abbot is now addressed as 'père abbé' instead of 'révérendissime père abbé'; at the Belgian Abbey of Maredsous the abbot's ring is no longer normally kissed by his brethren when they have audience of him. Various antique mortifications practised under obedience are on their way out; since 1967 the Poor Clare nuns have been allowed to sleep lying down instead of sitting up in special beds, as they used to.

The very heart of the religious life, the liturgy, is being overhauled perhaps more thoroughly than any other part of it. An Anglican superior has pointed out the difficulty for an active religious of reconciling his work with the need to say the sevenfold office each day; it has very often meant cramming a number of the offices together either before or after work so as to fulfil the quota ordained by tradition, 'which is as if a man should kiss his wife good morning and goodnight at the same time, in order to get it over and save him having to do so later on when the time comes.' His own order, the Community of the Resurrection, has experimentally dropped the lesser offices since the beginning of 1967 and now makes do with matins at 6.45 am, mass at 7.15 am, a 'midday office' at 1 pm, evensong at 7.0 pm and compline at 9.45 pm. The English Congregation of Benedictine monks, which tends to include a lot of schoolmasters, not only rises and retires now at the more academic hours of 7 am and 11 pm, but has altered its liturgy so that a hundred and fifty psalms are chanted in a fortnight instead of a week. The Dutch Augustinian friars have not only trimmed their offices; they have also re-bound their breviaries as loose-leaved books because they expect to be amending their forms and patterns of worship for some time to come. At the Benedictine monastery of Mount Saviour, in New

York, they have taken a leaf from Taizé's book by redistributing the psalms so that a hundred and fifty can still be chanted in a week while short periods of reflective silence are introduced into the office. At the Benedictine abbey of Bec, in France, they are conducting the most radical liturgical experiment of all. On Sundays women oblates, who live a modified Benedictine Rule in the world, sing part of the office and mass in the choir with the monks.

While experiments with the structure of the religious life have been carried out there have been moves to redirect it, where possible, to more effective employment in the world. In the United States three Franciscan Missionary Sisters have taken a downtown apartment in Portland, Oregon, where they teach remedial reading to backward children and counsel slum dwellers; forty Glenmary Sisters have detached themselves from their mother house in Cincinnati and started a new community in Appalachia to teach and nurse among the poor. In Britain the Anglican Community of the Resurrection closed its priory in a middle-class London suburb in 1968 and moved across the city to premises in a slum area; with the monks went a group of deaconesses to share in social and pastoral work there. Even ten years ago the idea of men and women religious joining forces in work, let alone sharing the same buildings to eat and sleep in, would have stunned anyone in the religious life, from a Carthusian nun to a Presbyterian minister doing his shift with the Iona community. It is, in fact, no more than a restoration of the dual community which existed in the early Middle Ages at Whitby and elsewhere. Yet nothing shows the extent to which some religious would re-adapt the life more than the pressure which Dutch Dominican novices successfully applied to their superiors in 1967 to let them study agriculture rather than theology, so that they might go after profession to work rather than to preach in underdeveloped countries.

Many of the changes now afoot are doubtless the result of much cross-fertilisation that has been quietly taking place during the past few years. As in the Church at large, denominational boundaries are counting for less and less – which is not, by any means, to say that they count for nothing yet – and are being crossed more and more frequently and with a greater sense of security. This is not just a matter of occasional visiting; it has, in some cases, meant residence over a long period. There have been Catholic and Orthodox priests at Protestant Taizé for two or three years now. Swedish monks of the Protestant Brotherhood of the Holy Cross have been living with the Benedictines of Ehrlach in Austria. At the abbey of Boquen, in northern France, American Episcopalians and Methodists have been sharing the common life and worship of the resident Trappist monks. And in the process of these visitations different ideas and outlooks have been channelled back and forth between the various sects of the Church involved. At the same time guests and hosts have discovered that not much of importance divides them in their understanding of what the religious life is and should be about. One of the Franciscans who has been attached to Taizé has written that 'If we did not have the separate Eucharist – the great sign of unity which still reminds us of our separation – there would be almost no difference between us.'

Other influences have been at work besides those exerted by itinerant individuals. Few things have shaped the present course of the religious life more than the philosophies of Taizé and of the Petits Frères, as they have been expounded in the writings of Roger Schutz, Charles de Foucauld and René Voillaume. They run so closely parallel as to make one almost suspect collusion, though neither Voillaume nor Schutz has ever acknowledged the existence of the other in print, so far as I am aware. Yet together they have damned the traditional concept of religious poverty for the sham thing it so often has been. Together they have rejected the idea of converting, in any accepted sense, the agnostic or half-believing world. Together they have insisted on the prime importance of contemplative prayer in the midst of worldly activity and have tried to exemplify this in their communities. Together they have argued that the Christian duty in the world is unself-consciously to take the next man as you find him and to offer him everything in the way of care and affection that he wants; nothing more, or less. In tandem these philosophies, the one Protestant, the other Catholic, are gradually being absorbed across the religious world.

They are not, perhaps, as codes of conduct, very distinguish-able from some that have been spawned by pure agnosticism; and agnosticism, too, can be seen pressing the religious world into a different shape. There never was a time when more mass movements driven by high humanitarian ideals were shifting without a thought for God across the face of the earth. Many American religious superiors have seen the unrest in their communities, the defections of people in vows and the compara-tively sudden lack of vocations, as a direct result of what they call the Peace Corps mentality. In the Peace Corps and in its equivalents in other countries (Voluntary Service Overseas in Britain, for example) the religious and potential religious of this generation can see a philosophy in action which is far closer to the precepts of the Christian gospel than most of the social patterns established by the Church; and if the Church cannot learn to follow this example then they will, heedless of official Christian sanctions. Thomas Merton has suggested another reason why, at this particular point of time, the religious world should have begun to move from its fixed positions again. He thinks that those who came to monasticism before the Second World War were comparatively little influenced by thinkers such as Marx and Darwin, Kierkegaard and Nietzsche, Freud and Jung, Adler and Sartre, Heidegger and Teilhard; most of this thought was not only banned from the monastery by the enclosure; it was for-bidden the average Catholic at any stage in his education. The end of the war not only prised open the enclosure a little but it also brought a crop of vocations in men already acquainted with writers who had all 'in one way or another concerned themselves very deeply with the predicament of modern man; with his special needs, his peculiar hopes, his chances of attaining those hopes. . . .'

The cross-fertilisation process is probably going to be taken many stages farther than most Catholics and Protestants can imagine at the moment – or, in many cases, would care to think of. For an attempt has been made to integrate the Christian and the Hindu religious life and it is at present quietly flourishing in the Kurisumala Ashram. This is a monastery in Kerala, in South-west India, founded jointly in 1958 by a Cistercian and a

Benedictine who had gone separately to the country in the hope of establishing some kind of contemplative life there. The Cistercian, the Belgian Dom Francis Mahieu, had already been involved in an experiment at Trichinopoly, in Madras, where two French priests, Father Monchanin and Father le Saux, had started an ashram (the Hindu term for a group of disciples living in community under a spiritual guide) on completely Hindu lines. The two priests had taken Hindu names, becoming Swami Paramarubananda and Swami Abhishiktananda. They had worn the saffron habit of the Hindu monk, had gone barefoot, and lived on a vegetarian diet in small thatched huts. They had worshipped in a chapel designed like a Hindu temple and their Christian liturgy had been in a mixture of Sanskrit, Tamil and Latin. It was far too bold an identification with its local religious culture for Indian Catholics and so it foundered for lack of vocations. But out of it came Kurisumala.

Kerala is a stronghold of that eastern branch of Catholicism, the Syrian Church, and this has added another ingredient to the intriguing mixture that has been made there. When Kurisumala was started:

The Rule of St Benedict was adopted as the basis and it was interpreted according to the strict Cistercian observance. The centre of the monastery's life became the Syrian liturgy with its emphasis on biblical theology. A quiet period of silent prayer varying from five minutes to a quarter of an hour is practised after each liturgical exercise. This is done in Indian fashion by sitting cross-legged on the floor. Other measures have been introduced to conform in general to the pattern of Indian life. The monks go barefoot, eat with their hands while sitting in the cross-legged position, sleep on mats on low wooden beds, and wear the kavi or saffron-coloured dress of the Indian sannyasin. For deeper spiritual contact with Indian tradition, they are studying Indian philosophy and religious systems, and practise some yoga exercises. They are cultivating their lands and developing a dairy farm and a medical dispensary.

There has been a small but steady trickle of vocations. A cynic might well suppose that the adoption of certain local habits of dress, diet and posture is merely a bait in order to proselytise more successfully. The only trouble with this theory is that it discounts the effect of the local environment and culture upon the proselyte's own system, when these are embraced as closely as they have been by the Christian monks of Kurisumala. Already the weightier monastic journals of Christendom have thoughtfully noted comparisons between classical Hindu literature, such as The Upanishads and the Bhagavad-Gita, and their Christian equivalents. And one of the Kurisumala monks, Dom Bede Griffiths, has reported back his own conclusions for the future:

It seems to me that it is the task of the Church in India to bring the light of Christ, of Christian revelation, to bear on this original intuition (of the classical Hindu philosophers), to complete the Vedanta, as it were, by introducing a new point of view. In this way we should not be simply introducing a new doctrine but continuing the work of Sankara, Ramanuja, Madhva and the other doctors of the Vedanta. But this means that we have first to enter into the intuition of the Upanishads, to understand Hindu doctrine as it were from within, and this is surely the work of a contemplative. No amount of conceptual skill will suffice, no attempt to graft St Thomas on to the Vedanta. There must be the discovery within ourselves, in the depths of our own souls, of the Self, the Atman; and what can this be but the discovery of Christ? Thus the study of Hinduism, if it is to bear any fruit, must lead us to a renewal in depth of our own religion, a rediscovery of that mystical presence of Christ in us which lies behind all our theology. But this discovery will be along lines which are indicated by the Hindu tradition.

And though talk of bearing fruit may still have an ominous sound to the cynic, no one ever entered someone else's intuition and came away unmarked.

The purely western religious life has enough problems of its own to sort out before it begins to take any strain which will be imposed if at some time in the future it tries to graft onto itself elements of other religious philosophies. The most formidable one, at present, is the condition of the individual. No one can be sure precisely what has motivated the increasing number of people who have abandoned their vows and walked out of the religious life in the past few years; it is likely that many are not sure themselves. Certainly some will have gone because they do not believe that the world (or God) is adequately served by the religious life in its present state. But many have opted out simply because they themselves can no longer endure the life; and the thing that ought, where it doesn't already, make religious authority ponder very deeply the elements of the life is the fact that so often the defections remove men and women of considerable experience, who have been monks, nuns or friars for several years. They have not gone back to the world after a small flirtation with religion, but after a thorough trial which may have lasted a decade or more. It is possible that this has always been the case and that until comparatively recently we never heard about it; it is rather more likely that until recently the sanctions of the Church seemed so terrible that they deterred anyone from breaking religious vows but the men or women who were past caring about the ultimate fate of their souls. The breach in the enclosure which admitted Freud and Nietzsche, Sartre and Teilhard and the rest also admitted doubts about the terrors promised defectors by the Church. It is the richest irony confronting the Church, both in the microcosmic world of religion and in the world at large, that to have invoked non-Christian thought in a genuine attempt to understand more clearly the Christian vocation on earth has meant enormous disillusionment with Christian practice and sometimes with the faith itelf; has meant, in the Church as a whole, a colossal loss of even nominal membership. It may seem inevitable to the non-Christian, but that doesn't relieve the confusion among the Christians.

The individual pressures which have caused people to leave the religious life in order to save themselves from what they have taken, consciously or not, to be a kind of personal destruction have been against a system which has traditionally been designed quite deliberately to suppress the distinctive quality of the individual. They have been pressures against a concept of obedience which has meant the total renunciation of will. They have been pressures against a concept of chastity which has meant that a demonstration of warmth and affection in any terms the world would recognise has been vilified as something not far short of promiscuity and which has seen to it that behaviour a long, long way short of that has been hallmarked as the norm.

They have meant, at last, that religious have seen themselves too often being moulded in the image not of Christ but of Tennyson's Maud – 'faultily faultless, icily regular, splendidly null.'

So the traditional view of the 'particular friendship' has been increasingly under attack this past two or three years. A pointer to the way ahead has been provided, yet again, by the Petits Frères. Standing pat not on twentieth-century psychology but on the habits of Christ himself, René Voillaume has indicated the impossibility of genuinely loving people in general without burnishing the capacity for love in a deep relationship with one or two in particular.

It is true that the love of friendship which unites us to our Lord also demands that we should love all our brethren in like manner. But this seems obviously impossible, unless indeed we are talking about something other than genuine friendship. The restrictions imposed by human life on earth make it impossible for us to acquire and exhibit feelings of friendship towards any considerable number of our brethren and, *a fortiori*, towards all those who cross our path. How, then, can it be possible for the love of friendship in our Lord's name and expressed towards all men to become the perfect fulfilment of the commandment to love? In fact, however, Jesus does not ask us to acquire a conscious feeling of friendship towards everybody, but to have a heart sufficiently open and humble and alert to others, and above all to be spontaneous enough to be cabable of friendship should it become possible here and now. We must understand the commandment to love and try to obey it in terms of what is possible in our human situation as it actually is, a situation so confined that in reality we are able to have a few friends only. Why should this surprise us? Was not our Lord so restricted by his circumstances on earth that he was unable to have more than a very few men and women as his intimate friends?

A Dominican has pushed the point even further and nearer the knuckle of the religious life. 'In the last resort,' he suggests, 'it is better to run the risk of an occasional scandal than to have a monastery – a choir, a refectory, a recreation room – full of dead men. Our Lord did not say "I am come that ye may have more safety and have it abundantly." Some of us would indeed give anything to feel safe, about our life in this world as in the next, but

In the Baroque splendour of Melk Abbey, high above the Danube in Austria, live a handful of Benedictine monks. *(Helga Schmidt-Glassner)*

The Cistercians had a powerful influence on the economy of medieval England because they were sheep-farmers. Today they still work their own flocks, for they have remained much closer than most orders to their origins. Brother Oliver of Nunraw Abbey in Scotland.
(John Bird)

Part of a life under vows. Trappist monks of Mount St Bernard Abbey, Leicestershire, shell peas for dinner – in community, always in community.
(Mount St Bernard Abbey, Coalville)

Some things have been untouched by time and one of them is the rule that the monk or nun eats from a common board in community as the Anglican sisters of St Mary's Convent, Wantage, England, are doing. *(Trevor Fry)*

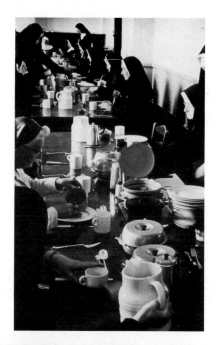

A young novice enjoys the greater freedom and mobility conferred by a bicycle and a shorter habit. *(Rex Features)*

Above A Benedictine monk hard at work in the kitchens of Nashdom Abbey. *Below* Meanwhile two fellow brothers relax with a pipe and a game of cards. *(Pershore and Nashdom Trust Ltd)*

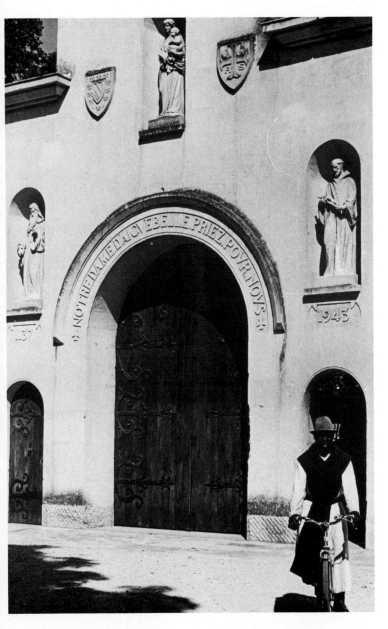

A Trappist monk outside the Cistercian Abbey of Aiguebelle, in France.
(Rex Features; Photo: Frank Monaco)

A novice of the Order of Poor Clares takes the veil in a solemn and moving ceremony. She will wear the bridal dress only once. *(Rex Features)*

Trappist monk at the kitchen sink; Aiguebelle, France. *(Rex Features; Photo: Frank Monaco)*

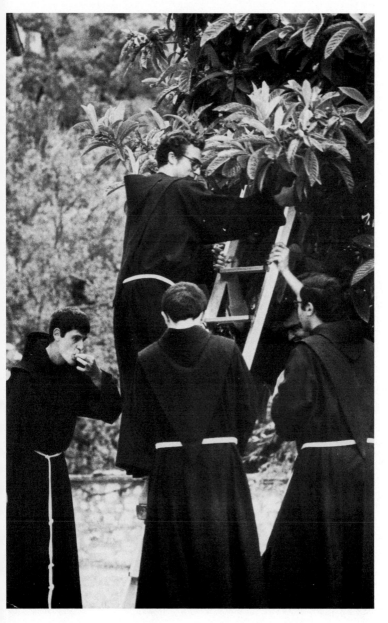

Franciscan friars picking fruit in the orchards of La Certosa.
(Rex Features; Photo: Frank Monaco)

One of the thirty-six nuns from different orders who were brought together for a business course. *(Rex Features; Photo: Peter Brooker)*

we cannot have it both ways: safety or life, we must choose.'

While the choice is being made the pressures continue to build up, the defectors continue to return to the world outside, and some of those remaining turn to psychiatry for salvation. In one case, at Cuernavaca in Mexico, a whole monastery put itself under the psychiatrist, an adventure that ended in its dissolution. It was an attempt by the prior, Dom Gregoire LeMercier, to resolve the tensions and the individual problems of the monastic vocation and it deserved better than its ultimate end. LeMercier is a Belgian who had been professed as a Benedictine at the abbey of Mont-César before the war. After serving as an army chaplain he went, on demobilisation, to Mexico and in 1951 established the monastery of Santa Maria de la Resurreccion near Cuernavaca, in accordance with the primitive Benedictine observance as practised at La Pierre Qui Vire and elsewhere. He was the only European in a community of Mexican Indians.

In 1960 he had an ecstatic vision, 'a host of brilliant, multi-coloured flashes of light, of extreme beauty, followed by a screen over which passed a succession of faces, stopping at one beautiful face radiating goodness. LeMercier began to weep, feeling his own inadequacy before God's love, a curious mixture of defeat, of God controlling him, and of great joy, which lasted several hours.' He called in a Freudian analyst, a Dr Quevedo, whom he knew to be interested in religious questions. After several months of treatment by Quevedo LeMercier felt able to say that 'The long ascesis of psychoanalysis has led me to a spiritual life which I had been unable to reach after thirty years of monastic life, filling me with a joy and confidence which nothing can destroy.' At about the same time it was discovered that he had contracted an operable cancer in his left eye; and medical opinion was that the cancer had begun at about the same time as LeMercier's vision.

LeMercier was so impressed with his general improvement at the hands of Quevedo that he decided to begin group therapy for his monks. It became a part of the novitiate and it was managed not only by Quevedo but also by a woman, Dr Frida Zmud. This was a deliberate choice by LeMercier. He argued that sexuality was too often ignored or suppressed by those offering themselves to the religious life and that confrontation with Dr Zmud on the threshold of their intended vocation would bring them face to face with the issue most crucial to their survival as human beings in the religious life. They would be forced to recognise their degree of sexuality and they would have to decide before they got anywhere near life vows whether this allowed them to cope with existence in a 'homosexual' society. The result of the early confrontations was that a number of professed monks left and returned to the world, sometimes to get married; many novices failed to complete their training. But by 1965, when the psychiatrists had been attending Cuernavaca for four years, thirty monks were in residence and LeMercier claimed that the life of the monastery had become more effective and more harmonious. Departures had diminished. In 1962 fifteen men had left, in 1963 sixteen, in 1964 five, in 1965 two. Vocations were increasing.

The astonishing thing is that the Vatican allowed the experiment to go so far before prohibiting it. The Archbishop of Mexico City had, after all, been calling LeMercier a demon and the Abbot Primate of the Benedictines at the time had said he was a shame upon the order. In fact, in 1961, when the psychiatric treatment had been going for only a few months, the Congregation for Religious had sent two observers to Cuernavaca to find out just what was happening there; it is said that they reported to Rome in LeMercier's favour. It was not until October 1965 that LeMercier received the imperial summons to present himself to Cardinal Ottaviani, at the head of the Curia. He was told that the experiment must end and that he must return to Belgium. He refused and asked that the matter should be put into the hands of the pope. The pope appointed three cardinals to examine the situation. In 1967 they delivered their verdict. LeMercier was to return to Cuernavaca but he was forbidden to dabble in psychiatry again; he was also to carry out spiritual exercises in the abbey of St Jerome as punishment for his obduracy. He did return, but not in the prescribed manner. In June 1967 he announced that he and his monks had renounced their monastic vows, had severed their connection with the Benedictine order, and would in future work in conjunction with the Emaus Psychoanalysis Centre.

The Vatican's verdict against LeMercier suggests not only

alarm at the upheaval that might be caused if psychiatry were let loose across the face of the religious world. It seems to be yet another refusal to look the facts of life straight in the eye. It is one more example of the Catholic Church's disinclination to acknowledge the existence of sex *qua* sex in the lives of its professional man- and woman-power. In the case of religious this is not confined to Roman Catholicism. There is no reason to suppose that, in degree at any rate, the sexual composition of a religious community is much different from that of any other sort; it will contain some who are highly sexed and some whose sexual drive is low; it will include both heterosexuals and homosexuals of different potencies. The fact that most of these at the beginning of their vocation are either unaware of their sexuality or are attempting to ignore it, with the whole weight of religious tradition actively encouraging them to do so, is the one thing that distinguishes them sharply from most other groups of people. Sexuality is not a thing that can be ignored or that can leave the individual unaware indefinitely. It can obviously be repressed, but at some cost. It can doubtless be channelled into something short of full physical expression, but again at some cost, if it is not to cause – in the terms of the religious life – some scandal. The cost of repression in the circumstances is sometimes scandal when sexuality asserts itself beyond control; more often it is an emotional and physical crisis which either causes the individual to abandon vows and walk out or which damages his personality for the rest of his life, turning him at best into something like Tennyson's Maud. A monk I know had to leave his order, with the connivance of his superiors and brethren, after medical and psychiatric treatment, because after many years under vows he had reached this critical point; for much of that time he had suffered a permanent headache; for the twelve months preceding his release he had endured a nightmare every single night and its pattern had always been the same – he or someone else had been killing him. If from the outset of his religious vocation he had been taught to channel his sexual energy in some way short of scandal he might have been able to continue as a monk – as he wanted to do, even when he recognised that he must and could not – with nothing more than a sense of loss; and perhaps the sense of lost sexual outlet is for the religious the imitation of Christ on earth, the small crucifixion which is to be borne without despair.

But all this needs to be recognised and if there is one thoroughly frightening thing about the religious life it is the general failure to recognise sexuality for what it is, for what it can be, and for the part it plays in personality. The most fundamental questions about sex are left unanswered, not only in literature written by religious for religious but in the verbal training of novitiates. What, for example, is the monk to do if he wakes up in the middle of the night bursting with sexual desire? Is he to masturbate? Is he to fling himself on the stone cold floor (as the handiest alternative to St Benedict's nettlebed) in the hope that this will cool his ardour? Or is he merely to seize his breviary and trust that prayer will drive the demon out? A superior, far less inhibited than most, says that every one of these methods has been tried though very few people in religion are prepared to admit the existence of the first – or even of a situation which may require it. Novices in that particular community are advised to try working themselves to exhaustion, or the cold floor, or prayer if need be. They are told that if none of these methods succeeds they will have to masturbate to relieve their tensions. They are also told that if by the end of the novitiate masturbation is still the only way of coping with their sex they had better pack up and return to the world. One cannot be sure, but one gets the impression that very few novices elsewhere have ever been given such straightforward advice. And from no one else have I ever heard it suggested that life vows will one day have to be scrapped altogether in favour of renewable vows over much shorter periods, purely because of the sexual problem.

An unflinching look at sex is the chief need of the religious life if the problems of the individual's condition are to be resolved. At the same time the whole ethos requires re-examination if monasticism and other forms of religious practice are not to founder slowly through lack of vocations from people who do not believe that these can any longer serve a valuable Christian purpose in their present shape. Again, this is the problem of the Church as a whole, in miniature. The Church has not yet shaken off the double standard applied to the world by St Augustine of Hippo, and the religious life has been pickled in it even more deeply than the secular. Augustine was not the first Christian to insist on it; Clement of Alexandria advanced the theory at the start of the third century, two hundred years before him; but Augustine was its supreme exponent, particularly in his book *City of God*, which was written under the influence of Christian Rome's capitulation to the barbaric Alaric in AD 410. Its opening words set the tone for what is to come. 'That most glorious society and celestial city of God's faithful is partly seated in the course of these declining times, wherein he that liveth by faith is a pilgrim amongst the wicked.' From there Augustine takes some time to get to the heart of his philosophy. But in the twenty-eighth chapter of his fourteenth volume he writes:

Two loves therefore have given origin to these two cities – self-love in contempt of God unto the earthly; love of God in contempt of one's self to the heavenly. The first seeketh the glory of men and the latter desires God only, as the testimony of the conscience, the greatest glory. That glories in itself and this in God. That exalteth itself in its own glory; this saith to God 'My glory and the lifter-up of my head'. That boasteth of the ambitious conquerors led by the lust of sovereignty; in this everyone serveth other in charity. . . . (In the earthly city) the wise men follow either the goods of the body, or mind, or both, living according to the flesh, and such as might know God honoured him not as God, but became vain in their own imaginations, and their foolish heart was darkened; . . . but in the other, this heavenly city, there is no wisdom of men but only the piety that serveth the true God and expecteth a reward in the society of the holy angels and men, that God may be all in all.

If any five sentences have fixed the Christian Church, and especially its religious life, in an attitude of superiority over the rest of mankind for the last fifteen hundred years then those are they. For the Church needed no pressure to identify itself with the heavenly city and inside the Church the progression was continued; the religious state was held to be more estimable than the secular, the contemplative higher than the active, the celibate worthier than the married. A number of biblical texts have been adduced to support some of these theories – St Paul's apparent penchant for celibacy and the Martha–Mary passage in Luke among them – by Christian philosophers ever since. But the arguments have always been made within the framework built by St Augustine, who in some of his other writings enlarged upon specific points. 'The mother,' he wrote elsewhere, 'will have a lower place in heaven than the daughter, because she is married, while her daughter is a virgin. . . . Both will be in heaven, but the one as a bright star, the other as a dim one.' This is a philosophy which has been challenged from time to time; St Thomas Aquinas insisted that the monastic life was no more than one of many ways of striving for perfection, not perfection itself or the only way to perfection; every word of Charles de Foucauld, René Voillaume, Roger Schutz and many other religious writing today makes the same point. Yet the philosophy has remained as the basis of the religious life, has been accepted as its justification. When, in 1950, representatives of all forms of Catholic religious life met in Rome for their first general congress they called themselves the General Congress on the States of Perfection. When, in 1967, the BBC made a television film of the Trappist monastery at Nunraw in Scotland, an old monk told his interviewer that he wouldn't stay in the cloister three days if he didn't think he was thereby going to heaven. A booklet which the Benedictines of Buckfast Abbey offer the tourists refers to 'the more perfect life of the monastery'. A French religious writes of 'the white-hot Christianity of monastic life'.

St Augustine is no longer good enough in a world which is no longer prepared to accept self-assertion as the only evaluation of either man or institution; which prefers to make its own judgements, and to make them on performance alone. Over the past decade the Church's realisation of this has quickened; it will be one overpowering reason why it has attended of late to the Bultmanns, the Bonhoeffers and the Teilhards, who much earlier than the official body of the Church sought to reorientate Christianity in a twentieth-century context; why it has thrown up more recently the writings of men like Kung and Robinson, working with the same end in view; why, within the sphere of Roman Catholic influence, many of its leaders were seen to be clamouring for adjustment to the age they live in at the Vatican Council.

Faithful Christians call all this the movement of the Holy Spirit, while the agnostic host sees it as an accommodation to a world which the Church can no longer hope to influence unless its ways are mended. Whichever it is, movement and accommodation are unmistakably there. They are also present within the religious life. It is being seen increasingly both by secular and religious Christians that the doctrines of Augustine must be replaced, that the Church's claims must henceforth rest upon a different theology, based less upon a notion of perfection than upon one of vision, less upon an attitude of superiority than upon one of service. Gradually the theology is being hammered out; but it has not yet been formulated into a code which the Church as a whole can assimilate. The question for religious, no less than for the Church of which they are a part, is whether it can be done fast enough before the whole structure crumbles irreparably. An American has already dared to suggest that his order, the Dominican, will have disappeared inside twenty years. The temptation, for the religious as well as for the Church, is merely to make adjustments to the existing order of things, either as a concession to popular demand or to provide a breathing space before a thorough overhaul. Yet the writing on the wall is too emphatic to allow either any longer. Its tale for the Church in general is one of increasing disobedience to the most rigid rules (in, for example, the growing number of Roman Catholics who practise non-Catholic methods of birth control) and of mounting unconcern for the more lenient requirements (in the dwindling congregations of Protestantism). Its tale for the religious life is one of scanty vocations and of vows being abandoned at a rate unheard of before. A few turns of the spanner in the religious works are not going to correct that. There must be, as Bishop Huyghe has pointed out, a complete re-reading of the Gospels rather than a return to the ideals expressed by the founders of religious orders.

There is a resistance to the notion of radical change in the religious life; there was bound to be. There is no reason to suppose that the reformers, who may be among the most articulate of religious, are anything but a small minority. There are cries for change from half a dozen countries of Europe and from the United States, but they have not been heard so far from

Spain, Italy or Ireland. A few years ago the Abbot of Montserrat was deposed on orders from Rome, for speaking out once too often against General Franco; which may be a straw in the wind of general change, or which may mean nothing more than the fact that the abbot was a Catalan and therefore a dabbler in purely local politics. And even where the religious radicals are reaching for their battering rams and their sapping equipment there are brothers in Christ preparing to withstand the siege. 'I know of enclosed nuns more than a thousand kilometres away from Paris,' writes a horrified Frenchman, 'who are so well informed about what goes on in the world that they find flats in the capital for their friends, who cannot succeed in doing so by their own efforts. The altruism which they display in this form is assuredly not the end for which they were enclosed.' That man would not only exorcise property advertisements from the convent but newspapers in general and intellectual preoccupations in particular, for 'the monastery is not a "thinking shop". To make of one's solitude the means, not of a truly spiritual life, but of an intellectual life, is one of the subtlest ways of adulterating it.' The opponents to change rarely express themselves as bluntly or as crudely as that. More frequently they appeal vaguely to history and to the sense of continuity which embellishes so much that is beautiful and awe-inspiring in the religious life. An Anglican contemplative monk says that 'Conservatism, then, as a looking back to past tradition, is a necessary element of monasticism; otherwise it could not remain true to itself.' An English Benedictine writes that 'any work which rules out manual labour and also takes monks habitually away from the enclosure and the choir can hardly be called Benedictine.' This is demonstrably true but it dodges the main question at issue, which is whether Benedictinism – among other forms of religious life – has anything more to contribute to the evolution of Christianity; whether it ought to be modified even more than it has already been, to a point at which it can no longer be called Benedictine. An Anglican has suggested that a particular difficulty facing reformers of the religious life within the Church of England is that in most of its communities there are still one or two people who can remember the founders and who see any change at all as a positive betrayal of someone they knew, admired and followed obediently. Judging by the regularity with which St Benedict's name is invoked without any supporting argument it sometimes seems as if many monks of his order can claim, across fourteen centuries, a similar acquaintance.

There is resistance to reform which speaks out point-blank against it. There is also acquiescence to the idea of reform which seems to speak of nothing more daring or dangerous than adjustments. No one has made more forward-sounding noises in print than the American Trappist monk Thomas Merton. His view of what ought to happen next to monasticism was set out in a paper which has circulated widely in religious circles in the United States and elsewhere since it was written in 1964.

The adaptation required by our time will not be effected by simple tightening up of the organisational structure and increased centralisation of control. On the contrary, more than anywhere else, a relative decentralisation would seem to be needed in the monastic order. Yet at the same time the idea of the Ordo Monasticus would seem to call for closer and more active inter-relationship between the various monastic communities of all the families now existing: Benedictine, Cistercian, Camaldolese etc. (It might be well for a change in legislation that would permit a change of stability allowing transfer from one of these families to another with no more complication than is now required to transfer from one monastery to another within the same order). Within the Order it should be recognised that different monasteries in diverse situations will have needs that greatly vary. Instead of detailed legislation in the matter of usages imposed on everyone, there should be greater respect for local differences, and the local abbot should be able to regulate details of horarium and observance for his own community. . . . Everything should be done to favour and encourage those who seek to maintain and to increase the silence and solitude of the monastic life, and its primitive simplicity. . . . Monastic silence should be maintained, along with enclosure, separation from the world etc., but in a somewhat different spirit; more flexible, less rigid, less forced. To this end, individual monks should have greater freedom in going apart from the others to read and meditate in their lectio time, the problem of machines in and near the monastery must be frankly confronted, and recreation should never become a formal observance. There is on the part of many monks an earnest and reasonable desire for experiments in a simpler, more primitive and more solitary form of monastic life. Furthermore, the insistence on absolute unification and perfect conformity of all in one form of observance should not be carried to the point where it may in fact interfere with the development of an individual monk who may have special needs; e.g., for greater solitude. Our cenobitic life should normally open up to a life of deeper solitude. For the sake of 'détente' and in rightful concern for human needs of modern man, which constitute a general problem, the following should be considered in general as *not acceptable solutions* – habitual use of TV in a monastic common-room; habitual smoking; recreation in the sense of conversation and play together; habitual use of cinema and radio in a common-room. But the following might be considered acceptable in accordance with the situation of individual houses – swimming; reading of works of literature (including novels of genuine value, under proper guidance); long walks (alone) in forest or countryside; ski-ing, horseback riding, boating, fishing. These of course would not normally be allowed to interfere with the obligations of the monastic life (including manual labour) but time could be made for them on certain feasts. General use of such recreation would not be encouraged but only special cases. Also the local abbot should allow his library to be suitably furnished with reviews which will enable the monk to keep up not only with current developments in theology and philosophy but also to get a general view of world trends. But habitual reading of newspapers and topical magazines should not be allowed. Examples of such magazines as would be permissible: *Etudes, Blackfriars, The Commonweal*.

There are many in the religious life today who will regard that as too radical for words, as a pollution of the pure, the authentic stream of monasticism; St Benedict, after all, would have had no truck with keeping abreast of current affairs in the world. There are many who will regard it as a very proper step forward, thoroughly in keeping with the times we live in without losing sight of the foundation on which the monastic life stands; a greater respect for local differences and a recognition that individuals have special needs do, after all, have a fine mid-twentieth-century ring. But there are some who will see it as no more than a half-hearted concession to popular noises off, in which tradition is not really undermined, in which nothing is really changed; and when there is to be no 'conversation and play' between brothers in recreation, when literature may only be read 'under proper guidance', one of the fundamental defects of the religious life for the individual will quite clearly remain unaltered.

It is difficult for an outsider, unburdened by the tradition, unconditioned by the life, not to accept the last diagnosis. Within the relatively narrow confines of monasticism, which is only a small part of the religious life, something much more drastic seems to be called for. This may mean a change in which some of its most distinctive marks – permanent or semi-permanent enclosure, a life of regularity, a strictly codified régime – will disappear forever. For it seems fairly certain that the present shortage of manpower will become more acute if things stay even as Thomas Merton would have them. Even his modified monasticism is so completely and unattractively at odds with the world, in terms of idealism and civilisation as well as hedonism, that it is very difficult to see where the next generation of recruits is to come from; they will have been reared on a variety of Christian doctrine which takes much greater account of the world as it is than the present one. And it is precisely because they have been thrown up by the twentieth century, and not by the nineteenth or the sixth, because they have genuinely tried to assess human needs in the twentieth century and to supply them, within the framework of Christ's teaching, that the Petits Frères, the Taizé Communauté, the secular institutes and the worker-priests seem to point most clearly the way ahead for the religious life as a whole.

It will engage more closely with the underprivileged world than it already does. Instead of sending a wealth of its manpower to non-Christian countries in order to convert these to the faith it will spend its people more freely in meeting obvious social needs at home; and where it does go on foreign mission it will regard conversion as a happy by-product of its primary task, which will be to help others to achieve health, education and dignity. It will close any gaps that remain in its social services; like the one in the Church of England, where no religious community cares for old, sick and lonely men, though several have been founded to look after women. It will make much greater use than now of an enormous asset in the potential mobility of its members, who are without the ties and obligations of family and who can drop everything on the instant and take up any job; some religious may not savour the comparison but they can be flung into some long-term emergency situation as effectively as the Salvation Army is apt to respond to brief disasters.

This may seem to be a prescription for active communities alone, leaving the contemplatives locked in some timeless solitude of their own. But if Voillaume and Schutz and the other radicals of the past few years have made two things very clear indeed, and one of these is the need for greater rather than less engagement in the world as it is, the other is the futility of separating the contemplative and the active life. Even the outsider who cannot understand the processes of prayer must recognise its significance in a Christian context; at the very least it is the channel of communication with the source of inspiration. It may also be, as contemplatives maintain, in itself an effective instrument upon the world; or a duty, with a quota per shift to be fulfilled by divine requirement. On the first count alone, the inspirational, the most intense form of prayer life in pure contemplation without the immediate distractions of work to be done and people to be seen is of obvious benefit. On the second count, the instrumental, it is difficult to see how it can be fully effective if contemplation is conducted in the vacuum conditions traditional to this vocation; a man can only pray intelligently for a world he is well aware of and he cannot be well aware of it insulated behind permanently closed doors. And if there is indeed a divine requirement for prayer then somehow it will have to be sustained by the community. The insistence by the most worldly actives, the Petits Frères, of attaching a hermitage to each community, to which individuals can go for contemplation in solitude at regular intervals, surely suggests a pattern for the future for the whole religious life. This is a pattern in which no exclusively contemplative communities will remain, or exclusively active ones either. Instead, all religious communities will be intensively engaged in the world's work; they will also have at their core the hermitage in which a proportion of their manpower will always reside, for the inspiration of intense prayer, for the application of prayer, for the duty of prayer; and while for a few individuals temperament may mean permanent or semi-permanent residence in the hermitage, for the majority it will be a place of periodic visitation.

Within the past decade a Benedictine has written that 'Monasticism has two things to offer to civilisation of the future: sanity and hope. By stressing the right order of values, monasticism, in a world of unbalance, stands for sanity. By keeping alive, in a world of mutual mistrust, an awareness of man's dignity and of his relationship in charity to the rest of the human race, monasticism brings with it hope.' More recently still the Belgian Cardinal Suenens has said of all forms of religious life that 'At a time when Communism is trying to impose by force a new social order which destroys the spiritual personality of man, it is more than ever important that the Church should be able to offer the world the picture of living communities, where a voluntary communism reigns, based on divine worship and brotherly love, as a foretaste of what in many aspects a society open to social Christianity and faithful to the Gospel would be.' At the moment both aspirations are within the realm of the possible rather than the probable. For monasticism badly needs to revise its human values if it is to stand for sanity; the way to sanity is not to be found by treating adults as if they were children, by prohibiting literature except under ominously proper guidance and by forbidding a free flow of conversation in the common-room. An awareness of man's dignity is not to be achieved by keeping mankind in general at even half-arm's length. It might be demonstrated more effectively than it is now not only by going out into the world more frequently but by bringing the world into the religious life more indiscriminately. If a community is to be a foretaste of a society open to social Christianity then it might well consider the possibility of including in its membership some regarded as outrageous misfits in the world outside; it will first have to be sure that it is itself, in human terms, balanced and sane and mature enough if it is to ease the misfit rather than be disturbed by him. And if a community is to exemplify voluntary communism then it will have to live voluntarily from start to finish; it will not have to maintain its membership under threat of penalty or even under the psychological pressure imposed by a permanent vow. It may well be that the East will be summoned to redress an imbalance in the

West at just this point, by way of Kurisumala and other places where Christian religious are absorbing something of Hindu and Buddhist philosophy. The Buddhist monastery is not just a place to which holy men are attached for life; it is also a school to which the faithful resort for various periods at a particular stage of their religious and human development.

Traditionalists will doubtless boggle at this prospect. They may comfort themselves with the thought that hardly any of it is utterly new. There is a precedent in the history of the religious life for almost all these changes. The Franciscans, after all, attempted for a time and up to a point to live at the lowest level of the people they were preaching to. The teaching and nursing canonesses of the eighth century lived in chastity and obedience while in community, but very often left to get married. The active community with a contemplative core and most of its population shifting from one to the other at intervals would be no more than a repetition of what Robert of Arbrissel attempted with his Order of Fontrevault at the end of the eleventh century. The traditionalists, however, will have to accept the fact that if reform takes this tack it will not be because anyone is modelling himself on the Franciscans, the canonesses or Fontrevault. It will be because the reformers intuitively believe this to be the most Christian course from their reading of the Gospels. And this is what distinguishes the present religious reformers from most of those who have preceded them.

The survival of the Christian religious life seems to depend on changes of this magnitude. But, then, so does the survival of Christianity itself. This may be an exciting time for some religious to be living in, for the ones who have fretted for too long under the impositions and pallid unworldliness of the old traditions and who can see the monolith beginning to move in the right direction at last. It is a time of some despair for others who are too old or ill equipped by temperament and training to accommodate themselves to more than small changes. It is not a comfortable time for any of them. The strains of the whole religious world at the moment are crystallised in a recent sentence written by an American. 'One older Jesuit in California reported to me tearfully that, as he sits down for meals in common with his fellow Jesuits, an abyss separates him from them, that the soldierly unity in the common cause of the defence of the Faith that has always knit into one the Companions of Jesus, has simply ceased to exist.' It is impossible for the outsider not to be saddened when he thinks what will have gone from the religious life by the time that abyss has been sealed and those ranks have been closed again, and are turned in another direction. Does it really mean that one day, before very long, there will be no more haunting beauty of Trappist monks pacing, in the dress of fourteen centuries ago, silently along a Gothic cloister? Does it perhaps mean that a little later the spellbinding liturgy of Taizé will be heard only on a plastic disc or a magnetised tape and not be seen and felt for the mysterious drama that it is? Can it be that monks and nuns and other religious will be indistinguishable from other human beings eventually, except in their community life and in their quiet profession of poverty, obedience and chastity for a part of their days and occasionally for a lifetime?

For although the form, the understanding and the duration of the threefold profession will change and the shape of community will alter, these alone, in their essentials, are the sure survivors of this turning-point in history. The worker-priests and some members of secular institutes have shown that some people can fulfil the ideals of the new social Christianity in isolation from their fellows. But not everybody can manage without the support of a closely integrated community; as Kierkegaard said, there will always be individuals with that need. The threefold profession in community is almost the definition of the religious life. It is also the reason why the world in general will always regard the life as supremely irrational, if not derisory. It represents, as a cold-blooded choice, the greatest sacrifice that a fulfilled human being can make. But people with an ideal of service driving them on can often give everything they have, in defiance of ridicule and contempt. And a man finding his way to salvation must sometimes fly in the face of reason.

BIBLIOGRAPHY

I should think that several hundred books – at least several hundred – with some bearing on the religious life have been written by now. The ones below are merely those I have read from cover to cover. The list includes all books referred to by title only in the Chapter source notes.

AMERICAN CATHOLIC EXODUS edited by John O'Connor (London: Chapman, 1968, and Washington: Corpus Books).

THE BENEDICTINE IDEA by Dom Hubert van Zeller OSB (London: Burns Oates, 1959).

BROTHERS OF MEN by René Voillaume (London: Darton, Longman and Todd, 1966).

THE CALL OF THE CLOISTER by Peter F. Anson (London: SPCK, 1964).

THE CALL OF THE DESERT by Peter F. Anson (London: SPCK, 1964).

THE COLLECTED WORKS OF ST JOHN OF THE CROSS edited by Kieran Kavanaugh OCD and Otilio Rodriguez OCD (London: Nelson, 1967, and New York: Doubleday, 1964).

THE COMPLETE MONKS by Dom Denys Rutledge OSB (London: Routledge and Kegan Paul, 1966).

CONJECTURES OF A GUILTY BYSTANDER by Thomas Merton (London: Burns Oates, 1968).

CONTEMPLATIVE NUNS SPEAK edited by Bernard Bro OP (London: Chapman, 1963, and Baltimore; Helicon).

THE DESERT MY DWELLING PLACE by Elizabeth Hamilton (London: Hodder & Stoughton, 1968).

DYNAMIQUE DU PROVISOIRE by Roger Schutz (Les Presses de Taizé, 1965).

GOD'S HIGHWAYS; THE RELIGIOUS LIFE AND THE SECULAR INSTITUTES by J. Perinelle OP (Blackfriars, 1958).

I CHOOSE THE CLOISTER by Rosemary Howard-Bennett (London: Hodder & Stoughton, 1966 edition).

I LEAP OVER THE WALL by Monica Baldwin (London: Hamilton, 1949)

INTRODUCTION TO SPIRITUALITY by Louis Bouyer (New York: Desclee Co., 1963).

THE LIFE OF A NUN by Françoise Vandermeersch (London: Chapman, 1967)

THE LIFE OF RAYMOND RAYNES by Nicholas Mosley (London: Hodder & Stoughton, 1963 edition).

LIVING TODAY FOR GOD by Roger Schutz (Baltimore: Helicon, 1963).

LOVE OR CONSTRAINT; PSYCHOLOGICAL ASPECTS OF RELIGIOUS EDUCATION by Marc Oraison (London: Burns Oates, 1959).

MATURITY IN THE RELIGIOUS LIFE by John J. Evoy SJ and Van F. Christoph SJ (New York: Sheed and Ward, 1965).

THE MEANING OF THE MONASTIC LIFE by Louis Bouyer, Cong Orat. (London: Burns Oates, 1955).

THE MONASTIC ORDER IN ENGLAND by David Knowles (London: Cambridge University Press, 1941 edition).

MONASTIC RENEWAL by Dom Columba Cary-Elwes (New York: Herder, 1966).

MONKS AND CIVILISATION by Jean Decarreaux (London: Allen & Unwin, 1964).

THE NEW NUNS edited by Sister Charles Borromeo CSC (London: Sheed & Ward, 1968).

THE NUN IN THE WORLD by Cardinal Suenens (London: Burns Oates, rev. edition, 1966).

OBEDIENCE edited by Père Plé (London: Blackfriars, 1953).

THE PARK VILLAGE SISTERHOOD by Thomas Jay Williams and Allan Walter Campbell (London: SPCK, 1965).

PRAYER by Hans Urs von Balthasar (London: Chapman, 1961).

PRIEST AND WORKER by Henri Perrin (London: Macmillan, 1965, New York: Holt, Reinhart & Winston Inc.).

THE RELIGIOUS LIFE by Sister Edna Mary Dss. CSA (London: Penguin, 1968).

THE RELIGIOUS ORDERS IN ENGLAND, 3 volumes by David Knowles (London: Cambridge University Press, 1955, 1955 and 1959 editions).

RELIGIOUS ORDERS IN THE MODERN WORLD, a symposium edited by Mgr Gerard Huyghe (London: Chapman, 1965 and New York: Newman Press).

THE RELIGIOUS ORDERS OF MEN by Jean Canu (London: Burns Oates, 1960).

THE RELIGIOUS VOCATION by R. M. Benson (Oxford: Mowbray, 1939).

RENOUVEAU COMMUNAUTAIRE ET UNITÉ CHRÉTIENNE by Annie Perchenet (Paris: Mame, 1967).

THE RISE OF PROTESTANT MONASTICISM by Francois Biot OP (Baltimore: Helicon, 1963).

THE RULE OF ST BENEDICT translated and edited by Dom Justin McCann OSB (London: Burns Oates, 1963 edition).

THE RULE OF TAIZÉ (Les Presses de Taizé).

SAINT BENEDICT by St Gregory the Great (being a new translation of the second book of the *Dialogues* by Dom Justin McCann, published by Princethorpe Priory, Rugby, 1941).

SECULAR INSTITUTES by Gabriel Reidy OFM (London: Burns Oates, 1962).

SEEDS OF THE DESERT by René Voillaume (London: Burns Oates, 1964).

THE SEVEN STOREY MOUNTAIN by Thomas Merton (New York: New American Library, 1948).

THE SILENT LIFE by Thomas Merton (Dublin: Clonmore & Reynolds, 1957).

THE SILENT REBELLION by Donald M. Allchin (London: SCM Press, 1958).

THE SPIRITUAL EXERCISES by Ignatius Loyola, translated by Fr T. Corbishley SJ (London: Burns Oates, 1963).

TEILHARD DE CHARDIN a biography by Rober Speaight (London: Collins, 1967).

TENSIONS AND CHANGE by Mgr Gerard Huyghe (London: Chapman, 1965 and New York: Newman Press).

A TIME TO KEEP SILENCE by Patrick Leigh Fermor (London: Murray, 1957).

LA TRAPPE IN ENGLAND by a Religious of Holy Cross Abbey (London: Burns Oates, 1946).

UNANIMITÉ DANS LE PLURALISME by Roger Schutz (Les Presses de Taizé, 1966).

A VALIANT VICTORIAN by anonymous authors among the Sisters of the Church (Oxford: Mowbray, 1964).

THE VISION OF GOD by K. E. Kirk (New York: Harper Torchbooks, 1966 edition).

THE WATERS OF SILENCE by Thomas Merton (London: Hollis and Carter, 1950).

WITNESS AND CONSECRATION by Sr Jeanne D'Arc OP (London: Chapman, 1967).

The most valuable reference work I have consulted is:

THE NEW CATHOLIC ENCYCLOPEADIA (New York: McGraw-Hill, ©
1967 by Catholic University of America, Washington D.C.).

Other useful ones are:

ANNUARIO PONTIFICIO (Vatican annually).

DIRECTORY OF RELIGIOUS ORDERS, CONGREGATIONS AND
SOCIETIES OF GREAT BRITAIN AND IRELAND (London: Burns
Oates, annually).

GUIDE TO THE RELIGIOUS COMMUNITIES OF THE ANGLICAN
COMMUNION (Oxford: Mowbray, 1962).

A GUIDE TO THE RELIGIOUS LIFE (London: Chapman, 1965).

Many religious communities publish their own periodicals. The ones I
have kept a regular eye on include:

C.R. (Community of the Resurrection), F.L.G. LETTER (Community of
the Love of God), SITIO (Benedictine nuns of Burnham Abbey),
NASHDOM ABBEY RECORD; all of which are produced by Anglicans.
Among Catholics there are PAX (Prinknash Abbey), AMPLEFORTH
JOURNAL, DOWNSIDE REVIEW, NEW BLACKFRIARS (English Domini-
cans), THE MONTH (English Jesuits), THE AYLESFORD REVIEW
(English Carmelites). There are several national or international reli-
gious reviews – MONASTIC STUDIES, REVIEW FOR RELIGIOUS, THE
AMERICAN BENEDICTINE REVIEW, LA VIE SPIRITUELLE, COLLEC-
TEANA CISTERCIENSIA, NOTES.

There are two or three other reviews which regularly contain
information about the religious world – HERDER CORRESPONDENCE,
NEW CHRISTIAN and (quite the most prolific and most reliable source of
statistical information) PRO MUNDI VITA.

Some fiction has been written around the religious life. Two pieces
which are better than most are:

THE TWO NUNS by Ann Huré (René Juillard, 1962 and Macdonald,
1964).

FOUND WANTING by Joseph Martindale (New Authors, 1967).

Finally, there is now a fair amount of Gregorian chant and other liturgical
music from religious communities available on gramophone records.
Three discs I would not wish to lose are:

GREGORIAN CHANT – MISSA VIII (DE ANGELIS) CUM CREDO III sung
by the German Benedictine monks of the Abbey of St Martin, Beuron
(Archive EPA 37112).

PSAUMES-CHORALS sung by the Taizé Communauté (Edition Studio SM – SM 4509).

MISSA LUBA, a Congolese Mass sung by an African choir trained by a Belgian missionary priest, which catches the mood (Latin words, *very* African music) of local free expression referred to on pp. 166–7 in Chapter 5 (Philips RL 7592).

SOURCE NOTES

Details of books not cited in full here are given in the bibliography. The author and publishers are grateful to all copyright-holders for their permission to reproduce material from other works.

CHAPTER 1
Page
19, line 23   UNANIMITÉ DANS LE PLURALISME, pp. 22–3
22, line 38   RULE OF TAIZÉ, p. 63
23, line 32   IBID, p. 71
23, line 37   TAIZÉ; COMMUNAUTÉ ET UNITÉ (Les Presses de Taizé), p. 10
24, line 30   THE RISE OF PROTESTANT MONASTICISM, p. 86
25, line 18   RULE OF TAIZÉ, p. 52
30, line 7   UNANIMITÉ DANS LE PLURALISME, p. 20
30, line 33   IBID, p. 56
31, line 24   IBID, p. 16
31, line 31   IBID, p. 49

CHAPTER 2
33, line 15   THE CALL OF THE DESERT, p. 12
34, line 19   ST MATTHEW'S GOSPEL, XIX, 21
34, line 22   IBID, XIX, 12
37, line 17   THE CALL OF THE DESERT, p. 29
37, line 30   SAINT BENEDICT, prologue
37, line 38   IBID, p. 14
38, line 5   IBID, p. 14
38, line 31   THE RULE OF ST BENEDICT, Chapter 1
38, line 35   IBID
38, line 38   IBID
39, line 8   IBID, Chapter 2
39, line 10   IBID, Chapter 33
39, line 37   IBID, Chapter 2
41, line 5   THE RELIGIOUS ORDERS IN ENGLAND, Vol. 1, p. 292

41, line 13   THE MONASTIC ORDER IN ENGLAND, p. 305
47, line 16   ST MATTHEW'S GOSPEL, X, 7–10
48, line 23   A HISTORY OF EUROPE by H. A. L. Fisher (London:
               Collins, Fontana, 1960, and Boston: Houghton Mifflin,
               p. 280
 5, line 4   THE RISE OF PROTESTANT MONASTICISM, p. 63
54, line 38   THE RELIGIOUS ORDERS OF MEN, p. 97
57, line 6   IBID, p. 112
59, line 25   ENGLISH ECCENTRICS by Edith Sitwell (London: Arrow
               Books, 1960. By permission of Denis Dobson), p. 34
59, line 34   IBID, p. 35
60, line 22   THE PARK VILLAGE SISTERHOOD, p. 3
61, line 10   IBID, p. 22
61, line 15   IBID, p. 25
63, line 9   THE CALL OF THE CLOISTER, p. 64

CHAPTER 3
68, line 33   THE LIFE OF RAYMOND RAYNES, p. 38
69, line 15   RULE OF THE COMMUNITY OF THE RESURRECTION,
               p. 5
70, line 31   REPORT OF THE ROYAL COMMISSION ON RITUAL
               (1867), Appendix B, p. 123
73, line 38   THE CHURCH OF ENGLAND by Paul Ferris (London:
               Gollancz, 1962), p. 197
74, line 20   THE CALL OF THE CLOISTER, p. 189
77, line 16   KIERKEGAARD'S JOURNALS (London: Collins, Fontana,
               1958), p. 130
78, line 1   THE RISE OF PROTESTANT MONASTICISM, p. 97
80, line 35   WHAT IS THE IONA COMMUNITY? by T. R. Morton,
               published by the Iona Community, p. 3
82, line 6   Figures from PRO MUNDI VITA, No. 19, 1967
84, line 11   BROTHERS OF MEN, p. 13 (The Biblical quotation is Luke
               chapter 14, verses 12–14)
86, line 29   IBID, p. 143
88, line 33   SECULAR INSTITUTES, p. 82
90, line 32   THE NUN IN THE WORLD, p. 30
90, line 38   NOTES, Dec. 1966, p. 50
91, line 6   NEW CATHOLIC ENCYCLOPAEDIA, Vol. 13, p. 674
92–3   Apart from the figures quoted from ANNUARIO PONTIFI-
               CIO and the BENEDICTINE CATALOGUE, all statistics on
               these pages are from PRO MUNDI VITA, No. 18, 1967;

PRO MUNDI VITA, No. 10, 1966, or THE NUN IN THE WORLD, pp. 30–1.

93, line 21   TENSIONS AND CHANGE, p. 45

93, line 29   NEW BLACKFRIARS, April 1967, p. 375

93, line 33   The decline among Anglican women and the rise in men was noted in an article by Mark Gibbard SSJE, NEW CHRISTIAN, April 7, 1966.

93, line 37   Survey by Fr Vincent Strudwick SSM. Results privately circulated.

94, line 17   THE NUN IN THE WORLD, p. 117

95, line 3   RELIGIOUS ORDERS IN THE MODERN WORLD, pp. 123–4

95, line 26   TENSIONS AND CHANGE, p. xii

96, line 4   HERDER CORRESPONDENCE, Vol. 2, No. 18, Aug. 1965

96, line 21   TENSIONS AND CHANGE, p. 41

97, line 23   DE ACCOMMODATA RENOVATIONE VITAE RELIGIOSAE (London: Catholic Truth Society, 1965), p. 7

97, line 37   Questionnaire appears in full as Appendix 4.

98, line 32   Figures from NEWSWEEK, Dec. 25, 1967, and TIME, Feb. 9, 1968

99, line 1   MONASTIC RENEWAL, p. 32

99, line 23   DE ACCOMMODATA, p. 18

CHAPTER 4

106, line 33   Figures from NEW BLACKFRIARS, April 1967, pp. 370–80

108, line 19   Figures from BENEDICTINE YEARBOOK (Ampleforth Abbey, 1967)

117, line 7   PRIEST AND WORKER, p. 192

117, line 32   Figure from NEW CHRISTIAN, June 15, 1967

118, line 14   RULE OF ST BENEDICT, Chapter 49

120, line 14   MONASTIC RENEWAL, p. 189

120, line 36   Inquiry reported in GOD'S HIGHWAYS, p. 290

121, line 10   SITIO, July 1959

122, line 5   Constitions of the Community of the Glorious Ascension, pp. 19–20

123, line 35   LA VIE SPIRITUELLE, July 1967

124, line 9   Quoted in a monastic journal which has asked to remain anonymous

130, line 35   COMMUNITY OF ST LAURENCE NEWSLETTER, No. 16, Easter 1966

133, line 26   NASHDOM ABBEY RECORD, No. 36, Winter 1967

134, line 27   THE RELIGIONS VOCATION, p. 310

CHAPTER 5
138, line 12   NEW BLACKFRIARS, April 1967
139, line 3   BROTHERS OF MEN, p. 79
139, line 24   THE MEANING OF THE MONASTIC LIFE, p. 130
140, line 1   INSIDE THE CLOISTER (Buckfast Abbey Publications),
                p. 9
140, line 31   F.L.G. LETTER, Feb. 1966, p. 6
141, line 18   CONTEMPLATIVE NUNS SPEAK, p. 220
141, line 25   HISTORICAL SKETCHES by J. H. Newman (London:
                Pickering), Vol. 2, p. 452
141, line 28   THE BENEDICTINE IDEA, p. 31
141, line 34   F.L.G. LETTER, March 1966, p. 3
142, line 2   IBID, Jan. 1966, p. 2
143, line 18   INTRODUCTION TO SPIRITUALITY, p. 93
144, line 24   SPIRITUAL EXERCISES, par. 47
144, line 29   IBID, par. 48
145, line 32   INTRODUCTION TO SPIRITUALITY, p. 68
146, line 2   IBID, p. 69
146, line 23   COLLECTED WORKS OF ST JOHN OF THE CROSS,
                pp. 68–9
147, line 31   IBID, p. 113
148, line 7   IBID, p. 373
148, line 32   INTRODUCTION TO SPIRITUALITY, p. 43
149, line 33   CONTEMPLATIVE NUNS SPEAK, p. 240
151, line 2   IBID, p. 28
151, line 9   IBID, p. 31
151, line 20   IBID, p. 59
151, line 22   IBID, p. 59
151, line 27   IBID, p. 68
154, line 1   A journal of a community of Anglican nuns. When permis-
                sion was sought to reproduce the extract the Mother
                Superior said this could be granted 'only on condition that
                it is entirely anonymous, because since that was written
                the Community has changed its custom and does not
                often use a grille now. This does not in any way invalidate
                what we said on the purpose of the grille where it is still
                retained.'
155, line 20   THE WATERS OF SILENCE, p. 273
157, line 30   THE RULE OF ST BENEDICT, chapters 16 and 18 (His
                biblical authority comes from Psalm 119, verses 62 and
                164)

162, line 11   St Luke's Gospel, X, 38–42
162, line 35   CISTERCIAN NUNS OF TODAY (Fowler Wright Books Ltd, Tenbury Wells, Worcs.), p. viii
163, line 17   'Openness and Cloister', paper by Thomas Merton, privately circulated, p. 2
164, line 27   'Monasticism in our Age', by a monk CSWG, privately circulated, p. 6
165, line 29   TENSIONS AND CHANGE, p. 34
166, line 3   IBID, p. 95
166, line 32   M. L. Algini in LA ROCCA, 23 (1964); quoted by Dom Jean Leclerq OSB in MONASTIC STUDIES, No. 4, 1966, p. 150

CHAPTER 6

All quotations from Canon Law in this chapter have been taken from the translation in THE SACRED CANONS, a commentary by John A. Abb and Jerome D. Hanna (St Louis: Herder, 1960).

176, line 13   THE DOWNSIDE CUSTOMARY, pp. 86–7
179, line 3   PAX, No. 315, Winter 1965
180, line 25   SUMMA THEOLOGICA, IIa IIae q186 art. 8
180, line 37   OBEDIENCE, p. 81
181, line 8   IBID, p. 85
181, line 18   IBID, p. 86
184, line 4   HERDER CORRESPONDENCE, Vol. 2, No. II, Nov. 1965, p. 323
185, line 5   RULE OF ST BENEDICT, Chapter 58
185, line 23   'The Religious Life – A Call to the Love of God', paper by Fr Hugh Bishop, to the Oxford Conference on the Religious Life, 1965
185, line 30   MONASTIC STUDIES, No. 4, 1966, article by Dom Emmanuel Schuurmans, Abbot of Zundert, Holland
186, line 4   MANUAL FOR NOVICES (Loughrea, Eire: M. S. Kelly)
188, line 3   THE MEANING OF THE MONASTIC LIFE, p. 151
188, line 8   IBID, p. 149
188, line 29   HOJA DEL LUNES, February 13, 1967
189, line 9   OBEDIENCE, p. 106
189, line 25   IBID, p. 214
190, line 1   IBID, pp. 191–2
190, line 16   IBID, p. 210
190, line 29   THE BENEDICTINE IDEA, p. 41
191, line 5   OBEDIENCE, p. 212
191, line 9   American nuns referred to in MATURITY IN THE RELIGIOUS LIFE, p. 151

191, line 26   TENSIONS AND CHANGE, p. 180
191, line 31   OBEDIENCE, pp. 55–6
192, line 3   MONASTIC STUDIES, No. 4, 1966, p. 100
192, line 6   RELIGIOUS ORDERS IN THE MODERN WORLD, p. 155
192, line 8   MATURITY IN THE RELIGIOUS LIFE, p. 275
192, line 11   RELIGIOUS ORDERS IN THE MODERN WORLD, p. 155
192, line 17   TEILHARD DE CHARDIN, p. 29
192, line 21   TENSIONS AND CHANGE, p. 234
192, line 22   MATURITY IN THE RELIGIOUS LIFE, p. 191
193, line 16   REVIEW FOR RELIGIOUS, Vol. 25, No. 3, May 1966,
               article by Joseph B. Simms on 'The Particular
               Friendship'
193, line 30   GOD'S HIGHWAYS, p. 142
194, line 11   REVIEW FOR RELIGIOUS, Vol. 25, No. 3, May 1966,
               article by James Griffiths SJ on 'Religious Censorship of
               Private Communications'
194, line 17   MATURITY IN THE RELIGIOUS LIFE, p. 143
194, line 25   THE RELIGIOUS VOCATION, pp. 306–7
194, line 33   WITNESS AND CONSECRATION, p. 64
195, line 1   TENSIONS AND CHANGE, p. 30
195, line 13   WITNESS AND CONSECRATION, p. 219 fn.
195, line 30   THE NUN IN THE WORLD, p. 47
195, line 34   For St Paul's views on women see, for example, I
               Corinthians, XIV, 34
195, line 37   OBEDIENCE, p. 115
197, line 13   Pius XII on Sept. 15, 1952, quoted in THE NUN IN THE
               WORLD, p. 143
197, line 27   OBEDIENCE, p. 199
198, line 1   THE NUN IN THE WORLD, p. 160
198, line 31   OBEDIENCE, p. 157
198, line 38   MATURITY IN THE RELIGIOUS LIFE, p. 289
199, line 13   THE LIFE OF RAYMOND RAYNES, p. 202
199, line 24   MATURITY IN THE RELIGIOUS LIFE, p. 243
200, line 8   'Monastic Vocation and the Background of Modern Secu-
               lar Thought' by Thomas Merton, privately circulated,
               pp. 13–14
200, line 38   RELIGIOUS ORDERS IN THE MODERN WORLD, p. 8
201, line 17   THE McCABE AFFAIR, Monica Lawlor and Simon
               Clements (London: Sheed & Ward, 1967)
202, line 29   THE TIMES, Jan. 5, 1968

CHAPTER 7
Except for the sources noted below, all the material in this chapter has

come from the answers to a questionnaire I composed and circulated among a number of religious communities – both men and women's, Catholic and Anglican – in Great Britain. The questions were as follows:

(A) You were called by God to your vocation as a religious. But what form did the call take? What was the pattern in your life beforehand that made you attend to this call; that made you sure this, and no other, was to be your vocation?

(B) In TENSIONS AND CHANGE Mgr Huyghe writes (p. 78) of the aspirant to the religious life: 'It is not sufficient to reject the world. . . . What would have been the candidate's attitude towards marriage if she had not had a religious vocation must be discovered.' What was your experience of human love before becoming a religious; to what extent was this satisfying? And what has been your experience of human love since then?

(C) Since becoming a religious has the certainty of your vocation been a constant in your life?

(D) What is the purpose of the religious life as practised by your community, bearing in mind that your own interpretation of this may not coincide precisely with that expressed by the founder(s) of your community?

207, line 1	ANATOMY OF A CHURCH: GREEK ORTHODOXY TODAY by Mario Rinvolucri (London: Burns Oates, 1966), p. 61
210, line 2	AN INTRODUCTION TO SPIRITUALITY, p. 197
210, line 13	TENSIONS AND CHANGE, p. 78
210, line 21	IBID, p. 79
223, line 33	The passage in St Matthew's Gospel reads 'For there are some eunuchs which were born from their mother's womb . . .'
236, line 5	TENSIONS AND CHANGE, p. 78

CHAPTER 8

246, line 23	BROTHERS OF MEN, p. 22 (Lancelot Sheppard's introduction)
247, line 17	RELIGIOUS ORDERS IN THE MODERN WORLD, p. 155
247, line 22	THE COMPLETE MONK, p. 213
247, line 29	MONASTIC RENEWAL, p. 192
248, line 10	Letter to THE TABLET, Aug. 14, 1965
248, line 20	BROTHERS OF MEN, p. 46
248, line 30	THE NUN IN THE WORLD, p. 142
249, line 3	THE RELIGIOUS LIFE, p. 315

249, line 23   'The Religious Life – A Call to the Love of God', paper by Fr Hugh Bishop to Oxford Conference on the Religious Life, 1965

251, line 16   AMPLEFORTH JOURNAL, Spring 1967, p. 19

252, line 28   'Monastic Vocation and the Background of Modern Secular Thought', by Thomas Merton, privately circulated, p. 3

253, line 21   MONASTIC STUDIES, No. 3, 1965, p. 200

254, line 10   MONASTIC STUDIES, No. 4, 1966, p. 131

256, line 13   BROTHERS OF MEN, pp. 52–3

256, line 32   TO HEAVEN WITH DIANA by Gerald Vann OP (London: Collins, 1960), p. 50

257, line 17   NEW BLACKFRIARS, Sept. 1967, article by Louis Allen

257, line 25   IBID

261, line 8   DE CIVITATE DEI, Healy translation (London: Dent, and New York: Dutton)

261, line 14   IBID

262, line 5   Sermo 354 ad continentes 9; PL 39 1568

262, line 9   SUMMA THEOLOGICA, a5 ad2

262, line 23   INSIDE THE CLOISTER (Buckfast Abbey Publications), p. 2

262, line 24   THE MEANING OF THE MONASTIC LIFE, p. 201

263, line 16   AMERICAN CATHOLIC EXODUS, p. 187

263, line 30   RELIGIOUS ORDERS IN THE MODERN WORLD, p. 107

264, line 8   THE MEANING OF THE MONASTIC LIFE, p. 135

264, line 17   IBID, p. 136

264, line 24   MONASTICISM IN OUR AGE, p. 8

264, line 27   THE BENEDICTINE IDEA, p. 46

264, line 34   'The Religious Life – A Call to Service', paper by Fr Michael ssf to Oxford Conference, 1966

265, line 14   'Adaptation of the Monastic Life', paper by Thomas Merton, privately circulated, 1964

269, line 3   THE BENEDICTINE IDEA, p. 229

269, line 10   THE NUN IN THE WORLD, p. 59

270, line 37   AMERICAN CATHOLIC EXODUS, p. 187

APPENDIX ONE

THE RELIGIOUS POPULATION AMONG ROMAN CATHOLICS

MEN	1967	1966	1962
Jesuits	36,038	36,038	35,086
Franciscans (Friars Minor)	26,940	27,009	26,876
Salesians	22,626	22,042	21,048
Christian Schools Bros	17,787	17,926	17,560
Franciscans (Capuchins)	15,710	15,838	15,708
Benedictines	12,070	12,500	11,500
Marist Brothers	10,221	10,356	8,974
Dominicans	10,003	10,191	9,841
Redemptorists	9,052	9,450	9,030
Oblates of Mary Immaculate	7,890	7,609	7,505
Vincentians	6,230	5,992	5,966
Society of the Divine Word	5,744	5,773	5,436
Holy Spirit, Congregation	5,147	5,200	5,200
Franciscans (Conventuals)	4,605	4,650	4,550
Augustinians (Hermits)	4,504	4,531	4,200
Passionists	4,340	4,135	3,935
Claretians	4,128	3,770	3,554
Discalced Carmelites	4,018	4,022	4,236
Christian Brothers of Ireland	3,900	3,814	3,500
White Fathers	3,749	4,013	4,055
Trappists	3,770	4,211	4,339
Marianists	3,434	3,490	3,250

	1967	1966	1962
Priests of the Sacred Heart	3,425	3,400	3,175
Missionaries of the Sacred Heart of Jesus	3,315	3,455	3,107
Brothers of the Sacred Heart	3,116	3,148	3,043
Holy Cross Fathers	3,110	3,352	3,127
Carmelites (Ancient Observance)	2,852	3,075	2,904
Piarists	2,501	2,540	2,455
Marists	2,446	2,343	2,277
Hospitallers of St John of God	2,318	2,504	2,527
Pallotines	2,281	2,400	2,250
Brothers of Christian Instruction of Ploermel	2,228	2,215	2,200
Picpus Fathers	2,135	2,052	1,962
Scheut Fathers	2,008	2,008	1,930
Premonstratensians	1,991	1,991	1,750
Montfort Fathers	1,985	2,000	1,722
Assumptionists	1,967	1,963	1,960
Brothers of Christian Instruction of St Gabriel	1,900	1,961	2,200
Society of African Missions	1,861	1,820	1,855
Viatorians	1,800	1,815	1,850
Servants of Mary	1,749	1,750	1,670
African Missionaries of Verona	1,703	1,710	1,570
Cistercians (Common Observance)	1,665	1,665	1,665
Franciscans (Third Order Regular)	1,650	1,592	1,420
Blessed Sacrament Fathers	1,641	1,645	1,580
Augustinians (Recollects)	1,571	1,615	1,490
Pious Society of St Paul	1,600	1,500	1,150
Brothers of Charity	1,566	1,559	1,567
Salvatorians	1,527	1,538	1,350
Oblates of St Francis de Sales	1,391	1,250	1,210
Maryknollers	1,381	1,356	1,442
Ministers of the Sick	1,309	1,380	1,297
Missionaries of the Holy Family	1,269	1,293	1,200
Mill Hill Fathers	1,207	1,204	1,152
Theatines	1,205	1,205	1,205
Little Workers of Divine Providence	1,202	1,090	1,055
Canons Regular of St Augustine	1,190	1,190	1,083

	1967	1966	1962
La Sallette Missionaries	1,175	1,179	1,069
Consolata Fathers	1,160	1,092	–
Mercedarians	1,061	1,230	1,163
Columbans	1,055	1,055	1,005
Carmelites of the Blessed Virgin Mary	1,028	1,028	–
Brothers of the Blessed Virgin Mary	1,000	1,000	1,041
Membership of Communities with fewer than 1,000 members	36,557	35,230	34,172
Total	332,997	332,993	319,006

WOMEN

	1967	1966	1962
North America	256,350	261,316	247,693
South America	107,358	82,945	73,885
Europe	576,814	591,360	591,577
Africa	30,702	45,616	25,408
Asia	101,710	79,443	74,010
World Total	1,072,934	1,060,680	1,012,573

The above figures are now of purely historic interest. They were issued by the Vatican and in some cases they were at variance with figures issued by specific orders in their own handbooks. Some years after they appeared in the first edition of *Against All Reason*, the Vatican stopped publishing figures for individual communities; it continued to provide only the most elementary statistics for the religious life as a whole. The latest (early 1986) available figures are those for 1981, as follows: Priests in religious communities: 154,148. Lay brothers: 70,621. Sisters: 952,043.

APPENDIX TWO

THE USAGES OF THE CISTERCIAN MONKS OF THE STRICT OBSERVANCE (THE TRAPPISTS)

(This edition of the Trappist Usages is the revision which came into effect in January 1964. In one or two details the practices outlined here have changed since then. The timetable is no longer the same in every monastery as it is laid down here; each house is making minor alterations to a rhythm of prayer and work best suited to its own conditions. The rules of silence have been modified, so that although the monks are not encouraged to talk any more than they have done in the past, they may now speak – if it is absolutely necessary – without obtaining permission. Eggs and fish are included in the diet more frequently than laid down here. And at least one monastery – Mount St Bernard, in England – has abandoned the Chapter of Faults and the tonsure; others may have done likewise. But all these changes are experimental; they are not yet official Trappist usage. At some subsequent date still to be fixed the General Chapter of the Order will discuss whether they are to be permanently incorporated in the next edition of this document.)

BOOK 1
THE RECEPTION OF THE BRETHREN

CHAPTER I   THE POSTULANCY

And the Lord said to Abraham: 'Go forth out of thy country, and from thy kindred, and out of thy father's house, and come into the land which I shall show thee.' (Gen. XII, 1)

1 The postulant who comes to the monastery will spend some time at the guest house during which time he will meet the Master of Novices.

> During his stay at the guest house, the postulant will assure himself by serious examination that it is really the spirit of God, namely, a desire to lead a more perfect life, that leads him into solitude.
>
> He will not make this examination, so important for his future, all alone. According to an old monastic custom, he will do so under the direction of an 'ancient', a monk possessing experience.

2 On the day when he is to enter the community, the Novice Master has him wait at the Chapter room door at the end of Prime.

> Initiation to the monastic life will take on a liturgical character for the postulant, in coming into the monastery, takes his place, as St Benedict says, in the School of the Master's service. Since he is being initiated into the divine service, it is natural that the ceremony will be marked by the seal of humility.

When the Abbot says 'Benedicite' the Novice Master brings in the postulant. The latter prostrates and the Abbot questions him in the following words: 'Quid Petis?' The postulant answers: 'Misericordiam Dei et Ordinis'. The Abbot adds: 'Surge in nomine Domini' at which the postulant rises and listens to the exhortation. At the conclusion of this the Abbot asks him if he is prepared to observe the Rule and persevere in his vocation. He replies: 'Yes, Reverend Father (or: 'Yes, Father' if it is the Prior) by the help of God's grace and the assistance of your prayers.' The Abbot adds: 'Qui coepit in te Deus perficiat.' The community answers 'Amen' and the Novice Master leads the postulant to his place.

> 'Moved by the spirit of God, Pachomius desired to become a monk. He was told where a certain anchorite named Palamon lived so he betook himself there to live with him in solitude. He knocked at his door. The old man, leaning out from overhead, asked "What do you want?" Nothing more because he was a man brief of speech. And Pachomius replied: "I beg you, Father, make me a monk".' (*Life of St Pachomius*)

3 When he enters the community the postulant draws up two lists of everything he brings with him. He keeps one and gives the other to the Novice Master after signing it. He deposits his personal items with the Secretary, or the wardrobe keeper, and he keeps nothing without permission. He also writes out and signs the following declaration: 'I, the undersigned, (family name and Christian name), declare that if for any reason whatever I cease to belong to the community of . . . , I will not claim any salary or compensation for the work which I have done, since this work will be simply the means whereby I participate as fully as possible in the spiritual life of the monastery, while contributing to its material upkeep.'

From the time of St Anthony, the Father of Monks, tradition has always considered detachment as an indispensable condition for perfect union with God.

'Anthony entered into a church. He noticed that the Gospel was being read at that moment and he heard the Lord say to the rich man: 'If thou wilt be perfect, go sell that thou hast and give to the poor; then come and follow me and thou shalt have treasure in heaven.'' Anthony believed that it was for himself this passage of the Gospel was read.' (*Life of St Anthony* by St Athanasius) But this abandonment of all created things will be of no use unless it is accompanied by interior affective detachment.

4 The postulant follows all the regular exercises but he does not assist at the chapter of faults. He stands second last in rank until the eighth day after his clothing.

5 The postulancy lasts a month. The Abbot admits the postulant to clothing after taking the consultative vote of his Council. The clothing is preceded by a retreat of eight full days.

Like St Benedict, whom St Gregory described as 'desiring solely to please God alone' the postulant will love to repeat these words of Scripture: 'Here I am, Lord, for thou didst call me. . . . Speak Lord for thy servant heareth.' (1 Kings, III, 9)

6 The order of seniority is determined by the time of entering the community and is not changed by the date of clothing, profession or ordination. However if the postulant is a priest he precedes the other postulants in the church at ecclesiastical ceremonies.

CHAPTER II   THE RECEPTION OF THE HABIT

7 On the day of the clothing, the wardrobe keeper brings to the chapter room the habit with which the postulant will be clothed by the Abbot.

'As a soldier of Christ the monk should be always in battle dress,

his loins girt. . . . There should be nothing in his clothing that
bespeaks vanity or pride. This is the teaching of the Apostle:
"But having food and wherewith to be covered, with these we are
content". Furthermore the clothing of the monk does not serve
merely to cover his body; its style harmonizes with his way of
life, it shows forth innocence and simplicity.' (Cassian)

After the prayers of Prime the Abbot says 'Benedicite' and the Novice
Master comes forward with the postulant who prostrates and makes his
petition as in No. 2 above.

Does the young novice realize from whence comes the joy that
inundates his soul? Pascal makes the Lord say: 'You would not
seek Me if you had not already found Me.' For the Lord allows
Himself to be found by him and this marks the beginning of his
joy.

After the usual exhortation, the religious rise at the same time as the
Abbot who dons a white stole and blesses the habit. The postulant
kneels during this time, and when the habit is blessed he kneels before
the Abbot who is seated and who clothes him, being assisted by the
Novice Master. During the ceremony the Cantor presents the book and
the Sacristan holds the crozier at the Abbot's left.

The ceremonies which accompany this rite show that the
postulant takes a step forward in separation from the world and in
being incorporated into the community.

When the postulant is being invested, the Cantor intones the 'Benedictus' on the 6th solemn tone and the two choirs continue it alternately.
They bow at the 'Gloria Patri', and only rise when replying 'Amen' at the
conclusion of the collect which follows.

'Blessed be the Lord God of Israel because he hath visited and
wrought the redemption of his people:

....

That being delivered from the hand of our enemies, we may
serve him without fear, in holiness and justice before him all our
days.

When he has received the habit the novice rises, bows profoundly, and
kneels in the same place as before. At the end of the canticle the Abbot
rises and sings the versicle and collect. When the ceremony is ended,
the novice bows profoundly and retires to his place.

The religious habit is only a symbol and the novice will try to
understand its meaning. 'Put ye on the Lord Jesus Christ,' says
St Paul (Rom. XIII, 14) who wished to see Christians 'put off the
old man and put on the new'. (Ephes. IV, 24)

The Abbot inserts the baptismal name of the novice in the collect, unless there is some reason for giving him another name.

> This was the old Cistercian usage laid down in the Ritual: 'In ipsa collecta exprimitur solum nomen in baptismo impositum, nec aliud adjungitur etiamsi plures fuerint in monasterio ejusdem nominis.' (VI, 1)

8 The Secretary then draws up the act of the reception of the habit. This is signed by the Abbot, the novice, two witnesses chosen from among the seniors and by the Secretary himself.

When official documents are being signed the monks add their family name to their religious name. If they wish to affix the abbreviations of the Order they add either OCR or preferably, OCSO.

9 A postulant who has already received the Cistercian habit takes it in private without any ceremony.

CHAPTER III THE NOVITIATE

> 'My son, if thou wilt attend to me, thou shalt learn; and if thou wilt apply thy mind, thou shalt be wise.
> If thou wilt incline thy ear, thou shalt receive instruction, and if thou love to hear, thou shalt be wise . . .
> Hear willingly every discourse of God.' (Eccles. VI, 33–35)

10 In conformity with the Constitutions the novices should live apart from the professed. Ordinarily they speak only to the Abbot and the Novice Master, to whom they apply in all their needs. If there is a Sub-master they speak to him in the measure determined by the Abbot.

The novices do not ask permission from each other.

> If silence has always been held in honour in our monasteries it is because it helps the life of prayer in a very special way. The soul needs silence to hear the voice of God: 'I wish to entice her, to lead her into the desert; and there I shall speak to her heart.' (Osee II, 14)

For Confession the novices will observe the prescriptions of Canon Law and the customs of the Order as outlined in No. 204.

11 During the two years of probation the novices shall learn the obligations of the monastic life and shall strive to understand and love the ideal of the Cistercian contemplative life to which God has called them.

In order to insure a thorough formation, no study properly so-called is permitted during the novitiate. Some revision of classical studies may be permitted during the second year if it is considered useful. The novices may be exempted from manual labour in part, but not to a greater extent than six hours a week.

> Our Cistercian ideal demands a hidden life because such is most favourable to the interior life. John XXIII recalled to Cistercian monks that their life should be 'altogether cut away from the world and completely consecrated to God'.
>
> 'Bernard, Bernard, why have you come here?' the Abbot of Clairvaux often asked himself during his novitiate, and to this he replied: To hide myself 'in the face of the Lord'.

12 The novices attend the conferences of the Novice Master, the programme of which is to be drawn up according to No. 16 of the Ratio Studiorum. The Father Master begins the conference with the words 'Divinum auxilium' to which all answer 'Amen'. He ends it with the verse 'Adjutorium, etc.' the novices replying: 'Qui fecit caelum et terram'.

The novices will undergo periodic examinations on their obligations and on the subjects mentioned in the Ratio Studiorum.

> The monastery is a school of the Lord's service (Rule, Pro.), and a 'school of charity'. (William of St Thierry)

13 In the church the novices are ordinarily placed in the front stalls, and they observe the same ceremonies as the professed. If, however, they use a single book in the middle of the choir, they face the altar, but they conform to the rest of the choir for the bows. When the novices are standing, bowed or sitting, they keep their cloaks crossed. When they stand in ceremony they let the arms hang down under the cloak.

14 As far as possible, the novices work apart from the professed, under the direction of the Novice Master or the Sub-master.

15 The novices should be allowed to receive visits only rarely and, like the professed, they may neither write nor receive letters without the permission of the Abbot.

> 'Forget thy people and thy father's house, and the king shall greatly desire thy beauty' says psalm 44.
>
> This forgetfulness is not, however, indifference. 'A monk is one who is separated from all and united to all' as on old monk, Evagre le Pontique, assures us; and we may affirm with St

Bernard, that parents who offer their son generously to the Lord, do not lose him: 'You do not lose him; quite the contrary; you acquire through him a great number of sons. All of us here at Clairvaux accept him as a brother and we accept you as our parents. Do not weep, do not cry, I shall be his father, I shall be his mother, I shall be his brother and his sister . . . I shall be everything and I shall arrange all for his physical well-being and his spiritual development.' (St Bernard, letter 110)

16 When the novitiate is ended, the novice must either make profession, if he is admitted, or return to the world, unless he becomes an oblate. The Abbot may, however, prolong the time of probation, but not beyond six months in ordinary cases (Const. 159) or a year if the novice is to make solemn profession immediately.

17 If a novice dies the same prayers are said for him and the same ceremonies observed as for a professed. That is why the novices, without being bound to it, should fulfil the obligations of the professed for the dead.

18 If a novice makes profession 'in articula mortis' he employs the following formula: 'Pater promitto tibi obedientiam secundum Regulam Sancti Benedicti'.
If he dies, he is buried in the novice's habit. If he recovers his health, he acts in all things as if he had not made profession.

19 Superiors should not give letters of recommendation to novices who leave the monastery. They may, however, give them a document stating the duration of their stay in the monastery, but in no case is the seal to be placed thereon.

CHAPTER IV   TEMPORARY PROFESSION

'If a man makes a vow to the Lord, or bind himself by an oath, he shall not make his word void but shall fulfil all that he promised.' (Numbers xxx, 3)

20 It belongs to the Abbot or his delegate, even in presence of Superiors of higher dignity, to receive the profession of his novices. To admit a novice to profession the Abbot asks the deliberative vote of the chapter. Some days beforehand the Abbot gives the voters the necessary information but exercises discretion regarding the past or the heredity of the candidate. Those who have doubts about the novice's fitness can expose them to the Abbot in private. All should cast their vote.

On the day of the scrutiny only the professed in solemn vows who have made stability remain in chapter. The Father Prior gives each one two balls, a white one for admission and a black one for rejection. If one of the voters is sick in the infirmary, the Father Prior goes to receive his vote accompanied by two other religious. The Abbot, assisted by the Prior and Subprior, counts the votes and the result is announced.

21 Before temporary profession, the novice disposes of his temporal goods, in conformity with the prescriptions of the Code of Canon Law and the Constitutions. He prepare for the making of his vows by a retreat of eight full days.

> During those days of retreat the novice will listen to God's word with a docile heart, he will ponder it in serious meditation and he will be come penetrated with it in the silence of prayer. It would be good for him to pass in review before God the ways by which grace led him into the desert, his dispositions when he commenced his novitiate, the ideals he then had of the religious life.
>
> Having now some experience of the Cistercian life, he will not underestimate its sacrifices and difficulties; but he has tasted also its charms and he knows its advantages. He will therefore ask God to help him realize the monastic ideal which St Bernard proposes to his monks: 'Solum inquirere Deum, propter ipsum solum.'

He writes the act of his profession in his own hand as follows:
'Ego, frater N (religious and family names), sacerdos (diaconus, sub-diaconus, acolythus, exorcista, lector, ostiarius, clericus or laicus), promitto stabilitatem meam, conversionem morum meorum et obed-iantiam secundum Regulam Sancti Benedicti Abbatis et ad normam iuris canonici, coram Deo et omnibus Sanctis ejus quorum reliquiae hic habentur, in hoc loco qui vocatur N (name of monastery) Ordinis Cisterciensium Strictioris Observantiae constructo in honorem Beatis-simae Dei Genitricis semperque Virginis Mariae, in praesentia Reverendi Domni N. hujusce monasterii Abbatis.'

If the second Superior receives the vows in the name of the Abbot, the novice will use the following formula: 'In praesentia Patris N. Prioris, in hac parte commissarii Reverendi Domni N. hujusce monasterii Abbatis.'

'Sede vacante', the formula before the Father Immediate, will read: 'In praesentia Reverendi Domni N. hujusce monasterii, sede vacante, curam habentis.'

And before a Superior ad nutum: 'In praesentia Reverendi Domni N. commissarii Reverendi Domni N. hujusce monasterii, sede vacante curam habentis.'

If the novice makes profession for another monastery, he says: 'pro loco qui vocatur . . .' etc.

22 On the day of his profession, the novice makes his petition in chapter as in No. 2 above. After the exhortation, accompanied by the Novice Master, he bows profoundly to the Abbot and kneels before him with his hands joined between those of the Superior, and says in an audible voice: 'Pater, promitto tibi obedientiam secundum Regulam Sancti Benedicti, ad normam juris canonici.' The Abbot adds: 'Et Deus det tibi perseverantiam', and the community answers 'Amen'.

> United to the sentiments of Christ, the novice will say: 'Ecce venio ut faciam voluntatem tuam' (Ps. 39; Heb. 10), promising God to live henceforth only for Him in an obedience full of love: 'Legam tuam in medio cordis mei' (Ps. 49).

If the Abbot is absent the promise of obedience is deferred until his return. 'Sede vacante' the following formulae are used:

(i) If the Father Immediate presides at the ceremony: 'Pater, promitto tibi pro tempore sedis monasterii nostri vacationis, obedientiam . . .'

(ii) If the Superior ad nutum presides: 'Pater, promitto Reverendo Domino N. nostri monasterii pro tempore sedis vacationis curam habenti, obedientiam. . . .'

The Abbot then embraces the novice, and the latter after bowing again, returns to the middle of the Chapter room where he stands and reads the schedule of his profession. He then signs it with his religious and family names and takes it to the Abbot. The novice then removes his cloak, and the Abbot, assisted by the Novice Master, takes off the cincture and white scapular, and puts the black scapular and leather belt of the professed on the novice, saying nothing. The newly professed dons his cloak again, bows profoundly to the Superior and kneels in the middle of the Chapter room. The Abbot and community rise, and the former sings 'Dominus Vobiscum' and the prayers 'Actiones nostras' and 'Deus qui nos'. When these are ended the Novice Master signs to the newly professed to rise and both bow profoundly to the Abbot.

23 The Secretary draws up the act of profession, which is signed by the Abbot, the newly professed, two senior monks as witnesses, and by the Secretary.

24 The professed in temporary vows have all the rights and privileges of monks of the Order, except the right to vote. They also have the same obligations.

If they are absent from the choir, to which they are bound, they must supply the Divine Office and the Office of the Dead, in whole or in part, according to the directives of the Abbot.

25 If temporary vows are to be renewed, this must be done at latest on the day on which they expire, and the renewal cannot be anticipated by more than one month. It takes place in chapter or before two witnesses. Temporary vows may be renewed once or several times, but not for more than three years in all. The following formula is used: 'Reverend Father, I renew my temporary vows for a period of . . .', or 'until such a date.' A record of the renewal should be kept.

26 The professed in temporary vows continue to follow the exercises of the novitiate for as long as the Abbot judges fit.

They may study Philosophy and Theology during the period of their temporary vows, but they must interrupt these studies for six months before solemn profession in order to live the monastic life fully. (Ratio, art. 25)

CHAPTER V   SOLEMN PROFESSION

'With Christ I am nailed to the cross. And I live, not now I; but Christ liveth in me. And that I live now in the flesh: I live in the faith of the Son of God, who loved me, and delivered himself for me.' (Galatians, II, 19–20)

27 The vote for admission to solemn profession is consultative only, and the Abbot is not bound to announce the result.

28 During the two months before his solemn profession, the professed in temporary vows must renounce, in favour of whomsoever he wishes, all the property which he actually possesses, on condition of his future profession. He may also indicate in writing what he wishes to do with any goods to which he has an actual right, and which could come to him by natural succession, direct or indirect. If he prefers, he may omit this, and in that case Canon 582,1, will apply. All necessary measures must be taken to ensure that this renunciation is effective in civil law.

'When one has caught a glimpse of how sweet the Lord is, how can one do otherwise than passionately desire to spend one's life in contemplating Him, in adoring Him, and in doing His will in all things, far removed from the vanities of the world.' (Father de Foucauld)

29 Solemn profession cannot be made before the day on which temporary vows expire. It is preceded by a retreat of eight full days.

The monk will reflect during this time on the grace of a monastic vocation. God has called him to share in a privileged life thus described by St Bernard: 'qui in claustro soli Deo Vivunt, semper Deo adherentes, ejus placitum considerantes.' If he has truly sought God and if it seems he has not sufficiently found Him, he will not be troubled and will say with St Gregory of Nyssa: 'To find God is to seek Him without ceasing. In fact, "seek" in this context is not one thing and "find" another. The fruit of seeking is to keep on seeking. The desire of the soul is fulfilled by the very fact that it remains insatiable, and to see God consists in being never surfeited in desiring Him.'

30 The professed should prepare the schedule of his profession beforehand, and write it on a sheet of parchment as follows: 'Ego, frater N. (religious and family names) sacerdos (diaconus, subdiaconus, acolythus, exorcista, lector, ostiarius, clericus or laicus), promitto stabilitatem meam, conversionem morum meorum et obedientiam secundum Regulam Sancti Benedicti Abbatis, coram Deo et omnibus Sanctis ejus quorum reliquiae hic habentur, in hoc loco qui vocatur N. (name of monastery) Ordinis Cisterciensium Strictioris Observantiae, constructo in honorem Beatissimae Dei Genitricis semperque Virginis Mariae in praesentia Reverendi Domni N. hujusce monasterii Abbatis.'

31 On the morning of the profession, the professed makes his promise of obedience in chapter.

He will make this promise of obedience in a spirit of faith, as a man who 'prefers nothing to Christ', and who knows that obedience 'will be pleasing to God and agreeable to men' only 'in so far as that which is commanded is performed without hesitation, without delay, without weariness, without murmuring

or any expression of resistance; because the obedience shown to
Superiors is shown to God, for He has said: "He who heareth you
heareth me." But the disciple must practise obedience with a
good heart, for "God loves the cheerful giver".' (Rule, ch. 5)
The professed comes to the middle of the chapter and prostrates: 'Quid
petis?' 'Misericordiam Dei et Ordinis.' 'Surge in nomine Domini.' He
listens standing to the exhortation. When he is questioned about his
determination to persevere he answers: 'Yes, Reverend Father, with
the help of God's grace and the assistance of your prayers.' The Abbot
adds: 'Deus qui coepit in te, ipse perficiat usque in diem Christi Jesu' and
all answer 'Amen'.

The professed then kneels before the Abbot, and with his hands
joined in his makes his promise of obedience: 'Pater, promitto tibi
obedientiam secundum Regulam Sancti Benedicti usque ad mortem.
The Abbot adds: 'Et Deus det tibi vitam aeternam.' All answer 'Amen',
and the Abbot embraces the professed.

32 The promise of obedience is made to one's own Abbot. If he is
absent it is deferred until his return.

33 If the professed has not already received tonsure all now go to the
church for the blessing of the monastic crown. The monks occupy the
presbytery stalls. On arriving in choir they kneel when the Abbot does.
When the latter rises, the Prior leads the professed from the choir of the
novices to the presbytery step, where, having bowed profoundly, he
kneels down. The monks are turned towards the altar all during the
ceremony, except for the singing of the 23rd psalm with its antiphon,
during which they are turned in choir.

34 The ceremony of solemn profession takes place in the church.
Solemn profession takes place in the church and during the Mass
so as to emphasise the sublimity of the offering which is being
made in union with that of Christ.
The act is likewise a complete and definitive aggregation to the
community and that is why all the brethren embrace the
professed. The detailed description of the ceremony shows that
there is here question of an act of divine worship which demands
all our respect.
The Abbot sings the Mass. After the Gospel the choir turn towards the
altar and the Abbot and his ministers sit at the presbytery step. If the
Abbot prefers to remain at the altar, he stands at the Epistle side with

his ministers at his left. The Prior now accompanies the professed to the presbytery step and then retires to his stall. If there is an exhortation all are seated during it.

When it is finished, the professed, having received his schedule from the Prior, stands at the presbytery step and sings the formula of his profession, ending it in the same manner as a prophecy. He then bows and accompanies the Prior to the Gospel side in order to sign the schedule on a table prepared there. He signs with his religious and family name after which he puts a cross.

Having bowed at the presbytery step, both prostrate on the knuckles on the lowest step of the altar. They then ascend, and the new monk having placed the schedule of his profession on the Epistle side, kisses the altar. They both bow at the foot of the steps when descending and again at the middle of the presbytery step. Then the Prior returns to his place.

The choir rise. The professed, standing in ceremony, sings the following versicle three times: 'Suscipe me Domine secundum eloquium tuum et vivam et non confundas me ab expectatione mea'. He prostrates on the knuckles after singing it each time. The monks repeat the verse after him and the third time they add the 'Gloria Patri' without bowing.

During this time the Deacon, at a sign from the Abbot, rises, bows to the latter and goes to the altar. He prostrates on the knuckles on the lowest step, ascends to the Epistle corner and takes the schedule of profession. He bows at the foot of the steps and carries the schedule in both hands to the Abbot to whom he bows. The Abbot gives the document to his secretary.

If the Abbot stayed at the altar, he would go now with his ministers to the presbytery step.

The choir bow on the misericords while the Cantor says: 'Kyrie eleison'. They rise after the Pater, and the Cantor immediately intones the 'Miserere' on the 6th solemn tone which the two choirs continue alternately. The newly-professed, accompanied by the Prior, goes and kneels before each of the professed, choir and lay, saying to him: 'Ora pro me, Pater (or Frater)'. The Choir monks reply while embracing him: 'Dominus custodiat introitum tuum et exitum tuum' and the Brothers say: 'Dominus tecum'.

He begins with the Abbot of the house and the other Abbots if there are any, and the ministers of the altar. He continues with the Prior and the monks on his side. Then he goes to the Subprior's side, kneeling before each of the professed, even before the temporary professed. If

the Prior is absent the newly professed begins with the Abbot's side of
the choir. In very large communities the professed kneels before two or
three together and they embrace him in turn.

> 'Ecce quam bonum et quam jucundum habitare frates in unum.'
> Yes, for the monks of a monastery are the sons of the same
> Abbot and are brothers closely united together. They love their
> Abbot with a sincere and humble affection and in honour they
> anticipate each other's needs. There is mutual emulation in
> obedience and they discharge the debt of fraternal charity by
> love. Thus, all marching together towards eternal life, they help
> each other on the way. (Rule)

The newly professed returns by the centre of the choir and prostrates
before the Abbot. The Prior meanwhile withdraws to his own stall. The
choir, having said the 'Gloria Patri' without bowing, turn towards the
altar and stand thus during the verses and prayers which follow.

After the fourth prayer the professed rises to his knees and the Abbot
blesses the cowl. Then the Abbot kneels facing the altar and intones the
hymn 'Veni Creator' which is continued by the whole community
kneeling, the Cantor intoning each verse.

> By his solemn profession the monk has just committed himself
> definitely to the religious life. He is entering into a new way of
> total consecration, and in order to receive all the graces of which
> he has need, we beg the Holy Spirit in the 'Veni Creator' to give
> him light and strength.

During this time the Abbot sits, removes the cloak from the new monk
and clothes him in the cowl. The latter immediately returns to kneel
before the presbytery step.

> As in Baptism, the new garment – the ample cowl of the monk
> with its hood – whose symbolism so pleased the ancient ascetics,
> is the exterior expression of the grace of Christ. . . . 'The
> religious soul is generously repaid in return: for having
> impoverished and despoiled itself of itself it is now enriched and is
> clothed with Christ as with a garment of glory that will never
> again leave it.' (Dom de Puniet)

At the end of the two prayers which follow the 'Veni Creator', the choir
rise and stand facing the altar. The Prior conducts the new monk to the
stall he is to occupy. The Abbot continues the Mass at which the newly
professed communicates even if he is a priest. The 'Te Deum' may be
sung after Mass.

35 The act of profession is drawn up and signed as in No. 23. An extract from the act should be sent to the pastor of the place where the newly professed was baptised.

36 If the Abbot cannot sing the Mass, he comes to perform the ceremony after the Gospel, vested in alb, stole and cope, and carrying the crosier. The Deacon and Subdeacon take part in the ceremony with him while the Hebdomadary remains alone at his stall in the presbytery.

> 'I also in the simplicity of my heart have joyfully offered all those things. . . .
> O God of Israel, keep us in this fidelity.' (1 Par. 29, 17–18)

CHAPTER VI   CHANGE OF STABILITY

37 No one should request a change of stability save for a grave reason and after mature reflection.

> 'Unknown before the time of St Benedict, stability in his Rule became the object of a vow: the monk attaches himself until the end of his life to his abbey and to the community of which he becomes a member.' (Dom Marmion)
> By his profession the monk contracts a bond of unity with his community of which the Holy Spirit is the link and which is a sign of the unity of the Mystical Body . . . In virtue of this significance, it is in itself indissoluble as is the unity which joins the members of the living body together. Thus tradition has not hesitated to establish a certain analogy between this altogether spiritual union and that of the spouse in marriage, the indissolubility of which is likewise founded on its being a sign of the mystery of Christ and the Church.

A change of stability is subject to the following conditions:

1 The acceptance of both Superiors.
2 The favourable vote of the Council of the Abbot who is receiving the religious.
3 At least one year's probation
4 The deliberative vote, taken towards the end of the period of probation, of the chapter of the monastery receiving the religious.
5 An indult from the Holy See.

A religious who is making his year of probation in view of the change of stability takes the rank that is assigned to him, and does not assist at the chapter of the professed. All his correspondence may be examined by the local Abbot, except in those cases mentioned in No. 258.

38 The professed in solemn vows who changes his stability makes his petition in chapter. He prostrates. The Abbot asks him: 'Quid petis?' He replies: 'Misericordiam Dei et vestram.' After the exhortation he kneels before the Abbot and holding his hands joined in his, says aloud: 'Pater, promitto tibi obedientiam secundum Regulam Sancti Benedicti usque ad mortem.'

The schedule is read after the Gospel of the Conventual Mass. The celebrant remains at the altar and turns towards the choir. The monk, accompanied by the Prior, as at solemn profession, comes to the middle of the presbytery step, salutes both choirs and reads his schedule, which is similar to that used for solemn profession with the following alterations: 'professus a votis solemnibus B.M. of . . . Ordinis Cisterciensium Strictioris Observantiae' and 'in hoc loco . . . ejusdem Ordinis'. He signs the schedule and places it on the altar on the Epistle corner, kisses the altar, bows to the celebrant and goes to the place indicated to him.

If the Abbot sings the Mass, as is fitting, the Deacon takes the schedule and gives it to the Secretary, who comes forward to receive it. Otherwise the Secretary goes himself at the end of the Offertory, takes it from the altar and brings it to the Abbot in choir.

39 If it is a case of one professed in temporary vows, the entire ceremony of the change of stability takes place in chapter. The candidate makes his petition as in the preceding number.

For his promise of obedience he uses the following formula: 'Pater, promitto tibi obedientiam secundum Regulam Sancti Benedicti ad normam juris canonici.' He then rises, bows again, and goes to the middle of the chapter room where he reads standing the schedule of his new stability, which is similar to that of one professed in solemn vows, but in which he describes himself as 'Professus a votis temporariis'. He signs this document and gives it to the Abbot. The Prior then conducts him to the place he is to occupy according to his rank in the Order.

40 If a delegate presides at the ceremony, the terminology at the end of No. 21 is used.

41 An act of the new stability is drawn up and signed as in No. 23 above. Mention is made in it of the consent of the former Abbot of the religious, of that of the community into which he has been received, and of the authorisation of the Holy See. An authentic copy of this act of new stability is sent to his former Abbot.

42 *Stability in a house newly erected into an Abbey or Priory.* After the execution of the indult canonically erecting the foundation into an Abbey (or Titular Priory), and before the election of the Superior, the monks who agree to remain there make their stability in chapter. They make their promise of obedience into the hands of the Father Immediate according to the following formula: 'Pater, promitto tibi pro tempore sedis monasterii nostri vacationis obedientiam secundum Regulam Sancti Benedicti usque ad mortem.' The professed in temporary vows say: 'Pater promitto tibi pro tempore sedis monasterii nostri vacationis obedientiam secundum Regulam Sancti Benedicti ad normam iuris canonici.' In the schedule they insert: 'in praesentia Reverendi Domni N., Fundatoris, necnon Patris Abbatis hujusce monasterii, sede adhuc vacante, curam habentis.'

43 *Stability of monks from a suppressed house.* Monks from a house which has been suppressed, ipso facto have stability in their Mother house. If they desire to make stability elsewhere, they are subject to the usual conditions.

44 *Stability of one elected Superior of a monastery not his own.* If a monk is elected Abbot or Titular Prior in another house, he acquires stability in that house by the fact of his confirmation.

If he resigns his charge, he may choose either this latter monastery or that of his profession. During the two months following the installation of his successor he must make a promise of obedience to the Abbot of the monastery he has chosen.

If he wishes to make stability in another monastery, he is subject to the usual conditions for change of stability.

45 *Monks sent to another monastery.* When a professed religious is sent to another monastery to render service there he is granted all the rights of stability except that of voting. If, at the end of a year, he desires to make his stability there the year which has elapsed may be counted as the year of probation.

If a religious is in another house for some reasonable motive, he need not be given the rights of stability, but a year which has elapsed may be counted as the year of probation.

A religious may be sent to another monastery to do penance despite his vow of stability. He occupies the rank assigned him and conforms to the directives of both Superiors.

The Abbot of a professed who is temporarily residing elsewhere is always considered to delegate all his authority to the Abbot of the place where the professed is. The latter however can always correspond freely with his own Abbot.

CHAPTER VII   OBLATES

46 Oblates do not canonically form part of the Order since they do not pronounce the vows of religion. They are received into it, however, according to the terms of their engagement. On entering, those destined to become oblates, write out and sign the declaration in No. 3.

47 *Admission to probation*. After spending at least a month in secular dress, the aspirant oblates are clothed in the habit, the consultative vote of the Abbot's Council having been taken first. The ceremony of clothing takes place in the novitiate, and for the blessing of the oblate's habit the 'Benedictio cucullae vestiumve regularium pro saecularibus' (as in Collectanea, ed. 1900, p. 273) is used.

An aspirant oblate who has already received the habit of the Order takes the oblate's habit without any blessing or ceremony.

48 *Admission to the ranks of the professed*. When the aspirant oblate has spent two years in the novitiate, the deliberate vote of the community is taken as to whether he is to be kept or sent away. If he is accepted, he may be allowed to join the professed; if he is refused he must leave the monastery.

49 *Engagement to the community*. If the vote of the community deciding that he be allowed to remain is favourable, the oblate may not be allowed to pronounce his engagement until the end of another three years' probation to be followed by another deliberative vote of the community. It is obligatory to take this vote at the end of the three years' probation.

This engagement is simply a promise of fidelity to the community and vice versa. It does not include any vow, either public or private.

The oblate always remains free to leave the monastery, even after his engagement.

If an oblate receives an unfavourable vote from the community he must leave the monastery.

50 The oblate prepares for his oblation by a retreat of eight full days. On the eve of the ceremony he should write out the act of his oblation as follows: 'Ego, frater N . . . , sacerdos, (diaconus, subdiaconus, acoly-thus, exorcista, lector, ostiarius, clericus, or laicus), ad majus obse-quium et gloriam Dei meipsum offero tamquam in hoc monasterio B.M. de . . . Ordinis Cisterciensium Strictioris Observantiae, in praesentia Reverendi Domni N. . . . hujusce monasterii Abbatis. Promitto pro tempore aggregationis meae observantiam Reguli Sancti Benedicti ad normam Constitutionum Ordinis in quantum Abbas mihi statuerit, ut sic per orationem et laborem, vitae spirituali et materiali monasterii parti-cipem.'

51 *Ceremony of Oblation.* The ceremony of oblation takes place in the chapter room. When the Abbot says 'Benedicite', the oblate comes forward and prostrates in the middle of the chapter. The Abbot says: 'Quid petis?' The oblate answers: 'Misericordiam Dei et Ordinis' and the Superior continues: 'Surge in nomini.' The oblate rises and listens to the exhortation of the Abbot. Then when he is asked if he is determined to observe the Rule, he answers: 'Yes, Reverend Father, with the help of God's grace and the assistance of your prayers.' The Abbot adds: 'Qui coepit in te Deus perficiat', and all reply 'Amen'. Then the oblate standing reads aloud the formula of his oblation, which the Prior hands to him. He signs it at a table which has been prepared for this, and then presents the document to the Abbot who gives him the kiss of peace.

The oblate returns to the centre of the room and kneels, while the Abbot and community rise. Wearing the stole, the Abbot recites 'Dominus vobiscum' and the prayer 'Actiones nostras'. After the prayer the Prior conducts the oblate to his place.

52 The Secretary draws up the instrument of the oblation, which is signed by the Abbot, the oblate himself, by two senior monks as witness and by the Secretary.

53 *Dismissal of an oblate.* An oblate who has made his oblation cannot be sent away except for grave reasons. The Abbot should be inspired by the enactments of Canons 646 and 647, and must ask the deliberative vote of his Council.

There is however no suspensive recourse against this dismissal, contrary to what is stated in Can. 647, 2.40.

Before his definitive admission an oblate may be sent away for reasons of health, but age or ill-health can never be used as pretexts for dismissal after he has made his oblation.

54 In choir and elsewhere, the oblates are placed after the novices. They are buried in their own habit and the same prayers and ceremonies are used as for a novice (17). For their part they should say the prayers for the dead prescribed in the Order.

55 *Particular cases.* If a novice becomes an aspirant-oblate after completing only part of his novitiate, he shall be deliberatively voted on by the community until he has spent twenty-four months in the novitiate whether as novice or aspirant-oblate.

If a novice completes his novitiate and is not proposed to the votes for admission to temporary profession, he cannot become an oblate without the favourable deliberative vote of the community.

If a novice completes his novitiate and the votes for his admission to profession are unfavourable, he may remain as an oblate on condition he is admitted by the deliberative vote of the community. The two years of his novitiate count as the years of probation for the state of oblate.

If a simply professed comes to the end of the three-year period of his temporary vows, and desires to become an oblate, he may do this only after the deliberative vote of the community. The Abbot may impose a further period of probation on him before granting him definitive admission to the community as an oblate.

If a temporary professed has been dispensed from his vows he cannot be received in any house of the Order as an oblate without the written permission of the Abbot-General.

BOOK 2
TIMETABLES: RINGING OF BELLS

CHAPTER I   TIMETABLES

Since he strives to divinise the ordinary affairs of life, the monk sees in the details of the daily timetable so many divine calls to fidelity and he does well in filially responding to these with punctuality.

It is by the accomplishment of things which are small, or which appear small, that he gives testimony of his attachment to things which are great, to things which are invisible. Furthermore, 'the accomplishment of these small things strengthens certain dispositions which are essential to every contemplative: the exacting demands of purity of soul, the submission of a child to his heavenly Father, immediately translated into submission to

Superiors and devotion to the Rule: finally there is that need for realism, for love is not content with mere dreams and ideas.'
(P. Regamey)
These timetables follow solar time.

56 *Working days*

2.15 Rise
2.30 Vigils, Mental Prayer, Lauds, Angelus, Masses, Lectio divina, Frustulum (Mixt)
6.15 Prime, Chapter, Making of beds, Lectio divina
8.00 Tierce, Conventual Mass, Work
11.00 End of work
11.15 Sext, Examen, Angelus
11.30 Dinner, Grace, Dish-washing, Lectio divina
1.15 None, Work
3.30 End of work, Lectio divina
4.35 (approx.) Vespers, Mental prayer
5.15 Collation, (Supper), Dish-washing, Lectio divina
6.15 Compline reading
6.30 Compline, Salve, Examen, Angelus, Retire

Note: During Lent, the Lenten Reading is held for three-quarters of an hour before either Conventual Mass or Vespers, according to the decision of the Abbot.

57 *Sundays and Feastdays*

2.00 Rise (if Vigils are sung)
2.15 Vigils, Mental prayer, Lauds, Angelus, Masses, Lectio divina, Mixt
6.30 Prime, Chapter, Making of beds, Lectio divina
9.45 (approx.) Tierce, (Blessing of Holy Water, Procession)
10.00 Conventual Mass
11.15 Sext, Examen, Angelus
11.30 Dinner, Grace, Dish-washing, Lectio divina
1.15 None, Lectio divina
3.00 Vespers, Benediction, Lectio divina
5.00 Mental prayer
5.15 Supper, Dish-washing, Lectio divina
6.15 Compline reading
6.30 Compline, Salve, Examen, Angelus, Retire

Note: On days which are kept as half-holidays, the above timetable is followed for the morning (rise at 2.15), and that of working days for the afternoon.

58 *Easter until September 14th.* The timetable given above in No. 56 may be followed. But the Abbot may also use one or other of the following modifications of it, beginning whenever he judges fit.

(1) *Conventual Mass after work*
       Quarter of an hour after Chapter: Work
 9.00 End of work, Lectio divina
10.20 (approx.) Tierce, Conventual Mass, Sext, Examen, Angelus

(2) *Prolongation of the time of work*
(a) if the Conventual Mass is celebrated before work
 7.30 Tierce, Conventual Mass, Work
11.00 End of Work . . . etc.
12.45 None, Work
 3.30 End of work, Lectio divina
(b) if the Conventual Mass is celebrated after work
       Quarter of an hour after Chapter: Work
 9.30 End of work, Lectio divina
10.20 (approx.) Tierce, Conventual Mass, Sext, Examen, Angelus, etc.
12.45 None, Work
 3.30 End of work, Lectio divina

Note: The timetables under 1 and 2 above can include the short siesta (half-hour) authorised by the Decree of 27 June 1956.

59 For this period of the year (Easter to September 14) we may also use the following with a full siesta.

(1) *Working days*
2.30 Rise
2.45 Vigils, Mental prayer, Lauds, etc.
. . . . Conventual Mass and work, or vice versa as in No. 58, 1 or 2
1.30 End of siesta
1.40 None, work
4.30 End of work, Lectio divina
5.35 (approx.) Vespers, Mental prayer
6.15 Supper, Dish-washing, Lectio divina
7.15 Compline reading
7.30 Compline, Examen, Angelus, Retire

(2) *Sundays and Feastdays*
....
2.00 End of siesta
2.10 None, Lectio divina
4.00 Vespers, Benediction, Lectio divina

6.00 Mental prayer
6.15 Supper, Dish-washing, Lectio divina
7.15 Compline reading
7.30 Compline, Examen, Angelus, Retire

60 *Christmas Eve*
.... The timetable for the morning as for working days
1.15 None, Lectio divina
3.00 (approx.) Vespers, Mental prayer
3.45 Collation, Dish-washing, Lectio divina
4.30 Compline, Salve, Examen, Angelus, Retire
9.00 Rise
9.15 Vigils
If this day falls on a Sunday:
1.00 None, Lectio divina
2.30 Vespers, Benediction, Lectio divina
3.30 Mental prayer
3.45 Supper, Dish-washing
4.30 Compline, Salve, Examen, Angelus, Retire

61 *Christmas Day*
Midnight: Conventual Mass, Lauds, Retire
5.45 Rise
5.55 Angelus, Prime, Masses
Remainder as on Sundays

62 *Holy Thursday*
 2.15 Rise
 2.30 Vigils, Mental prayer, Lauds, Angelus, Lectio divina, Frustulum
 6.15 Prime, Chapter, Making of beds, Lectio divina
 8.00 Tierce, Work
10.30 End of work, Lectio divina
11.00 Sext, Mandatum of the Poor, Examen, Angelus
          (11.15: Sext, Examen, Angelus, if there is no Mandatum of the
          Poor)
11.30 Dinner, Grace, Dish-washing, Lectio divina
 1.15 None, Lenten reading
 3.15 (approx.) Mandatum, Reading of Gospel
 3.45 Mental prayer in presbytery stalls
 4.00 Conventual Mass
 6.00 Collation, Dish-washing

  6.30 Compline, etc. (56)
Note: The Abbot will decide whether or not to have Mandatum of Poor
(G. Chap. 1960)

63 *Good Friday*
  2.15 Rise
  2.30 Vigils, Mental prayer, Lauds, Angelus, Discipline, Lectio,
          Frustulum
  6.15 Prime, Psalter for two hours
  9.30 Tierce, Lectio divina
11.15 Sext, Examen, Angelus
11.30 Dinner, Grace, Dish-washing, Lectio divina
  2.00 Lenten reading
  2.45 None, Liturgy of the day
  5.15 Mental prayer
  5.30 Collation, Dish-washing, Lectio divina
  6.30 Compline etc. (56)
Note: The Abbot may arrange morning timetable according to needs of
community.

64 *Holy Saturday*
.....   As on Holy Thursday, up to:
10.30 End of work, Lectio divina
11.15 Sext, Examen, Angelus
11.30 Dinner, Grace, Dish-washing, Lectio divina
  1.15 None, Work
  3.30 End of work, Lectio divina
  4.40 (approx.) Vespers, Mental prayer
  5.15 Collation, Dish-washing
  5.45 Examen, Angelus, Retire
10.30 Rise
10.45 Paschal Vigil, Retire
Note: The Abbot may arrange morning timetable according to needs of
community.

65 *Easter Sunday*
5.00 Rise
5.15 Regina Coeli, Mental prayer, Masses, Mixt
7.30 Prime, Chapter, Making of beds, Lectio divina

66 *Vigil of Pentecost*
(1) *Timetable without siesta*: as on working days, except:

```
 8.00  Tierce, Work
10.30  End of work, Lectio divina
11.15  Sext, Examen, Regina Coeli
11.30  Dinner, Grace, Dish-washing, Lectio divina
 1.15  None (in Vigils choir), Conventual Mass, Work
 4.00  End of work, Lectio divina
```
(2) *Timetable with siesta*: as on working days, except:
```
10.15  Tierce, Lectio divina
11.15  Sext, Examen, Regina coeli
11.30  Dinner, Grace, Dish-washing, Siesta
 1.30  End of siesta
 1.40  None, Conventual Mass, Work
 5.00  End of work, Lectio divina
```

67 Any habitual modification of these timetables must be submitted to the Father Immediate.

Other permanent timetables may be submitted for approval to the General Chapter, if those given above are not suitable to the country or the climate.

CHAPTER II   RINGING OF BELLS

68 In keeping with tradition, our churches should have two bells of different dimensions.

69 The Abbot will confide the task of ringing the bells to a monk who is noted for punctuality, so that all may be done at the correct time. He will also appoint a second bell ringer who will assist the first when necessary.

70 The time for rising is announced with the dormitory bell.

If the monk charged with waking the community rings too late, he stands in ceremony at the presbytery step at the beginning of the Office and waits there for some time. He then makes a profound inclination to the altar and goes to his place.

71 The bell for an Office or for any other exercise is rung* for the space of a 'Pater' and 'Ave' unless otherwise stated.

* Throughout this section, 'ring' means to cause the bell to give forth a sound by swinging it on its axis, so that the tongue strikes the sides of the bell: 'toll' means to cause the bell to give forth a sound by striking it with the tongue or hammer in such a way that the bell itself does not move.

72 *First bell.* Each office is announced a quarter of an hour beforehand by the ringing of the great bell. But this first bell is omitted if the Office is preceded by sleep or by a community exercise.

If the Abbot considers it useful, he may also have a warning bell rung a few minutes before the time of the Office.

73 *Second bell.* The second bell is rung at the time of the Office. In the case of the Little Hours, this is done with the small bell. For Vigils, Lauds, Conventual Mass and Vespers, the great bell is used. On Feasts of Sermon these last names are announced with both bells. Both bells are likewise rung for every solemn Mass and whenever the Abbot judges it expedient.

When two hours of the Canonical Office follow each other immediately, there is no bell for the second.

74 *The Conventual Mass.* Before the Office which precedes the Conventual Mass three strokes of the great bell are tolled to summon the ministers of the altar and to call the community to choir. The bell is rung again when the ministers leave the sacristy.

The bell is rung again for the Conventual Mass when the Office which precedes it is completed, or after the procession, if there is one. During this Mass the great bell is tolled from the 'Sursum corda' to the 'Sanctus' and three strokes of the small bell are tolled before the elevation of the Host and again before the elevation of the Chalice.

75 *Some other bells*
1° The end of work, supper, collation, and Compline reading are announced with the great bell.
2° At Benediction of the Blessed Sacrament three strokes of the small bell are tolled when the priest turns to give the blessing and three further strokes when he puts back the Blessed Sacrament on the altar.
3° For the Mandatum, five strokes are first of all rung to notify the servers and the community; the exercise itself is announced by the small bell.
4° If mental prayer or the particular examen are separated from an office, they are announced with three strokes of the great bell.
5° Chapter is announced with the great bell after the verse 'Fidelium' of Prime if the Brothers are to attend.

76 *Angelus and Regina Coeli.* The Angelus is rung three times daily: after the night Office, before dinner, and after the examen following the Salve. Three strokes of the great bell are tolled three times with the space of an 'Ave' between them. For the Regina Coeli the space between each three strokes is shorter. Finally the bell is rung for the space of a 'Pater' and 'Ave'.

77 *Rites for the sick and the dead.* For the Sacrament of the Sick or Viaticum, the great bell is rung twice, each time for the space of a 'Pater'. The bell is rung again a third time for the same space when the Cantor begins the psalms.

For the prayers for the dying, at the time indicated by the Abbot, the great bell is rung four times for the space of a 'Pater', with a short interval between each ringing.

When the sick person dies, the knell is sounded for five minutes by ringing the great bell and tolling the small bell at the same time. This is done again after the midday Angelus for the space of a 'Miserere', also at the time of the burial and when the community leave for the cemetery during the psalm 'In exitu'.

When Requiem Mass or Office of the Dead is sung, it is announced in the same fashion. The bell for the latter is rung during the Canticle of the Office preceding it, or a few minutes before the end of mental prayer.

At the death of a guest, the small bell is rung twice, with a short interruption between each ringing. At the burial of a guest the small bell alone is rung.

78 *Liturgical reception of visitors.* When a dignitary is to be given a liturgical reception, the great bell is rung to summon the community to the church. The two bells are rung for whatever length of time the Abbot decides, while the visitor is being conducted to the church in procession.

BOOK 3
ECCLESIASTICAL RITES IN GENERAL

CHAPTER I   ORDER IN CHOIR

'Let the Oratory be that which its name indicates.' (Rule)
'My house is a house of prayer.' (Luke XIX, 45)

79 The first Superior occupies the first place in choir on the right side and the second Superior the first place on the left. The Subprior stands beside the Abbot in the return stalls. In the absence of the Abbot or the Prior no one may occupy their stalls. All the others occupy the stalls on each side according to their rank of seniority. Priests take precedence of the other monks in choir and in ecclesiastical ceremonies only.

> By reason of the sublime functions of their office, the priests of
> the monastery, more even than the other monks, should cultivate
> humility (Rule, ch. 62), but their brothers, who are not priests,
> should never forget the character with which they are invested.
> 'The Sacrament of Orders gives not only a particular grace
> proper to this state and function, wrote Pius XII, but also an
> indelible character that likens sacred ministers to the Priest,
> Jesus Christ.' (Mediator Dei)

The novices likewise observe the order of seniority in the front stalls (6), but they never stand in front of the Abbot or the Prior.

80 The Abbot General always occupies the first place, and at the Generalate his place may not be occupied by anyone, even in his absence.

81 When an Abbot of our Order comes to one of our monasteries, the local Abbot yields him his place and takes that of the Prior. However, a local Abbot does not yield his place to an Abbot from a monastery of his filiation; the latter occupies the place of the Prior and only takes that of the Abbot in his absence.

82 When several Abbots meet in one monastery they take their rank in choir as follows: Abbots de regimine following the seniority of their abbeys; other Abbots; Titular Priors; Superiors ad nutum and Definitors.

83 In his own monastery the claustral Prior yields his place only to Abbots de regimine, Titular Priors, Superiors ad nutum and Definitors. If he is visiting another monastery he stands beside the Prior of the place.

84 A monk who is in another monastery, ordinarily takes the rank of seniority that he has in his own house.

CHAPTER II DIFFERENT LITURGICAL POSTURES

85 Our Cistercian rite has many liturgical postures which are rich in significance.

'Those external and visible bodily movements intensify the interior and invisible movements of the soul without which they are impossible.' (St Augustine)

86 The most frequent posture, especially during the Office, is that of standing upright; the monks stand erect in their stalls turned in choir or turned towards the altar. They keep their hands in the sleeves of the cowl before the breast.

87 On certain occasions they allow the sleeves to hang down by the side: they are then said to be 'in ceremony'. This posture is never assumed when not wearing either cowl or cloak; the hands would then be held inside the scapular above the belt.

88 When 'on the misericords' they are bowed down with the hands crossed on the knees in the sleeves of the cowl; if previously in ceremony the sleeves are lowered and crossed.

89 There are three different kinds of bows: the profound bow in which we incline until the hands are crossed on the knees, the moderate bow involving a sufficiently pronounced movement of the head and shoulders, and the slight bow which consists in bowing the head only.

90 There are also three kinds of prostrations. For the first the body is extended on the ground, the hands crossed on the breast, the forehead against the floor and the head uncovered.

In both the Old and New Testaments the prostration was a sign of adoration symbolising the nothingness of man before his God. 'God appeared to Abraham in the vale of Mambre . . . Having raised his eyes, he prostrated on the ground.' (Gen. xviii, 1–2) 'This is my beloved Son . . . And the disciples hearing fell upon their face and were very much afraid'. (Matt. xvii, 5–6)

The second consists in going on our knees, with the hands brought close together, and bowing down in such a way that the knuckles are placed on the ground near the knees. We call this 'prostrating on the knuckles'.

'. . . et ecce manus tetigit me et erexit me super genua mea et super articulos manuum mearum. . . .' (Daniel, x, 10)

The third kind of prostration is made by kneeling in the stalls leaning against the desks with the sleeves raised. This is called 'prostrating against the desks'. Those who have not desks before them simply kneel upright facing in choir.

91 When kneeling we face the altar, keeping the body upright, the hands in the sleeves, the feet covered and in the stalls as far as possible.

92 When seated we keep the sleeves raised on the knees. We raise and lower the seats with the hand nearest the altar.

93 The genuflection consists in bending the right knee down to the ground near the left foot, while keeping the rest of the body erect and the hands resting on the left knee.

94 We make the sign of the cross reverently, with the body erect, giving it its full extension and covering the hand with the sleeve of the cowl or the border of the cloak, except, obviously, when signing ourselves with holy water. During community exercises we make only those signs of the cross that are prescribed in those Usages.

> 'Properly understood, the sign of the cross means: I adore You, O God, by the cross, by Jesus on the cross, with Jesus on the cross, as Jesus on the cross. . . . I ask You for all that is necessary to me in the name of the cross, that is, in the name of that same remembrance, of those same merits to which I humbly unite "that which is wanting to them" according to the invitation of the Apostle.' (P. Sertillanges)

CHAPTER III   COMMON CEREMONIES

95 When entering the church we take holy water, except on Sundays before Tierce and whenever we are walking in procession.

We make a profound bow to the altar when entering the church and when leaving it.

We never enter the church without kneeling for a moment unless the second bell for an Office has begun.

If we pass before an altar during the Consecration or while Communion is being distributed we at least genuflect.

When walking in the church we are always in ceremony.

96 When going to choir we make a profound bow to the altar at the entrance to the stalls or in the middle of the church if we have to cross it. We make the same bow when we turn our back on the altar; when we come to the presbytery step either to stand there or to ascend it; when we stop in the presbytery, or cross it if the Blessed Sacrament is not on the altar; when we pass before the Hebdomadary in the presbytery stalls or before a relic of the True Cross solemnly exposed.

97 When crossing the presbytery we genuflect if the high altar has a Tabernacle. If the Blessed Sacrament is exposed, we go on the knuckles when we enter or leave the presbytery. We make the same reverence on the lowest step when about to ascend the high altar if the Blessed Sacrament is present there, unless we have previously stopped in the presbytery.

98 We make a moderate bow when we pass before an altar, before the principal door of the church and before the image of Our Lady in the reading cloister. We also make this bow when we meet a priest going to say Mass or coming therefrom. We omit this bow when we are walking in community.

99 We make the slight bow whenever we hear the holy names of Jesus and Mary unless we are already bowed down or unless they occur too frequently.

100 Those who wear the calotte should remove it during the singing or reading of the Gospel, from the Preface until after the Communion, when the Blessed Sacrament is on the altar, when they serve Mass or go to Confession. They should likewise remove it to receive ashes or holy water, to offer the candles at the Purification, when genuflecting and on entering the presbytery.

101 At the sound of the bell we recite the Angelus silently, prostrate on the knuckles and turn in choir. We rise at the signal of the Abbot. From Saturday evening until after Compline on Sunday, we recite it standing in ceremony and turned towards the altar.

During Paschal time we say the Regina Coeli standing instead of the Angelus.

Those who are not in choir when the Angelus rings observe the same ceremonies as far as possible wherever they may happen to be, taking care to turn towards the church.

The Angelus recalls the Incarnation of the Word three times

daily, that is to say, the greatest event in history and the source of all graces.

102 When we go from the church to another community exercise, having occupied the lower stalls, the Abbot leads down the middle of the choir, and the community follow him leaving the stalls by the lower opening. If we are coming from the presbytery stalls, we leave by the upper opening.

In large communities the Abbot may allow the monks to walk in two lines but he himself remains in the middle.

CHAPTER IV   THE CHANT

103 The entire Office should normally be sung on feasts of Sermon, and the whole Office except the responsories on Sundays. On half-holidays we begin to sing at Prime. Exceptions to this rule may not be made habitually without the consent of the Father Immediate.

On ordinary days the Abbot may also have part of Vigils and Lauds sung; whether the Invitatory or the hymn, or the 'Te Deum' and Lauds, or Lauds alone, or Lauds beginning at the capitulum.

An old proverb says: 'He who sings well, prays twice.' (Pius XII)

104 The signing may be sustained by a schola in the middle of the choir. It is preferable that the verses of the Gradual and Alleluia be sung by it alone. The schola may also sing the Tracts alternately with the choir. For the remainder the Abbot will decide, but he must take care that the schola does not supplant the choir.

105 The singing of the Mass and the Office may be sustained by an organ, except during the Tridum Sacrum. On feasts of Sermon and other solemnities, the organ may be played during the Mass but not during the Canon.

106 It is forbidden to sing anything whatever, either at the Office or at Mass, Processions or Benediction of the Blessed Sacrament, etc., on a tone other than that which is appointed in the books of the Order.

CHAPTER V   GENERAL NORMS FOR THE OFFICE

'I frequently experience a great joy during the Divine Office in recalling that the Holy Spirit prays in us "with unspeakable

groanings", and that in the psalms I have the consolation of saying to the Heavenly Father all that I have to say. The psalms are so full.' (Dom Marmion)
The liturgy has us say things to God that we should never dare to say of ourselves.

107 We open the books before the beginning of the Office.
During the second bell for an Office we stand in the stalls turned towards the altar.

108 From the beginning of the last bell for an Office no one enters the choir from the side where the seniors are except the first two Superiors or, in their absence, the first monk on either side.

The Abbot presides at all the Offices. When in his stall at the beginning of the Office, or when he arrives afterwards, the first monk and the first novice of both choirs salute him, unless they are bowed down, in ceremony, or seated; those who come later salute him also if there is no one between them and the Abbot. We also salute the Abbot whenever we pass before or beside his stall, the community being assembled. If there are several Abbots in choir we salute only the one who presides.

We do not bow to the Abbot if the bell for the Office has not rung or if the Blessed Sacrament is on the altar: neither do we salute him if he arrives when the choir is seated, in ceremony or bowed down.

When we salute the Abbot we salute Christ whose place he holds in the monastery. That is why when Christ is actually present on the altar we no longer salute His representative.
'After I had heard and seen, I fell down to adore before the feet of the angel, who shewed me those things. And he said to me: See thou do it not, for I am thy fellow servant, and of thy brethren. Adore God.' (Apoc. XII, 8–10)

109 After the 'Dulce nomen' of the antiphon of Our Lady, we come out of the stall, turn towards the altar, make the sign of the cross and bow profoundly. In ceremony, and still turned towards the altar, we respond to the 'Deus in adjutorium' (to the 'Domine labia mea aperies' at Vigils). Then we bow profoundly turned in choir for the 'Gloria Patri' and re-enter the stalls at the 'Sicut erat'.

110 We stand in the stalls, turned in choir, during the psalms, hymns, canticles and common antiphons, unless otherwise indicated.

We stand in the stalls, turned towards the altar, during the second bell for an Office, the Invitatory and psalm 'Venite', the versicles, the first blessing of each Nocturn, the short lessons, the little chapters, the commemorations at Vespers and Lauds.

111 During the Office we sit down only after the first verse of the psalm, and we rise after the mediant of the last verse, or towards the end of the responsory, so that all can bow together at the 'Gloria Patri'.

112 We bow out of the stalls for the 'Gloria Patri', and for the doxology of hymns which have one.

We likewise bow out of the stalls for a collect if the preceding antiphon was sung out of the stalls.

113 On feasts of Sermon we are in ceremony for the antiphons and hymns of Lauds and Vespers as well as for the antiphons of the 'Benedictus' and 'Magnificat'. We are also in ceremony for the commemoration of a feast of Sermon.

114 In the church, and even elsewhere when in community, the monk who has to sing or recite anything is uncovered in ceremony, except for certain exceptions noted later.

He who intones an antiphon stands out of the stall, turned in choir and in ceremony. His neighbour adopts the same posture when intoning a psalm. He who has intoned the antiphon remains in ceremony until the mediant of the psalm verse; he then makes a profound bow to the altar and re-enters his stall.

When a psalm or a canticle begins with the same words as the antiphon, these words are not repeated when intoning the psalm or canticle.

> St Benedict considered it an honour for a monk to intone a psalm or antiphon, so much so that a prohibition to do so was regarded by him as a severe penance: 'In the oratory, he said, the guilty one will intone neither psalm nor antiphon, nor will he recite a lesson until he has made satisfaction.' (Chap. 24)

115 When the last person in choir has intoned an antiphon, the succeeding antiphons are intoned by those next above him in retrograde order, although they may already have intoned theirs.

For the psalms, however, the general rule is that they be intoned by the one next below him who intoned the antiphon, except when the latter is last on his side, in which case the psalm is intoned by the one next above.

116 Prelates intone only those antiphons designated in these Usages. They never intone psalms.

117 When two psalms follow each other without an antiphon, the second is taken up by the choir opposite that on which the preceding ended.

118 The 'Kyrie eleison' is intoned by the Cantor on the Invitator's side, except at the prayers of Prime, and at Grace before and after meals when it is intoned by the whole choir.

119 From the 'Kyrie eleison' at the end of the Office we bow on the misericords. If it is a ferial day on which the liturgical colour is violet we prostrate against the desks, but if there is a commemoration we do not again prostrate. The Abbot remains bowed when reciting the verse 'Fidelium'.

120 If a blessing is given at the end of an Office the choir stand in the stalls turned towards the altar.

121 When the Office is ended we noiselessly close the books with the edges towards the altar. At the signal of the Abbot we bow and retire.

122 The 'Magnificat', the 'Benedictus', the 'Te Deum', the 'Gloria in excelsis', the 'Credo', the 'De profundis' in chapter, the 'Miserere' and 'Laudate' in the refectory, and the penitential psalms are always intoned on the Abbot's side.

123 Only the Cantors may sing when walking in choir. The Hebdomadary or Invitator do not fulfil any of their functions when they are not at their places.

124 No one should leave the choir without necessity or without permission. In order to ask this permission, the monk presents himself before the Abbot; however, the two monks who are nearest to him may ask this permission from their places. If we are not going to return to choir, we advise our neighbour of the fact by a bow of the head.

   We do not leave the choir by the side of the seniors.

CHAPTER VI   COMING LATE: FAULTS IN CHOIR

'Let nothing be preferred to the love of Christ' – 'Let nothing be
preferred to the Work of God.' (Rule, ch. 4 and 43)
'St Stephen had such reverence for the Divine Office that he left
all his material preoccupations at the door of the Oratory and only
resumed them when he came out again.' (Great Exordium, 1, 20)

125 When a fault is committed in the service of God it is fitting that
satisfaction be made.

There are three kinds of satisfactions in the Cistercian rite: the great
satisfaction, which is made by prostrating fully, the moderate satisfaction which consists in 'prostrating on the knuckles' (90) and the little
satisfaction in which we touch the ground with the knuckles without
going on the knees.

We are turned in choir when making the little satisfactions; if seated
we rise fully before making it, but we sit down again without fully
resuming an upright position.

126 When a monk arrives late, but before his stall is due to be
occupied (127) he makes the little satisfaction at his place.

When the choir are bowed down or out of the stalls, we do not pass
before them without necessity; we wait at the end of the choir until they
re-enter the stalls.

We do not walk in the church without necessity during the 'Deus in
adjutorium', the 'Gloria Patri' or the doxology of the hymns.

127 We occupy the stall of one coming late or one who is absent after
the 'Gloria Patri' of the Invitatory at Vigils (of psalm 94 on days when
there is no Invitatory), after the 'Gloria Patri' of the 'Deus misereatur' at
Lauds, after the doxology of the hymns at the Little Hours, after the
'Gloria Patri' of the first psalm at Vespers and after the 'Gloria Patri' at
the beginning of Compline.

128 If a monk arrives after his stall has been occupied (127) he makes
the little satisfaction at the presbytery step and remains there for a few
moments before coming to choir. If several are making this satisfaction,
the senior takes the middle place, but if he is an Abbot, the others go
behind him.

129 When someone arrives after his stall has been occupied he
remains the last on his side, exception being made for only the Cantor

and Subcantor. And even for the latter, the choir should not be disturbed if seated.

> 'If someone arrives (late) . . . he will not take his accustomed place in choir, but will stand . . . after all the others.' (St Benedict, ch. 43)

130 Those who return from the fulfilment of a liturgical function make no satisfaction when arriving in choir; the same applies to those who leave the church and return again.

If we arrive in the church when the choir are seated we remain standing for the space of two verses.

131 Those who arrive after the Office has begun should immediately join in with the choir. They afterwards make up the part of the Office which they have missed unless their coming late was due to the fulfilling of a liturgical function.

132 If we make a mistake in the pronunciation of the text during the Divine Office, we make the little satisfaction at our place. This satisfaction is not made for a mistake in the melody. It is omitted when we are kneeling, bowed down, prostrate against the desks, or in ceremony. It is likewise omitted when the mistake is general. The little satisfaction is not made outside the church.

We also make a little satisfaction at our place when we make a considerable noise or disturb the good order of the choir.

133 When a monk makes a mistake, nobody should correct him except the Cantors or the Superiors.

If he takes one little chapter, a collect, a short responsory, a versicle, etc., for another, and if he perceives this before finishing, he corrects his mistake if he can do so without causing disturbances or a notable interruption; if not he should leave the correction to the Cantor.

134 When one is thus corrected by the Cantor he goes and prostrates at the presbytery step. He rises without awaiting the signal of the Abbot.

BOOK 4
THE DIVINE OFFICE AND CONVENTUAL MASS

CHAPTER I   THE DIVINE OFFICE

'We believe that God is present everywhere and that the eyes of
the Lord behold the good and the bad in every place. Let us
firmly believe this especially when we take part in the Work of
God. . . . Let us stand to sing so that our mind may be in
harmony with our voice.' (St Benedict, ch. 19)

Antiphons of the Blessed Virgin before the Divine Office

135 Before each hour of the Divine Office except Compline an
antiphon is sung in honour of Our Lady. Before Lauds we sing the 'Sub
tuum' kneeling.

By singing this antiphon of ancient Greek origin, one of the oldest
in honour of the 'Theotokos', the monks have recourse to their
Protectress at the very beginning of the day and invoke her aid
for all the great intentions of the Church.

136 When the signal is given the community prostrate on the knuckles
and the Abbot says: 'Ave Maria, gratia plena, Dominus tecum'. The
community rise and re-enter the stalls saying: 'Benedicta tu . . .' Then
the antiphon is sung. We face the altar for the versicle and bow on
the misericords for the collect which the Hebdomadary sings and for
the 'Dulce nomen' which is added by the Abbot still bowing on the
misericords.

'Above all let it not come to pass . . . that the cult of Our Lady,
Mother of God, which in the opinion of the saints is a sign of
predestination, be under-estimated.' (Pius XII, Mediator Dei)

Vigils when sung

'Super muros tuos Jerusalem constitui custodes; non tacebunt die
noctuque, neque cessabunt laudare Dominum.' (Isiais, LXII, 6)

137 After the 'Dulce nomen' the Office begins with the usual ceremonies (109). We re-enter the stalls after replying to the 'Domine, labia
mea . . .' intoned three times by the Hebdomadary on the tone chosen
for psalm 3.

138 On feasts of Sermon, two monks designated by the Cantor assist
the Invitators to sing the Invitatory and psalm 'Venite'.

139 After the Invitatory and the hymn the Abbot intones the first antiphon and the first monk on the Invitator's side intones the first psalm; in the absence of the Abbot this monk intones the first antiphon. The second antiphon is intoned by the first on the Hebdomadary's side the third by him who intoned the first psalm on the Invitator's side, and so on. We sit at the odd-numbered psalms.

140 After the last antiphon of each Nocturn the choir turn towards the altar. We sit down when we have answered 'Amen' to the blessing. After the blessing of the third Nocturn, however, we remain standing in ceremony and turned towards the Deacon until the 'Et religio'.

141 If the responsories are sung, the lessons of the first Nocturn are sung by monks from the Invitator's side, beginning with the juniors; those of the second Nocturn by monks from the other side. For the third Nocturn, the 9th lesson is sung by the Deacon of the week, the 10th and 11th by the seniors, and the 12th by the Prior. The Abbot sings the Gospel. In his absence, the Prior replaces him and the Subprior sings the 12th lesson.

> 'All Egypt and all the Thebaid kept the number of twelve psalms both for the evening Office and for that of the night; these were followed by two lessons, one from the Old and one from the New Testament. If this number of very ancient origin was so scrupulously adhered to by all the monasteries of Egypt, it was because the ancients averred that it did not originate through human initiative but came from heaven, being transmitted to the Fathers through the ministry of an angel.' (Cassian, Inst. 11, 4)

142 The monk who is to sing a lesson bows in the middle of the choir between the two openings and goes to the reading desk. He asks the blessing bowed towards the Abbot. The latter gives the blessing in ceremony, but if there is a blessing before each lesson, the first blessing only of each Nocturn is given in ceremony. The reader begins his lesson only when the choir are seated. At the end he says 'Tu autem'. He then bows to the altar and returns to his place, making the little satisfaction between the two openings if he has not been correct to the letter.

Those who sing the last three lessons of each Nocturn leave their places during the verse of the preceding responsory.

143 When the responsories are not sung, all the lessons of the first Nocturn are sung by the Invitator, those of the second Nocturn by the

Invitator of the preceding week and those of the third Nocturn by the Deacon of the week. If the latter is absent he is replaced by the deacon above him (or below him if he is the first on his side).

When several lessons are thus together, there is only one blessing and only one bow at the end.

144 Each responsory is sung by two monks. As far as is convenient, the Cantor appoints religious from the Hebdomadary's choir for the responsories of the first Nocturn; for those of the second, religious from the Invitator's side, and for those of the third Nocturn religious chosen indifferently from both choirs. The 12th responsory, however, is sung by the Abbot assisted by the two Cantors, and in his absence by the Cantors alone.

The two monks designated bow profoundly together on arriving at the stand. They intone the responsory in ceremony and sing the verse in the same way. If they have to sing the 'Gloria Patri' they bow only after the 'et Spiritu Sancto'.

145 At the end of the repetition of the last responsory of each Nocturn, we rise so that we can bow at the 'Gloria Patri' and we raise our seats. When the responsories are not sung we do not raise our seats after the first Nocturn.

From Passion Sunday until Easter in the Office of the season the 'Gloria Patri' is not said after the last responsory of each Nocturn. Instead the Cantor begins the responsory again, while the choir, standing, continue as far as the verse.

146 If it is not possible to have the responsories sung by two monks, he who is to sing one remains at his place. He raises his seat and intones the responsory in ceremony turned in choir. He then re-enters his stall where he remains standing, turned in choir with the sleeves raised, while the choir continue the responsory. Then he sings the verse in ceremony turned in choir. After the verse, or after the last if there are several, or after the 'Gloria Patri' of the last responsory of each Nocturn, he bows to the altar.

147 After the 12th responsory the Abbot intones the 'Te Deum' which is sung alternately by both choirs, the Cantor on the Abbot's side continuing 'Te Dominum'. We bow at the words 'Sanctus, sanctus, sanctus, Dominus Deus Sabaoth' and rise again at 'Pleni sunt'. We also bow at 'Quos pretioso Sanguine redemisti'. Both choirs say the words of the last verse 'Non confundar in aeternum' together. Then we stand out of the stalls and face whoever is singing the Gospel.

148 The Superior sings the Gospel (wearing a stole if he is an Abbot). He makes the sign of the cross when saying 'Sequentia . . .' and the community do likewise when answering 'Gloria tibi Domine'. At the end all answer 'Amen', turn in choir and re-enter the stalls. Then the Superior intones the hymn 'Te decet laus', the Cantor adds 'Te decet hymnus', and the two choirs continue it. We bow on the misericords at the collect sung by the Superior.

149 If the Superior is an Abbot, he then gives the blessing. The choir stand in the stalls facing the altar for the versicles 'Sit nomen . . .' and 'Adjutorium . . .' They bow out of the stalls towards the Abbot at the words: 'Benedicat vos . . .'

150 After the Gospel the Superior makes the little satisfaction between the return stalls if he has not been correct to the letter.

Lauds when sung

> 'O Lord, may our lips praise You, and may our soul and our life praise You also; and since it is to You we owe our existence, may our lives be all Yours.' (Leonine Sacramentary)

151 The psalm 'Deus misereatur' is sung standing and 'in directum'. We sit during the first, third and fifth psalms. We turn in choir at the repetition of the short responsory.

On days of XII lessons and above, the Cantor pre-intones the 'Benedictus' antiphon to the Abbot. He stands in ceremony, bows his head to the Abbot and then intones the antiphon.

After the last 'Kyrie eleison' the Abbot sings the 'Pater noster' in ceremony and we all answer 'Sed libera nos a malo'.

We stand for the commemoration or the 'Benedicamus Domino', after which we bow on the misericords. Then having closed the books we recite the Angelus.

Vigils and Lauds when not sung

152 When the Office is not sung, the Invitator says the Invitatory at his place. On ferial days when there is no Invitatory we say the psalm 'Venite' after psalm 3.

153 At Vigils, the first monk on the Invitator's side intones the first psalm of the first Nocturn. The others are intoned alternately as in the sung Office.

154 We conform to the preceding numbers for the rest, except that at Lauds the choir do not rise for the 'Benedicamus Domino', which is said by the Hebdomadary.

155 When the Office of the Dead follows Lauds, we are bowed at the 'Dicinum auxilium'; then we stand erect in the stalls.

Prime

156 We bow out of the stalls at the words of the hymn 'Deum precemur supplices'. We sit for the first and third psalms, and after the 'Fidelium' we go to Chapter.

157 When the monks arrive in chapter they make a moderate bow to the crucifix at their places, sit down and mutually salute each other. The Invitator sings the martyrology at the lectern. When he announces a feast of Sermon of Our Lady, we rise and bowed down in choir say the 'Ave Maria' secretly. We do the same on the eve of All Saints. If such a feast is transferred we say the 'Ave Maria' on the eve of the day it is celebrated.

When the Invitator has said 'Et alibi . . .' all rise and answer 'Deo gratias'. We turn towards the crucifix and the Hebdomadary sings the verse 'Pretiosa . . .' with the prayers which follow. At the 'Gloria Patri' and 'Kyrie eleison' we bow turned in choir. The Superiors, the Invitator and those at the end of the chapter room bow towards the crucifix. At the verse 'Et ne nos . . .' we rise and stand facing the crucifix until the collect 'Dirigere' during which we again bow turned in choir. We rise on saying 'Amen'. We face the crucifix for the verse 'Adjutorium' but we are turned in choir for the blessing which follows. We sit down after it.

The Invitator then sings a passage from the Holy Rule and at the end he adds 'Commemoratio . . .' This passage may be read in the vernacular when the Laybrothers are present. The Abbot sings 'Requiescant in pace' and all reply 'Amen'.

The community rise when the Cantor intones the 'De profundis' which is sung alternately with flexes by the two choirs facing each other. After the verse 'Requiem' we bow still turned in choir while the Abbot, uncovered and standing in ceremony facing the community, sings the versicles and collect. We then bow to the crucifix and retire.

If Prime is not sung, neither are the prayers in chapter.

Tierce, Sext, None

158 Tierce, Sext and None are sung like Prime, except that the choir are never seated.

Vespers

159 The first antiphon of Vespers is intoned by the Invitator, the second by the first monk on the Hebdomadary's side, the third by the Sub-invitator and the fourth by the one who intoned the second psalm. We sit for the first and third psalms.

When there is a long responsory it is sung in the middle of the choir by the two Cantors with the same ceremonies as for a responsory at Vigils (143). We are turned in choir during the singing of the responsory but face the altar at the intonation of the verse.

We kneel, turned in choir, during the first verse of the Hymn 'Ave maris stella'.

The Abbot intones the 'Magnificat' antiphon on feasts of XII lessons and above. For the rest we act as Lauds.

If the Vespers are pontifical, the Abbot gives the solemn blessing, even though Benediction of the Blessed Sacrament is to follow immediately.

Compline reading

160 Compline reading takes place in the cloister or chapter room according to local circumstances. The monks take their places in order of seniority on either side of the Abbot's seat, the Prior being on his right and the Subprior on his left. The Laybrothers are placed after the choir monks. In the cloister the choir novices and oblates sit on either side of the reader, and after them the lay novices and oblates.

On arriving at his place, each one sits down and bows to his neighbours. At the signal of the Abbot, all rise, and the reader asks the blessing. When it is given, we sit and cover. No one should pass before the Abbot's seat once the reading has begun. After about a quarter of an hour's reading the Abbot says 'Tu autem', the reader continues 'Domine miserere nobis' and all rise while answering 'Deo gratias'. We then turn towards the Abbot's seat. The latter says the verse 'Adjutorium' with a flex, and all reply 'Qui fecit coelem et terram'. We then bow moderately to the crucifix and proceed to the church.

Compline

161 If the reading before Compline is replaced by the short lesson 'Sobrii estote' this is sung by the Invitator, the community meanwhile standing in the stalls facing the altar until the 'Deus in adjutorium' of Compline.

> The sentiments expressed by the psalms of Compline are most apt to that hour. The first is a psalm of thanksgiving, the second renews in us a sense of confidence in the divine protection and the third gives us an occasion to unite ourselves to all those who sing God's praises during the night.

The psalms of Compline are sung standing and 'in directum'. We make the sign of the cross at 'Pater et Filius, etc.' of the verse 'Benedicat'. Then we rise and solemnly sing the 'Salve Regina' during which we face the altar in ceremony. We answer the versicle still standing in ceremony and bow out of the stalls for the collect. The Abbot sings this on the solemn tone, standing and in ceremony. The choir re-enter the stalls on answering 'Amen' and remain bowed on the misericords during the versicles which follow. The Abbot takes the posture of the choir during those versicles.

Immediately afterwards we make the examination of conscience.

Repose

162 At the end of the examen, the Angelus is rung and the Abbot gives the signal. Then he stands at the door of the church near the holy water font and sprinkles each member of the community who bow profoundly before him. On receiving holy water each one covers and goes to the dormitory. The Abbot takes holy water himself by touching his forehead with the aspersory before giving it back to the server.

The Office of the Dead

> 'It is a holy and wholesome thought to pray for the dead that they may be loosed from their sins.' (II Mach. XII, 46)

163 The Office of the Dead comprises one Nocturn, Lauds and Vespers and is regularly discharged twice a month. It begins with the

Nocturn which may be anticipated except on November 2nd. In this case we say the 'Pater' versicles and collect after the third responsory and Lauds is recited after Lauds of the Divine Office. If the Nocturn is not anticipated, then it is recited with Lauds after the morning mental prayer and Lauds of the Divine Office is said before Prime.

Office of the Dead not sung

164 We sit for every other psalm, counting from the first of each Hour. We sit after the first verse and rise at the verse 'Requiem' of the psalm. The Sub-invitator intones the first psalm of each Hour, the first monk on the other side the second, and so on.

At the Nocturns the choir, turned towards the altar, answer the versicle after the psalms and then incline on the misericords during the 'Pater'. We sit at the signal of the Abbot for the lessons and responsories. The Invitator reads the lessons and responsories. At the verse 'Requiem' of the third responsory the choir rise and remain standing until the 'Pater'. From the 'Pater' to the end we are bowed on the misericords.

If Lauds follows the Nocturn we remain seated until the end of the first psalm of Lauds.

At Lauds and Vespers we stand during the canticle. From the 'Pater' till the end we are inclined on the misericords.

Office of the Dead when sung

165 The Office of the Dead is sung on November 2nd, on the four solemn anniversaries, and for one whose body is present.

166 The Invitator intones the first antiphon of each Hour; the first monk on the Hebdomadary's side intones the second, the Sub-invitator the third and so on alternately. At the Nocturns the Invitator sits after each lesson. The Cantor intones the three responsories and signs the verses (145); he is seated during the lessons. The canticles of Lauds and Vespers are sung on the simple psalm tones. For the rest we conform to No. 164.

CHAPTER II   THE MASS

'The sacred liturgy, then, is the public worship which our
Redeemer, the Head of the Church, offers to the heavenly

Father, and which the community of Christ's faithful pays to its
Founder and through Him to the Eternal Father; briefly it is the
public worship of the Mystical Body of Jesus Christ, Head and
members.' (Pius XII, Mediator Dei)

The Conventual Mass when sung

167 The Conventual Mass, which is sung daily, is the centre of the
monastic day.
   'The summit, we may say the centre, of the Christian religion is
the Mystery of the Most Holy Eucharist, instituted by Christ the
High Priest and by His command renewed perpetually in the
Church through His ministers.' (Pius XII, Mediator Dei)

168 At the three strokes for the Office which precedes the Mass, the
monks go to choir and stand facing the altar in the presbytery stalls,
while the Celebrant and his ministers go to vest.

169 During the singing of the Introit we stand in the stalls turned in
choir, except during the 'Gloria Patri' when we bow. If time permits we
may repeat the Introit alternating it with one or two verses of the psalm
and the 'Gloria Patri'. The repetition is always done by the whole choir.
   At Masses of Our Lady which begin with the words 'Salve Sancte
Parens' we prostrate on the knuckles while the Cantor intones these
words.

170 The 'Kyrie' is intoned by the Cantor on the Invitator's side and
continued by the choir on the same side. Both choirs end the last 'Kyrie
eleison' together and then turn to face the altar.

171 If there is a 'Gloria in excelsis' we turn in choir when the Cantor
sings 'Et in terra pax hominibus'. We bow out of the stalls at the words
'Adoramus Te' and 'Suscipe deprecationem nostram'. We make the sign
of the cross at 'Cum Sancto Spiritu' and after 'Amen' we face the altar.

172 On days when the Deacon sings 'Flectamus genua', we prostrate
on the desks and rise only after 'Levate'.

173 At Quarter Tense, the prophecies of the Mass are sung by the
clerics, beginning with the juniors. Those appointed go to the presbytery step, bow profoundly, and standing on the top step at the Epistle

side, sing the prophecy facing the choir. They end it with the proper conclusion, bow profoundly to the altar and retire. The choir are seated during the prophecies.

174 We face the altar from the 'Dominus vobiscum' ('Pax vobis') until the 'Oremus' of the collect, during which we bow on the misericords. On feasts of Sermon, however, we bow out of the stalls for the collect. At the end of the collect we rise and remain turned towards the altar until the Celebrant is seated.

175 We sit in choir during the Epistle, the Gradual, the Tract or Alleluia, until the Gospel. If the words 'In nomine Jesu omne genu flectatur coelestium, terrestrium et infernorum' occur in the Epistle, we bow the knee towards the altar until 'infernorum' inclusively.

176 The 'Alleluia' is intoned by the Cantor. After the singing of the verse it is taken up by the whole choir.

At the words 'Veni Sancti Spiritus' of the Alleluia of the Mass of the Holy Ghost, we prostrate on the knuckles when the Cantor intones these words; we conclude the verse in ceremony. For the repetition we stand in the stalls.

177 The Tracts are sung by the two choirs together, the Cantor intoning each verse. For the 'Benedictus es' of Quarter Tense, the Cantor or the schola sing the first part of the verse and the choir sing the refrain.

At the words 'Veni Sancte Spiritus' of the Tract of the Mass of the Holy Ghost, the choir prostrate on the kuckles and then enter the stalls to continue the verse.

178 The community rise and stand in ceremony for the Gospel, facing the Deacon. We make the sign of the cross while replying 'Gloria tibi Domine'. If we genuflect during the Gospel, we do so towards the book. After the Gospel we re-enter the stalls and remain facing the altar.

179 If there is a 'Credo' we turn in choir when the Cantor sings 'Patrem Omnipotentem'. We prostrate on the knuckles at 'Et homo factus est'. We bow out of the stalls at 'Simul adoratur' and when both choirs have sung the 'Amen' we turn to face the altar.

180 When the Cantor intones the Offertory antiphon we turn in choir

in the stalls. This antiphon may be repeated in the same manner as the
Introit.

181 If the choir is to be incensed, each side stands out of the stalls in
ceremony facing the Deacon. After the incensation we salute him with a
bow of the head.

182 When the priest says 'Orate fratres', if the singing of the Offertory is finished, we bow on the misericords and remain there until the
Preface. After replying 'Amen' at the end of the Secret, we stand up and
remain facing the altar until the Sanctus, except during the words:
'Gratias agimus Domino Deo nostro', during which the two choirs bow
profoundly towards each other out of the stalls.

183 At the end of the Preface we bow out of the stalls when the Cantor
intones the 'Sanctus' and rise at 'Pleni sunt'. We make the sign of the
cross at 'in nomine Domini'. After the second Hosanna we face the altar
and kneel at the same time as the Deacon.

184 We prostrate on the knuckles after the elevation of the Host, and
kneel upright when the bells sound again before the elevation of the
Chalice.
> 'In the sacrament of bread and wine . . . the Saviour of men has
> concentrated at once all His teaching and all His love.' (Pius XII,
> 16 Sept. 1953)

185 We stand facing the altar until the end of the 'Pater'. Then we
bow on the misericords until the 'Agnus Dei' which is sung turned in
choir.

186 Those who are to communicate at the Conventual Mass leave
their stalls after the last 'Agnus Dei' and stand in single file at the
presbytery step, on the Epistle side. The deacons lead if they are
vested in stole. The Subdeacon (or Deacon) gives the Pax to the first in
line, who gives it to the next and so on. He who gives the Pax stands on
the step, and without bowing, places his hands on the shoulders of the
one below the step, and his left cheek against his, saying 'Pax tecum'
after which he bows to him. The one who receives the Pax makes first a
moderate bow to the other and, placing his hands under the elbows of
the latter, answers 'Et cum spiritu tuo'. He then bows again, ascends
the step and gives the Pax to the one who comes after him. According as

they receive the Pax the communicants go and kneel in the presbytery on the right-hand side.

In large communities the communicants may come to receive the Pax in several lines, and in this case the minister gives it to the first in each row.

If the Mass is not sung, the Pax is given as above.

When the Celebrant says 'Ecce Agnus Dei', all the communicants say: 'Domine non sum dignus, etc.' aloud, while striking their breasts. Then they rise, come forward in single file, prostrate on the knuckles in plano and kneel on the top step of the altar, unless local circumstances or the large number of monks call for some other arrangement.

The Deacon holds the paten under the chin of each communicant and the Subdeacon holds the end of the cloth, the other end of which is attached to the altar. If there are no sacred ministers, the communicants use a Communion plate which they leave on the corner of the altar, while the server holds the cloth. If there is only one for Communion, the priest may himself hold the paten under the communicant's chin. If the Celebrant is a Bishop or an Abbot, we kiss his ring before receiving the Sacred Host except in Requiem Masses.

The days on which the professed priests communicate they do so after the sacred ministers, but priest novices keep their ordinary rank. The inferior ministers of the altar precede the monks of the choir, even those in sacred orders. Secular clerics wear a surplice when communicating. Priests and deacons wear a stole which is either white or the colour of the day.

As soon as we have communicated, we descend the step, drawing back a little to the right, and make a profound bow to the Blessed Sacrament. Then we return to our places in single file passing behind the altar with grave and measured step.

187 When the priest communicates, or after the 'Domine non sum dignus' if there are other communicants, the Cantor intones the Communion antiphon, which may be repeated if necessary, alternating it with one or two verses of the psalm and the 'Gloria Patri'. It is sung standing turned in choir.

188 At the Postcommunion all is done as at the collect.

189 When the Celebrant gives the blessing, we bow profoundly out of the stalls. Prelates bow moderately.

190 During the last Gospel we observe the same ceremonies as during the first; we genuflect at the words 'Et Verbum caro factum est'.

On Sundays, after the last Gospel, the choir re-enter the stalls for the blessing of the reader of the refectory.

191 When the Celebrant has left the presbytery, we close the books and at the signal of the Abbot bow profoundly to the altar and retire, or if necessary go to the lower stalls.

Conventual Mass not Sung

192 If by way of exception, the Conventual Mass is not sung, the bells are rung as above at the Preface and Elevation.

If such a Conventual Mass is a Dialogue Mass, the directives of the Holy See (Musica Sacra, Nos. 31 and 32) are observed. The Abbot will determine the degree of participation. Whatever be this degree of participation we observe the following ceremonies: we kneel during the prayers at the foot of the altar, stand when the priest ascends the altar, sit during the Epistle (prophecies, etc.), stand out of the stalls at both Gospels, stand or kneel from the Gospel to the end of the Mass, except during the Consecration and the blessing of the Celebrant when we observe the usual postures.

If this Conventual Mass not sung is not a Dialogue Mass either, we nevertheless follow the directives just given.

Daily Masses De Beata and Pro Defunctis

193 A Mass is celebrated every day in honour of Our Lady and another Pro Defunctis except during the Triduum Sacrum. At least once a week these Masses are offered for members of the Order, their relatives, benefactors and associates, living and dead.

BOOK 5
SOME OTHER RITES

CHAPTER I   THE BLESSING OF WATER

194 On Sunday at Tierce, after the 'Dulce nomen' of the antiphon in honour of Our Lady, the Celebrant blesses water at the middle of the presbytery step. The community stand in the stalls facing the altar, and reply to the exorcisms and collects. As the priest asperses the fount of the altar, we turn in choir and the Cantor intones the antiphon which is repeated as often as necessary, alternating it with one or several verses of the psalm and the 'Gloria Patri' at which we do not bow. When the Celebrant comes to the presbytery step after aspersing the altar, we leave the stalls by the upper opening and approach in pairs to receive the holy water, bowing profoundly to the Celebrant when doing so.

The Abbot comes first alone, then the sacred ministers before the priests of the choir and the inferior ministers before the deacons and subdeacons of the choir. We return by the centre and re-enter the stalls by the lower opening. During the versicles and collect which follow, the choir face the altar.

CHAPTER II   PROCESSIONS

195 Processions ordinarily take place in the cloisters.

196 There is a solemn procession with stations on Palm Sunday, Ascension Thursday, and Corpus Christi, on feasts of Sermon of Our Lady and on the feast of our holy Father, St Bernard.

197 When the incense has been blessed, all together bow profoundly towards the altar when the Cantor intones the responsory, and leave the church. The monks walk in the following order: the choir novices, the choir professed juniors first, the Celebrant before the Abbot, the Laybrethren with the seniors first, the lay novices and the guests. We walk in two lines except the Abbot and the Celebrant who are in the middle. The Abbot carries the crosier and the Celebrant may carry the relics. If the two choirs have to cross they do so on re-entering the church.

On arriving at a station the community stop at the same time as the ministers and turn in choir with the exception of the Abbot and Celebrant.

At the end of the third station the Abbot, or in his absence, the Cantor intones the antiphon which is repeated if necessary, and we re-enter the church omitting the usual bows. If something still remains to be sung, it is finished in the stalls turned in choir.

Processions with Litanies

198 The Litanies of April 25th and the Rogation days may be sung either in the cloisters or outside. They may also be sung in the church, standing and turned in choir.

The antiphon 'Exurge' is first sung and we are turned in choir in the presbytery stalls. Meanwhile the Celebrant and his ministers vest. We bow at the 'Gloria Patri'. When the antiphon has been repeated, the choir kneel and two monks appointed by the Cantor begin the Litanies, kneeling in the middle of the choir.

The invocations as far as 'Christi exaudi nos' inclusive are repeated. Then we answer 'Miserere nobis' or 'Ora pro nobis'. At 'Sancta Maria' all rise, bow to the altar and the procession begins. The two Cantors stand in the middle before the Celebrant. On the return of the procession we again kneel in the presbytery stalls and rise only after the collects.

The Litanies of April 25th are of obligation on all those bound to the breviary. But there is no obligation to supply in private for the Litanies of the Rogation days.

CHAPTER III   BENEDICTION OF THE BLESSED SACRAMENT

'What an excellent and salutary devotion! As the faithful bow their heads in veneration, the priest raises the Bread of angels towards heaven and, making the sign of the cross with It over them, entreats the heavenly Father graciously to look upon His Son crucified for love of us, and for His sake and through Him who willed to become our Redeemer and our brother, to pour out His Supernatural gifts upon those whom the blood of the spotless Lamb has redeemed.' (Pius XII, Mediator Dei)

199 On Sundays and Feastdays of the Order, Benediction of the Blessed Sacrament is given after Vespers. If, however, we work during the afternoon of a feast of Sermon, it is for the Abbot to decide if there will be Benediction and at what hour.

200 At Solemn Benediction, that is, at second Vespers of feasts of Sermon, or even at first Vespers if it is a Sunday, the Celebrant is assisted by a Deacon and Subdeacon in dalmatics; otherwise he is accompanied only by the Sacristan in cowl.

201 The choir kneel in the stalls turned towards the altar. We always begin Benediction with an antiphon or hymn in honour of the Eucharist, which the Cantor intones when the Blessed Sacrament is exposed. We may then sing some motet in keeping with the feast or the season. We then add another honour of Our Lady, and finally we sing the 'Tantum ergo' immediately before the actual benediction. During the blessing we prostrate on the knuckles. Benediction ends with the 'Mane nobiscum' or the 'Laudate', or some similar piece.

If there is a 'Te Deum' it is always sung standing, in two choirs, with the proper collect, before the 'Tantum ergo'.

We always kneel in the stalls when the Blessed Sacrament is being exposed, and during exposition we do not sit in choir except during Vigils and Lauds. Outside the time of Office there should always be two adorers who are appointed by the Cantor.

CHAPTER IV   CONFESSION

'By the Sacrament of Penance the Church offers its members, who have fallen into sin, a salutary remedy; and this not only with a view to their own salvation, but also to keep far from other members of the Mystical Body all danger of contagion: better still to lead them to virtue by example.' (Pius XII, Mediator Dei)

202 It is desirable that in keeping with the traditions of the Order confessions should not ordinarily be heard in rooms.

203 Following the Constitutions, every member of the Order should confess at least every eight days. The professed, even those who are still following the exercises of the novitiate, may choose their confessor from among the priests approved by the Abbot.

One or more ordinary confessors must be appointed to hear the confessions of the novices, and some other priests must also be nominated to whom the novices may freely go in particular cases. At least four times a year the novices shall be given an extraordinary confessor to whom all shall present themselves at least to receive his blessing.

As far as possible we avoid making our confession during the community exercises or in the evening after the time for retiring.

204 For confession we observe the following rite. The penitent kneels down and the confessor, seated, says 'Benedicite'. The penitent answers 'Dominus' and the priest then says 'Deus nobiscum'. The penitent answers 'Amen' and goes on his knuckles and says 'Benedic mihi, Pater Reverende, quia peccavi'. The confessor joins his hands and blesses him: 'Dominus sit in corde tuo et in labiis tuis, ut integre, veraciter et humiliter confitearis omnia peccata tua, in nomine Patris et Filii et Spiritus Sancti. Amen'. He then covers.

After the priest's blessing the penitent, still on his knuckles, says: 'Confiteor Deo, Beatae Mariae et omnibus Sanctis et tibi, Pater, quia peccavi nimis cogatione, locutione et opere, mea culpa'. At 'mea culpa' he strikes his breast, rises on his knees and accuses himself briefly of his sins, adding at the end: 'De his et omnibus aliis meis peccatis me reum confiteor et veniam deprecor.'

The penitent then goes on his knuckles again while the priest says: 'Misereatur tui omnipotens Deus, et dimittat tibi omnia peccata tua, liberat te ab omni malo, conservet et confirmet in omni opere bono et perducat ad vitam aeternam.' The penitent answers 'Amen'. The confessor making the sign of the cross over him adds 'Indulgentiam et remissionem omnium peccatorum tuorem per gratiam Sancti Spiritus tribuit tibi omnipotens et misericors Dominus.' The penitent again answers 'Amen', rises to his knees and listens to the advice which the confessor, who has uncovered, gives him. He goes on his knuckles again to receive absolution.

The confessor covers and, extending his hand over him, absolves him in these words: 'Dominus noster Jesus Christus te absolvat, et ego auctoritate ipsius absolvo te a peccatis tuis in nomine Patris et Filii et Spiritus Sancti. Amen.' When the confessor adds: 'Vade in pace et jam amplius noli peccare', the penitent answers: 'Retribuit tibi Dominus vitam aeternam' and retires after bowing to the priest who returns the salute.

205 At the confession which is intended to fulfil the Paschal duty, and whenever the confessor thinks fit, he shall make use of the following formula of absolution appointed in the Ritual: 'Dominus noster Jesus Christus te absolvat, et ego auctoritate ipsius absolvo te ab omni vinculo excommunicationis, (suspensionis), interdicti in quantum possum et tu indiges. Deinde ego te absolvo ab omnibus peccatis, etc.' ut supra. The confessor then uncovers and joining his hands says: 'Passio Domini nostri Jesu Christi, merita Beatae Mariae Virginis et omnium Sanctorum, quidquid boni feceris et mali patienter sustinueris, sint tibi in remissionem peccatorem et augmentum gratiae et praemium vitae aeternae. Amen.'

> Speaking of the absolution of a sinner, St Augustine does not hesitate to say: 'Majus opus ex impio justum facere quam creare coelum et terram.'

206 The monks shall remember that in the sacred Tribunal they converse only on matters of conscience.

The confessors can commute the Communion, visits and prayers prescribed for gaining indulgences, in favour of the aged and sick.

BOOK 6
THE LITURGICAL YEAR

'David . . . in all his works gave thanks to the holy one, and to the most High words of glory. With the whole heart he praised the Lord and loved God that made him. And he set singers before the altar, and by their voices he made sweet melody. And to the festivals he added beauty, and set in order the solemn times . . . that they should praise the holy name of the Lord and magnify the holiness of God in the morning. The Look took away his sins and exalted his horn for ever.'

(Eccles. XLVII, 9–13)

Advent

207 During the third week of Advent we sing the solemn 'O' antiphons out of the stalls. We bow on the misericords or, on ferial days, prostrate on the desks for the collect.

Christmas Eve

208 On Christmas Eve we prostrate on the desks only at Vigils, the remainder of the Office being celebrated according to the rite of XII lessons. Lauds is sung and the 'Benedictus' antiphon is intoned by the Abbot.

When the Invitator announces the feast in chapter we prostrate. We rise at the signal of the Abbot and when all are seated again the Invitator continues the reading of the martyrology. The sermon for the feast is given on this day.

The Conventual Mass is abbatial and the rite of Sunday is used. Compline reading is replaced by the short lesson.

At Vigils we rise for the four blessings for the homilies.

Christmas Day

209 The bell for assembling in choir is rung so that the Mass may begin at midnight. The two bells are rung at the 'Gloria in excelsis' up to 'Domine Deus, Rex coelestis'. After Mass we come down to the lower choir and begin Lauds immediately.

The Angelus is rung ten minutes after the morning bell for rising. Prime follows, after which the martyrology and the Holy Rule are sung without going to chapter.

The Purification

210 On the feast of the Purification of Our Lady, the Abbot blesses the candles after Tierce and the Sacristan distributes them to the community and guests. During the distribution we are turned in choir. The Cantor intones the antiphon 'Lumen' and the canticle 'Nunc dimittis', which the two choirs continue, interposing the antiphon between every two verses.

When the 'Nunc dimittis' is finished, we have the procession as usual. Those on the right carry the candles in the right hand, the others in the left. On the return of the procession all place their lighted candles in the place prepared for them which should be accessible. During the Gospel we hold the candles in our hands, afterwards replacing them as above. When the Celebrant comes to the presbytery step all go to give him their candles, kissing his hand as they do so.

If the feast of the Purification falls on a Sunday, the blessing of the holy water is omitted.

Ash Wednesday

211 Before entering the church for the Office of Tierce we remove our shoes, and, if the climate permits, our stockings also.

Tierce is sung in the presbytery stalls.

When it is ended, the Cantor intones the antiphon 'Exurge'. We bow at the 'Gloria Patri'. When we have repeated the antiphon, we turn to the altar and respond to the versicle 'Ostende nobis . . .' After the versicle we prostrate on the desks and say the 'Kyrie eleison' together, and then the 'Pater noster' silently. At the end we reply: 'Sed libera nos a malo' and the Cantor begins the psalm 'Deus miseratur . . .', which the two choirs chant alternately with flexes, ending it with the 'Gloria Patri'. After the prayer we rise and stand facing the altar.

The blessing of the ashes takes place in the middle of the presbytery. When the ashes are blessed the Hebdomadary imposes them on the Abbot who kneels at the presbytery step. The Hebdomadary then receives the ashes himself and immediately returns to the sacristy. At this moment the choir begin to sing the antiphons and all come to receive the ashes from the Abbot, the Deacon leading. The ashes are placed on top of the head.

Lent

212 On ferial days we prostrate on the desks at the verse 'Adjuva nos . . .' of the Tract 'Domine non secundum . . .' and at the prayer over the people. While the Deacon sings the verse 'Humiliate capita . . .' before it, we bow on the misericords.

Lenten reading. On the first Sunday of Lent the books which have been chosen, or at least approved by the Abbot, are distributed. When receiving them, we bow to the Cantor. The Lenten reading begins next day and takes place daily except Sundays. It is announced with the small bell. During the reading, which lasts forty-five minutes, we observe a stricter silence than during the rest of the day. We do not leave the reading without permission, except during the last fifteen minutes which may be devoted to prayer.

The Second Sunday of Passiontide, or Palm Sunday

213 On the second Sunday of Passiontide, the 'Benedicamus Domino' and the hymns of the Little Hours are sung on the tone of feasts of Sermon.

The blessing of the Palms takes place after Tierce, the time of which is accordingly advanced. As soon as the blessing is ended, the Cantor intones the antiphon 'Pueri Hebraeorum'. The other antiphones are sung and, if necessary, repeated, until the Sacristan has distributed all the palms. We face the altar for the singing of the Gospel, which we listen to standing out of the stalls, holding the palms in our hands.

At the procession, those on the right carry the palm in the right hand, the others in the left. At the last station, when the Cantor intones the antiphon 'Ave Rex noster', all except the Deacon and acolytes prostrate on the knuckles facing in the direction of the cross. After the words 'Fili David' the community rise and continue the singing turned towards the cross. Towards the end of the antiphon, those who are to sing the 'Gloria laus . . .' go and stand before the cross and sing the hymn facing it. The two choirs face each other. When we enter the church we leave the palms in the place prepared for them.

The Mass is celebrated solemnly by the Abbot. The relics may be exposed. The 'Kyrie' used is that of Lent. The Passion is sung either on the Gospel tone or one of the other tones approved by the Order. At the words 'Emisit, etc.' all prostrate and rise at the signal of the Abbot.

Benediction is simple.

The Triduum Sacrum

214 Vigils and Lauds are sung during the Triduum Sacrum. At the beginning of Lauds the servant of the church lights a yellow candle at the presbytery step. All the lights of the church are extinguished at the beginning of psalm 150 except this candle which is extinguished at the beginning of the 'Benedictus'.

Those who are not present at the liturgical ceremonies on Holy Thursday and Good Friday are bound to recite Vespers privately.

From the 'Gloria in excelsis' of the Mass of Holy Thursday until that of the Paschal Vigil, no bell should be rung. The bell ringer uses a rattle or clapper to announce the Offices, for the Angelus, etc.

Holy Thursday

215 The Conventual Mass is solemnly celebrated by the Abbot and the entire community communicate at it. The Mass is not announced but at the 'Gloria in excelsis' the two bells are rung as at Christmas (209). For Communion we leave the stalls by the upper opening after the last 'Agnus Dei'. After Communion, the deacon who is to act as cross bearer goes to the sacristy with those appointed to carry the canopy.

At the end of the Mass all remain standing until the Celebrant kneels, and then all kneel, each holding a lighted candle in his hand. When the Celebrant receives the ciborium from the Deacon, the Cantor intones the 'Pange lingua' and we go in procession to the altar of repose by the longest route.

On arrival at the chapel, the priests station themselves nearest the altar and all kneel as the Blessed Sacrament passes before them. The Cantor does not intone the 'Tantum ergo' until the Blessed Sacrament is actually on the altar.

As soon as the Deacon places the Blessed Sacrament in the Tabernacle, all the lights of the church are extinguished, but a lamp is left burning before the altar of respose until the Blessed Sacrament is removed. The community make their thanksgiving in the chapel and also come there for mental prayer and the examen if local circumstances permit.

From the stripping of the altars until the adoration of the Cross on Good Friday, we bow profoundly whenever we pass before the high altar, even though the Blessed Sacrament is not reserved.

It is for the Abbot to decide whether or not the *Mandatum of the Poor* should be held. If it is the Ritual is followed.

Great Mandatum The Abbot performs the Great Mandatum assisted by one or two monks. If the community is numerous, one or several seniors are appointed to wash the feet of those whom the Abbot does not wash, and each has a junior assistant. The Prior presides and occupies the abbatial seat. In the absence of the Abbot, the Prior performs the ceremony and the Subprior presides.

When the antiphon 'Dominus Jesus' is intoned, the Abbot and those performing the Mandatum come in order of seniority and in single file before the abbatial seat. They uncover and all together bow profoundly to him who presides. We do not stand up when they enter. The Abbot washes the feet of twelve monks, choir and lay. His junior assistant carries the water and the other presents the towel. The Abbot washes the feet, dries and kisses them. The other assistants do likewise. After the washing of the feet, the Abbot and those who performed the ceremony with him stand before the presiding Superior, bow profoundly and retire in the same order in which they entered, while the community continue singing the antiphons.

When they arrive at the place from which they came, the Abbot and the assistants wash each other's feet, the Abbot receiving this service last of all. All don their cowls and return in the same order as before, walking uncovered and in ceremony. On arrival before the presiding Superior, they bow profoundly. The community rise and the Prior vacates the abbatial seat. Then the Abbot sits and the community do likewise.

The deacon appointed by the Cantor sits in the reader's place and reads the Gospel of the Mass and its continuation either in Latin or in the vernacular. He continues until the Abbot rises at the words: 'Surgite eamus hinc'. He neither asks the blessing nor announces the chapters. At the end neither the 'Tu autem' nor the versicle 'Adjutorium' is said.

Good Friday

216 We recite the Psalter for two hours, either after Prime, which is followed by chapter as usual, or after Tierce. The Abbot may have the Psalter recited by different groups.

We come to None barefoot. When the Office is ended we go to the presbytery stalls and stand facing the altar. When the Celebrant is seated the choir also sit, and one of the seniors sings the lesson 'in tribulatione'. The choir rise and bow on the misericords at the collect 'Deus a quo et Judas', and they sit again for the lesson 'Dixit Dominus ad Moysen' and the Tract 'Eripe me'.

During the Passion we do as on Palm Sunday.

For the solemn prayers, we stand facing the altar during the monitions, and bow on the misericords for the collects. Towards the end of these solemn prayers the two priests or deacons who are appointed for the Office of the Cross, go to the sacristy to vest in alb and take the Cross from behind the altar.

During the 'Popule meus' we are turned in choir and those who are to sing the 'Agios' go to the middle of the presbytery step. They kneel when this is indicated in the books. The choir do likewise at 'Sanctus Deus' facing the desks.

We prostrate on the knuckles facing the Cross when the priests intone 'Ecce lignum'. When the Cantor intones the psalm 'Beati immaculati . . .', we rise on our knees and continue the psalm in this position and then the antiphon after it, which the priests intone anew. After the antiphon we rise and sing the hymn 'Pange lingua' facing the altar. The Cantor intones each stanza and they are repeated if necessary.

Those who go to adore the Cross, leave the stalls by the lower opening. They prostrate on the knuckles two by two at the entrance to the novices' choir, or towards the middle opening, according to the locality, then at the presbytery step. When they arrive at the Cross they prostrate fully and kiss the feet of the crucifix. They rise together and genuflect to the Cross as the next two prostrate, taking care to withdraw slightly to one side so as not to impede them. They return to their places going down by the novices' stalls and entering by the middle opening. Care should be taken to have the distances between the places of the prostrations mentioned above more or less equal, so that they may be traversed with gravity and measure, and the ceremonies performed together.

When all have adored the Cross, the priests raise it on the prie-dieu, and intone the antiphon 'Super omnia'. At these words the choir prostrate on the knuckles facing the altar. They rise immediately and continue the antiphon kneeling while the priests place the Cross on the altar. From this moment until the Mass of the Paschal Vigil we salute the Cross exactly as we do the Blessed Sacrament in the Tabernacle at other times.

When the Celebrant returns with his ministers from the sacristy to the altar, the choir kneel when he does and wait thus until the Deacon brings the ciborium from the altar of repose. The choir then rise with the Celebrant and stand facing the altar. All recite the 'Pater noster' to the 'Amen' inclusively, aloud with the Celebrant. The latter then recites alone the 'Libera nos . . .' and the choir answer 'Amen'.

As the Celebrant communicates, the whole community, the priests and deacons wearing red (or white) stoles, go directly to the presbytery for Communion. Prostrate on the knuckles, all recite the 'Confiteor . . .' aloud, then answer 'Amen' to the 'Misereatur' and 'Indulgentiam' and rise to their knees for the 'Domine non sum dignus'.

During the three prayers following Communion, we stand facing the altar. When the priest withdraws we remain in choir for some time for thanksgiving.

Holy Saturday

217 Vespers of Holy Saturday are celebrated according to the rite of ferial days in Lent, and this evening the Angelus is recited prostrate on the knuckles.

The Paschal Vigil

218 The Celebrant and his ministers come to the middle of the presbytery step where they bow profoundly. The whole community bow with them and follow the Celebrant to the end of the church, the seniors walking first, and everyone carrying an unlighted candle. During the blessing of the New Fire and the Paschal Candle we stand around the Celebrant, the seniors nearest to him. All lights should remain unlit until after the third 'Lumen Christi'.

When the procession moves towards the choir, the seniors lead behind the Celebrant. Each time the Deacon sings 'Lumen Christi', we genuflect towards the Paschal Candle while replying 'Deo gratias'. After the second 'Lumen Christi' the candles of the community are lighted. After the third we enter the stalls and take our places in the presbytery choir. We remain standing until the Deacon begins the 'Exultet'. During the latter we stand out of the stalls holding the lighted candles in our hands. After the 'Exultet' we put the candles, still lighted, in their receptacles, as on the feast of the Purification.

The lessons are sung on the presbytery step by the seniors. The choir sit at the same time as the Celebrant. After the lessons the two monks appointed for the Litanies go to sing them, standing, at the middle of the presbytery step. The community, also standing, and turned in choir, give the responses. At the 'Propitius esto' we turn towards the altar for the blessing of the water.

During the renewal of baptismal vows which follows, we stand out of the stalls holding the lighted candles in our hands. All reply together to the interrogations of the Celebrant. Then we go to the presbytery step to be aspersed with holy water as on Sundays, carrying the lighted candles in our hands. After the versicles and prayer, the candles are extinguished and we continue the Litanies.

When these are ended the Solemn Mass begins. At the 'Gloria in excelsis' the bells are rung as at Christmas (208). We bow out of the stalls at the collect. After the Epistle we stand, turned in choir and repeat the 'Alleluia' three times after the Celebrant on the same tone and we remain thus for the verse 'Confitemini'. We sit for the Tract. From the Gospel until the 'Orate fratres' we stand facing the altar, as likewise after the 'Pax Domini'.

When the priest takes the first ablution, the senior of the choir intones the antiphon 'Alleluia' and the Cantor intones psalm 150 on the sixth tone. We sing the antiphon out of the stalls.

The Celebrant intones the antiphon 'Et valde mane' and the Cantor the 'Benedictus'. We stand out of the stalls for the antiphon.

The Paschal Candle is left lighted until after Compline on Easter Sunday.

Those who are bound to the Office and are not present at the liturgy of the Paschal Vigil are bound to recite Vigils and Lauds as they are in the breviary.

> 'It is impossible to present a more pleasing gift to God than to offer Him ourselves with full knowledge of the mystery.'
>
> (St Gregory Nazianaan)

Easter Sunday

219 When we come to chapter on Easter Sunday morning we remain standing and uncover for the announcement of the solemnity by the

Cantor. Then we sit, cover, and salute each other, while the Invitator begins the martyrology.

Easter Monday

220 Even though this day is kept holy we are not bound to sing Vigils or Lauds.

Paschal Time

221 During Paschal time the Paschal Candle is lighted at least on Sundays and feasts of Sermon during Conventual Mass and Vespers. On ferial days the hymns are sung on the tone of days of three lessons.

The Ascension

222 The Paschal Candle is lighted from first Vespers until after Compline on the feast day.

Vigil of Pentecost

223 After None the bell is rung for the Conventual Mass which is solemn and is celebrated by the Abbot. The choir ascend to the presbytery stalls for the Mass.

Pentecost

224 On the feast of Pentecost and during the octave, we sing the first stanza of the hymn at Tierce 'Veni Creator' kneeling facing the altar. We sing the remainder standing in ceremony turned in choir. For the intonation of the 'Veni Sancte Spiritus' at Mass we are on the knuckles. We continue the verse in ceremony and re-enter the stalls at the second 'Alleluia'.

Whit Monday

225 All is done as on Easter Monday (220). The Octave of Pentecost, and with it Paschal time, ends at None on Saturday, the eve of Trinity Sunday. That evening we resume the Angelus.

Trinity Sunday

226 At Prime we sing the 'Quicumque' standing; it is intoned by the Sub-invitator.

Corpus Christi

227 The cloisters may be decorated with flowers and greenery for the procession of the Blessed Sacrament.

After Mass we stand in the stalls facing the altar, each one having a lighted candle in his hand. We kneel when the Celebrant does, and at the same time the canopy is brought out by those appointed by the Cantor. As soon as the Deacon puts the Monstrance into the Celebrant's hands, we rise and begin the singing. Having bowed profoundly, we leave the church for the procession which includes the usual stations. At the beginning and end of each station, all those who precede the canopy genuflect towards the Blessed Sacrament.

On the return of the procession to the church, we kneel in the stalls facing the altar and remain thus until the ministers retire. We extinguish our candles when the Monstrance is placed on the throne. The Blessed Sacrament remains exposed until Vespers.

At the reposition of the Blessed Sacrament only the 'Tantum ergo' is sung. The Celebrant gives the benediction after the prayer 'Deus qui nobis . . .' We then sing 'Mane nobiscum' while the Deacon places the Blessed Sacrament in the Tabernacle.

Feast of the Sacred Heart

228 On the feast of the Sacred Heart the Blessed Sacrament is exposed from the end of the Conventual Mass until after Vespers.

Vigil of the Assumption

229 On the Vigil of the Assumption of Our Lady, the Conventual Mass is abbatial, and the rite is that of Sunday.

All Souls' Day

This commemoration of the dead is of monastic origin.
'St Odilon, Abbot of Cluny, under the inspiration of the Holy Spirit, prescribed that his monks hasten through their pious

supplications, the entry into heavenly joy of their deceased
brothers who were still expiating the faults of their life time.'

(Leo XIII)

230 On All Souls' day the Conventual Mass is sung by the Abbot. After
Mass there is a procession to those places where there are graves – the
church, cloisters and cemetery. When the Celebrant has donned the
cope, the Cantor intones the 'Libera'. We begin the Penitential psalms
as we leave the cemetery. On arriving in choir we kneel in the
presbytery stalls facing the altar and terminate whatever psalm we had
begun by the verse 'Requiem'. The Celebrant and his ministers go into
the presbytery to the altar where the Deacon replaces the cross. The
Celebrant says the versicles and the prayer 'Fidelium', after which we
retire.

BOOK 7
THE CONVENTUAL PLACES

'Paradisus claustralis, vere, claustrum est paradisus.' (St
Bernard)
'Every one of your religious houses should reflect the image of
the heavenly home, a place full of beauty and of peace.' (John
XXIII)

The Church

231 All the churches of our Order are dedicated to Our Lady and
consecrated in her honour.

They are normally built in the form of a cross as was that of Citeaux,
our Mother.

The upper part, where the high altar is situated, is called the
presbytery. It is elevated above the floor of the church by at least one
step. The high altar, which should be one or two steps above the level of
the presbytery, should be sufficiently far from the wall of the apse to
enable one to walk around it easily. This end wall is decorated with an
image of Our Lady. On the high altar is a crucifix along with the number
of candles required by the rite of the day. On either side is a large
candelabrum. On the Epistle side is the credence table and three stalls
(or a bench) which are occupied by the Celebrant and ministers during
the Tierce and the Conventual Mass.

Separated from the presbytery by the transept, the central nave forms the second part of the church. The choir is composed of the stalls with their 'desks' or book stands. The seats of the stalls are movable and are furnished with small projections called 'misericords' on which we rest during certain parts of the Office. The front choir or novices' choir is also furnished with stalls but need not have desks, depending on local circumstances. At the end of the choir the stalls make a right angle towards the centre of the nave and thus form what we call the 'return stalls'. The Superiors and some of the seniors occupy these stalls. Immediately behind these is a 'jube' or ambo, an elevated platform from which the lessons of Vigils are read. If there is no ambo, a lectern is placed between the stalls of the Abbot and Prior.

Finally at the end of the nave is a third section behind the 'De Beata' and 'Pro Defunctis' altars, in which are places for the Laybrothers and the sick.

A lamp burns before the Blessed Sacrament day and night.

> 'The holiness of the unbloody Sacrifice of the New Law demands that the place where it is celebrated be worthy and dignified. The careful attention which the Catholic Church has always given to the choice of such a place, proves this amply.' (Pius XII)

> 'Let the oratory be what it is called,' says St Benedict, 'and let nothing else be done or stored there.' (Ch. 52)

The Sacristy

232 In the sacristy is a piscina to receive water which has been blessed or used for ritual ablutions. There are also one or more wash basins with towels.

In keeping with the Holy Rule and the spirit of poverty, no monk should have a chalice, missal or vestments for his exclusive use.

The Cemetery

233 As far as possible the cemetery is situated behind the apse of the church. It is surrounded by a wall or hedge and should be tended with care. The graves which are orientated according to the quality of the dead person, are surmounted by a simple cross. On each is inscribed the religious name of the deceased, his rank (priest, deacon, etc.) and the date of his death.

The cloisters

234 The main monastic buildings are traditionally laid out in the form of a square and thus form an inner court surrounded on four sides by an arcade. This arcade is the cloisters. The cloister beside the church is called the reading or Compline cloister. Towards the middle of this cloister is an image of Our Lady, and under this is the abbatial seat, with that of the reader facing it.

> Our Fathers required that the monks behave in the cloisters almost as they would in the church, keeping there the same silence as the same recollection was expected to be found there. For them the cloister was a place of silence and a place of prayer, giving access to the principal conventual places and this less for the sake of convenient communication than to provide the monks who might pass with an occasion for more intimate contact with God.
> 'The cloister is a parlour wherein converse is held with the Holy Spirit . . . auditorium Spiritus Sancti.' (Adam of Perseigne)

The Auditorium

235 Since we do not speak in the cloisters, there is an auditorium or speaking room near the chapter room. Here the Abbot listens to those who have only a few words to say to him and here also he distributes the work. Likewise it is in the auditorium that the novices, oblates and those who have not made stability, gather to recite the 'De profundis' when they leave chapter before the community. Besides the auditorium, there are also several other small speaking rooms or closets throughout the monastery.

The Chapter Room

236 The chapter room is in a certain sense the central community room of the monastery. As far as local circumstances allow, the Abbot's seat should be towards the East, with the Prior's place on his right and that of the Subprior on his left. Those of the community are down each side of the room. Over the Abbot's seat is a crucifix which we salute on entering and leaving.

It is in the chapter that the Abbot gives his instructions, that we receive the habit, make temporary profession, etc. It is here also that the monks assemble to deal with the business of the monastery.

The Scriptorium

237 Every monastery has a scriptorium where the monks engage in intellectual work. This room is well supplied with all the books necessary for lectio divina and the study of the sacred sciences. There will also be stationery, paper, etc. and other items for common use there. There should be several class-rooms, for the students, so separated from the community that they will not prove detrimental to silence.

The Novitiate

238 As far as possible the novitiate should be in a part of the house which is separated from that occupied by the professed. It includes a scriptorium and some other rooms for conferences and singing classes.

The novices should have a separate dormitory. One or two rooms may also be assigned for their use in case of illnesses which do not necessitate their entering the infirmary.

The Dormitory

239 The monks sleep in a common dormitory. The beds are separated by partitions, and the entrance to each cell, on which the name of its occupant should appear, is closed by a curtain. The bedding is composed of a hard mattress, stuffed with straw or fibre or some such material, and placed on boards; there is a pillow of the same material as the mattress, sheets, and an adequate number of blankets. There is in each cell a crucifix, a holy water font, one or two pictures and a few pegs. Nothing may be added without permission.

The Refectory

240 In the refectory the principal table is raised one step. The Abbot, Prior and Subprior sit there, and also distinguished guests who may be admitted to the refectory. We do not use tablecloths and the table covering and service should be in keeping with poverty. The monks are seated on one side of the table only. A pulpit is provided for the reader.

When we enter or leave the refectory, we bow moderately to the crucifix.

The Kitchens

241 No one except the cellarer, the refectorian, the guestmaster and the infirmarian may enter the kitchens without permission. Further, we avoid speaking there without necessity.

BOOK 8
MONASTIC OBSERVANCES

CHAPTER I   COMMUNITY LIFE

242 The monk's external behaviour should be governed by religious modesty and good manners. While avoiding affectation, he should be careful about personal cleanliness and neatness in clothing. We should also take good care of the objects given us for our use. Likewise we will look to the cleanliness and good order of the monastery in general – closing doors and windows correctly, not hanging clothes out to dry at the windows, etc.

243 We wear the cowl at the Divine Office. The Abbot will decide whether we should wear it at lectio divina and at meals, depending on the country and the season. Outside the church we keep the sleeves of the cowl raised. If we are in scapular for the community exercise, we keep the hands under the scapular above the belt, at least when we are not seated.

244 We are covered whenever we walk in community. We cover also for meals, the procession for Grace after meals, the prayers of Prime in chapter, the Compline reading and the Mandatum. The Abbot may allow us to uncover at some of these exercises.

245 When we meet we salute each other with a moderate bow except during the great silence and in those places specified by the Abbot. It is proper that the junior salute the senior first. In our relations with one another we avoid all unbecoming familiarity.

> 'Loving one another with the charity of the brotherhood, with honour preventing one another,' as the Apostle recommends. Sincere respect and Christian charity are contained in these few words, as is also that mutual obedience recommended by St Benedict.

246 Discretion demands that we do not busy ourselves unduly with the affairs of others. To open the desk of another and to remove anything whatever therefrom must be considered a grave fault. For a novice this could be a sufficient reason for dismissal, and this should be pointed out to them from the beginning. This is all the more true when

there is question of personal notes. Likewise we should not unnecessarily enter workshops, etc. where we are not employed.

247 The professed priests are called 'Father', and also all the solemnly
professed, even the non-priests, unless this is contrary to the custom of
the country. The others are called 'Brother'.

248 The Abbot, since he holds the place of Christ, is called Dom.
When we meet him we uncover and bow profoundly except during the
great silence. Each Abbot can further specify those places or circumstances in his own monastery where the monks do not bow to him.

We kneel to receive his blessing, which we normally ask whenever
we go to see him in his room. We give the same honours to a visiting
Abbot.

> These marks of respect become clear when we realize that an
> Abbot is not intended merely to govern his monastery, but to
> lead those souls who have committed themselves to his care,
> along the path of salvation. As Father of the monastic family he
> has a right to the fullest confidence of all his monks. As Superior
> of the monastery, the Holy Rule wishes that we obey him in all
> things, that we have for him 'a humble and sincere love', and that
> we surround him with that respect which flows naturally from the
> thought that his authority comes from God and that he takes the
> place of Jesus Christ.

249 If the hierarchy of functions is to be safeguarded, no subordinate
Superior should give a permission which has been refused by the Abbot.
Whenever a permission has been refused by a Superior or officer, we
should not ask it of another without informing him of the refusal.

250 If a monk has to leave a community exercise, he asks permission
of the one who is presiding, except in case of urgency. To do this he
uncovers and brings his hand, covered with the sleeve of the cowl, or
the edge of the cloak, or the extremity of the scapular, towards his lips.
Permission is granted by a nod or by a sign of the hand. The one who has
requested the permission then bows to the Superior.

If we wish to call anyone from a community exercise we approach the
one who is presiding.

The weekly officers named by the Invitator in chapter, the Sacristan
and the ministers of the altar, do not ask this permissiin in the church
when they are going to perform their functions.

CHAPTER II   SOLITUDE: SILENCE: LECTIO DIVINA: PRAYER

St Benedict, who desired his monks above all to become men of prayer, could not forget that the means most apt to facilitate the practice of the interior life are solitude and silence. And so, according to the testimony of St Gregory, he lived 'alone with himself under the gaze of the Lord'.

Faithful observers of the Rule, our Fathers of Citeaux did not neglect these means, and prescribed that all our monasteries be established 'in places remote from the haunts of men', and that the monks therein ordinarily guard silence so as the more easily to remain recollected.

Solitude

'Martha had a sister called Mary, who sitting at the Lord's feet, heard his word.' (Luke x, 39)

251 Since we have freely left the world, we must take care that the world does not reach us. Hence if there are doors in the cloisters, chapter room or church which communicate with the guesthouse, they must always be kept closed. The same holds for all other doors which would allow seculars free access to the interior of the monastery. We should especially avoid bringing anyone into the cloister during the time of the lectio divina.

252 In principle correspondence with the outside world should be rare. It is for the Abbot to decide on the frequency and opportuneness of letters and to give the necessary permissions to write them. Letters are handed in open and are received in the same way. All, however, have free correspondence with higher Superiors, that is, with the Holy See, the Papal Legate in the country, the Abbot General, the Father Immediate, and one's own Abbot or Superior when he is absent, or when we ourselves are away from the monastery. Replies may be freely received unopened from all these persons. These letters and replies need not necessarily pass through the hands of the local Abbot.

253 We receive visits ordinarily only from our near relatives. These should not be too frequent nor habitually prolonged beyond three days.

Do not let us see in this petty restrictions or something more or less contrary to charity. 'In the monastic Orders, separation from the world has a meaning only when it prepares and already realizes a more perfect spiritual union with all those who are in the world, and responsibility for whom we henceforth accept by each of our thoughts, by each of our acts and by each of our desires.' (Louis Lavelle)

'You are completely cloistered with God – "inclusistis cum Deo". He is truly alone to whom God is not present. But the monk who is with God is never less alone than when alone.' (William of St Thierry)

Silence

254 The solitude of the monk is completed in silence. And so we do not communicate directly with each other, either by word or in writing, without permission. Only the Abbot or the Superior replacing him can give this permission, and we should respect its limits by not speaking of other topics.

The one wishing to speak says: 'Benedicite' and the other says: 'Dominus'. Only the Superiors, Father Masters and Cellarer may omit this 'Benedicite'.

> If monks still preserve this very ancient usage, it is because they believe, like their forebears, that an occasion of speaking easily becomes an occasion of sin. So it is that before speaking they wish to draw down grace by an act of humility. 'Give me your blessing': 'No, but let the Lord Himself bless you.' And now that the name of the Lord has been invoked, it is in His presence that conversation is held. There were two, now there will be three.

If two monks have something to communicate to each other, they do so by signs, and they should avoid accompanying these signs with words.

> Monastic silence leads to recollection. On the contrary, Scripture tells us that lack of control in the use of speech easily leads to sin: 'And if any man thinks himself to be religious, not bridling his tongue, but deceiving his own heart. . . . If any man offend not in word, the same is a perfect man.' (James 1, 26: 3, 2) St Benedict, nourished on this doctrine, expressed himself as follows: 'Therefore, because of the importance of silence, let permission to speak be rarely given to perfect disciples even for good and holy and edifying discourse, for it is written: 'In much talk thou shalt not avoid sin.'

255 Ordinarily we speak only to the Abbot and the Prior. If, however, the two first Superiors cannot easily be found, we may also speak to the

Subprior. The students can also speak to the Magister Spiritus. The novices and those professed who are still in the novitiate speak to the Abbot and the Novice Master. They may also speak to the Sub-master in certain cases (10). These directions will be further specified for each house by the Abbot.

> Our silence is something more than a mere mortification, and that
> is why God receives it as acceptable praise. 'Tibi silentium laus.'

256 It is obvious that no one speaks to outsiders without permission; we even avoid speaking or making signs in their presence.

257 The use of the telephone will be regulated by the Abbot.

258 Silence, however, does not consist merely in abstaining from speech. It also demands that we avoid everything which could disturb the peace, calm and recollection of the monastery, such as calling others loudly, banging doors, walking noisily, etc. We particularly avoid breaking silence, at least without necessity, in the regular places, and especially in the church, cloisters and scriptorium.

> It was in an atmosphere of silence that our Fathers found that
> remarkable peace which impressed those who visited them. 'At
> Clairvaux, in a valley peopled with monks, there was the silence
> of the night in the middle of the day; one only heard the noise of
> labour, or of the praises of God if the brothers were then chanting
> them. Those who visited the place, would not dare, out of
> respect, to utter a word out of harmony with the surroundings.'
> (Life of St Bernard)

259 When we have permission to speak, we go to the auditorium or to one of the appointed places. Those who have permission to speak because of their employment or for some similar reason, should use this permission only in the place of work and as little as possible in the presence of their brethren.

260 Finally, in connection with monastic silence, there is a special privileged time during the night when we observe the 'great silence'. This is stricter than during the day, and is observed from the evening Angelus until the collect of Prime. During this time we do not speak even to the Abbot without an urgent reason.

> 'When the calm of night brings on a profound silence, prayer
> ascends more freely and more purely. . . . It mounts more

securely by night as there are not witnesses but God alone
and the holy angel who receives it to offer it on the celestial
altar. . . . The dust of earthly cares does not soil it.' (St Bernard)
   During the day, those who are not in choir avoid speaking during the
Divine Office.

Lectio divina

'Not on bread alone doth man live but on every word that
proceedeth from the mouth of God.' (Matt. IV, 4)

261 The monk begins his lectio divina by a prayer, which should be
said as far as possible kneeling. When reading Holy Scripture, he should
also kneel for the first few verses out of respect for the word of God.
   It is especially in Holy Scripture that the monk will seek the
knowledge of God and Him whom He has sent, Jesus Christ,
recalling the words of St Jerome: 'To be ignorant of the
Scriptures is to be ignorant of Christ'.
   The Lord, all alone, could enable us to discover the true sense of
Scripture; and He will do so if we are among the number of those
'little ones' to whom it pleases Him to reveal Himself. Let
us expect more light from His goodness than from our own
knowledge. 'Was not our heart burning within us when he spoke
to us on the way and when he explained to us the Scriptures,' said
the disciples of Emmaus.

262 The scriptorium, the sanctuary of the lectio divina, should be
plentifully provided with books. The library also, apart from reserved
sections, should be easily accessible, but there should be some control
on the removal of books therefrom.
   'He who is of God hears the words of God.' (John VIII, 47)

263 Following the example of our Fathers, we should have great
respect for books. They should be treated with care and replaced at the
end of reading time. In a spirit of charity we should avoid keeping books
too long for our personal use.

Mental prayer

264 The community make mental prayer together in choir twice daily;
in the morning after Vigils for a half-hour, and in the evening before

supper or collation for a quarter of an hour. We may sit during mental prayer.

These moments given to prayer seem very short for religious whose lives are dedicated to seeking God. It is obvious that monks cannot, and do not wish to restrict themselves to these periods. The goal they seek is to arrive at a life of prayer. St Benedict regulated all in the monastery with a view to establishing and maintaining a life of prayer, and this is the end pursued by the monk. 'Little by little the soul ascends to God, and prayer becomes for it the breath of life; an habitual union, full of love, is established and a very simple but very stable contact is made with God, who becomes the life of the soul. If the monk keeps silence, it is in order to hold interior converse with God; if he speaks, he does so to God or of God and for the glory of God. This was the practice of the holy monk, Hugh, Abbot of Cluny: "Silens quidem, semper cum Domino; loguens autem, semper in Domino loquebatur".' (Vita Hugonis Clun) Let us be convinced, like Mary, that it is especially in prayer that we discover the sense of Scripture: 'Maria conservabat omnia haes, conferens in corde suo' . . . 'Ipsum adutie' she says to us. It is to the school of Christ that we must go to learn.

CHAPTER III   CHAPTER MEETINGS

265 The monks come together in chapter daily. The Abbot explains the Holy Rule there, but he may omit this explanation if there is a sermon or conference or whenever he judges fit. If, for the sake of the Brothers, he prefers to defer the explanation of the Rule to the time of the reading before Compline, he may do so.

266 After the prayers of Prime the Abbot says 'Benedicite' and all answer 'Dominus'. Then the usual instruction follows.

From St Benedict's point of view the Abbot then appears, first of all, as Pastor. . . . And what is the first duty of a pastor? It is to feed his flock: 'Nonne greges a pastoribus pascuntur' (Ezech. XXXIV, 2). And what is the food that he must give them? God answers us by the mouth of the prophet: 'they shall feed you with knowledge and doctrine – Et pascent vos scientia et doctrina' (Jer. III, 15). Christ Jesus Himself declares: 'Not in bread alone doth man live, but in every word that proceedeth from the mouth of God' (Matt. IV, 4: Luke IV, 4). And St Paul re-echoes this when he writes in several places: 'The just man liveth by faith', 'My just man liveth by faith'. (Hebr. x, 38: Rom. i, 17: Gal. iii, 11)

(Dom Marmion)

267 If a message is read from the Sovereign Pontiff to the Order or the community, we listen to it standing. If the message comes from the Head of State, the Bishop, the Abbot General, the Father Immediate, the Visitor (Visitation card), from the Abbot of the monastery who may be absent, or from any other person of rank, we bow at the beginning of it.

Those to whom the Abbot gives some particular command likewise bow, as do also the weekly officers when their names are announced by the Invitator on Saturday mornings.

268 If the Abbot is going to hold a chapter of faults, if the close of a Tricenary is to be announced, if an obituary notice is to be read, or if prayers are to be asked for a deceased person, he announces it thus: 'Loquamur de Ordine nostro'. He gives absolution for the dead by saying: 'Requiesca(n)t in pace' to which the community answer 'Amen'.

269 On Thursdays the rubrics and ceremonies of the Mass or other practical liturgical questions are explained. The Abbot may then hold a chapter of faults for the priests and those in Sacred Orders, even novices. This chapter is concerned only with faults committed in the exercise of the functions of the altar.

270 If by way of exception the Abbot decides to assemble the whole community to treat of some important matter, everyone, even the sick as far as possible, should come to chapter. The Abbot opens the proceedings with the verse 'Divinum auxilium' and explains the matter. If he consults those present he begins with the juniors. Each one stands up to give his opinion, which he does candidly but modestly. The meeting ends with the verse 'Adjutorium'.

If there is question of a conventual chapter strictly so-called, only the solemnly professed Choir monks who have made stability are present. The acts are drawn up and entered in a special register.

Everything that is said or done in the conventual chapter, either ordinary or extraordinary, if it is a matter of chapter, should remain secret.

CHAPTER IV   FRATERNAL CORRECTION AND PENANCE

'For which cause comfort one another; and edify one another.'
(Thess. v, 11)

271 The chapter room is the traditional place of fraternal correction, since it is there that we hold the chapter of faults and have proclamations.

Chapter of faults

272 The Abbot will decide on the frequency of the chapter of faults. It should not be held on Sundays, feasts of MM or feasts of Sermon.

After the explanation of the Holy Rule the Abbot hears successively the accusations and proclamations of the oblates, the novices, the professed who have not made stability and the professed of the monastery.

Those who wish to accuse themselves of some fault kneel at their place. When the Abbot says: 'Quid dicitis?' they reply: 'Mea culpa'. They rise at the words 'Surgite in nomine Domini' and remain standing. The Abbot calls those whom he wishes to hear while the others sit. Those who are called come to the centre and accuse themselves briefly and in a manner intelligible to all. They mention their external faults without revealing the motives which inspired them. Vague and general accusations should be avoided. If someone has committed a fault which has disedified the novices or oblates, he should accuse himself of it in their presence. When we have finished our accusations, we kneel to hear the admonition of the Abbot and to receive our penance. We then retire to our place.

If someone wishes to proclaim one who is accusing himself, he does so immediately after the accusation.

A few texts from Scripture will perhaps help our generosity. 'He that hideth his sins shall not prosper: but he that shall confess and forsake them, shall obtain mercy.' (Proverbs xxviii, 13)
'A wise son heareth the doctrine of his father: but he that is a scorner heareth not when he is reproved.' (Proverbs, xiii, 1)
'Such as I love, I rebuke and chastise. Be zealous, therefore and do penance.' (Apoc. iii, 19)

Proclamations

273 Proclamations should concern faults which are external and

certain, and never doubts and suspicions. We speak only, and that
briefly, of what we ourselves have seen or heard. We never proclaim for
personal matters; neither do we proclaim one who has already been
proclaimed that same day.

> 'My son, reject not the correction of the Lord: and do not faint
> when thou art chastised by him: For whom the Lord loveth, he
> chastiseth: and as a father in the son he pleaseth himself.' (Prov.
> III, 11–12: Hebr. XII, 5–6)

274 When the Abbot asks for proclamations, he who wishes to make
one rises and says 'I proclaim Father X. or Brother Y.' The one who is
proclaimed kneels at his place and listens to the fault for which he is
proclaimed. If another wishes to proclaim him, he does so at this
moment. The Abbot makes his comment, gives a penance, and receives
the other proclamations, the number of which he may limit. He can also
deprive a monk of his right to proclaim others.

> Fraternal correction is an act of charity, the exercise of which is
> difficult and almost always painful. Is this a sufficient reason for us
> to omit it? We should not allow ourselves, however, to be guided
> by our own petty interests which we may think to have been
> slighted. Let us be prompt to forget completely whatever may
> have caused us suffering: 'Let all bitterness and anger and
> indignation and clamour and blasphemy, be put away from you,
> with all malice. And be ye kind one to another; merciful, forgiving
> one another, even as God hath forgiven you in Christ.' (Ephes.
> IV, 31–32)
> But when the interests of our neighbour are at stake, let us
> overcome all timidity, all cowardice, and let us try to do him
> good.
> 'Why do you correct your brother? Because you suffer from the
> fact that he has offended you in some way? God forbid! If you
> correct him out of love for yourself, you do something which is
> worthless. If you correct him from love of himself, you do
> something which is excellent. If he hears you, you have gained
> your brother.' (St Augustine)

275 When the Abbot has heard the accusations and proclamations of
the oblates, he bids them leave, unless he then terminates the chapter.
He does likewise with the novices and the professed who have not made
stability. They all recite the 'De profundis' together in the auditorium.
The versicles and collect are said by the senior of the group, even

though a novice, unless there be someone in Orders, in which case he says them.

276 It is considered a fault to excuse oneself, especially in chapter, even if one is not guilty. However, there are cases when we can, and even should, give a humble explanation to the Abbot in private.

277 If we have noticed a grave and scandalous fault in one of our brethren, we should tell the Abbot about it in private, and let him decide whether or not it is a matter for proclamation.

Penances

278 For external faults mentioned in chapter there are certain penances which are of long usage in the Order. These are done either in the refectory or the church, but never on a Sunday, a feast of MM or a feast of Sermon, nor are they ever done during supper.

> These penances, disagreeable to nature, do not, however, sadden us, because they serve for our purification: 'As sorrowful, yet always rejoicing.' (2 Cor. VI, 10)
> 'My brethren, count it all joy when you shall fall into divers temptations.' (Jas. I, 2)

279 He who is to perform a penance in the refectory stands at his place uncovered with his hands in his sleeves or under the cloak, until the Abbot gives the signal for the meal to begin.

280 The most usual penance is the recitation of some prayer. To do this we kneel before the principal table and recite the prayer silently, with the hands in the sleeves, unless the Abbot has told us to hold our arms extended in the form of a cross.

281 Another penance is to take our soup on the floor. This is done by taking our soup sitting on a stool in the middle of the refectory and then going to our place when we are finished.

282 It can happen that for a grave fault a monk may be told to kiss the feet of the community. He begins with the Abbot, then goes to the Prior and then kisses the feet of all the monks and novices on that side. Then he does the other side, beginning with the Superior. He kneels before two monks at a time and kisses one foot of each, which should be covered. He then salutes them.

This penance should not be done by several on the same day.

283 If a monk is to kneel at the door of the church as a penance, he leaves the refectory when grace after dinner begins. He goes and kneels at the door of the church, uncovered and facing the community, and remains there until all have passed.

284 He who is to prostrate during the Sacred Mysteries, leaves his stall towards the end of the Preface and goes to the presbytery step where he prostrates at the Sanctus. He rises only at the 'Per omnia' before the 'Pater'.

285 If a monk as penance has been deprived of the whole or part of the regular habit, he takes his place everywhere after the last novice. He does not preside at any exercise and may neither read in public nor intone anything unless the Abbot allows him to do so.

The discipline

286 There is another penance unconnected with the chapter of faults, which is performed by the whole community, namely the discipline. The instrument of this penance is a scourage of five small cords, each having five knots. Each monk takes it personally on his shoulders every Friday of the year immediately after Lauds in the dormitory for the space of a 'Miserere'.

We omit this penance from Christmas until January 13th inclusively, during Paschal time and whenever a feast of Sermon occurs.

We keep the discipline concealed under the mattress or pillow.

CHAPTER V   MANUAL LABOUR

'And the Lord took man, and put him into the garden of Eden to cultivate and keep it.' (Gen. II, 15)

287 Monks, who are poor with the poor Christ, live by the labour of their hands. As soon as the signal for work is given, we go to the auditorium where the Abbot assigns to each one his task. We tie up our robes modestly or put on work clothes – an apron, smock or overalls, according to the nature of the work. We also change the shoes if necessary.

In so far as it is painful, manual labour is the principal penance which an offended God exacts from sinful man: 'In the sweat of thy face thou shalt eat bread.' (Gen. III, 19) Man must submit to this: 'Hate not laborious works nor husbandry ordained by the Most High.' (Eccles. VII, 16)

Jesus, who wished to have 'in all things the likeness of man' worked with His hands (Mark, VI, 3). Mary did likewise. So did the Apostles. The monk realises this and has heard St Paul's recommendation to the Thessalonians (1 Thess. IV, 11): 'And that you use your endeavour . . . and work with your own hands, as we commanded you.' Which prompted St Benedict to write: 'for then are they monks in truth, if they live by the work of their hands, as did also our forefathers and the Apostles.' (Rule, ch. 48)

288 We go to work in single file, following the Abbot. If we arrive after the others we present ourselves to the one who is presiding. If we must leave the work, we ask permission to do so.

If we complete some particular task before the end of work time, we go to the common work or to the work room. No one should absent himself from manual labour.

Does one object that manual labour is unbecoming for a priest? St John Chrysostom did not think so, he even considered it quite in order for priests engaged in the care of souls: 'You may see our brethren here, now training the ox under the yoke of the plough, then ascending the sacred pulpit and cultivating the souls entrusted to their care; or you may see them with bill-hook in hand cleaning the thorns from the soil, and later by their preaching, purifying souls from their sins. They are not ashamed to work just like ordinary people do.' (St John Chrysostom)

289 If we damage something we accuse ourselves to a Superior or at the next chapter of faults.

The monk will not try to justify himself by quoting the old adage: 'It is only he who does nothing who breaks nothing'. Besides it is evident that nobody wishes to reproach him for negligence when there has only been awkwardness. He is simply invited to make an act of the virtue of poverty, to recall that the object he uses is not his own.

290 He who presides may grant a period of rest about the middle of the time of work. During the rest period we do not do any reading properly so-called.

> This respite may be regarded as necessary if the work is difficult; but it serves another purpose also. It allows the monk more easily to resume contact with God if the attention given to his work took his mind off Him for whose sake he became a monk.

291 When we hear the bell for the end of work, we stop immediately unless this would result in serious inconvenience. If we are working at a distance from the monastery, he who presides will end the work sufficiently early to allow us to arrive back at the monastery in time. Those who work inside do not remain at their employments during the time of lectio divina.

> 'To the monk heaven was next door; he formed no plans, he had no cares; . . . He went forth in his youth "to his work and to his labour" until the evening of life; if he lived a day longer, he did a day's work more; whether he lived many days or few, he laboured on to the end of them. He had no wish to see further in advance of his journey than where he was to make his next stage. He ploughed and sowed, he prayed, he meditated, he studied, he wrote, he taught, and then he died and went to heaven.'
> (Newman)

292 If necessary the work may be prolonged beyond the usual time. But if an Abbot wishes to prescribe extraordinary work habitually, he must obtain the authorisation of the General Chapter, which will be given only within the terms of No. 102 of the Constitutions. Those who say the Office in the fields may anticipate or defer the regular time for it, according to need. As far as possible they should face the church and observe the postures of the choir. The Office in choir should be assured by those remaining in the house, including the sick, if they are able to attend.

It is in keeping with the Rule that the community be given extra food during the time of extraordinary work. (Ch. 39)

293 We do not work on feasts of Sermon, nor on Easter Monday nor Whit Monday. If necessary, however, the Abbot may prescribe work on feast days which are not of precept. Feasts of MM Major, as well as the feast of the Exaltation of the Holy Cross are, in principle, kept holy in the morning, but exception is made for the Tuesdays after Easter and Pentecost.

294 If the Abbot considers it necessary, he may have the community prepare the vegetables during the Compline reading, provided everyone takes part and that the work does not distract from the reading. The monks would then assemble in some other place besides the reading cloister or chapter room.

CHAPTER VI   MEALS

Ceremonial

295 We go to the refectory in single file unless the community is very numerous. At the entrance we wash our hands slightly, and on arriving at our place we bow moderately to the crucifix. At the signal the Cantor intones the 'Benedicite' and the monks add with flexes the verse 'Oculi' at dinner and 'Edent' at supper, and the 'Gloria Patri' during which we are bowed in choir. We stand upright when replying 'Amen' to the blessing of the table, and face the crucifix while the Abbot blesses the reader.

> 'Not in bread alone doth man live, but in every word that proceedeth from the mouth of God.' St Benedict deduced from this that reading should never be omitted at table when the brethren take their meals. (Ch. 38)

As soon as we have answered 'Amen' we sit down with our hands covered on the edge of the table and wait for the signal which the Abbot gives after the first sentence of Holy Scripture. After the signal each one looks to see if anything is wanting to his neighbours. Then after this act of charity, he unfolds his napkin, part of which he places under his plate, allowing the other part to fall on the front of his habit, or fastening it in front of him. If he notices that one of his brethren has been left short of something, he informs the servant of the refectory. We may not ask for anything for ourselves except bread, water and salt. He who is served anything makes a moderate bow to signify his thanks. The food may be served either in individual portions or dishes. In the first case each one is provided with a large spoon to take what he needs.

If we break something, or make a noise liable to upset the reading, or spill a quantity of food or drink which we cannot conveniently clean up, we go and kneel before the Abbot's table and show him the broken object, if necessary.

When we have finished eating we wash the knife, fork and spoon in our cup, gather up the crumbs, and arrange our napkin, etc. according to custom. Then, with our hands covered on the edge of the table we await the signal.

296 If any comes to the refectory after the blessing of the reader, he uncovers, presents himself before the Abbot and remains standing until he receives the signal to retire.

He then bows, goes to his place and says the Grace with the same ceremonies as the community, but without making the sign of the cross while reciting the collect 'Benedic . . .' as the food has been blessed before.

Latecomers serve themselves.

297 If someone has not finished eating when the community rises from table, he rises with them and when they leave the refectory, he continues his meal. When he is finished he says the Grace indicated in No. 300.

298 The Abbot may shorten the time of reading during supper. In this case we may leave the refectory individually when the reading has ended. Grace before supper is always 'Edent'. Afterwards each one recites the verse 'Retribuere' privately.

299 When the Abbot wishes to conclude the reading, he rings the bell and says: 'Tu autem'. The reader finishes the versicle and all reply 'Deo gratias'. Then all rise and stand facing the crucifix. At the 'Gloria Patri' we bow turned in choir and after answering 'Amen' we rise and bow moderately to the crucifix. When the Cantor intones the 'Miserere' which is sung in ceremony with flexes, we walk to the church in the same order as for a procession. The Superior who has presided at the meal walks last in the middle between the two choirs. We finish the psalm standing in the presbytery stalls facing the altar. We bow turned in choir for the 'Gloria Patri' and then end Grace bowed down on the misericords. At supper Grace is said in the refectory.

300 Those who do not eat with the community say Grace as appointed for all. After the meal they say 'Agimus' or 'Benedictus', 'Laudate Dominim omnes gentes', 'Gloria Patri', 'Retribuere', 'Benedicamus Domino' and 'Fidelium'.

301 When we take the mixt or frustulum we say 'Largitor' in private standing in our place. The priests make the sign of the cross towards the table, the others on themselves.

For collation we go to the refectory in the same order as for dinner. The Cantor says 'Benedicite' and the Hebdomadary adds 'Largitor . . .' with flexes, making the sign of the cross before him as he says 'Benedicat'. There may be reading for about ten minutes. No one should leave before the end of the reading.

For Grace after mixt, frustulum and collation we say 'Retribuere'. Each one says it in private when he is finished and leaves without waiting for the others.

CHAPTER VII   FOOD AND FASTING

Food

'Give us this day our daily bread.' (Matt. VI, 11)

302 No one other than those appointed by the Abbot, should concern himself about the food.

'Eat such things as are set before you,' said Jesus to His disciples when He sent them on their mission. (Luke X, 8)

The monk also will eat what is set before him, and without distinction whether it be good or less good, just as would a poor man which is what the monk wishes to be. 'I believe there is greater virtue in eating without choosing just what is given to you and in the order in which it is given and whether it be according to your taste or not, than in always choosing the worst. For even though this latter course may appear more austere, the former entails more resignation, for in it we renounce not only our taste but also our choice.' (St Francis)

Meat, fish and eggs are forbidden as portions for the community. All milk and vegetable products may be served both as portions and as condiment. However, we abstain from milk products and from cheese on the following days: Mondays, Wednesdays and Fridays of Advent and Lent; Quarter Tense; the vigils of Pentecost, the Immaculate Conception and Christmas; and all Fridays out of Paschal time: an exception is made, however, when any of the foregoing days happens to be a feast of Sermon.

The bread served to the community is the ordinary bread of the country. A sufficient quantity is served at dinner and supper, but at mixt, frustulum and collation the amount is limited. Potatoes may always be served with bread.

The drink is the usual drink of the country. If the beverage is cider or beer, about half a litre is served; of wine slightly less. (1 litre = 1.7 pints.)

Dessert consists of fruit, preserves, honey, cake, etc., according to the country. Cheese may also be served on days when abstinence from milk products is not prescribed.

303 Fish, eggs and milk products may be served as 'indulgence'.

'Black bread and pure water, cabbage and vegetables without special preparation, nothing to flatter the taste. But aided by the love of God, as well as by an appetite for interior joys, it is remarkable what a hearty meal these can provide for a stomach that becomes accustomed to them.' (William of St Thierry)

'The Spartans were accustomed to spice their food with hunger and work; these also are the condiments of the Order.' (Helinand de Froidmont)

Fasting

'Everyone who striveth for the mastery, refraineth himself from all things: and they indeed that they may receive a corruptible crown; but we an incorruptible one.' (1 Cor. ix, 25)

304 Although the Church has considerably mitigated the practice of fasting for the generality of Christians, monks should preserve the traditional note of austerity at their table.

If the Church has mitigated the practice of fasting, she continues nevertheless, to emphasise its advantages and she has changed nothing in the Lenten Preface where she has us say to the Lord: 'By the fast which we inflict upon our bodies, restrain Thou our passions, elevate our souls, and bestow upon us the merit and the reward.' Note how this text makes it clear that it is not from fasting in itself that we hope for graces but from the bounty of the Lord on the occasion of our fasts.

St Augustine relates the following fable: 'I am going off to Jerusalem. My flesh, which is my steed, heeds not the bridle and I am almost thrown to the ground. The only way to subdue it is to give it less food. It drags me along and tries to turn me away from my path which is Jesus Christ. Shall I not curb it in its rearings and jumpings?'

But fasting does not only subdue the flesh. It also elevates the soul, and does so especially when in a spirit of charity we consider it as a voluntary participation in the sufferings of our neighbour – in the sufferings of those multitudes who in our day are hungry in certain countries.

In the light of these considerations we understand better the depth of St Benedict's thought when he prescribed that his sons 'Love fasting'.

Besides the fasts which are prescribed by the Church, and which are still obligatory in some countries (fasts of the Church), we also keep other fasts prescribed by the Rule of St Benedict. We call these 'fasts of the Order' or monastic fasts. They are of two kinds:

The major monastic fast which is observed during Lent, Quarter Tense, and the vigil of Pentecost. (Note: In some English-speaking countries these, and of course the vigils of Christmas, and the Immaculate Conception, are fasts of the Church.)

The minor monastic fast, which is observed on the following days: from the 14th of September until the beginning of Lent; the Wednesdays and Fridays from Trinity Sunday until September 14th, unless the Abbot dispenses from it because of the work or the heat, as the Holy Rule allows him to do; the vigils of the Assumption and Nativity of Our Lady. There is no fast, however, if a Sunday, feast of Sermon or MM Major falls on these days.

'And when you fast, be not as the hypocrites, sad. For they disfigure their faces, that they shall appear unto men to fast. Amen, I say unto you, they have received their reward. But thou when thou fastest, anoint thy head and wash thy face. That thou appear not to men to fast, but to thy Father who is in secret: and thy Father who seeth in secret will repay thee.'

'Then Jesus was led into the desert by the spirit, to be tempted by the devil. And when he had fasted forty days and forty nights, afterwards he was hungry.' (Matt. VI, 16–18: IV, 2)

By his fasts, the monk is united to Jesus, and this is not the least advantage of this mortification.

305 The fasts of the Church and the major monastic fasts are observed by the choir monks and by the Laybrothers. The minor fasts of the Order are kept by the choir monks only. Although the obligation of the major monastic fast is less grave than that of a fast of the Church strictly so-called, the reasons for dispensing from it should still be more serious than those which suffice for a dispensation from the minor monastic fast.

306 The diet on fast days of the Church and on major monastic fast days is the same, i.e. Lenten fare.

Should the monk some day feel wanting in courage, he may stimulate himself by saying with St Bernard: 'Prayer obtains the grace to fast, and fasting obtains the grace to pray. Fasting nourishes prayer, and prayer strengthens fasting and presents it to the Lord.'

Measure of Food

307 The mixt consists of about 180 grammes of bread with drink; the frustulum about 60 grammes of bread with drink. (Note: 30 grammes = 1 ounce.)

308 At dinner, two portions and dessert, with bread and drink, are served. On the first three Fridays in Lent, only one portion with the usual drink is served. On the fourth and fifth Fridays of Lent, only bread and water are served, to which potatoes may be added, if the Abbot decides. If a feast of Sermon falls on these days, the usual dinner is served. On Good Friday bread and water alone are served at dinner.

309 For supper there are two portions with bread and drink.

310 For collation, about 180 grammes of bread with dessert or a small portion are served, along with the usual drink. The dessert or small portion may be replaced by cheese on days when milk products are permitted.

311 The Abbot can have a supplementary portion, called the 'indulgence', served in the community refectory to those who need it. It may be served every day of the year without exception, morning, noon and evening, according to need.

312 We do not eat outside the refectory or infirmary without permission.

CHAPTER VIII THE MANDATUM

313 The servants of the refectory who are finishing their week's duty and those who are appointed to succeed them, complete their service by performing this act of charity which is called the Mandatum. This takes place every Saturday of the year before the Compline reading. It is a beautiful lesson of charity and humility which Christ willed to leave us on the eve of His death.

> 'Having loved his own who were in the world, he loved them to the end. And when supper was done . . . he riseth, and layeth aside his garments, and having taken a towel, girded himself. After that he putteth water into a basin and began to wash the feet of the disciples and to wipe them with the towel with which he was girded. . . . Then after he had washed their feet and taken his garments, being set down again, he said to them: Know you what I have done to you? . . . You also ought to wash one another's feet. For I have given you an example that as I have done to you, so you do also.' (John XIII, 1–15)

The whole community are present and all the professed, choir and lay, take part in it. At the sound of the bell we go to the cloister or chapter room, according to the locality, and take our places as for the Compline reading. When the servants of the refectory enter, we do not rise, and the Abbot, or in his absence, the Cantor, intones the antiphon 'Postquam'. The community continue the antiphon and repeat it. The other antiphons are always intoned by the Cantor. We bow moderately to the servers when they have washed our feet. When the ceremony is almost ended, the Cantor intones the antiphon 'Benedicat'. This antiphon, like the first, should never be omitted.

CHAPTER IX CLOTHING: TONSURE

314 The habit of the monk is of wool or some similar material, but of common quality. The underwear may be of any material, and should be changed at least weekly.

315 The cowl reaches to within 5 cms of the ground in front and a little more behind. It is closed on all sides and sewn up under the sleeves. Its average circumference is about three metres. The sleeves are one metre in circumference and come at least 12 cms below the knees. The hood is about 30 cms deep.*

The robe is a little shorter and slightly smaller than the cowl. The scapular is slightly shorter than the robe and at least 35 cms wide and covers the shoulders. The belt is of leather of natural colour and is about 5 cms wide. It terminates at one end in two parallel buttonholes

---

* 1 metre = 40 inches (approx.): 1 cm. = two-fifths of an inch.

and at the other in two pendants about 50 cms long, which are fastened
in the buttonholes by means of knots of interlaced leather. We may also
use a belt with a metal buckle without pendants. The belt is worn over
the scapular.

For underwear and stockings we conform to local usage and the
directives of the Abbot.

> 'Let the monks not worry about the colour or texture of all these
> things; but let them accept such as can be found in the country
> where they lie and that can be bought more cheaply.'
>
> (Rule, ch. 55)

316 The temporary professed wear the same habit as the monks, but
they retain the novice's cloak until solemn profession.

317 The novice's habit, which is white, has the same form as that of
the monks, but in place of a cowl, they wear a cloak with a hood
attached. Its length is the same as that of the cowl, and its circumference at the bottom is about 3.60 metres. The cincture is of white cloth.

318 The oblates wear a habit similar to that of the novices, but in place
of the cloak they wear a short mantle which reaches to their knees, and
their scapular has no hood. For work time they are given a little hooded
cape which ends in a point behind and is rounded in front.

319 The monastic crown is renewed at least once a month on the day
appointed by the Abbot. The crown is about 2 cms in width. The beard is
shaved as often as necessary to appear clean.

CHAPTER X   REPOSE

320 Just as we pray and work in common, so we take our rest in
common. Therefore we do not go to the dormitory without necessity
nor take rest there without permission. During the night, no one should
leave the dormitory without necessity. When entering, if the community are resting there, we should have the charity to avoid all noise.

> 'When the signal is given, they will rise without delay and hasten
> to outstrip each other to the Work of God, yet with all gravity and
> decorum.' (Rule, ch. 22)

321 When the timetable with full siesta is followed, those who wish to
take the siesta go to the dormitory after the dish-washing.

322 Our night attire has the form of the regular habit, but may be of very light material. In regard to underwear we conform to the directives of the Abbot.

323 One or several lamps are lighted in the dormitory at bedtime and burn until morning. Each day after chapter we go to make our beds. If we cannot do so at this time we go as soon as possible. On Fridays we make our beds immediately after the discipline.

The curtain is open when we are not in our cell. No one except the Superiors and the Infirmarian may open the curtain of another cell.

CHAPTER XI   JOURNEYS

324 When a monk has to go on a journey, which should happen only in cases of real necessity, he asks the instructions of his Abbot and receives his blessing. If he is to be absent several days, he will ask the prayers of the community; this is not to be taken literally in the case of the Abbot and the Cellarer.

To ask the prayers, he goes to the presbytery step at the end of the Hour of the Divine Office which immediately precedes his departure. He bows profoundly, then bows moderately to the two choirs right and left, without turning his back on the altar, and remains bowed while the Hebdomadary gives out the versicles and prayer. The choir stand meanwhile facing the altar.

325 The monk who is on a journey will observe the directives of the Abbot about meals.

326 On his return, he should first make a brief visit to the church. He then goes to the Abbot to ask his blessing and give an account of his journey. At the end of the first Office he attends, he asks the prayers of the community, prostrate at the presbytery step without bowing to the choirs. The Hebdomadary and the community act as in No. 324 above.

The monk should be very discreet with his brethren about his journey.

> Nature is filled with much that merits admiration and raises the soul to God. But the sacrifice of such pleasures is more beautiful still. 'To say that men go away to admire the peaks of mountains, the mighty waves of the sea, the sweeping stretches of rivers, the winding beaches of the ocean, the revolutions of the heavens, and then pay no attention to themselves,' remarks St Augustine sadly. (Confessions, Bk 9, ch. 8)

BOOK 9
THE WEEKLY OFFICERS

327 Each monk in turn has the honour of fulfilling certain offices in choir, and the opportunity of serving his brethren in community life. Those holding these offices and performing these services for the following week are named in chapter every Saturday morning.

> Fidelity and punctuality are religious virtues which the monk must have at heart to cultivate: in everything he does there is question of God's service. As a rule what the Lord asks of us is to do very small things with a very great heart.

CHAPTER I   THE HEBDOMADARY

328 The Hebdomadary when celebrating the Conventual Mass is as it were the representative of the community at the altar.

329 In choir he sings the versicle and collect of the antiphon of Our Lady which precedes the Divine Office. He intones all the hours, says the Capitulum, the 'Dominus vobiscum', the collect and the versicles which follow, but not the verse 'Fidelium', nor the 'Benedicamus Domino' at Vespers and Lauds when the Office is sung, nor the 'Dulce Nomen' after the antiphon of the Blessed Virgin, nor the 'Divinum auxilium' after the Salve.

> 'How proud I was to be Hebdomadary at the Divine Office and say the prayers aloud in choir. I would reflect that the priest was reciting the same prayers at Mass and that like him I was privileged to speak aloud before the Blessed Sacrament, to give the blessings, the absolutions, and to read the Gospel when I was first chanter.' (St Therese of the Child Jesus)

330 When a collect outside the Office ends with the short conclusion, the Hebdomadary makes the final flex only after the 'Per Christum Dominum nostrum'. When several prayers sung on the simple tone follow each other, the first are each ended with a punctum and the last one with a flex.

The Hebdomadary lowers the pitch at the verse 'Divinum auxilium'. When the Office of the Dead is sung, he sings the collect on the tone of the little hours.

331 When he recites anything in the church, chapter or refectory, he stands upright. At the Office he stands out of his stall facing the altar when fulfilling his duty. He bows after the little chapters only.

332 In chapter he sings or recites the prayers of Prime in ceremony facing the crucifix. He says the 'Gloria Patri' alone with a flex at the mediant and at the end. He sings the collect 'Dirigere', and for everything else he observes the same ceremonies as the choir.

333 In the refectory he blesses the table. At the end of the Pater he sings 'Et ne nos', and when the community have replied 'Sed libera nos a malo', he makes the sign of the cross in the direction of the principal table, saying 'Benedic Domine'.

At Grace after dinner he sings 'Agimus', facing the crucifix. Then in the church he says the versicles 'Et ne nos', 'Dispersit' and those that follow. He ends with the Fidelium on a slightly lower tone. After supper he says 'Benedictus Deus' facing the Cross.

334 When the Hebdomadary is absent he is replaced everywhere by the priest above him in choir, or by the one below him if he is first on his side.

In the absence of the Superiors, he gives the blessings, recites the prayers and presides at all the exercises.

335 The following week he says the Mass 'De Beata', and the third week the Mass 'Pro Defunctis'.

CHAPTER II   THE INVITATOR

336 The Invitator as his name indicates invites us to the praise of God, and it is his duty to intone, sing or recite alone various parts of the Office. He is on the side of choir opposite to the Hebdomadary's.

> 'What the voice sings the heart must believe, and what the heart believes, private and public conduct must reflect.' (Pius XII, Mediator Dei, 20 November 1947)

337 Whenever he intones or recites anything, the Invitator stands in ceremony facing the altar. But all antiphons are intones turned in choir. He makes a profound bow towards the altar:
(1) After a veriscle.
(2) After a short lesson.
(3) After completing a short responsory with its verse.
(4) After singing the 'Benedicamus Domino'.

338 In his absence, the Invitator is replaced by the one above him in the church, and this holds even in the chapter room.

339 When the Office is sung, he goes with the Invitator of the preceding week to the lectern placed at the middle of the presbytery step, or if necessary nearer the choir. On arriving there they bow profoundly to the altar. Then they sing the entire Invitatory. When the choir has repeated it, they sing each verse of the psalm 'Venite'. They bow again only after repeating the Invitatory as far as the asterisk, and then return to their places. When the Office is not sung, the Invitator recites the Invitatory at his place, bowing only at the end.

He says the versicle of the nocturns, unless he is at the lectern for the reading of the lessons. If the Office is sung he intones the antiphon of the second nocturn, if there is only one, and always of the third.

When there is only a short lesson, he recites it at his place, out of his stall.

When the responsories are not sung, he recites or sings the lessons of the first nocturn. He also recites those of all three-lesson offices, unless they consist of a homily in which case they are the responsibility of the Deacon of the week.

He intones the antiphon at Lauds and the first antiphon at Vespers. He sings the short responsory, the long responsory during the Triduum Sacrum (unless the cantor does so), the versicle after the hymn, and the 'Benedicamus Domino'. At the little hours he intones the antiphon and sings the versicle.

At Compline he sings only the versicle. But if there is no Compline reading he sings the short lesson in choir.

The Office of the Dead when not sung

340 At the nocturn he says the versicle, the lessons and the verses of the responsories. After the third antiphon of the nocturn he rises and says the versicle. After the Pater, he begins the first lesson. He does not ask a blessing before the lessons or say 'Tu autem' after them. He bows only after the verse 'Requiem'. From the Pater until after this verse he remains out of the stalls, facing the altar.

The Office of the Dead when sung

341 The Invitator intones the first antiphon of the nocturn, Lauds and Vespers and the antiphons of the Benedictus and Magnificat. He sings the lessons on the ordinary tone, with a proper ending. After each lesson he bows and ten sits while the responsories are being sung. All else is done as in the preceding paragraph.

Chapter

342 When the community go to chapter, the Invitator stands at the lectern. When all are in, he uncovers, and sings the Martyrology standing in ceremony. If the Office of Prime is recited, so is the Martyrology. A transferred feast is announced twice, but an office of the dead is announced only on the eve of the day on which it occurs.

During the prayers in chapter, he observes the postures of the choir, but bows towards the crucifix. When the Hebdomadary has said the verse 'Adiutorium', the Invitator bows profoundly, asks the blessing, and then sings a passage from the Holy Rule. This passage may be read in the vernacular if the Brothers are present. He announces only the title of the chapter, and if it is a division it is sung without title. On the first Sunday of Lent he sings Chapter 49 of the Rule, 'De Quadragesimae Observatione', to which he adds the latter part of Chapter 48 – 'In Quadragesimae vero'.

After the reading of the Holy Rule, he adds 'Commemoratio omnium fratrum . . .' When the community has answered 'Amen' to the versicle 'Requiescant in pace', he bows profoundly. If the Abbot is going to explain the Rule, the Invitator goes to him and presents the book with both hands. He salutes the Abbot and goes to his place, where he sits and salutes his neighbours. Every Saturday, after the reading of the Rule, he sings or reads (157) the list of officers for the coming week. He gives the title 'Nonnus' to all the solemnly professed, and 'Frater' to all others including himself. The following titles are used:

For the Abbot	Reverendus Domnus Abbas
For a resigned Abbot	Reverendus Domnus N . . .
For a Titular Prior	Reverendus Domnus Prior
For a Superior ad nutum	Reverendus Domnus Superior
For a Claustral Prior	Nonnus Prior
For a Subprior	Nonnus Subprior

343 The following week he sings the Invitatory with the Invitator of the week, and reads or sings the lessons of the second nocturn.

CHAPTER III   THE SUB-INVITATOR

344 The Sub-invitator is the monk standing immediately below the Invitator in choir, or immediately above him if he is last on his side.

345 When the Sub-invitator intones a psalm or antiphon, he is in ceremony facing the opposite side of choir. Whenever the Invitator intones an antiphon, the Sub-invitator intones the psalm or canticle that follows.

When the Office is not sung, he intones the psalm or canticle, the antiphon of which would be intoned by the Invitator were the Office sung.

346 At Vigils he intones the psalm 'Domine quid multiplicati sunt'. He recites the short responsory which is said after the short lesson in summer, at the end of the first nocturn.

He also intones the following:

At Lauds: the psalm 'Deus misereatur' and the psalm following it.
At Vespers: the first psalm and the third antiphon.
At Compline: the psalm 'Cum invocarem'.
At the Office of the Dead not sung: the first psalm, the Benedictus, and the Magnificat, in ceremony.

347 When the Invitator is absent and there is no one above him to take his place, the Sub-invitator continues his own duties until something occurs which has to be given out by the Invitator; he then begins to supply for him and the next below becomes Sub-invitator. But if the Sub-invitator knows that the Invitator cannot come to choir, as for instance when acting as Deacon he is Invitator from the beginning of the Office.

CHAPTER IV   THE SERVANTS OF THE CHURCH

The functions of the Servants of the Church, whether at Mass or at the Office, are those of Acolytes.

It is in seemingly insignificant things that we can show the most love, because they are hidden and, having scarcely any natural consequences, reveal nothing but the delicacy of our love.

A. The First Servant

348 If the Invitatory at Vigils is to be sung, the Servant of the Church prepares the lectern.

If there is a Te Deum, he goes to the lectern in due time, bows to the Abbot when he arrives, presents the stole for him to kiss, and puts it on him. During the Gospel he stands behind the Abbot at his right. He bows to him when he withdraws and then closes the lectionary. The stole is not used unless an Abbot sings the Gospel.

Chapter

349 Towards the end of Prime he goes to the chapter room to prepare the Martyrology and on Saturday the list of officers.

The Conventual Mass

350 It is the duty of the Servant of the Church to assist the Celebrant and ministers to vest.

If there is a Solemn Procession he brings the cope to the Celebrant at the end of Tierce.

He lights the candles for Mass after Tierce or after the Procession if there is one. It is preferable that he do this from behind the altar. He begins on the Epistle side with the candle nearest the Cross. When extinguishing them he begins on the Gospel side with the candle farthest from the Cross. He lights candles as follows:

six	all solemn Masses
four	Sundays
	feasts of MM
	during the three Octaves
	on the Vigils of Christmas and the Assumption
two	all other days

After the last Gospel he extinguishes the candles and covers the altar. If the relics are exposed he leaves two candles lighted until they are removed.

Vespers

351 He lights two candelabra of the sanctuary for the first and second Vespers of Sunday and feasts of Sermon.

Compline

352 He lights the candelabra for the Salve and extinguishes them after the Fidelium. Towards the end of the examen he opens the door of the church and stands near the holy water font. When the Superior arrives the Servant kisses the aspersory and gives it to him, kissing his ring, or his hand if the Superior is not an Abbot. He stands beside the Abbot while the latter sprinkles the community. He receives holy water himself after the community, and takes back the aspersory, kissing the ring of an Abbot or the hand of the Superior, then kisses the aspersory and bows profoundly.

Benediction of the Blessed Sacrament

353 When there is Benediction of the Blessed Sacrament, he lights the candles in due time. He extinguishes them afterwards, and covers the altar.

Blessing of Holy Water

354 Every Sunday before Tierce he places a lectern at the middle of the presbytery step, and to the right of it a small table covered with a cloth, on which he puts the vessel containing the water, a shell containing a little salt, and the aspersory. Nearby he puts an empty holy water vessel and another aspersory. As soon as the priest finishes the blessing the Servant of the Church removes the lectern and moves the table towards the Gospel side, so that the Celebrant may have it on his right during the actual aspersion. He puts some holy water into the empty vessel to be used for aspersing the monastery, and presents it and the aspersory to the Subdeacon. Then he receives holy water himself in his own rank. Towards the end of the aspersion, he goes to the presbytery step and receives the aspersory from the Deacon. He carries it and the table to the sacristy.

Feast of the Purification

355 After Tierce on this feast he places the Collectaneum open on the lectern in the middle of the presbytery. After the prayer which follows distribution of the candles, he removes the lectern and takes the Collectaneum to the sacristy.

Ash Wednesday

356 After Tierce he places the Collectaneum open on the lectern in the middle of the presbytery. After the blessing of the ashes he removes the lectern, takes away the book and lights the candles for Mass. The book is taken to the sacristy.

The Second Sunday of Passiontide

357 After Tierce he arranges the Collectaneum as in the preceding paragraph. After the blessing of the palms, he removes the lectern and takes the book to the sacristy.

Holy Week

358 On the last three days of Holy Week he lights the candle at the presbytery step towards the end of mental prayer. He extinguishes it when the Benedictus antiphon is intoned. At the beginning of Psalm 150 he extinguishes the sanctuary lamp.

Holy Thursday

359 He lights the candles at the Altar of Repose before the Procession. After the Blessed Sacrament is in the tabernacle and the ministers have departed, he extinguishes the candles and all the lights of the church, except one lamp which he takes care to keep burning before the Blessed Sacrament until the following day.

Good Friday

360 As soon as the ministers arrive at the altar, he places the lectern on the presbytery step at the Epistle side, and on it the epistolary open at the Office of the day. After the prophecy he removes the stand. He lights the candles at the altar of repose towards the end of the Adoration of the Cross.

Paschal Vigil

361 The Servant of the Church lights the new fire and from it lights several coals which have never been used before. When the Deacon removes his violet stole after the blessing of the Paschal Candle he brings the stole to the presbytery where the Deacon will need it again after the Exultet. When the Abbot arrives at the presbytery, the Servant takes his candle from him with the usual ceremonies, and places it in the receptacle prepared for it on the credence table. Then he lights four others prepared in the same place. When the incense has been blessed for the Exultet, he gives a candle to the Subdeacon for presentation to the Abbot and then gives him another for himself. After the Exultet he places the uncovered lectern at the Epistle side of the presbytery step, with the epistolary open on it. After the prophecies he takes the book to the credence. At the 'Propitius esto' of the litanies he lights the candles for Mass.

Paschal Time

362 The Paschal Candle remains burning through Easter Sunday, and is extinguished by the Servant after Compline. He lights it on the other days indicated. (22)

On the feast of the Ascension he lights it at first Vespers, and extinguishes it only after Compline.

Corpus Christi and Feast of Sacred Heart

363 On these feasts he lights the candles for exposition towards the end of the Conventual Mass.

The Dying and the Dead

364 When the bell rings for the Sacrament of the Sick, he goes to the sacristy and takes the Ritual and a lighted candle. In going to the presbytery step and thence to the infirmary, he walks on the Sacristan's left. In the sick-room he stands near the table on which are the Holy Oils.

If Viaticum alone is administered he takes a cruet of water and one of wine instead of the candle and the Ritual. He goes to the infirmary walking before the acolytes and ringing a small bell.

As soon as the bell for the agony sounds (77), he goes to the infirmary carrying the Paschal Candle and kneels beside the sick-bed. He gives the lighted candle to the Infirmarian. When a deceased person is brought to the church, he lights a candle at the feet of the corpse.

B. The Second Servant of the Church

365 The Second Servant of the Church assists and supplies for the first in everything. He lights the candles of the community before processions on Holy Thursday and Corpus Christi.

On the feast of Dedication of the Church he lights the candles at the consecration crosses, for first and second Vespers, for Lauds, and for the Conventual Mass.

When Viaticum is administered immediately after the Sacrament of the Sick, he goes with the priest and acolytes to the sacristy, where he takes a cruet of water, one of wine and a little bell. Then he goes to the presbytery step and thence to the infirmary, walking before the acolytes and ringing the bell.

CHAPTER V   THE READER AT TABLE

366 'There should always be reading at the monastic table.' The Reader begins his task each Sunday by asking the prayers of the community. Towards the end of Mass he goes to the presbytery step at the Epistle side and having bowed to the altar unless he did so previously in crossing before it, he salutes both choirs. When the last Gospel is finished he sings the following versicle in ceremony three times alternately with the choir: 'Domine labia mea aperies et os meum annuntiabit laudem tuam'. When the choir have repeated the verse for the last time, the Reader bows to receive the blessing. He rises only after 'Amen', and having bowed to the altar withdraws.

When the Mass is pontifical, the blessing is asked at the end of Sext.

367 He receives the Mixt every day, except on fastdays of the Church.

368 He goes to the refectory before the community. When the latter arrive, he stands uncovered and bows to the Abbot as he passes before him. He sits during the prayers. At the end of the collect 'Benedic' he asks the blessing in the same way as at the Office.

369 At the signal of the Abbot he begins the Holy Scripture, either singing it in Latin on the tone of the lessons, or reading it in the vernacular.

In announcing a title, if it is the beginning of a chapter he says for example: 'Libri Genesis * caput primum +.' If it is the continuation of a chapter he says 'Sequitur in capitulo primo * Libri primi Regum +.'

He reads the Holy Scriptures in this order:

From the First Sunday of Advent to the Circumcision: Isaiah.

From the Circumcision to Septuagesima: Epistles of St Paul.

From Septuagesima to Passion Sunday (I): Genesis and the other books which follow, as far as the First Book of Kings.

From Passion Sunday to Easter: Jeremia and Baruch.

From Easter to Pentecost: Acts of the Apostles, Apocalypse, and the Canonical Epistles.

From Pentecost to the First Sunday of August: The Books of Kings, Paralipomenon and Esdras.

From the First Sunday of August to the First Sunday of September: the five Books of Wisdom.

From the First Sunday of September to the First Sunday of October: Job, Tobias, Judith and Esther.

From the First Sunday of October to the First Sunday of November: The two Books of Machabees.

From the First Sunday of November to the First Sunday of Advent: Ezechiel, Daniel and the twelve minor prophets.

The reading of the Scriptures ends at the signal of the Abbot.

370 The Reader may cover for the reading of the Menology and the book appointed by the Superior. He announces the title and subtitle in such a way that the hearers can easily recall where he stopped. When the Abbot gives the signal and says 'Tu autem', the Reader adds while rising 'Domine, miserere nobis'.

He says the prayers before and after his meal as prescribed for those who do not eat at the same time as the community. (300)

371 The following week he has the Compline reading. At the signal, he asks the blessing in the same way as at the Office.

CHAPTER VI   THE SERVANTS OF THE REFECTORY

372 The brethren should serve one another, especially in the refectory where serving at table is a source of great merit and an increase of charity.

'Goodness and humility are almost the same thing. When a man is good, he feels impelled to give himself, to sacrifice himself, to make himself little, and that is humility.' (Lacordaire)

373 On the Saturday preceding his week of duty, the Servant of the Refectory performs the Mandatum with the one whom he succeeds. When they hear the five strokes they remove their cowls and don aprons. They take the basin, towels and warm water which have been prepared in advance. At sound of the little bell they go to the chapter room or the cloister, according to the location. He who is entering on his week goes first, carrying an empty basin with the towels, while the other carries the warm water. They put down everything before the abbatial seat, uncover and bow.

They begin the washing of the feet with the Abbot and continue with the next in dignity and the religious on the same side. The one who is ending his week washes the feet and the other dries them. They bow to each monk only after washing his feet, but bow profoundly to the Abbot both before and after. When all is finished, they make a profound bow, cover, and in the same order as before carry the basin and towels to the appointed place, wash their hands and re-assume their cowls. Then they return before the abbatial seat, walking uncovered and in ceremony, single file, and in such order that they will not have to cross to go to their places. They bow profoundly to the Abbot, bow to each other, raise their sleeves, and sit down. Then they salute their neighbours and cover.

374 On Sunday towards the end of Lauds the Servant who is ending his week goes to the presbytery step at his own side of the choir, bows profoundly to the altar and salutes both choirs. After the verse 'Fidelium' he sings in ceremony and the verse 'Benedictus es Domine Deus qui adiuvisti me et consolatus es me' which he repeats three times alternately with the choir. After the blessing which he receives bowed, he salutes the altar and returns to his place.

Meanwhile the Servant of the coming week goes to the presbytery step on the opposite side. He acts as above, singing the verse 'Deus in adiutorium meum intende. Domine ad adiuvandum me festina.'

When he has received the blessing he withdraws to one of the front stalls of the upper choir. If the Office is not sung, neither are the verses above.

375 The Servant goes to the refectory some time before dinner, depending on the number of monks. He removes his cowl, dons an apron and serves the portions. If he is not finished when the community enter, he waits until all are seated. The first portion should normally be served before the meal, and the second may be served after the prayers.

The Servant says the prayers with the community and observes the same ceremonies. He is uncovered when serving. After the blessing or after serving the second portion he goes around the refectory to see if anything is lacking, and to clean the tables if necessary. Then he reassumes his cowl and begins his own meal.

If he has forgotten to serve a portion, he kneels before the Abbot after repairing his omission. If anything else is lacking, he advises the refectorian. If someone has not yet arrived at the end of the Scripture reading, the Servant sees that his portions are kept hot.

When the community rise from table, he opens the refectory door, and when they depart he serves the Reader.

Without love there can be neither humility nor obedience.

376 At supper or collation he begins serving in sufficient time to be finished before the community come to the refectory.

BOOK 10
THE SICK AND THE DEAD

CHAPTER I   THE INFIRMARY

'Before all and above all care must be taken of the sick, because in them Christ is more especially served.' (St Benedict, Chap. 36)

377 A special part of the monastery is set aside for the sick, towards whom monastic tradition has always shown great solicitude. And since according to the Rule monks do not even have disposal of their own bodies, they will have the simplicity to make known their infirmities to their Superiors. Then they will only have to follow their directions and those of the Infirmarian.

An old tradition says that the monk who is suffering should be treated in such a way that he will not regret the absence of his mother; but the monk must take care not to become demanding, since the fact that he is approaching death does not dispense him from tending to perfection.

378 The Abbot will see to it that the fare in the infirmary is more substantial than that served in the common refectory. The sick may take fish, eggs and dessert every day of the year. The Abbot can have meat served to those who need it.

379 When a monk returns to the common refectory from the infirmary he is given the indulgence for whatever time is necessary.

> We should not be surprised at these concessions because 'charity requires that we show condescension for the corporal and spiritual infirmities of our neighbour.' (St Bern., De Div., S.36, No. 1)

380 The sick take their meals as far as possible at the same time as the community. The senior says 'Benedicite' and the others continue 'Oculi' or 'Edent' recto tono. If he who acts as Hebdomadary is a priest he blesses the table with the sign of the cross, otherwise he signs himself. Grace is said after meals as in No. 300.

There is reading for a short period at the beginning of the meal, unless the reading of the common refectory is transmitted by loud speaker.

381 The sick speak to the Infirmarian only in the infirmary. Apart from an urgent case they do not do so during the office or when they are at table. They may not enter the cell of another without permission. In principle those who are in the infirmary only for sleep and for meals do not speak to the Infirmarian.

382 The sick recite their Office as far as possible at the same time as the community. They assist at the Conventual Mass, unless their illness prevents this. The Abbot will decide at what other exercises they will assist.

> 'In order to save our souls, it suffices to support patiently all the infirmities of the body; but perfection consists in embracing them voluntarily and with fervour.' (St Bern., De Div., S.35, No. 5)

Communion of the Sick

383 When the sick cannot go to the church or infirmary oratory for Holy Communion it is brought to them in their cell. On a table covered with a cloth are prepared a cruet of water and a cruet of wine, a vessel of holy water with an aspersory, a corporal and a purificator. The coverlet of the bed should be white. If the patient is a priest, he wears a white stole.

384 For the ceremony we follow the Ritual. The priest comes, preceded by two torch-bearers, before whom walks a monk carrying the Ritual and ringing a little bell. The priest, who says his part alone, recites the Miserere alternately with another.

At the entrance of the sick-room they say the Gloria Patri, even though the psalm is not yet finished, and the ringing of the bell ceases. The priest says 'Pax huic domui', and the assistants answer 'Amen'. The acolytes kneel at either side of the table and respond to the priest. The third monk removes the humeral veil, folds it, and after giving the Ritual to the priest, kneels down.

If the patient is able he recites the Confiteor with joined hands:

'Confiteor Deo, Beatae Mariae et omnibus sanctis, et tibi Pater, quia peccavi nimis cogitatione, locutione et opera, mea culpa' – to which he adds: 'Ideo precor vos, orate pro me'.

The assistants say:

'Misereatur tui omnipotens Deus, et dimittat tibi omnia peccata tua, liberet te ab omni malo, conservet et confirmet te in omni opere bono, et perducat te ad vitam aeternam.'

The patient replies 'Amen' alone to the 'Misereatur' but all reply 'Amen' to the Indulgentiam which the priest says alone.

After Communion the patient takes the ablution if he can do so. The priest recites the collect and gives the blessing and all return to the sacristy in silence, in the same order in which they came.

'O my dear Lord, though I am so very weak that I am not fit to ask You for suffering as a gift, and have not strength to do so, at least I will beg of You the grace to meet suffering well, when You in Your love and wisdom bring it upon me.' (Newman)

CHAPTER II   ANOINTING THE SICK AND HOLY VIATICUM

'Let the Abbot take the greatest care lest the sick should suffer from any negligence,' says St Benedict. This inspires the Abbot of Clairvaux to remark: 'I cannot help suffering when you suffer, and I could not hear of your sufferings without sharing them.'

385 For the anointing of the sick the Infirmarian prepares the table as for Communion, putting on it in addition a piece of bread and a vessel of water. At the appointed time the great bell is rung twice (77) and the community go to the church and stand in the presbytery stalls facing the altar.

When all is ready the bell is rung again and the Cantor begins Psalm

40, 'Beatus qui intelligit', to which he adds Psalms 42 and 141. These are recited recto tono with the Gloria Patri at the end of each, and the last is repeated if necessary. We leave the church at the bginning of the first psalm, and go in procession to the infirmary, the seniors leading, following the Abbot who carries the crosier.

On arrival at the sick-room the community kneel in such wise as not to impede the priest. All reply 'Amen' to 'Pax huic domui' and to the prayer 'Omnipotens'. The patient recites the Confiteor with joined hands if he is able (384). If not the Infirmarian says it for him. The community say the Misereatur (384) with the priest, and the sick brother answers 'Amen'.

After the anointing the choir recite Psalm 102, 'Benedic', with the Gloria Patri at the end. The Cantor intones 'Kyrie eleison' and the community continue 'Christe eleison', and say the Pater silently. After the prayers, and the special blessing for the sick, the community retire, unless Viaticum is to be administered immediately.

In that case the priest appointed goes to bring the Sacred Host, as in No. 384.

386 If the Sacrament of the Sick is administered in the church, the community stand in the presbytery stalls and recite Psalms 40, 42 and 141 turned in choir, while the officiating priests vest in the sacristy, the sick monk sits in the middle of the choir.

Holy Viaticum

387 At the approach of death this Sacrament is administered solemnly if circumstances allow, even though the sick person has already communicated that same day.

The great bell is rung twice to assemble the community in church as for the anointing. While going to the infirmary we recite the Seven Penitential Psalms, and interrupt them with the Gloria Patri on arrival at the sick-room. The community act as above (384).

The Agony

388 When a sick brother nears death, the community will assemble in a spirit of fraternal charity to assist him with their prayers. Everyone will pray fervently for his brother, who without doubt will soon appear before the Lord and who meanwhile, perhaps, is suffering much.

God sends us suffering only for our sanctification. That is not
cruelty, but a lesson and a challenge.

At sound of the bell (77) all go to the infirmary, reciting the Credo in
an audible voice, which is repeated until the sick-room is reached. The
sacristan brings the items specified in the Ritual. The community kneel
around the sick-bed and answer the litanies and prayers which are
recited by the Abbot.

If the agony is prolonged the Penitential Psalms may be added. Then
if the patient is not on the point of death, the community retire. The
Paschal Candle is left burning in the sick-room, and a crucifix and
aspersory are left there also. The Abbot leaves some of the religious to
pray beside the patient, and appoints a priest to suggest some consoling
words to him.

CHAPTER III   FROM DEATH TO BURIAL

Monks are saddened at the thought of being separated from a
much loved brother, but their souls, like that of the sick person,
remain in great peace.
'I could never be brought to believe that one can fear the good
God . . . When I am playing on the road and my father calls me to
come back into the house, I am not afraid of my father.' (Peguy)

389 If the sick brother dies while the community are present, they
rise and the Cantor intones the responsory 'Subvenite'. The Community bow for the 'Kyrie' which the Cantor says alone, and then all add
'Christe' etc. They remain bowed during the Pater, the versicles and
the prayer 'Tibi Domine'.

After this the community leave the sick-room, and if the place
permits it, stand in choir around the Abbot, who says the prayers of the
Ritual. If these are finished before the completion of the preparation of
the body, the Cantor begins the psalter which is continued alternately
recto tono. Meanwhile the Infirmarian and his assistants proceed with
their work. If the community do not remain as just stated, a priest says
the prayer 'Suscipe', etc.

The corpse is placed on a bier, and the bells are rung. A dead priest
may be vested in violet stole.

390 If death occurs during the night, or at a time when the community
cannot go immediately to the infirmary, a priest says the 'Subvenite'

and the prayer 'Tibi Domine', and also the prayers said during the preparation of the body.

All go to the infirmary at the time indicated by the Abbot for the removal of the body.

391 When the preparation of the body is completed the Infirmarian and his assistants carry it to the place where the community are assembled. After the aspersion with holy water and the incensation, all bow for the Pater, the versicles and the prayer 'Deus cui coli'. The Cantor then intones the responsory 'Libera'.

The body is then brought to the church in procession in the following order: holy water bearer, thurifer, monk carrying the lighted Paschal Candle, Deacon carrying the cross, the choir novices, the professed, juniors first, the Abbot wearing the stole and carrying the crosier, the body borne by monks of the same rank as the deceased, who are appointed by the Prior, the Laybrethren, seniors leading.

On arrival at the church the community occupy the presbytery stalls. The body is placed in the middle of the choir, the feet towards the altar. The monk carrying the candle and the Deacon carrying the cross stand at the head of the corpse; the thurifer and holy water bearer stand at the feet beside the Abbot.

After the responsory the community bow during the Pater, the versicles and the prayer 'Commendamus tibi'. Then the Deacon re-places the cross on the altar. A lighted candle is placed at the head of the corpse; and the holy water vessel and the aspersory at the feet.

392 The body is not brought to the church on Sundays and feasts of Sermon, during Holy Week, the Octaves of Easter and Pentecost, Ash Wednesday, nor the Vigils of Christmas and Pentecost. On these days it is placed in chapter or in an oratory. But if it is impossible to sing a Conventual Requiem Mass for the deceased, the body should be brought to the 'Pro Defunctis' altar while a Mass is being offered for him there because no one should be interred without at least one Mass having first been celebrated for his soul.

393 The Abbot should take great care that the body is never left alone nor without a light. Outside the times of Mass, the Office, and Mental Prayer, two monks appointed by the Cantor should recite the psalter or the Office of the Dead, either in Latin or the vernacular. If the body is not in the church, those who are praying beside it interrupt the psalter when they hear the bell for the Office, and say the Office where they are. Then they resume the recitation of the psalter. If the community is small, however, they may go to choir and be replaced by Laybrothers.

When we interrupt the psalter to say the Office, we mark the place in the psalter and note also what part of the Office of the Dead we have finished.

394 During the night the monks appointed relieve each other every two hours. They begin by reciting their Office together. One of them goes to awaken those who are to succeed them, and then they go to rest, rising only after they have taken the same amount of sleep as the community.

395 Those praying by the dead recite the Office of the Dead after each psalter as follows:

during the night	the three Nocturns
from dawn to midday	Lauds
from midday to night	Vespers

They say the collect 'Deus cui proprium est . . . te supplices', but for a priest or an Abbot they say 'Deus qui inter . . .'

At the end of each psalter they say the verse 'Requiem', and they sit during all these prayers.

396 A Requiem Office is always sung for a deceased. If the rubrics do not permit this before the burial, it is done on the first free day. It is announced with both bells. The third responsory of the Nocturn is 'Libera'.

397 All Masses celebrated between death and burial should be for the deceased, except the Masses 'De Beata' and 'Pro Defunctis', where these Masses are offered daily for the intentions of the Order. If a priest is impeded from making this application there is no obligation to supply it later.

398 The deceased is absolved in the first chapter following his death, and this holds for all who are buried in our monasteries.

CHAPTER IV   BURIAL

399 No burial should ever take place unless the time demanded by the laws of the country has elapsed after death.

On certain more solemn days, indicated below, the burial is deferred until after Vespers, or if convenient, even until the morrow.

400 At the time of burial the bells are rung (77), and the community occupy the Mass stalls. When the Officiant arrives they turn in choir. After each of the prayers the Cantor begins the responsory and the 'Kyrie'. All stand during the first three prayers and the responsory which follows. They bow only during the Pater, the versicles and the last collect, 'Annue'. They rise at 'Amen'.

401 When the Cantor intones the 'Chorus Angelorum', the monk beside him intones the psalm 'In exitu', during which the bells are rung. We go to the cemetery in the following order: holy water bearer, thurifer, acolyte carrying the candle, Deacon carrying the cross, choir novices, the professed (juniors first), Subdeacon carrying the Ritual, the Abbot with crosier, the body of the deceased on a bier or in a coffin according to the custom of the country, the Laybrothers (seniors leading).

When Psalm 113 ends during the procession, the choir sing the antiphon 'Chorus Angelorum'. Then the Cantor intones the antiphon 'Aperite' followed by Psalm 117, 'Confitemini'.

402 At the cemetery, the holy water bearer stands at the foot of the grave, and the community stand on either side, as the locality permits. The bearers put the corpse near the grave, feet towards the east, but in the case of a priest the feet are towards the west.

After repetition of the antiphon 'Aperite', the Officiant sings the prayer 'Pio recordationis', to which all reply 'Amen'. The Cantor immediately intones the antiphon 'Ingrediar' followed by Psalm 41, 'Quemadmodum', during which the Officiant blesses the grave, which he sprinkles and incenses.

After repetition of the antiphon 'Ingrediat', the Officiant sings the prayer 'Obsecramus'. Then the Cantor intones the antiphon 'Haec requies mea', followed by Psalm 131, 'Memento'. During this time the Infirmarian descends into the grave and the bearers remove their cowls or cloaks and lower the body into the grave. The Infirmarian receives it and disposes it becomingly, crossing the arms, and covering the face with the hood. Then he comes up out of the grave.

After the repetition of the antiphon 'Haec requies mea' the Officiant sings the prayer 'Dues apud quem'. When the Cantor intones the 'De terra' followed by Psalm 138, 'Probasti me', the Officiant throws a little earth on the body, and the bearers begin to cover it without precipitation, shovelling the earth gently down the sides of the grave and beginning with the feet, so that the body may only little by little disappear. They may then be replaced by the Laybrothers.

After the repetition of the antiphon 'De terra', the Officiant sings the prayer 'Temeritatis' at the foot of the grave. He then returns between the two choirs and sings the exhortation 'Oremus fratres', followed by the collect 'Deus qui humanarum'.

The Cantor then begins the antiphon 'Clementissime'. At the end of this, at least if the state of the ground permits, all prostrate on the knuckles to sing three times the verse 'Domine miserere'. Then all rise and bow during the Pater, versicles and collects.

> Until the day of Resurrection we shall not see again this brother laid to rest in the cemetery. But his memory will not be forgotten. It is even probable that we shall be better able to appreciate his virtues now that we are separated from him. 'The olive and the grape yield their substance only after passing through the press.' (Life of Blessed Anne of St Bartholomew) Similarly there are souls who, like violets, yield their full aroma only when they have been ground.

403 The acolyte who carries the candle extinguishes it now, and the Cantor begins the Seven Penitential Psalms which are recited alternately in two choirs while returning to the church in the same order in which we came out.

404 The Officiant and ministers enter the presbytery and go up to the altar, where the Deacon replaces the cross, and the community occupy the stalls as for Mass. All kneel facing the altar, and at the end of the psalm which they are actually reciting, say the verse 'Requiem' and end the recitation. The Officiant says 'Pater noster', the versicles and prayers 'Satisfaciat'. Then all retire.

> 'Did not the Christ have to suffer these things before entering into his glory?' (Luke xxiv, 26)
> 'I am not dying, I am entering into life.' (St Therese of the Child Jesus)

CHAPTER V   THE BURIAL OF GUESTS

405 Guests should normally be buried in the parish cemetery. If however a guest is buried at the monastery, we follow our own rite with the changes mentioned in the Ritual. If the deceased is a priest, he is dressed in vestments or simply in surplice and stole, and is thus laid out until the time of burial.

The corpse of a guest is never alone or without a light, and should be buried in a coffin.

406 The Officiant at the burial may wear the cope and stole over his cowl or his alb. We always sing at the burial of a priest or a religious from another order. We may even place the body in the monastic choir, but all other deceased are placed outside the choir, and for them we sing only what is prescribed by the Abbot.

407 No guest is ever buried without there being a Requiem Mass for him. If the Office of the Dead or a conventual Mass is said between the time of death and of burial, the proper collect is inserted. At the burial, after the 'Clementissime' we say neither 'Domine miserere' nor the Penitential Psalms.

Priests say one collect for the deceased, and non-priests recite the Penitential Psalms or a Rosary.

408 If a deceased person is brought to the monastery, we go to meet the remains at the door where we sing 'Subvenite', followed by the responsory 'Libera me' as we come inside in procession.

CHAPTER VI   DUTIES TOWARDS THE DEAD

409 In addition to what has been done for the deceased before his burial:
1 we say the collect 'Deus qui inter apostolicos' or 'Inclina' at the Office of the Dead for thirty days when the rubrics permit. This collect is also inserted at the daily Mass 'Pro Defunctis' and at the Conventual Mass.
2 Every professed priest of the monastery, whether he has made stability or not, present or absent, offers three Masses.
3 The non-priests say fifty psalms.
4 During his tricenary a crucifix is kept at the deceased's place in the refectory. His dinner and supper are served if there are poor persons to whom the food can be given. If not, an alms is given for the same intention.

This monastic custom is very ancient. The Lord having assured us that we shall be judged on our charity towards the poor and the suffering (Matt. xxv, 35) we are quite willing to give alms in this way on behalf of our deceased brother.

On the thirtieth day, counting from the day of burial exclusively, the Cantor announces in chapter the conclusion of the tricenary, which ends after Compline.

410 If a professed dies in a monastery other than his own, he has a right in justice only to the Masses and prayers of his own community. If he had come to render services, however, it is equitable that everything be done for him as for a professed of the house, without prejudice to what is done for him in his own monastery.

411 The death of a member of one of our communities is announced to every house of the Order, as well as to those of the Sacred Order of Citeaux, and to our affiliated monasteries. The following formula is used:

'Die . . . mensis . . . anni Domini . . . obiit in nostro monasterio
Beatae Mariae . . . Ordinis Cisterciensium Strictioris
Observantiae in diocesi . . . , in . . . (name of country), Nonnus
. . . (Sacerdea or Frater, pro etc.) cuius anima vestras precamur
orationes et sacrificiorum suffragiis ex caritate et orabimus pro
vestris.'

For every person whose death is thus announced in chapter, each one recites the 'De Profundis' three times. Priests may replace this by a collect in the Mass, saying one collect for each deceased.

412 On the death of the Sovereign Pontiff or of the Abbot General, a Requiem Office and a Solemn Requiem Mass are sung for him in every house of the Order. All daughter houses do likewise on the death of the Father Immediate.

413 Even though the Solemn Anniversary of the month of January is celebrated for all Superiors who have died during the preceding year, an anniversary Mass may still be celebrated annually for the last deceased Superior.

'Precious in the eyes of the Lord is the death of his faithful ones.'
(Psalm cxv, 15)

The Anniversaries of the Order

414 The Solemn Anniversaries of the Dead are celebrated:

In January for all the Superiors of our monasteries of monks and nuns.
In May for all the deceased relatives of members of the Order.
In September for all the members of the Order, benefactors, and associates who have died during the year.
In November for all the deceased of the Order.

415 Professed priests are bound to apply Mass for the Dead on the Solemn Anniversaries, except the hebdomadaries of the 'De Beata' and 'Pro Defunctis' Masses, where these are applied daily for the intentions of the Order. The application of the Mass should be made on the day fixed by the Ordo.

A priest who is impeded from saying Mass on that day for this intention is not obliged to supply it on another day.

On the day of the Office of the Month, only the Conventual Mass is applied for the intention of the Order.

Prayers for Deceased Relatives

416 On the death of the father, mother, brother or sister of a member of the community, the absolution is asked in chapter.

The priests say a collect for the deceased, and the others recite the Penitential Psalms or a Rosary.

If there are several brothers by blood in the same community, this must be taken into account in computing the prescribed prayers.

CHAPTER VII   THE GREAT TRICENARY

417 In our Order, it is during the Great Tricenary from September 17th to October 17th that we pray in a more special manner for the dead.

The Great Tricenary opens on September 17th with the Solemn Absolution which takes place in chapter. On this day the Invitator does not say the 'Commemoratio'. After the reading of the Holy Rule the Cantor comes to the centre of the chapter room, bows profoundly, and sings on the tone of the lessons: 'Absolvatis animas fratrum, sororum, familiarium et benefactorum nostrorum hoc anno defunctorum.' He bows again and goes to his place.

The community then rise and the Abbot uncovered sings 'Animum fratrum, sororum, familiarium et benefactorum nostrorum hoc anno defunctorum requiescant in pace.' All reply 'Amen', and the Cantor intones the 'De Profundis', which is sung with flexes. After the verse 'Requiem' he says 'Kyrie eleison' and the choir add, bowing, 'Christe eleison' etc., and immediately say the Pater silently. The Abbot standing sings 'Et ne nos inducas' and the versicles 'A porta inferi', 'Requiescant in pace', 'Domine exaudi', 'Dominus vobiscum', with the prayer 'Deus veniae', using the short conclusion. The community sit again and the Cantor comes once more to the centre of the chapter room and says recto tono: 'Absolvatis animas patrum, matrum, fratrum, sororum et consanguineorum nostrorum hoc anno defunctorum'. Remaining seated the Abbot says 'Requiescant in pace' and all answer 'Amen'.

If there is some deceased person to be absolved or an obituary notice to be read, the Cantor does it at this moment.

The Abbot then recalls our various obligations to the dead.

At the end of chapter, the 'De Profundis' is said recto tono, and in place of the collect 'Deus veniae' the collect 'Fidelium' is said with the short conclusion.

418 According to the ancient statutes of the Order every priest should apply twenty Masses for the dead. By an Indult of 11 March, 1859, this obligation has been reduced to three Masses. Each Abbot is free to make use of this Indult, and the monks should conform to his decision.

The non-priests recite the psalter three times. The Abbot can commute the obligations of the Tricenary into other practices of piety or penance.

419 Every day during the Tricenary three dinners are served in memory of the dead on a separate table, and on Sundays and feasts of two meals, three suppers also in the same place, if there are poor persons to whom the food can be given. Otherwise an equivalent amount of alms is given.

420 The Tricenary ends October 17th after Compline. That morning in chapter the Cantor says 'Hodie finitur tricenarium solemne defunctorum'. The Abbot adds 'Requiescant in pace' and the community respond 'Amen.'

> Holy Virgin Mary, who stood at the foot of the Cross to offer
> your Son to the Heavenly Father in the name of all, it is by your
> hands that I wish to unite the hour of my death to that of Jesus on
> Calvary.

Foundation Masses

421 No foundation Masses may be accepted without the consent of the community and of the General Chapter or of the Abbot General. The conditions (length of time, etc.) to which these foundations are subject are those stated by the General Chapter of 1948.

BOOK 11
THE OFFICERS OF THE MONASTERY

CHAPTER I   THE OFFICERS IN GENERAL

422 In the monastery, a mystical body in miniature as it were, each member has his own function, and all contribute to the common good. Those who hold the principal offices are the core of the community.

For the Abbot the necessary conditions of age and profession are stated in the Constitutions. The Prior, Subprior, and the Cellarer should be solemnly professed and have made their stability in the monastery. If in case of necessity a monk who has not made stability or who is in temporary vows must be appointed to one of these offices, the permission of the General Chapter or of the Abbot General is required.

423 St Benedict's counsel to the Cellarer – that he care for his own soul – applies to all the officers. If they are impeded by their duties from prayer or lectio divina, they will supply these at the first opportunity.

They should also make a day's retreat each month.

If they cannot follow the community retreat as they should, the Abbot will allow them a week at another time of the year to make it.

This holds also for the time of rest. Those officers who are unable to take their sleep with the community will do so at another time designated by the Abbot.

The fact of being in charge does not authorise anyone to procure those things which he needs for his personal use. He should ask the same permissions as the rest of the community.

Each of the officers mentioned here should keep his department in a proper state of cleanliness.

CHAPTER II   THE ABBOT OR TITULAR PRIOR

424 The Abbot, who is the one principally responsible before God, has the full and entire administration of his monastery, spiritual and temporal. He nominates all the officers, sharing among several monks, if necessary, the functions allotted to one in these Usages.

As his name indicates, the Abbot is a father. He is the father of a monastic family. He has all the corresponding rights, but the duties and responsibilities as well. His children consider that he holds amongst them the place of Christ, and that is why it is he who teaches them by word, leads them, draws them by his example. He is truly their father, and loves them as sons.

425 The Abbot celebrates pontifically on the most solemn feasts. Unless impeded, he sings Mass on feasts of Sermon, on the Vigils of Christmas, Pentecost and the Assumption. He officiates on Palm Sunday and during the Triduum Sacrum. He sings the Mass on the Solemn Anniversaries of the Dead, and on the day of burial of a member of the community.

He presides at Solemn Benediction of the Blessed Sacrament.

He blesses the candles and the ashes. He gives the Last Sacraments to members of the community, and presides at their burial.

The other abbatial functions will be found in the Ritual.

426 If necessary he may act as Hebdomadary. He holds chapter and asks for accusations as often as he wishes. Apart from illness the Abbot sleeps in the common dormitory and eats in the community refectory. He dines with guests only by way of exception.

427 *Resigned Abbots* When an Abbot resigns his charge, we should give him the same honours and have for him that respect which is his due. He always occupies a place of honour. When the community is divided into two choirs, he stands beside the Abbot before the Subprior. When the community walk in single file, he is immediately behind the Abbot. In the absence of the Abbot he presides in choir, where he supplies for the Abbot in everything. This also holds for the procession after dinner. Without a special mandate, however, he does not give the Last Sacraments or perform burials. Every other community exercise is presided over by the Prior or Subprior. In their absence a resigned Abbot is regarded as the senior. If the Abbot is not in choir, we salute the resigned Abbot as we would the Abbot.

He is incensed separately after the Abbot at Conventual Mass. He may act as Hebdomadary if he wishes, but he is not appointed to other duties.

He should observe the rule as far as he is able, and conform to the directives of the Abbot of the place. He is given a private room.

428 *Titular Prior* The Titular Prior has the full spiritual and temporal administration of his monastery, just as an Abbot. Even outside his house he intones the antiphons at the Magnificat and Benedictus if there is no Abbot in choir.

429 *Resigned Titular Prior* If a resigned Titular Prior remains in the house of which he was Superior, he takes the first place after the President. In every other monastery he takes his rank of seniority.

CHAPTER III THE CLAUSTRAL PRIOR

430 The Prior is the aid and deputy of the Abbot in the government of the monastery. He must therefore watch that his words and actions are always in conformity with the thought of the Abbot.

431 Together with the Cellarer, he is charged with the care of the Abbot's health.

He takes his turn as Hebdomadary, Invitator, and Servant of the Refectory, except when the Abbot is absent from the monastery or confined to the infirmary. If he presides at an Office, the Sub-invitator replaces him for the reading of the lessons and of the Martyrology.

He has a room where he receives the monks. He procures for them whatever they need. He gives the signal for work, and presides at it in the absence of the Abbot.

When the Abbot is at home, the Prior does not speak to guests without permission.

432 When the Abbot is absent from the monastery, the Prior unless he has special instructions deals only with current affairs, or with those matters which cannot be deferred. His conduct should be inspired by the intentions of the Abbot, and on the latter's return he gives an account of his administration. Without a special mandate he cannot receive anyone to clothing or temporary profession, or send them for Orders.

He replaces the Abbot when the latter cannot preside at the exercises. On these occasions he also sings the Masses on the most solemn feasts, presides during the Triduum Sacrum, blesses the candles, ashes and palms, administers the Last Sacraments and officiates at burials.

433 Normally the Prior should be a priest. If by an exception he is not, he does not give the blessings in church, and fulfils only those functions proper to the Orders he has received. This holds also for the Subprior.

CHAPTER IV   THE SUBPRIOR

434 The Subprior, 'Custos Ordinis' as tradition calls him, watches discreetly to see that everything is done according to the Rule, especially during the Office and lectio divina. He occupies everywhere the third place, unless there be a resigned Abbot in the house.

435 When he thinks that a monk has not heard the bell for rising, the Subprior goes to awaken him or to inquire into his indisposition.

It is his duty to remedy the mistakes of the Cantor, the Sacristan, and the Servants of the Church, and to alert the officers who do not leave choir in time to fulfil their duties. Ordinarily he speaks to the religious only within the limits of No. 255 of these Usages.

436 When the Prior is absent or in the infirmary, the Subprior replaces him in everything.

437 In Titular Priories the Second Superior takes the name Subprior, and the third that of President. It is the same in non-autonomous foundations, where the Superior is in fact a claustral Prior, with special delegation from his Abbot.

CHAPTER V   THE MASTER OF NOVICES

438 The Master of Novices, who must be an experienced monk, 'skilled in winning souls' (St Benedict, Ch. 58), is charged with the formation of the Novices. He may be in charge of both choir and lay novices together.

He always has a private room.

439 The Father Master concerns himself with the postulants in the guest-house to the extent determined by the Abbot. By means of discreet inquiry and medical examination he will obtain the necessary information about their physical, intellectual and psychic capacities. More solicitous for quality than numbers, the Novice Master will be on the watch to eliminate those subjects for whom our way of life, with its silence and solitude, is not suitable – those with difficult characters, or who lack docility; those who attract attention by singularity, by a tendency to melancholy, or the like.

We may receive candidates for the choir who will become monks without becoming priests. They must have, however, the level of classical and spiritual culture demanded by the Ratio Studiorum. (No. 10, 1° and 2°.)

An indult of the Holy See is required to receive candidates mentioned in No. 145 of the Constitutions.

440 When a postulant enters the community, the Father Master shows him his place at the various functions, has him sign the necessary documents with the Secretary, and informs those in charge of the wardrobe, refectory, etc. For the taking of the habit, he sees that everything is made ready, assists the Abbot during the ceremony, and afterwards brings the novice to the church for an act of thanksgiving.

441 In keeping with No. 16 of the Ratio Studiorum he gives conferences several times a week to the choir novices, and similarly to the lay novices if he is in charge of them. If he considers it useful and the Abbot approves, he may give some conferences to the two groups together. The programme should be drawn up in advance and be in conformity with the above-mentioned statute on the formation of novices.

He takes special care to see that the novices occupy usefully the time of lectio divina.

He holds a chapter of faults from time to time.

He obtains for the novices whatever they need, and for this he can sign tickets to the various officers of the monastery. If a novice is not at Vigils, he goes to inquire the reasons for his absence. If one is ill, the Father Master informs the Abbot, takes him to the infirmary and visits him often.

He prepares the novices for profession and explains the ceremonies.

442 *The Submaster* A Submaster may be appointed to assist the Novice Master in his work. His role is determined by the Abbot, observing Canon Law (c. 559), if he is truly Submaster.

He should normally be with the novices in the absence of the Father Master.

CHAPTER VI   THE MAGISTER SPIRITUS AND THE PREFECT OF STUDIES

443 According to the 'Ratio Studiorum', the Magister Spiritus is responsible for continuing the monastic formation of the students and of seeing to their priestly formation at the same time. By that very fact he has permission to speak to them. He has a private room. The Abbot will consult his council before appointing him, and will give him directives regarding the conferences that he is to give.

The *Prefect of Studies* is responsible for organising studies and classes. He may speak to the Professors and students to the extent fixed by the Abbot. The Abbot will consult his council before appointing him, and will also ask the 'Nihil obstat' of the Abbot General.

The Magister Spiritus and the Prefect of Studies are ex officio members of the Council of Studies of the monastery.

CHAPTER VII   THE MASTER OF THE LAYBROTHERS

444 The Father Master of the Laybrothers is responsible for the temporal and spiritual care of the professed Brothers. He gives them conferences several times a week in which he explains Christian doctrine, monastic spirituality, the Holy Rule, the Constitutions, Usages, etc. He also holds chapter of faults.

445 Apart from conferences, he speaks to the Laybrothers only in his room, or in the speaking places. From time to time, however, he visits them at the work, and more frequently if they are in the infirmary. If he sees that some particular employment is causing serious inconvenience to a Brother, the Father Master makes it known to the Abbot.

446 He can give the Brothers tickets to obtain whatever they need for their personal use, but not the things they require for their work. In this case they apply to the Cellarer. If there is question of an important permission he sends the Brothers to the Abbot.

CHAPTER VIII   THE SACRISTAN

447 It is the Sacristan's duty to preserve in our churches their Cistercian note of simplicity and poverty.

He arranges for the celebration of Masses, furnishing each altar with those items listed in the liturgical books. The candles are of white wax, especially on feast days. During Advent and Lent, and for Offices of the Dead, we use unbleached (yellow) wax candles.

Apart from real necessity, the Sacristan will see that only Conventual Masses are celebrated at the high altar.

A visiting priest may not celebrate in one of our churches without the permission of the Abbot or of the Guestmaster whose duty it is to inspect the 'celebret' of the visitor, unless he is known. Such priests must follow our Ordo.

448 For Conventual Mass the Sacristan prepares the vestments for the ministers, and everything that is required in the Ceremonial. If the Conventual Mass is not sung he prepares the chalice and the Missal on the altar, and the chasuble on the credence. On Sunday before Tierce he empties and cleans the holy water fonts of the church, and makes ready in the sacristy everything necessary for the blessing of the water.

He likewise prepares whatever is needed for other ceremonies – Benediction, processions, burials, etc.

449 For the candles at Benediction he observes the following:
(1) Exposition with the ciborium   six candles
(2) Exposition with the monstrance twelve candles
(3) Solemn exposition   twenty candles

When there is Benediction he goes to the altar following the thurifer, and carrying the humeral veil on his left arm. He is on the Celebrant's right for simple Benediction, but if he is neither a priest nor a deacon he is replaced by the Deacon of the Week. At Solemn Benediction he is on the Subdeacon's left.

The Sacristan should see that the Sacred Species are renewed weekly.

450 The Sacristan may expose the Holy Relics on the high altar for Conventual Mass on feasts of Sermon, Palm Sunday and at profession Masses in the manner stated in the Ceremonial. Two candles remain lit while the relics are exposed. The same holds if a relic of the True Cross or some other relic is exposed at the presbytery step. But if these are left exposed all night, a night light may be substituted for the candles. During Benediction of the Blessed Sacrament the relics are covered with a veil.

451 The Holy Oils should be kept in a silver vessel which is locked in a little safe or press near the altar or in some other accessible place, the key to which is easily available. A supply of cotton wool and everything necessary for the administration of the Sacrament of the Sick in case of urgency should be kept with the oils. The Holy Oils are renewed annually and the old ones burned in the piscina.

452 The Sacristan will have special care for the sacred vessels, the altar linens and the liturgical vestments. He will see that everything needing it is blessed before use.

The purificators are changed every week. He puts aside corporals and palls which have been sufficiently used. The water in which these linens have been washed is disposed of in the piscina in the sacristy. He also washes the chalices and patens from time to time.

He provides three towels in the sacristy – one for the priest and sacred ministers before Mass, one of them after Mass, and the third for the other ministers. He takes care that the albs fit the priests properly. Vestments which can no longer be used should be burned.

453 *Christmas* On Christmas Eve the Sacristan prepares on each altar a little vessel of water, covered with a pall, for Christmas Masses.

454 *Purification* Before Tierce the Sacristan prepares a table covered with a cloth near the lectern in the presbytery. On it he puts the candles and the holy water vessel. He also prepares the processional cross. When the candles are blessed, the Sacristan and his assistant distribute them to the community and the guests. He removes the table immediately after the distribution.

At the Offertory he comes to the altar step at the same time as the Abbot, in order to take the candles from the Deacon and acolytes. He extinguishes them and removes them after the ceremony.

455 *Ash Wednesday* Before Tierce he places two dishes of ashes, made from last year's palms, in the presbytery. He puts the holy water beside it and on the credence a ewer of water and a bowl. He brings the stole and crosier to the Abbot at the appointed time. He also prepares a violet stole at the Prior's place.

456 On the *First Sunday of Lent* after Compline he covers the crucifixes, statues and images in the church and sacristy with violet veils.

457 *Palm Sunday* Before Tierce the Sacristan prepares the palms which are to be blessed, on a table at the right of the lectern. In the sacristy he prepares violet vestments for the solemn Mass and violet stoles for those who are to sing the Passion. He also prepares a red cope, tunic and dalmatic, and stoles of the same colour for the Celebrant and Deacon. He prepares a red veil for the Gospel stand. Before Tierce he uncovers the processional cross and also the cross on the high altar if it be distinct from the former, and he does not cover the altar cross again until after Compline. When the palms are blessed he distributes them. After the procession he removes them, as also the red veil from the Gospel stand. Then he arranges three lecterns, without cover, for the Passion.

458 *Spy Wednesday* The Sacristan prepares the altar of repose without superfluous ornamentation. Four white candles are placed thereon, and it is decorated with hangings and a carpet. The Tabernacle, veiled inside with silk, should have a lock. There is no cross on the altar.

459 *Holy Thursday* Before Lauds the Sacristan places a yellow wax candle at the middle of the presbytery step, and this is done also on the next two days. The altar is prepared as for solemn Masses. The cross is covered with a white veil, but after Mass this is replaced by violet.

In the sacristy are prepared the canopy, sufficient hosts for Communion for today and tomorrow, white vestments for the Mass, a cope, and a dalmatic and white stole for the crossbearer. The Sacristan leaves a stole at the place of each priest and deacon who is to communicate. He distributes the candles to the community.

When the Celebrant incenses the Blessed Sacrament after Mass, the Sacristan gives the humeral veil to the Subdeacon. If there are several ciboria, it is the duty of the Sacristan to remove them to the appointed place, and he also sees that all the altars are completely stripped.

460 *Good Friday* Before the Office the Sacristan covers the cross which is to be used for the adoration, with a red veil, and places it behind the altar. He covers the altar with a white cloth, and places a cushion or bookstand in the middle, and a little vessel of water near it. He also prepares a Missal on the credence or near the seats of the ministers. The credence should be covered with a plain cloth, and on it are placed a red burse with a corporal, a purificator, and the Epistolary. Nearby is prepared a red cope. In the presbytery he arranges a bookstand for the Deacons of the Passion.

In the sacristy the following are laid out: a red chasuble and stole for the Celebrant; red stoles for the Deacon and for those singing the Passion, amice, alb and cincture for all the above as well as for those who are to sing the 'Popule meus', and for the acolytes. In choir he leaves out stoles (red or white) for the priests and deacons who are to communicate. He brings the tabernacle key, the candles of the acolytes, and a white humeral veil to the Altar of Repose.

Towards the end of the solemn prayers, the Sacristan spreads a carpet in the presbytery in plano, near the altar steps, on which he places a prie-dieu covered in red, with a Missal open on the rest, and a red cushion on the step. He removes all after the Adoration of the Cross. When the Celebrant has left the church, he removes the Sacred Species and uncovers the altar and the Altar of Repose.

461 *Holy Saturday* During the evening the Sacristan uncovers the statues and images. He prepares what is needed for the new fire. In the place where the Paschal Candle is to be blessed he prepares a lectern and the appointed text; also to one side a table for the new fire, with forceps, matches, aspersory and stylus. Nearby he puts a white stole and dalmatic for the Deacon. Near the credence he puts five candle-sticks with unlighted candles, and a white stole and cope for the Celebrant. In the middle of the presbytery he places the stand for the Paschal Candle, and to one side a lectern covered with a white veil, and the text of the 'Exultet'.

The altar is prepared as for solemn Mass and if an antependium is used it should be violet. The credence is covered with a violet veil. He also prepares the candles for distribution to the choir before the ceremony, and water for the blessing.

In the sacristy is prepared everything needed for the Holy Sacrifice, and also the following: violet cope and dalmatic and three violet stoles; amice, alb and cincture for the Celebrant and his ministers; processional cross; Paschal Candle; five grains of incense in the form of nails on a tray; a small candle; thurible and boat.

When the Celebrant returns to the sacristy towards the end of the litanies, the Sacristan removes the violet antependium, and the violet veil from the credence.

462 *Corpus Christi* On the eve of the feast the Sacristan prepares with becoming simplicity all that is needed for exposition of the Blessed Sacrament, and also the canopy and two thuribles. On the feast itself he prepares a white dalmatic and stole for the crossbearer, and leaves out two large hosts for the Conventual Mass. At the end of Mass he distributes the candles for the procession. He gives the humeral veil to the Subdeacon and takes it back after the procession.

463 *Feast of Dedication* On this day the Sacristan prepares candles at all the consecration crosses.

464 *All Souls' Day* On the eve of the feast the Sacristan prepares a vessel of water covered with a pall on each altar. On the day itself at the end of the Conventual Mass, he brings a black cope to the Celebrant at the Epistle side and assists him to vest.

465 *Clothing* For the ceremony of clothing the Sacristan brings a white stole, holy water, the Ritual, and the crosier to the chapter room. When the Abbot rises to bless the habit he puts the stole on him and gives him the crosier.

466 *Solemn Profession* On the day of a solemn profession, the Sacristan prepares everything needed for the giving of the tonsure, the signing of the schedule and the blessing of the cowl. He arranges the seats for the Abbots and ministers at the presbytery step after the Epistle, and removes them when the Celebrant returns to the altar.

467 *Liturgical Receptions* On the occasion of such receptions, the Sacristan places a covered prie-dieu with two cushions on it in the middle of the presbytery, and another similar one at the door of the monastery. He prepares the processional cross, the candles of the acolytes, and the thurible in the sacristy.

468 *Opening of Regular Visitation* He prepares in the sacristy a white stole for the Rev. Father Visitor, and also a burse and corporal with the tabernacle key.

469 *Holy Communion Outside Mass* When Holy Communion is to be brought to someone (a sick monk, guest, etc.) he prepares a purificator and a little vessel of water near the Tabernacle. He disposes of this water in the piscina when the priest has purified his fingers in it.

470 *Anointing the Sick* When a sick person is to be anointed, the Sacristan prepares in the sacristy an alb, violet stole, small violet veil, a cross, six tufts of cotton on a tray, a morsel of bread, a blessed candle, the Ritual and the holy water. He goes to the altar before the priest and after genuflecting takes the oils. He places them on the tray, covers them with the violet veil, and walks behind the cross.

On arrival in the infirmary he puts the oils on the table before the crucifix and kneels. After the exhortation he rises, uncovers the oils and presents them to the priest for the anointing. He takes the cotton as it is used. After the last anointing he replaces the oils on the table and washes the priest's fingers. After the ceremony he burns the cotton and disposes of the ashes and the water used by the priest, in the piscina.

471 When *Holy Viaticum* is to be given immediately after the Anointing of the Sick, the Sacristan prepares the following in the sacristy: alb, stole, chalice and pall (or pyx), burse with corporal, purificator, tabernacle key, and two torches for the acolytes. On the altar he puts a small vessel with water and a purificator.

The Sacristan, humeral veil on arm, accompanies the priest when he goes to get the Blessed Sacrament. When the priest has purified his fingers he puts the veil on him, places the corporal in the burse, and carrying this follows the priest. On arrival in the infirmary, he spreads the corporal on the table and kneels. After the Communion the Sacristan pours the ablution of wine and water over the priest's fingers and then disposes of it in the piscina unless the patient drinks it.

If the Sacrament of the Sick is administered in church, he prepares a seat for the sick brother in the middle of the choir, and to one side a table covered with a cloth, on which he places a ewer, and a morsel of bread and two candles.

472 *Agony, Death and Burial* For the commendation of a soul, the Sacristan brings a violet stole and Ritual to the infirmary. During the preparation of the body he places yellow candles on the altar, and takes a black stole to the infirmary. At the end of the collect which is said in church, he takes this stole from the priest. For the burial he prepares a black cope and two black stoles.

CHAPTER IX   THE CANTORS

473 The Cantor is responsible for the worthy execution of the Divine Office. He stands on the Abbot's side of choir, near the middle, and may pass to the other side whenever necessary. He and his assistants always keep the place in choir assigned because of their office.

It belongs to the Cantor alone, with the agreement of the Abbot, to regulate the pitch and the movement.

474 If someone mistakes one capitulum, versicle, etc. for another, he lets him finish what he has begun, and then corrects his mistake. When a psalm is intoned on a pitch that is too high or too low, the Cantor on the side of intonation lowers or raises the pitch at the mediant. If the Cantor is not a priest, it is for the Subprior (if a priest) to correct the mistakes of the Hebdomadary. If the Cantor fails to correct a mistake, the Subprior does it.

475 The Cantor is always in ceremony when intoning, unless the Office is not sung. The hymn and the 'Kyrie eleison' are always given out by the Cantor on the Invitator's side. The solemn responsories at Vespers are sung by the Cantor and Subcantor together. If the Office is recited the Cantor himself gives out the 'Benedictus' and 'Magnificat'. If the Office is sung, the Abbot intones these antiphons on days when the rite is above three lessons. The Cantor of his side prompts him discreetly and, in the place where he is, intones the Canticle. On days of three lessons and ferial days when the Office is sung the Cantor intones the antiphons of the 'Benedictus' and 'Magnificat'.

When Vigils are sung he draws up a list of those appointed to sing the lessons and responsories. During the twelfth lesson he goes to the Abbot and invites him by a bow to come and sing the last responsory at the lectern.

When the Cantor intones something outside the church, he should be uncovered and in ceremony, if his hands are free. He intones kneeling that which is sung on the knuckles.

476 If the Mass is sung by a priest alone, the Cantor appoints a cleric to sing the Epistle. If not all the clerics are capable of singing the prophecies at Quarter-Tense, he designates beforehand those who are to do so.

The Cantor and Subcantor come to receive the ashes and to adore the Cross after the novices.

At the last station in solemn processions, the Cantor pre-intones the antiphon for the Abbot just as the community are about to enter the church. Whenever the Abbot says any public prayer and is not accompanied by a minister, the Cantor holds the book open before him.

477 Every Friday the Cantor draws up the list of officers for the following week, and presents it to the Abbot. The officers are named in the following order: Invitatorium, Missam Maiorem, Missam de Beata, Missam pro Defunctis, Evangelium, Epistolam, Servitor Ecclesiae,

Lector mensae, Servitor Coquinae. Only those are appointed who can perform the various offices edifyingly. Novices are not appointed Hebdomadary or Servant of the Refectory. The Cantor preferably appoints as Deacon and Subdeacon those who have only these Orders.

478 The Cantor regulates the reading of the Bible in the refectory according to the liturgical seasons. If a book does not end in the time appointed, he notes where the reader stopped so that it can be begun at the same point in the following year.

If the Reader fails to come to sing 'Domine labia mea' at the end of Mass, the Cantor supplies for him. He likewise supplies for the Servants of the Refectory if the Cellarer is absent.

479 The Cantor gives the novices singing classes, unless someone else is charged with this duty. He also holds class for the whole community whenever the Abbot thinks fit.

480 He has the care of the choir books. If they need repair he will have done this. It is also for the Cantor to watch that no change be made in the musical text without authorisation. He distributes the processionals for the Mandatum and processions.

481 On the First Sunday of Lent the Cantor distributes the Lenten books in chapter. He offers the Abbot his book with both hands, and bows profoundly to him. He continues with the monks on the same side, bowing moderately to each after giving him the book. The Subcantor does the same on his own side, and each is accompanied by an assistant cantor.

482 On the Second Sunday of Lent, the Cantor reads in chapter the statute on detraction, and on the Third Sunday he reads that on enclosure. Before Holy Week he posts the list of those who are to sing the 'Gloria Laus', the Passion, etc. – 483.

484 On Easter, after the community enter the chapter room and before the Invitator begins the Martyrology, the Cantor announces the Paschal Solemnity at the lectern. He does not read the Martyrology, but goes to his place after bowing profoundly.

485 At Quarter-Tense the Cantor reads the last Visitation Card in chapter, and also the decisions of the last General Chapter.

He reads the Constitutions once a year on a day appointed by the Abbot.

486 When the agony of a sick brother is announced, the Cantor brings the processionals to the infirmary. He draws up a list of those who are to pray beside the dead, assigning a particular time to each.

487 If absolution is to be asked for a deceased person, the end of a tricenary to be announced, or an obituary notice read, the Cantor does this in chapter.

When the Abbot says 'Loquamur de Ordine nostro', the Cantor comes to the middle of the room and says, 'Absolvatis animam fratris nostri N. defuncti'; or 'Absolvatis patrem (matrem, fratrem, sororem) fratris nostri N. nuper defunctum (-am)'; or for a guest, 'Absolvatis animam N. defuncti', or 'Absolvatis animam Reverendi Domni N. sacerdotis defuncti'.

To announce the end of a tricenary he says 'Hodie finitur tricenarium fratris nostri N.', adding his rank of priest, etc.

Obituary notices should be read in the first chapter after receipt. The Cantor then puts them on the board and after eight days removes them.

488 The Subcantor stands on the left side in choir, about the middle. He intones the hymns and 'Kyrie' on that side in the same manner as the Cantor. On feasts of Sermon he sings the long responsory at Vespers with the Cantor at the lectern, and also the twelfth responsory at Vigils.

If the Cantor is absent or cannot perform his duties, the Subcantor supplies for him in everything, except in those cases mentioned in these Usages. He corrects those on his own side who make mistakes, as in No. 474. When the Cantor is acting as Hebdomadary the Subcantor gives out the commemorations at Lauds and Vespers, and the 'Benedicte' at Collation.

489 The Assistant Cantors stand beside the Cantors.

If the Cantor is absent the Assistant Cantor from the same side pre-intones the antiphons of the 'Benedictus' and 'Magnificat' to the Abbot, and then intones the Canticle. He also intones in the Cantor's place whatever is sung alternately by the two choirs.

If the Cantors are absent they are replaced by the Assistant Cantors, each on his own side. If the latter are also absent, they are replaced by the monks above them in choir.

CHAPTER X   THE MASTER OF CEREMONIES

490 The Master of Ceremonies holds class in this subject for the whole community and for the ministers of the altar whenever this is necessary. He appoints those ministers whose nomination is not reserved to someone else in the Usages.

He may give the necessary instructions before or during a ceremony. Apart from this he speaks only as permitted by the Abbot.

He corrects the faults of the ministers in choir and on the altar. The Abbot can allow him to take chapter or rubrics and of liturgy for the whole community.

CHAPTER XI   THE LIBRARIAN

491 The Librarian has charge of the library and should keep a catalogue of all books in the house. He keeps note of the books which are taken from the library, and does not give books from the reserved sections without the permission of the Abbot. He suggests the books for refectory and Compline reading to the Abbot.

CHAPTER XII   THE SECRETARY AND ACCOUNTANT

492 These functions may be given to several monks, depending on circumstances.

493 The Secretary or Notary draws up and countersigns all acts of profession, letters of association, and other authentic documents issued by the Abbot. He affixes thereon the seal of the monastery or of the Abbot, as the case requires. He keeps copies of important letters and documents which he sends out.

After the solemn profession or ordination to subdiaconate of a monk he informs the pastor of the parish where the monk was baptised. When someone dies in the house he issues notice of it as required by the laws of the country.

He keeps a register in which he enters the name, age, quality, nationality and names of parents of everyone admitted to the monastery, with the time of their entering, clothing, profession (or departure, and the reasons for it), ordination and death. The dates should always be written in full. He keeps a special register of everything that is deposited with him by the postulants, such as valuables, important papers, etc. He has the postulants sign this register. If they leave he returns their belongings to them, and gets a receipt.

The Secretary (or Archivist) keeps the archives (maps, documents, photos, etc.) carefully and he also keeps a written account of the principal events in the life of the house.

494 The Accountant, who is distinct from the Treasurer, keeps the financial accounts exactly, and at the end of the year draws up a general report. He should show the accounts to the Abbot whenever the latter wishes. He should also show them annually to the Visitor who signs them.

CHAPTER XIII THE CELLARER

495 All temporalities of the monastery, the buildings and agricultural undertakings, are normally confided to the care of the Cellarer. He provides for the upkeep and support of the community.

The Cellarer must guard against taking the attitude of a proprietor. The goods of the monastery are entrusted to him, but they do not belong to him. St Benedict wished him to be 'as a father to the whole community', which is quite a different thing. (Ch. 31)

He considers it one of his principal duties to assist the poor.

He speaks to the Brothers about the work, and to the choir monks to the extent determined by the Abbot. He speaks also to the workers and to all who come to the monastery on business, but not to those who come for other reasons, such as retreatants, visitors and guests.

If one of the Servants of the Refectory is not present to receive the blessing on Sunday after Lauds, the Cellarer supplies for him.

CHAPTER XIV THE REFECTORIAN

496 The Refectorian takes care of the pantry and cellar. He serves the correct amount of bread for the meals, mixt, frustulum and collation. He prepares the drink and serves the dessert if any. He should see to it that no one on indulgence is overlooked.

CHAPTER XV THE INFIRMARIAN

497 The Infirmarian, whom St Benedict wishes to be 'God-fearing, diligent and careful', looks after the sick with that charity which they have a right to expect from a brother. He keeps them informed of announcements in chapter. If their illness is such as to permit occupation he gives them work according to their strength.

When a patient is in danger, the Infirmarian should visit him before going to Vigils, even if there is someone watching with him. It is the duty of the Infirmarian, along with the Abbot, to see that the sick receive the Sacraments in time.

The Infirmarian may speak to the cook and to those who watch with a sick brother. He asks the Cellarer for whatever is needed for the Infirmary by means of tickets. He also communicates in this way with the wardrobe keeper, and for the needs of the Laybrothers and novices with their respective Father Masters.

Every Friday he presents to the Abbot a list of those on indulgences.

498 *The Assistant Infirmarian* The Infirmarian is normally given a Laybrother to assist him, so that he himself will be absent from choir as little as possible. Apart from the remedies prescribed by the doctor, he gives nothing to the sick without informing the Infirmarian.

CHAPTER XVI   THE WARDROBE KEEPER

499 All the clothing and linen are confided to the care of the monk who is in charge of the wardrobe. He takes special care of postulants' effects, which he keeps until they make solemn profession. He organises the work in the wardrobe and laundry and may speak to those employed there.

For each monk he should have two cowls, two robes, and all necessary underwear, all marked with each one's number. He should not make new clothing without consulting the Abbot. Clothing and bedclothes should be adapted to the climate of the country and to the season.

He distributes the underwear weekly and also gives each one whatever is required to enable him to change when he needs, especially during warm weather. He changes the other garments and the bedclothes as often as necessary.

He may enter the cell of each monk in order to put clothing, etc., there.

He changes the napkins in the refectory weekly and the towels at the washbasins several times a week. He gives aprons and the necessary cloths to the Sacristan, Refectorian, those who wash up after meals and any others who need them for their work. On Saturday he prepares what is required for the Mandatum. He gives suitable clothing to those going on a journey, and if necessary to those going to the guesthouse.

CHAPTER XVII   THE GUESTMASTER

500   The Guestmaster receives most amiably everyone who comes to the monastery.

> He receives them as he would Christ Himself to the end that the Latter may one day say to him, 'I asked hospitality of you and you received me.' (St Benedict, Ch. 53)

He keeps a register in which he enters the names, addresses and dates of arrival and departure of guests. If necessary he makes inquiries about those who may wish to stay at the monastery.

The guests are served at table according to local custom, but without any departure from monastic simplicity. They do not speak at table, and there is reading at least at the beginning of the meal.

Guests should not ordinarily remain longer than three days in the guesthouse, unless they are on retreat. Ladies, other than relatives of the religious, are not received at the guesthouse to spend the night there, nor are they admitted as retreatants properly so-called, nor as permanent paying guests.

501   Guests should rarely be allowed to eat in the community refectory. If the Abbot permits this, the Guestmaster will place what is necessary at the principal table, and will give the guests the necessary directions. At the time of the meal he brings them to the door of the refectory, where he presents a ewer to the Abbot, who offers it to the guests to wash their hands, and the Guestmaster presents them with a towel.

502   The guests assist at Conventual Mass and the Salve daily. If clerics are permitted to come to choir, they should be in surplice. Guests do not ordinarily come to chapter, but may assist at certain ceremonies such as the Great Mandatum and burials.

The Guestmaster instructs the guests not to enter places reserved for the monks, nor to go where they are working, nor to speak to them. When conducting guests about the monastery he avoids bringing them where the community are assembled, and gives necessary explanations quietly and briefly.

503 The Guestmaster may speak to the Cellarer, the Porters and the brethren in the kitchen. He communicates by note with the confessor for externs and with the wardrobe keeper.

BOOK 12
SOME SPECIAL OCCASIONS

CHAPTER I LITURGICAL RECEPTION

504 If guests in general should be received as Christ Himself, with much greater reason should those who, under various titles, represent His authority, as, for example, the Apostolic Nuncio or Delegate, the Bishop of the diocese, the Abbot General or the Father Immediate. It is traditional that on the occasion of their first visit to the monastery these dignitaries be received more solemnly, and we do this by giving them a liturgical reception.

505 When such a reception is to take place, the great bell is rung and all go to their places in the presbytery stalls. When all is ready we go in procession to the door of the monastery in the following order: thurifer, Subdeacon carrying holy water, Deacon carrying the cross and accompanied by acolytes, the Abbot, the professed Choir monks, seniors leading, the novices, oblates, the Lay brethren and lay novices. Meanwhile the bells are rung. We walk two by two in silence. The Abbot, who like the ministers is in cowl, will send one or two monks ahead to meet the Prelate.

When the latter arrives at the door, all bow profoundly except the Deacon and acolytes. The Abbot presents holy water to the Prelate, has him bless the incense, and then incenses him. He may now offer a few words of welcome. The Cantor immediately intones the responsory from the processional and, if necessary, the canticle 'Benedictus' which is sung on the 5th tone. The community return to the church in the inverse order, that is, the ministers, lay novices, etc. The Prelate walks last accompanied by the Abbot who is on his left.

On arrival at the church we again occupy the presbytery stalls. The ministers leave the cross, holy water, etc. in the sacristy and come to their places in choir. The Prelate kneels at the prie-dieu. When the responsory or the 'Benedictus' is ended, the Abbot invites him to give his blessing, unless he is going to chapter immediately, in which case he will give his blessing after addressing the community.

506 If the above-mentioned dignitaries come to the monastery again they are given a simpler reception. The abbot, accompanied by some of the seniors, goes to receive them at the door of the church, where he presents the aspersory.

CHAPTER II   THE REGULAR VISITATION

507 In order that the Regular Visitation may be the more fruitful the Abbot will have the appropriate chapter of the Spiritual Directory read some days beforehand.

508 Unless the community are in choir or taking their rest, the arrival of the Visitor is announced by a pealing of the bells. He is received by the Abbot accompanied by some of the seniors, who bring him to the church and then to his room.

509 At the time appointed the bell is rung for the opening of the Visitation chapter. The novices may assist at the first part of the chapter but they retire at the usual formula: 'Loquamur de Ordine nostro'.

The Visitor occupies the abbatial seat with the Abbot on his right and his secretary on his left. If he is delegated the document of delegation is read, and on his invitation the Cantor goes to the lectern and asks the blessing which the Visitor gives saying: 'Divinum auxilium . . .'. Then all sit and the Cantor reads the statute 'De forma Visitationis' in the vernacular. If the Visitation is being made by the Abbot General the Cantor adds the second chapter of the Chart of Charity.

Then the Visitor indicates the times when the monks may speak to him in private and asks each one to recite 'Veni Creator' and the 'Pater' for the success of the Visitation. Chapter ends with the verse 'Adjutorium' which is said facing the crucifix.

The community go from the chapter room to the church and kneel in the presbytery stalls. The Sacristan conducts the Visitor to the sacristy where he gives him water with which to wash his hands and a white stole which he dons over his cowl. Meanwhile the Servant of the Church lights two candles on the altar. Accompanied by his secretary and the Sacristan, the Visitor inspects the Tabernacle and the sacred vessels. Before closing the Tabernacle he blesses the community with the Ciborium. The latter prostrate on the knuckles and retire when the Prelate leaves the sanctuary.

510 The Abbot gives the Visitor the last Visitation Card and also a list of the members of the community with the employment of each one on it. During the scrutiny each professed in the house goes to see the Visitor individually. Afterwards the Visitor speaks to the novices all together; unless he sees them individually.

511 When the scrutiny is finished, the Visitor inspects the conventual places and carefully examines the account books and Mass registers. Finally he draws up the Visitation Card, having first consulted the Abbot with regard to what he intends it to contain, and having asked his advice about adding to it or modifying it for the good of souls.

512 At the time appointed for the closing of the Visitation, the bell is rung for chapter. The professed of the house attend to hear the reading of the new card. The Secretary of the Visitation reads it and the Visitor adds his comments. He can depose officers if he considers it necessary, after consulting the Abbot.

513 A plenary indulgence on the usual conditions is attached to each Regular Visitation. The Abbot fixes the day on which this favour may be gained.

CHAPTER III   THE GENERAL CHAPTER

514 On the day on which the General Chapter opens we sing the Mass of the Holy Spirit in each of our monasteries, in union with all the Abbots of the Order assembled at Citeaux, and for their intentions.

On receipt of the text, the definitions and decisions of the General Chapter are read in chapter before all the professed. This text should afterwards be left at the disposition of the professed.

CHAPTER IV   THE ELECTION OF AN ABBOT

515 As soon as a church of our Order becomes vacant through the death of its Abbot, the Prior will inform the Abbot General and the Father Immediate in the name of the community. He will exhort the community to pray for the happy outcome of the election.

The Father Immediate takes over the administration of the abbey until the election of a new abbot. Meanwhile the Prior cannot change any of the officers without his consent; neither may he read, sort out, remove or destroy the papers of the late Abbot. This also holds for the

Secretary and every other member of the community. All the papers of
the Abbot, as well as his seal, should be consigned to the Father
Immediate, who will keep them intact for the new Superior.

516 The election may not be held sooner than fifteen days after the
vacancy occurs, and may not be deferred for longer than three months
without a just cause. The Prior must take care to convoke all the voters
in good time. Those who are absent may not vote by letter or by proxy.

517 When the President of the election arrives at the monastery, the
Prior, Subprior, Cantor and Cellarer and those designated by the Prior
go to meet him. They conduct him to the church and then to the grave of
the deceased Abbot where the prayers appointed by the Ritual are said.

518 On the eve of the election the voters assemble in chapter after
Vespers at the sound of the small bell. As soon as the President arrives
at his place, the Cantor goes to the lectern, asks the blessing and reads
the texts appointed by the Ritual. When this is done the President
explains briefly the importance of the act they are about to perform.

> 'But let him who is to be elected be chosen for the merit of his life
> and the wisdom of his doctrine.' (St Benedict, Ch. 64)

He may then have the chapter elect the scrutators by secret in order
to shorten the proceedings on the morrow. All retire after the verse
'Adjutorium'.

519 A table is prepared in the middle of the chapter room and on it are
placed the book of the Gospels, the Ritual and the voting urn. Around it
are six seats for the scrutators, the notary and the witnesses. At the
end of the chapter room several small tables are arranged, isolated from
each other, and on them are placed writing materials.

520 On the day of the election the President, or one appointed by him,
sings the Votive Mass of the Holy Spirit. The whole community should
attend as well as the notary and the witnesses. The voters communicate at the Mass, but those who are priests may say Mass as usual.

521 At the sound of the great bell the electors, the notary and the
witnesses all go to the chapter room. Those who are not taking part in
the election leave the church and cloisters. The Sacristan locks the
doors and gives the keys to the President.

If the election takes place after Prime, chapter begins with the reading of the Martyrology and the usual prayers. When the witnesses have taken the oath, the list of the voters is read out. As each one hears his name, he rises and says audibly 'Adsum'. He then bows moderately and sits down.

During the 'Veni Creator' we kneel facing the crucifix. As soon as the President has taken the oath, the senior elector approaches, kneels and takes it also, according to the formula in the Ritual. He puts both hands on the Sacred Text while saying the last words. All the other electors then come to take the oath in the order of seniority. It is sufficient if the full form is said by the first voter alone, and the others say only the last phrase 'Sic me Deus adjuvet . . .' while placing their hands on the text.

522 If the scrutators were not chosen the evening before, this is done now. In either case they now take their particular oath. When the President calls them, they come before him, the senior first. The latter then stands between the other two and all bow profoundly. After the exhortation of the President, the senior kneels to take the oath. Then he rises, bows to the President and goes to the table. The other two do likewise, each in turn, and then go and sit on either side of the senior scrutator.

523 When the scrutators have taken their places, the Cantor replaces the Gospel book on the table. Then at a signal from the President, and assisted by the Subcantor, he distributes the ballot papers, which have been made out according to the form in the Ritual. They begin with the scrutators and then each continues the distribution on his own side. The junior scrutator uncovers the urn and the senior turns it upside down to show that it is empty, after which the junior covers it again.

At the indication of the President the first scrutator goes to one of the small tables and fills in his ballot paper secretly as follows:

Ego, frater N . . . .
eligo vel postulo in abbatem (priorem) hujus nostri monasterii BM de Domnum N . . . .

In giving the name of the candidate he will add whatever precisions are necessary to obviate any element of uncertainty. He also writes a sign or device on the space provided for this on the paper. He then folds the ballot paper in such a way that his name and device are not visible, and seals it. Then he folds it again so as to conceal the name of the candidate, but does not seal it. He returns to the principal table, holding the ballot paper in his right hand, which is uncovered and slightly raised, and puts it in the urn which the junior scrutator uncovers and then covers immediately.

Each of the other two scrutators fills in his ballot paper at the small table and puts it in the urn as above and then resumes his seat. All the other voters then come to vote in order of seniority and having done so each one bows profoundly to the President and goes out into the cloister to await the signal recalling the assembly.

If a voter is in the infirmary, the scrutators go with the notary and witnesses to bring him his ballot paper and have him take the oath. The first scrutator carries the Gospels, the second the urn in a prominent fashion and the third the Ritual and ballot paper. They are followed by the notary and the witnesses. The patient takes the oath, writes his ballot paper as above, and puts it in the urn which the scrutators bring back to the chapter.

524 The first scrutator shakes the urn so as to mix the ballots and then proceeds to count the votes as follows. The second scrutator uncovers the urn and the first scrutator takes out the ballots and counts them. If the number of ballots is higher or lower than the number of voters, the first scrutator informs the President, who recalls the electors, declares the voting null and proceeds to another ballot.

If the number of ballots is as it should be, the first scrutator puts them all back in the urn, then takes them out singly, reads each one in private and then informs the other two scrutators. Each of the three then draws up a list of names of those who have received votes.

525 When all the votes have been checked, the ballot papers are put back in the urn. Each of the scrutators counts the number of votes each of the candidates has received, and then they compare the three lists to see if they agree.

In order to be elected Abbot, a monk must get an absolute majority of the valid votes. If no one has obtained a majority the first scrutator rises and says: 'Reverende Pater, non habemus electionem'. Then the President sends one of those present to recall the electors to chapter where the balloting begins again. If someone has obtained a majority the first scrutator rises and says: 'Reverende Pater, habemus electionem' and the President recalls the electors to chapter.

526 When the electors have assembled in chapter again, the first scrutator asks if they agree that the result of the balloting be published. All reply together: 'Placet. Volumus.'

If the number of votes is such that if the elect (or the one postulated) has voted for himself, this vote could be the determining one, the President has the ballot checked. He asks the elect what device or sign he has written on his ballot paper and then opens the lower part of the papers until this is found. Then only is the upper part of the ballot paper opened to verify the name of him who has written it. The scrutators carry out this verification.

When the elect has given his consent, all answer 'Amen'. The notary draws up the instrument of the election and reads it aloud. Only then is it signed and in the following order: the President, the electors, the elect, the witnesses and the notary. The text is kept carefully in the archives of the house and a summary is sent to the Abbot General, giving the result of each balloting, to obtain his confirmation. If the election does not take place after Prime, the President closes the proceedings with the verse 'Adjutorium'.

Before his installation, the elect may not perform any act of jurisdiction, nor does he occupy the abbatial seat, but takes the next stall, or stands after the Abbots and Titular Priors.

527 *Installation* When the election has been confirmed by the Abbot General, the day for the installation of the Abbot elect is fixed. The great bell is rung at the appointed time and the community go to chapter. The elect recites the profession of faith aloud. When he receives the keys, all answer 'Amen'.

Immediately afterwards the professed Choir monks come to make their promise of obedience, their hands in his, saying: 'Pater, promitto tibi obedientiam secundum Regulam obedientiam secundum Regulam Sancti Benedicti ad normam juris canonici'. Then the Laybrethren make their promise using the formula given in their Usages. The notary draws up the act of the installation, which is signed at least by the President, the elect, the witnesses and the notary.

All then go in procession to the church, singing the 'Te Deum' while the bells are rung. They enter by the lateral door and stand in the Vigils stalls. All bow on the misericords during the veriscles and collects. When finished they salute the altar and retire.

528 *The Abbatial Blessing* The choir stand in the presbytery stalls facing the altar during that part of the blessing ceremony which precedes the Mass.

Before the 'Alleluia' after the gradual, or before the last verse of the Tract, we kneel facing the altar and sing (or recite) the antiphon 'Ne reminiscaris' and the penitential psalms, unless this has been done the evening before. The Litany of the Saints follows, during which the choir remain kneeling. It is sung by two monks, who interrupt the singing after the verse 'Ut omnibus fidelibus . . .' When the Prelate kneels again the Litany continues. If the Litany is not sung, the Prelate himself recites it and the choir answer.

When the Litany is ended we stand facing the altar. When the Prelate goes to the altar or the throne, we continue the Mass, singing the 'Alleluia' or the last verse of the Tract.

Towards the end of the Mass, the Prelate conducts the new Abbot to his stall and enthrones him. Then he intones the 'Te Deum' and the new Abbot goes around the church giving his blessing while the bells are rung. When he returns to his stall, all the professed of the house come up, bow profoundly, kneel, kiss his ring and embrace him.

During the versicles and prayer which follow we face the altar. These prayers, in fact, are for the new Abbot that God may bless his reign.

Alphabetical Index to Appendix 2
The Numbers Refer to Paragraphs

APPENDIX THREE

THE RULE OF THE COMMUNITY OF THE SISTERS OF THE LOVE OF GOD*

THE MONASTIC STATE

All Christians, whether monastic or secular, are called to sanctification. The Christian life may be manifested in many forms but it is one in its acknowledgment of a total commitment of its members to the service of God. For the monastic this commitment must be a witness to the necessity of separation in order to fulfil the vocation of a following of the way of Christ bound by the Vows of Poverty, Chastity and Obedience.

There is one Christian way, there is one monastic life of total commitment in which the Monastic Vows are an underlining of the Christian baptismal life. Here lies its unity and its witness both to the Church and to the world. In function, nevertheless, there are differences of application as the life is directed either to an active ministry made fruitful through prayer or, as in the contemplative life, to one separated not *from* but *for* the world to a way of living that is disciplined for the work of prayer. Therefore the Vows of Poverty, Chastity and Obedience shall always be regarded by the Sisters as the foundation of their life and of their witness to the Church and world. The requirements of the Vows shall always be exactly fulfilled in spirit as in letter.

Profession under the Holy Vows provides unity. It is the redirection to God of the natural life of man in its ownership of things, in the exercise of all creative powers and in the complete control of all self-interest.

* Anglican contemplative nuns.

THE AIM OF THE COMMUNITY

The Community of the Sisters of the Love of God shall have for its aim the glory of God. The Community is called to witness both to Christ's repairing of man's disobedience and to the Divine Will for unity by the sanctification of the individual lives of its members through their union with the mysteries of the life of the Incarnate Son of God.

Contemplative life and prayer is to be the realisation in time of man's union with the purposes and will of God. Therefore the Sisters shall have the visible unity of Christ's Church as a central theme of their prayer and offering.

The Sisters, while cherishing all that is distinctive in their own life and calling, shall offer special intention and intercession for the increase and perfection of the Priesthood and for the Monastic Life in all its forms.

They shall strive by their discipline and prayer and constant self-oblation to fill up what is behind the afflictions of Christ for His Body's sake, and to use their privileges of enclosure and of silence as a means to lead them to a growing union with God through Christ in the power of the Holy Spirit.

RECONCILIATION

There is in true contemplation an urgency to love God for himself and also a desire that all men should be drawn to respond to his mercy, to acknowledge and accept the reconciliation accomplished by, with and in Christ.

Asceticism is not an end in itself but a disciplined training for the renewal of the life in Christ to witness Christ in and for the world. The ascetic way both for the individual and for the community is a preparation whereby through grace all may participate in the re-creating ministry of Christ.

To be in Christ's reconciliation means to open the whole being in the common life to God through the stripping of self, and to gather and hold to his love the concerns of the temporal and the many requests for intercession which are brought to the Community. It is through Christ in the fellowship of the Spirit that the wholeness of spiritual power proceeds for the healing of the ills of mankind and of the world's disorders.

It will be by continually remembering that God has called each member of the Community into this common life, that the order and discipline of the individual life will bear the fruits of Christ's victory over sin and death. (St John xv)

ENCLOSURE AND SEPARATION FROM THE WORLD

The Sisters of the Love of God are constituted as a Monastic Community which observes enclosure.

Enclosure in answer to the Divine call is a withdrawal from the secular estate to witness a more complete offering of the whole self, body, soul and spirit, to do God's will and to be the means of extending his love into the world.

The function of the withdrawal of the enclosed life is for the preserving and deepening of prayer in the Church. It is within this withdrawal that the needs of the world can be most completely seen in the light of God.

The practical application of this principle of enclosure both in regard to those who are permitted within the enclosure, and the occasions on which the Sisters may go out of enclosure, shall be stated in the Customary. The Bishop, or at least the Warden, shall have knowledge of and give permission for these exceptions. In emergency the Prioresses of the Convents may act in accordance with the principles laid down in the Rule.

THE MOTHER GENERAL

In the hierarchy of obedience the leadership of the Mother General shall be the unifying source and directive for the common purpose and life of the Community.

The Mother General must remember that more than anyone else she is responsible for the maintenance and exposition of the distinctive spirit of the Community.

THE MOTHER GENERAL AND THE MOTHER PRIORESSES

The principal duty of the Mother General and the Mother Prioresses is to lead those under their care with justice and charity, and to maintain a strict and faithful observance of the Rule and Statutes of the Community.

They shall always be careful to set a good example of such observance, regarding themselves as being bound, within the limits compatible with their office, by the ordinances of the Community.

They shall be careful to keep a strict impartiality in their administration both of those spiritual and temporal goods of the Community of which they are stewards during their tenure of office.

ENTRY INTO THE COMMUNITY

Those who seek admission to the Community shall always be received with courtesy and sisterly kindness as sharers in a common hope.

No consideration of wealth or poverty shall be allowed to influence the acceptance or rejection of any candidate provided that the Community has reasonable hope of being able to maintain her; nor shall any such contribution be regarded as entitling her to any favour or privilege.

Candidates who are accepted for probation shall be admitted as Postulants immediately upon their arrival, that they may have full privilege of entry into the enclosure.

They shall during the time of their postulancy be instructed by the Novice Mistress in the duties and obligations of the Novitiate.

NOVICES

Those who are admitted to the Novitiate shall bear in mind its twofold purpose of probation and training, and shall accordingly be entirely open with the Novice Mistress in all that concerns their daily life, while they give a cheerful obedience to all that she may enjoin. The demands of the life shall be accepted readily and joyfully as a means towards the purification of life which may entitle the Novice to hope for the privilege of Profession in due time.

The Novices shall be instructed by the Novice Mistress in the various exercises of the Monastic Life and in the Rule and Statutes of the Community, and in such other matters as she shall consider appropriate to their calling.

The simplicity and thoroughness of a good Novitiate is the foundation of the Professed Life.

PROFESSION

Throughout the time of Noviceship, the Sisters shall accustom themselves to look forward to their Profession as being the pledge of the acceptance of their offering to God by, with and in Jesus Christ in the unity of the Holy Spirit. Profession shall, therefore, be always regarded as a signal token of the love of God, and the utmost diligence shall be given to preparation for it. The offering must be thoroughly purified if it is to be brought for Divine acceptance.

No one shall be permitted to take the first Temporary Vows unless it be her intention to proceed to Final Vows if the privilege is granted in due time. Thereafter the offering continues until it is consummated in death.

The Professed shall be careful to maintain the spirit of sacrifice in its integrity, looking forward to, and preparing for its consummation with the same zeal with which she formerly sought its acceptance. All shall endeavour continually to be united with our Lord's offering in order that all their actions, words and thoughts may be permeated with the spirit of sacrificial love in the fellowship of the Spirit.

The daily dying to self is the necessary condition of that risen life in which the Professed is called to dwell with Christ.

POVERTY

Poverty as a call means far more than a simplification of life in a community of common ownership. It means possessing *nothing* for self, an entire dependency on Christ in whom all things are gathered up and in whom all things are possessed.

The positive application of Poverty is the cultivation of the virtue of holy indifference – to claim the possession of nothing but to use all things and opportunities to deepen that dependence on God wherein is true liberty.

In accordance with the spirit of their consecration to the mysteries of the life of the Incarnate Word, the Sisters shall always have in regard the Vow of Poverty. Its requirements shall be recognised throughout the daily life both in the appointments of the Convents and in the conduct of the Sisters.

No one who enters the Community shall claim anything for her private use, but everything shall be received from the common stock and shall be regarded as belonging to the Community. The careful and reverent use of all Community goods shall be recognised as an essential part of true poverty.

As far as possible the Sisters must avoid asking for dispensations. They shall shun all deviations from their common usages that are not absolutely necessary; all singularity shall be carefully avoided.

In daily life such small hardships and deprivations as may occur through the faithful maintenance of this standard of Holy Poverty shall be welcomed by the Sisters as offering fresh opportunities for realising the conditions of their consecration.

CHASTITY

The distinctive dedication of the Community to the mystery of the Love of God must always be regarded by the Sisters as emphasising the dignity and power of holy Chastity.

Chastity is the submission of every creative faculty to their re-creation in Christ that the Sisters may take their part in our Lord's reconciliation.

It is by the faithful observance of this Vow, and the cultivation of the virtue, that the soul of the contemplative must seek to be trained for the vision of God promised to the pure in heart. All the faculties of mind and spirit must be purified by penitence and trained to familiarity with the things of God. There must be a continual exercise of love and desire reaching out towards God.

Chastity is the answer to man's selfish and destructive use of his natural powers both over nature and in his relationship with other men. The application of Chastity for the monastic includes voluntary perpetual celibacy.

In Chastity, which is the whole being set on God, we have the hidden joy that is beyond all natural attainment. It is there that all relationships are made perfect both in this world and in the whole unseen world. Herein is the wonder of the monastic life and of the whole family in God.

OBEDIENCE

Obedience is the means whereby the human will is re-established in its true purpose to be one with the will of God. Obedience must always be recognised as a free response of love.

Through all the authorised channels of leadership and in her relationship of mutual obedience and co-inherence with her Sisters throughout the Community, each Sister shall make her obedience as complete and generous as possible. The virtue of obedience can only be acquired by its detailed practice in small things as well as in great.

If any conscientious difficulty is felt about obedience it shall be stated.

No position of seniority in the Community shall excuse a Sister from fulfilling her obligation of obedience.

The Sisters shall seek by the faithful observance of Holy Obedience to keep themselves free from all self-pleasing and self-will that the spirit of sacrifice may be the more perfectly attained.

SILENCE

Silence, which is always to be regarded as one of the chief privileges of the Community, shall be observed with all possible strictness and its spirit must be faithfully cultivated, for it prepares the way for the union of the soul with the will of God and is an offering of perpetual reverence to his Majesty.

It should be remembered that silence must cover all the levels of the conscious life, for there must be an outward silence of speech and movement, a silence of the mind for the overcoming of vain imaginations and distractions, and a silence of the soul in the surrender of the will to be still and know that God is God, leading to a silence of the spirit which is the preparation for the fullness of contemplation.

Failure in silence is a real failure in chastity, just as failure in humility is a failure in poverty.

Silence can be broken not only by speech and gesture but also by idle curiosity, for it is in stillness that the spirit should be trained to deepen recollection. Remembrance of the morning's Eucharist, intercession, thanksgiving and adoration should fill the silent hours, while the mind brings its own contribution of thought stimulated by spiritual and other reading and instruction.

In order to maintain the spirit of silence throughout the day, the necessary speaking shall be brief and quiet. Silence must be guarded by each for others so that none shall invade another's silence thoughtlessly and without real necessity.

Silence should never be made an excuse for lethargy, whether mental or spiritual, but the life of the contemplative should be trained to exercise itself after the likeness of the Seraphim and Cherubim that worship round the Throne of God.

THE CELL

The Sisters of the Love of God shall endeavour to remember that the poverty and simplicity of their cell are meant to remind them of the poverty of Bethlehem and of the sacred solitude of the holy sepulchre and completed Sacrifice.

They shall, therefore, learn to regard their cell as a place where the Holy Spirit will reveal to them the mysteries of God and manifest to them the compassion and love of the Saviour.

The cell shall always be kept clean and tidy, and no one shall enter the cell of another without leave nor stay there longer than is necessary for the purpose for which she has been sent.

Immediately upon rising every Sister shall make the following act of self-oblation:

'All glory be to thee, my God, for that thou art, three Persons, one all holy God, very love.

'My God, I desire to love thee with all my heart, with all my mind, with all my soul and with all my strength. I here renew the consecration of my life to thee in union with the supreme oblation of Jesus Christ my Lord.'

THE SACRAMENT OF PENANCE

Confession has for its object the more complete purification of the soul for the glory of God and it should always be accompanied by great watchfulness and care with regard to all matters which generally make the subject matter for confession.

The Sisters shall therefore be very careful to avoid all known occasions of temptation, and must be prompt to resist it at once, and with all the resources at their command. They shall ever bear in mind our Lord's will for their perfection, and upon every occasion seek to unite themselves with him in his temptation, that they may with confidence dispel anxiety, fearfulness and scruples.

After any fault a Sister shall, if possible, make an avowal of it and instantly turn to God with an act of contrition, and that done she shall dismiss all fear and discouragement, nor should the remembrance of the fault be allowed to create an atmosphere of despondency and gloom. She shall rather seek to make amends for her failure by resuming her work and prayer with renewed vigour and watchfulness.

THE EUCHARIST

In the Eucharist the People of God thank God for what he has done and revealed to us through Christ who is both Word and Sacrifice, with whom we participate, priest and people alike, in the one Sacrifice of the one Body and Blood. Therefore to participate in this central activity of the Church's offering is the first duty of the Sisters, whereby they unite themselves with the oblation and satisfaction of our Blessed Lord, our great High Priest. All prayer and offering is in him, and in the eucharistic action all are drawn by the Holy Spirit to be offered by, with and in Christ in his offering to the Father for the sin and need of the world.

THE DIVINE OFFICE

The recitation of the Divine Office shall always be regarded not only as a fundamental duty in the Community but also as a privilege. Because of man's incorporation in Christ's risen life, the Divine Office is an extension of the holy Incarnation both in worship and mediation. Therefore the greatest care must be given to render it with a dignity which unites each individual in the corporate offering.

The recitation of the Divine Office shall be binding upon all those who are admitted to Profession whether under Temporary or Final Vows; and the Sisters shall recite their Office when absent from Choir.

In cases of necessity dispensation may be granted by the Warden or, in emergency, by the Mother General.

Novices, though bound to the recitation of the whole of the Day Hours, may be excused from the recitation of the Night Office by the Novice Mistress with the approval of the Mother General.

Strict silence must always be observed from the time of the ringing of the first bell, and all work should immediately cease; and no one shall enter the Choir after the second bell has rung without asking and obtaining leave.

The Psalter shall be recited or sung rhythmically and without haste, all the words being carefully uttered. All shall endeavour to take their part in such a way as to preserve a corporate uniformity.

LECTIO DIVINA

The study of scripture to form the basis of their prayer should be the first charge upon the Sisters' attention outside the Divine Office. Nothing can take the place of this.

The reading of commentaries, exegeses, and the writings of spiritual masters should be undertaken in such time as may be available for reading and study. Attention should also be paid to doctrine and to books which may help to the more intelligent use of the Liturgy and Divine Office in order that the Sisters may learn to pray with the understanding. Any tendency to pass lightly from one subject to another should be resisted.

The Sisters shall take care that spiritual reading does not degenerate into a matter of merely intellectual interest or of formal duty. The exercise of reading shall be begun with prayer and carried through in a prayerful spirit.

Sisters should from time to time consult the Mother General about their reading.

PRAYER

Prayer is the growth of a personal relationship between man and God. It must be directed so that every faculty of man is brought into the obedience of fulfilling the will of God. This requires both time and discipline and it is through the growth of the prayer that the true potential of each individual life may be realised.

Ideally the whole life is to be made prayer, but there must be times set apart for its solitary exercise. The prayer which the Sisters carry out in Chapel or cell apart from their participation in the corporate Liturgy and Divine Office, is not regarded as a contrast to but as a continuing expression of this corporate offering.

An hour shall be appointed each morning for prayer with a further hour of recollection in the afternoon. A distinction should be drawn between the two hours. In the morning the prayer should be orison, whether the actual form be simple petition, pondering meditation or affective or contemplative prayer. A greater liberty is allowed in the use of the hour in the afternoon as long as the attention is set wholly on God. Sisters should consult the Mother General as to their use of this time.

In all their prayer the Sisters shall remember that the primary purpose is the worship of God rather than their own consolation or enlightment, and that they are equally called to sacrifice themselves in their prayer, as in their lives, for the sanctification of their neighbour.

INTERCESSION

Contemplation gives both strength and purpose to intercession. As contemplative prayer is waiting upon God to be taught of God, both of the wonder of himself and of his will for the world, so intercession is the uniting of man's will to be one energy with the will of God.

The intercessor both perceives and realises the knowledge of God's love and, with compassion, is concerned with the suffering and lack of purpose in the world. The intercessor sees the world in the light of God to hold it to the love of God for its healing and restoration.

It shall be remembered that the intercessory activity extends to the whole conduct of life in the Community, and forms an integral and important part of it. After the example and in the power of the Incarnate Lord every member of the Community should regard her life as called and set apart for this work of mediation, and should find in it further inspiration for faithfulness in obedience and generosity in self-sacrifice.

The power of the prayer will depend not on any intimate knowledge or carefully detailed exposition of the subject matter, but rather upon a comprehensive and penetrating sense of the majesty and mercy of him to whom the prayer is made and of the merits and compassion of him through whom the Sister pleads.

The Sisters are committed to pray for the dead and dying, remembering the countless numbers of those who have passed from this life spiritually uncared for and who specially need our prayers.

RETREATS

In order to maintain in its integrity the corporate sense of their vocation, the Sisters shall observe annually two separate weeks of corporate retreat, of which one shall be unconducted. They shall also keep a corporate day of retreat monthly. A Sister before her Profession anniversary shall in addition have a day of retreat.

Upon these days at least three hours shall be given to solitary prayer, and it is desirable that the opportunity should be taken for special examination upon the observance of the Rule.

The Superior may at her discretion grant leave for a Sister to have a period of retreat in the local 'desert' of each Convent.

FASTING AND MORTIFICATION

It is the common life that provides the primary means of self-loss, and the Sisters shall therefore accept with simplicity and fortitude any physical discomforts that may come to them through its poverty and strictness.

While the true spirit of mortification is in the affections and will, external and physical penances have value in so far as they contribute to that which is more perfect. Fasting and mortifications are traditional accompaniments to growth in the life of prayer and penitence to which the Sisters are committed.

RECREATION

All recreation should be regarded as part of the repairing of man's selfish and irresponsible attitude towards pleasure. Everyone shall enter fully into the spirit of recreation, contributing to the refreshment and enjoyment of all, and should realise the danger of any forms of withdrawal as detracting from the expression of love in the fellowship of the common life.

At formal recreation no Sister shall absent herself without permission. At these times conversation shall be general and private conversation shall be avoided.

MANUAL WORK

In the tradition of monastic custom manual work has its place in the sanctification of the natural world and is a sharing in the common lot of man. It completes man's offering to God in body and mind.

Every Sister shall accept with generosity and simplicity whatever work is given her in the Convent. Quietness of movement, recollection of mind and a consecrated energy should be accounted as part of the offering enjoined.

SICKNESS

The discipline of ill-health, pain and weariness must be accepted by the Sisters as offering opportunities for deepening their participation in Christ's re-creation through the Sacred Passion and Resurrection. These experiences should be definitely offered as part of the inter-cesory activity of the Community.

The sick shall make it part of their offering to avoid giving unnecessary trouble, and they shall accept with loving gratitude the care and kindness bestowed upon them.

A Sister should report anything that seems really prejudicial to her health that, if advisable, some alteration may be made, but she shall in any case accept at once the decision made on her behalf.

Only those who have permission or are appointed for it, shall visit the sick whether they be in their cell or in the infirmary: in any case the sick-room shall not be made a place of undue relaxation of silence or other rule but suitable means of recreation shall be provided as needed.

Those who tend the sick shall remember, as St Benedict says, 'care must be taken of the sick so that they may be served in very deed as Christ himself.'

CHAPTER OF FAULTS

The Chapter of Faults, an ancient monastic custom, gives the Community an opportunity for the deepening of mutual responsibility in the observance of the corporate vocation. It is an instrument for the increase of fraternal charity and for the mutual respect and knowledge of each other.

THE TIMETABLE

The timetable as arranged shall be of obligation and shall be acknowledged by all as the expression of the Community corporate offering.

THE RULE

Every Sister and Novice shall have a copy of the Rule for her own use and it shall be the subject matter for prayerful consideration and study.

The Rule when finally accepted may not be altered except by the authority of the governing body of the Community, according to the provisions set forth in the Statutes.

THE SPIRIT OF LOVE

As the heavenly City is builded of innumerable stones, each possessing its own intrinsic beauty and its own due place, so the living Church of Christ on earth is ever being builded by the perfecting of individual souls and their due relationship to one another in the oneness of charity.

This is especially true in the Religious family, where all depend for their growth in holiness upon the perfection of their relationship to one another in mutual obedience and holy love.

From their first entry into the life of the Community, therefore, the Sisters shall study to develop themselves in the spirit of love, setting the wellbeing of their Sisters and the perfection of the Community as a whole above any personal aims and desires of their own.

It will be within the safe protection of the life thus lived, that each will look to find her own spiritual life deepened and enlarged according to the spirit of Jesus Christ her Lord.

The Sisters shall pray for each other daily.

They shall always be watchful to use opportunities of unselfishness as far as the conditions of the life of Rule admit, bearing one another's burdens and avoiding laying burdens on others to relieve themselves.

No unkind, derogatory or critical words shall ever be used by one Sister of another, nor shall blame be imputed to another by any unless it be part of a Sister's duty herself to give correction or to report some grave irregularity; such correction shall always be administered with courtesy and the firmness of true Charity.

When anything is needed or when any complaint has to be made, the Superior or Sister appealed to shall always attend to the request with courtesy and consideration.

While the spirit of silence serves to separate each individual life unto God, the spirit of love must ever be binding all together in God, that in the unity of the Spirit all may seek their perfection by holy charity.

APPENDIX FOUR

THE DOMINICAN QUESTIONNAIRE*

Father Aniceto Fernandez, Master General of the Order of Preachers, sends his greetings with a blessing to the Provincials, Priors, Superiors and to all the Brethren of the Order of Preachers.

When we come to tackle the difficult task of the appropriate revision of the Constitutions of the Order, we should begin by turning our attention to what Vatican II or the Holy See have already laid down. Among other things the following may be usefully noted.

1 The right 'to establish norms and laws' and to 'make allowance for adequate and prudent experiment' with a view to 'appropriate renewal' belongs to 'competent authority and in particular to General Chapters', as Vatican II (*Religious* 4) indicates, adding a phrase about the approval of the Holy See if required by law.

2 'The principal part in the renewal and adaptation of religious life belongs to the Institute itself, by means of General Chapters' (Motu Proprio *Ecclesiae Sanctae* Normae II.1): here is a principle that evidently concerns us in view of the place of General Chapters in our tradition.

3 'In order to bring about an appropriate renewal . . . there should be within two, or at most, three years, a special Chapter . . . which could be held in two sections not more than a year apart . . .' (loc. cit., n. 3). For us this will be verified in the General Chapter appointed for Jerusalem in 1968: whether a special Chapter will also be necessary will be discussed then.

4 All members of the Order are in some way to be consulted – 'in

* See pages 97–8.

decisions which involve the future of an Institute as a whole.' (Vat. II: *Religious* 4)

5 'The General Council (of an Order) in preparing for this Chapter, should arrange for the consultation of members on a wide scale and with freedom, and for the co-ordination of the information resulting from it, to provide guidance for the Chapter. This can be done by reports from communities, by questionnaires, etc.' (*Ecclesiae Sanctae* II, 4). Our own General Council has therefore to carry this out in accordance with the spirit of our Constitutions. This is the questionnaire, but it is no more than a sample: any of the brethren are free to raise other matters: and the Provincial is free to arrange for the consultation of the brethren as above, or in any other way.

In order to achieve the best results of the consultation, the following seem to us to be recommended:

(I) First of all there must be co-operation of all superiors and members regarding (a) the renewal of the religious spirit in themselves; (b) the preparation of the spirit of the Chapters; (c) the carrying out of the Chapters; (d) the faithful observance of the regulations decreed by the Chapters (cf. *Ecclesiae Sanctae* II, 2).

(II) In considering and answering the questions, everyone should bear in mind (a) all the documents of Vatican II, especially the sections on the Liturgy, the Church, the Bishops, Religious Life, Priestly Formation, the Priesthood and the Missions; (b) the subsequent directions of the Holy See for the implementation of the Council, especially *Ecclesiae Sanctae* and the liturgical directives; and (c) the Acts of the General Chapter of Bogota.

(III) In the above documents, the following features could profitably receive special notice:

(A) 'Since the religious life is intended above all else to lead those who embrace it to an imitation of Christ and to union with God through the profession of the evangelical counsels, the fact must be honestly faced that even the most desirable changes made on behalf of contemporary needs will fail of their purpose unless a renewal of spirit gives life to them. Indeed such an interior renewal must always be accorded the LEADING ROLE even in the promotion of exterior works.' (Vat. II, *Religious* 2e; tran. Abbott, p. 469)

(B) 'Since the fundamental norm of the religious life is a following of Christ as proposed by the Gospel, such is to be regarded by all communities as their supreme law'. (Vat. II, *Religious* 2a; tran. Abbott, p. 468)

(C) Next, recognition should be given, and an effort made to preserve, the spirit of St Dominic, the ideals that are proper to our Order, and its sound traditions, for all these things are our own heritage. (cf. Vat. II, *Religious* 2b; *Ecclesiae Sanctae* II, 2a)

(D) Regarding the adaptation of our Order to the changed conditions of the times, the character, objects and means of the Order should be clearly defined and expressed; its original spirit should be faithfully preserved; things alien to our religious life should be eliminated, and it should be freed from things that are outmoded. (cf. Vat. II, *Religious*, 2 and 3)

(E) Things should be judged outmoded which are not part of the nature and purpose of the Order, which have become meaningless or useless, and which in fact are no help to religious life. Yet it must be borne in mind that a religious order, according to its particular function, is pledged to bear witness before the world. (cf. *Ecclesiae Sanctae* II, 17)

(F) things moreover which are of their nature not permanent, and belong to the customs of a particular age or place, should also be eliminated from the Constitutions. But things demanded by the present age, or by the physical, mental or social circumstances of today, should be placed in appendices or 'customaries' or suchlike. (cf. *Ecclesiae Sanctae* II, 14)

(IV) 'A Chapter is not held merely to pass laws: it is to encourage spiritual and apostolic vitality.' (*Ecclesiae Sanctae* II, I)

Well, brethren, it is a difficult and important task, calling for a strong and upright spirit, a desire for God's glory and the good of the Order, a zeal and a readiness to accept the sacrifices that may be involved in this collaboration. But we approach it with joy and trust in God, whose will has been shown in the Council and the other documents, and who will help us if we are ready to do what we ought to do. Furthermore, it is encouraging for us to see how closely the traditions of our Order coincide with what the Council has proposed with regard to the idea of the Church, the liturgy, the lay apostolate, ecumenism, missions, work among non-Christians, developments in theology from the pastoral and scriptural angles, with help from the Fathers and not least from St Thomas, the revival of preaching, etc.

What we all desire is good; but let us not forget St James's warning that 'every perfect gift is from above, coming down from the Father of light' (James I, 17) nor St Paul's 'By the grace of God I am what I am' (I Cor. 15) and let us remember that God gives his grace to those who ask it of him.

We therefore ask all brethren, nuns, sisters, tertiaries and members of Dominican confraternities, to pray every day for God's help until the next General Chapter. Let them use whatever prayers they like, but let them daily pray for a proper adjustment of our Dominican life and may this common intention lead us all to pray all the more fervently. We would also suggest that superiors should sometimes offer conventual Mass for this intention. And let us not forget to ask the intercession of Our Lady, of St Dominic, and of the Saints of our Order, that they may join their prayers to our own.

Fr. Aniceto Fernandez OP, Master General, Santa Sabina, Rome
19 November 1966

INSTRUCTIONS FOR ANSWERING THIS QUESTIONNAIRE

1 Each question must be answered on a separate sheet (28 × 22 cm). Only one side of the paper must be used. For any additional questions (invited at the end of the questionnaire) separate sheets must again be used for each question.

2 Answers should be typewritten.

3 Answer in Latin if possible; otherwise in English, French, German, Italian or Spanish.

4 Arrange each answer in the following way:
(a) the code letter(s) of the questions (A, B, AA, AB, etc.)
(b) the name of your province, thus 'Provincia Angliae'.
(c) your own name, with proper title and position in the Order
   e.g. Father Abraham Small, MA, STL
      Lector at Oxyard
      Brother Isaac Stout
      Student at Hawkford
      Brother Jacob Tallboy
      Solemnly professed Brother at Woodcastle

5 The direct answer to the question may not occupy more than *five* lines of typescript. A maximum of *ten* more lines may be used to provide proof or explanation of the answer. Any further discussion of the point must be placed among the 'additional questions' at the end.

6 Answers should reach the Secretary General of the Order before 1 May 1967.

QUESTIONNAIRE

The following documents are frequently referred to:
Vatican II; *Liturgy* = the Constitution on the Liturgy

Vatican II; *Bishops* = the Decree 'Christus Dominus'
Vatican II; *Priestly Formation* = the Decree 'Optatem Totius'
Vatican II; *Religious* = the Decree 'Perfectae Caritatis'
The Motu Proprio *Ecclesiae Sanctae*
Bogota = the Acts of the General Chapter of the Order at Bogota

I The Basic Idea of the Order

(A) What is the special character of the spirit and life of St Dominic, and what was his intention in founding the Order?

(B) How is the Order to set about a searching self-examination, as the Church is doing, especially in the light of Vatican II, *The Church* (Ch. V and VI) and *Religious*?

(C) What are the questions raised for the Order today by the document of Vatican II on *The Church in the Modern World*?

(D) How should we define today the end, or object, of the Order?

(E) And then, what in practice, are the essential means to this end?

(F) In view of *Eccl. Sanct.* II, 12, how should our Constitutions be arranged? Evangelical and theological principles, basic ideas of Dominican life, applications to particular circumstances?

II The Life and Government of the Order; Questions Regarding Formation

(G) Is it necessary to revise the methods of preparing candidates (e.g. Apostolic Schools) and the conditions of admission to the Order (with regard to age, maturity, mentality and education)?

(H) Should the traditional type of novitiate be altered? At what stage should it begin and how long should it last? And what of the duration and the nature of temporary vows?

(I) What of the position of the Novice-Master? Should this be altered?

(J) What of the present type of Study House? How best would the young men there be prepared for the religious life, for the apostolic work and community life which they will subsequently practise elsewhere?

(K) What of the position of the Student-Master? Is there need for alteration here, and in the part played by the lectors in the general formation of the students?

(L) How are we to put into practice the direction of *Eccl. Sanct.* II, 36 that the instruction of our young men should 'not be merely theoretical but should be completed by the gradual introduction of some actual practice, as part of the training, in the work proper to the Institute'?

(M) Should there be a revision of the conditions laid down in the

Constitutions for solemn profession (age, maturity, previous vows, etc.)?

Questions regarding the Laybrothers

(N) What is it that marks off the vocation of the Laybrother in our Order, in the context of the Church and the men of today?

(O) Should there be a modification of the direction of *Bogota* 130 about the Laybrothers' Office?

(P) How in practice are our Laybrothers to receive the theological, spiritual, educational and technical instruction needed for their place in the life of the Church today (cf. *Eccl. Sanct.* II, 35 adapted)?

(Q) Within the basic structure of the Order, how is it to be arranged that 'those members who are called "conversi", co-operators, or by some such name, are to be given a vote in certain community affairs and in elections, and to be able to be appointed to certain positions; so that they become more closely integrated into the community, and at the same time free the priests for their own proper tasks' (*Eccl. Sanct.* II, 27)?

Questions Regarding 'Regular Life'

(R) In the light of Vatican II *Religious* how is our mode of life to be renewed

    (i) regarding the vow of chastity? (*Religious* 12)

(S) (ii) regarding the vow of obedience, and in particular Dominican obedience and that active and responsible obedience which involves 'a co-operation in undertaking and carrying out a task' (*Religious* 14)?

(T) (iii) regarding the vow of poverty, and in particular Dominican poverty, and 'the eager search for new forms, fitting the Institute, and the practice of which today will bear witness more powerfully to poverty' (*Eccl. Sanct.* II, 23; cf. *Religious* 13)?

(U) In order that every community should be 'a true family gathered together in the Lord's name' (*Religious* 15) should there be a revision of the way the categories are divided in a community? To what extent should this be done?

(V) What of penitential observances proper to our Order? These things show that religious are more ready to undertake penance and mortification than others. Should we therefore accept new forms which belong to the life of today? (cf. *Eccl. Sanct.* II, 22)

(W) To what extent can or should certain elements of our Regular Life (e.g. various observances, silences, enclosure, etc.) be adjusted to the requirements of today's apostolate?

(X) What of the special problems of the religious life affecting those brethren who because of their work are living alone (e.g. nuns' chaplains, teachers in positions outside the Order)?

Questions Regarding Government

(Y) Is any change needed in the manner of appointing superiors (i.e. any kind of superior)?

> (i) regarding the duration of that office?
> (ii) regarding the qualities required for voters in their election?
> (iii) regarding the membership of Chapters, General, Provincial and Conventual, and the frequency of their occurrence?

(Z) With regard to the above Chapters, how can Vatican II *Religious* 14 (last paragraph) be put into practice: 'Let chapters and councils faithfully acquit themselves of the governing role given to them; each should express in its own way the fact that all members of the community have a share in the welfare of the whole community and a responsibility for it' (tr. Abbott, p. 477)?

(AA) Is any change needed in the manner of appointing members of the General Council, and in the definition of their functions? And what of the relation between the General Council and a General Chapter?

(AB) In the government of a Province, is any change needed with regard to a Provincial Chapter, the Diffinitory, the Provincial Council and the relations between these bodies?

(AC) What should be the constitution, membership and function of the Conventual Chapter in relation to the government of the house (see *Bogota* 220) and of the Provincial Chapter regarding religious life in community and the apostolate? And what of the relations between the Conventual Council and the Conventual Chapter?

(AD) In view of various local problems, especially of the apostolate, should the Provincials have increased powers, and in which direction?

(AE) Are modifications needed of the offices of those who assist the Provincial, such as Vicar Provincial, Socius, Treasurer, Secretary, various Promoters, etc.?

(AF) In connection with *Bogota* 239, 240, 253, should emphasis be laid on the relationships between Provinces within the same nation or Episcopal Conference, or having the same language? What legislation would be needed to establish such relationships?

III *Preaching the Word*

(AG) How is renewal to be brought to the traditional ministry of the

Order (preaching, teaching, confessions, parish-work, confraternities, social work, missionary work) and how are we to meet the repeated invitations of the Council to the apostolate (to non-Catholics, atheists, workers, and regarding justice and peace, etc.)?

(AH) In this effort of renewal and adaptation, which areas of apostolate present special problems, and how are they to be solved?

(AI) In view of the variety of religious institutes, and of the special character of our own apostolate, which area should, in your opinion, receive priority today? And then, how should our work in that area be tackled by individual houses, by the Provinces and by the whole Order, and made effective?

(AJ) In view of the above-mentioned priority, and the special demands of certain localities, how are we to deploy and co-ordinate the forces which we have at present?

(AK) With regard to the religious life and the apostolate, what are the problems which arise out of the relationships between an exempt Order and the organised apostolate of a diocese, or an Episcopal Conference (cf. Vat. II, *Bishops*, 33–5, and *Eccl. Sanct.* I, 22–41)?

(AL) How can our Missions meet the requirements of Vatican II on *Missions* ('Ad Gentes') and the direction for their fulfilment in *Eccl. Sanct.* III?

IV *Liturgy*

(AM) In view of Vatican II, *Liturgy* 18, is the liturgical life of a house to be directed to both the increase of our own contemplative life and the active participation of the faithful? And if so, how?

(AN) How is the pattern of prayer to be adapted to the conditions of today? (cf. *Religious* 3)

      (i) regarding Divine Office?

(AO) (ii) regarding other extra-liturgical prayers (cf. *Eccl. Sanct.* II, 21)

(AP) (iii) regarding mental prayer?

(AQ) Is our own Dominican Rule to be preserved?

If so (1) How? Wholly or in part only?

      (2) How, in the light of sound tradition, should it be reviewed and
      endowed with new vigour (cf. Vat. II, *Liturgy* 4)?

(AR) How should our Constitutions (n. 568) on attendance in choir and on habitual dispensation from choir, be adapted to the conditions of today?

V *Studies*

(AS) With the object of preaching the Gospel to men of today, how are we to define the special function of the Order in the intellectual field, and remain faithful to the Word of God which we received through our own traditional teaching? What in present conditions is our obligation of fidelity to the teaching of St Thomas?

(AT) What is to be the object of the intellectual formation of our men? And what means are to be used by an individual man, a house, or a Province, to secure that this formation should be continuous and should affect the man's whole life, both contemplative and active?

(AU) What should be done to bring about an intellectual sharing on the part of the Order with the universities and among learned men? What should be done by the Study Houses, by the Provinces, by the Provinces grouped within a nation, by the Order as a whole?

(AV) With regard to our own Ratio Studiorum, how is the decentralisation demanded by Vat. II, *Priestly Formation* 1, to be fitted in? What common elements are to remain? What kinds of experiments should be allowed?

(AW) What kind of concentration of our studies should be considered, in order to obtain a better training for our students and a greater degree of specialisation for our lectors?

(AX) If a concentration is achieved 'by the fraternal collaboration of several (Institutes)' – *Eccl. Sanct.* II, 37 – how shall we preserve the features which are proper to ourselves?

(AY) In our Study Houses, should a clearer distinction be made between the training of those who are to become lecturers and scholars, and that of the others?

(AZ) How are we going to put into practice the direction of Vat. II, *Priestly Formation* 17, about the revision of teaching methods, so that this instruction may produce 'a genuine and deep formation of students' (tr. Abbott, p. 453)?

(BA) In the application of *Priestly Formation* 14, 15 and 16, how are we going to organise our courses and rearrange the material?

(BB) How are we going to implement *Priestly Formation* 19–21 on specific pastoral formation?

VI *Dominican Nuns and Sisters*

(BC) What does the Order expect from the Nuns today?

(BD) Would it be possible to determine more accurately the moral links which bind us to the Nuns, and to strengthen these links by new legislation, by granting for instance (a) that they should have the right to send petitions to the General Chapter; (b) wider powers to the Master General and his delegates in their regard; (c) representation within the Order of federation of monasteries of nuns?

(BE) What does the Order expect today from the Congregations of (Third Order) Sisters?
(BF) How can the Brethren help our Nuns and Sisters to fulfil ever more faithfully their own vocations?

VII *Tertiaries*
(BG) What, in your opinion, should constitute the image of the Secular Tertiary, especially in view of the documents of Vatican II on *The Church*, *The Church in the Modern World*, and *The Apostolate of the Laity*?
(BH) In what terms should we think of the collaboration of Tertiaries in the apostolic vocation of the Order?

VIII *The Economic Question*
(BI) How should the use and administration of material things be managed, so that the whole community should bear witness to religious poverty and each of the brethren should really lead a life of poverty?

Additional Questions
(BI bis) Are there any additional questions you would like to ask?
(BI ter) In view of *Eccl. Sanct.* II, 6, are there any particular experiments you would like to see asked for at the next General Chapter?

INDEX

Aachen, conference of abbots at (817), 41, 178

Abbeys, see Monasteries and Convents

Abbots, Aelred, 44; Baldwin, royal physician, 40–1; Biscop, Benedict, 40; Clowns, William, 50; de la Mare, Thomas, 49; Hor, 36; Hugh of Cluny, 42; Odilo, 42; Wilfrid of Lindisfarne, 40; responsibility of, 39–40; live separately from monks, 40; congregational meeting of, 174–5; power of, 175–6

Abelard, Peter, 46

Active Orders (see also Benedictines, Dominicans, Franciscans, Jesuits, etc.), distinguished from contemplative, 106–7, 162–3; difficulties of prayer in, 249

Africa, Dominicans in, 48; the dance as prayer in, 166–7

Albigensians, 47

Alexandria, early religious sects in, 33 *et seq*

Alms, canon law on collection of, 171–2

America, arrival of Benedictines in, 65; Anglican Benedictines in, 73; postwar growth in, 90; 2,000 nuns abandon vows in, 98; Camaldolese hermit-monks in California, 104; Trappists in Kentucky and Utah, 106; wealth of communities in, 119–20; false poverty in, 247–8; liturgical reforms in, 249–50; redeployment of religious in, 250; unrest in, 252; Jesuits in, 270–1

Anglicans, *see* Church of England

Annuario Pontificio, 67

Aquinas, *see* St Thomas Aquinas

Arrupe, Fr Pedro SJ, Superior General of Jesuits, 173

Art, at Taizé, 25–6; medieval monastic, 41; treasury at Kremsmünster, 104–5

Ascent of Mount Carmel, 146–8

Athos, Mount, 208

Augustinians (Austin Friars), 51; founding of, 47–8; liturgical reforms, 249

Austin Friars, *see* Augustinians

Austria, 107; Benedictines in, 105–6, 251; monastic granges in, 124

Austrian Empire, contemplatives suppressed in, 57

Authority, *see* Obedience

Current and forthcoming titles from Sceptre

MARY RENAULT

THE KING MUST DIE

GALINA VISHNEVSKAYA

GALINA

MARY RENAULT

THE MASK OF APOLLO

JOHN COLVILLE

THE FRINGES OF POWER VOLUME I

PIERS PAUL READ

THE VILLA GOLITSYN

BOOKS OF DISTINCTION